Princess Resurrection

Yasunori Mitsunaga

Translated by
Satsuki Yamashita

Adapted by
Joshua Hale Fialkov

Lettered by
North Market Street Graphics

DEL
REY

Ballantine Books • New York

Princess Resurrection volume 1 is a work of fiction. Names, characters, places, and incidents are the products of the author's imagination or are used fictitiously. Any resemblance to actual events, locales, or persons, living or dead, is entirely coincidental.

A Del Rey Trade Paperback Original

Published in the United States by Del Rey, an imprint of The Random House Publishing Group, a division of Random House, Inc., New York.

Publication rights arranged through Kodansha Ltd.

First published in Japan in 2006 by Kodansha Ltd., Tokyo,

ISBN 978-0-345-49664-5

Printed in the United States of America

www.delreymanga.com

9 8 7 6 5 4 3 2 1

Translator: Satsuki Yamashita
Adapter: Joshua Hale Fialkov
Lettering: North Market Street Graphic

Contents

That is not dead
which can eternal lie,
and with strange eons
even death may die.

Honorifics Explained

Throughout the Del Rey Manga books, you will find Japanese honorifics left intact in the translations. For those not familiar with how the Japanese use honorifics and, more important, how they differ from American honorifics, we present this brief overview.

Politeness has always been a critical facet of Japanese culture. Ever since the feudal era, when Japan was a highly stratified society, use of honorifics—which can be defined as polite speech that indicates relationship or status—has played an essential role in the Japanese language. When addressing someone in Japanese, an honorific usually takes the form of a suffix attached to one's name (example: "Asuna-san"), is used as a title at the end of one's name, or appears in place of the name itself (example: "Negi-sensei," or simply "Sensei!").

Honorifics can be expressions of respect or endearment. In the context of manga and anime, honorifics give insight into the nature of the relationship between characters. Many English translations leave out these important honorifics and therefore distort the feel of the original Japanese. Because Japanese honorifics contain nuances that English honorifics lack, it is our policy at Del Rey not to translate them. Here, instead, is a guide to some of the honorifics you may encounter in Del Rey Manga.

-*san:* This is the most common honorific and is equivalent to Mr., Miss, Ms., or Mrs. It is the all-purpose honorific and can be used in any situation where politeness is required.

-*sama:* This is one level higher than "-san" and is used to confer great respect.

-*dono:* This comes from the word "tono," which means "lord." It is an even higher level than "-sama" and confers utmost respect.

-*kun:* This suffix is used at the end of boys' names to express familiarity or endearment. It is also sometimes used by men among friends, or when addressing someone younger or of a lower station.

-chan: This is used to express endearment, mostly toward girls. It is also used for little boys, pets, and even among lovers. It gives a sense of childish cuteness.

Bozu: This is an informal way to refer to a boy, similar to the English terms "kid" and "squirt."

Sempai/
Senpai: This title suggests that the addressee is one's senior in a group or organization. It is most often used in a school setting, where underclassmen refer to their upperclassmen as "sempai." It can also be used in the workplace, such as when a newer employee addresses an employee who has seniority in the company.

Kohai: This is the opposite of "sempai" and is used toward underclassmen in school or newcomers in the workplace. It connotes that the addressee is of a lower station.

Sensei: Literally meaning "one who has come before," this title is used for teachers, doctors, or masters of any profession or art.

[blank]: This is usually forgotten in these lists, but it is perhaps the most significant difference between Japanese and English. The lack of honorific means that the speaker has permission to address the person in a very intimate way. Usually, only family, spouses, or very close friends have this kind of permission. Known as *yobisute,* it can be gratifying when someone who has earned the intimacy starts to call one by one's name without an honorific. But when that intimacy hasn't been earned, it can be very insulting.

Princess Resurrection

1

Yasunori Mitsunaga

Contents

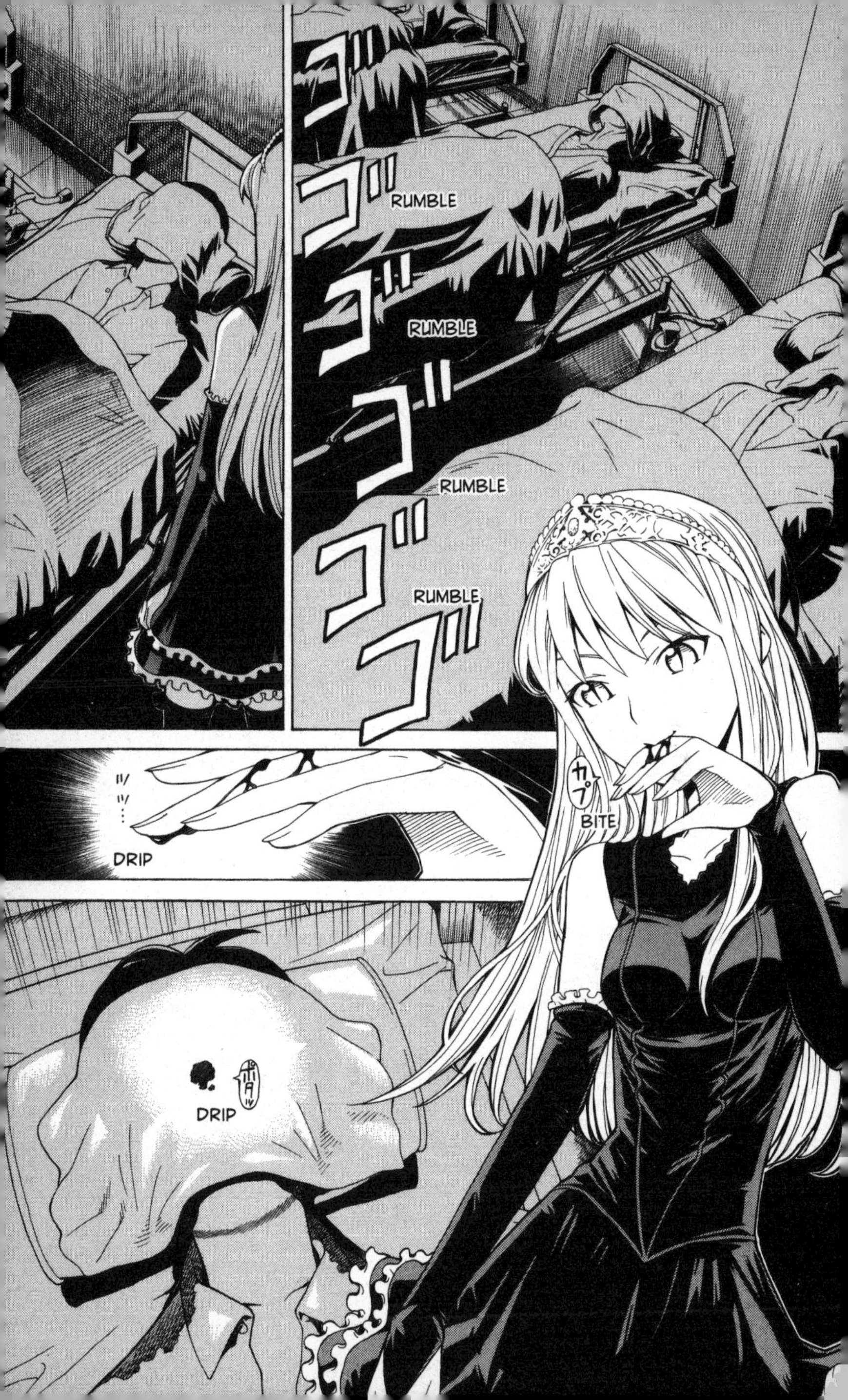
ゴゴ
RUMBLE
ゴゴ
RUMBLE
ゴゴ
RUMBLE
ゴゴ
RUMBLE
カプ
BITE
ツツ…
DRIP
ポタッ
DRIP

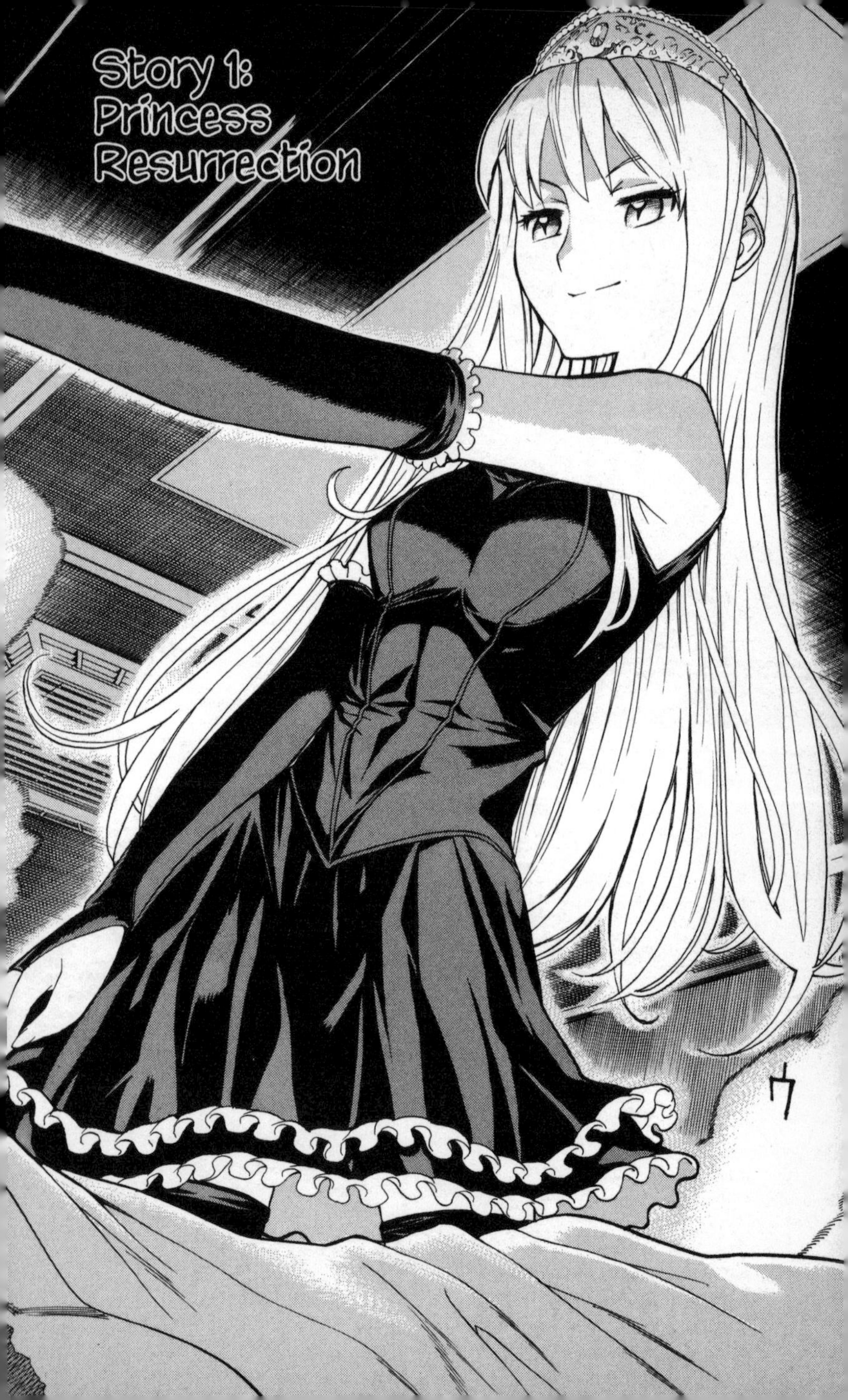
Story 1:
Princess
Resurrection
ウ

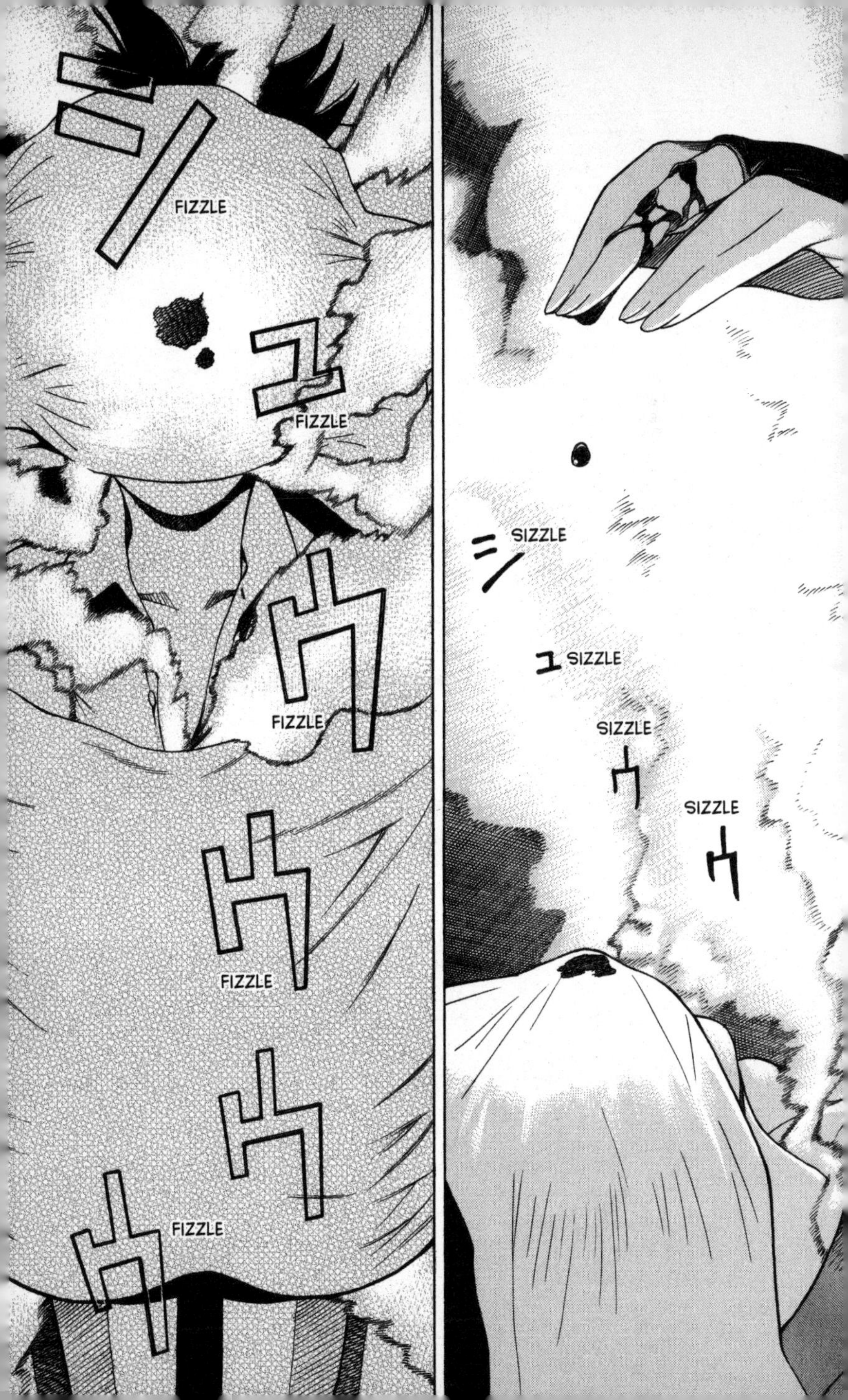
SIZZLE
SIZZLE
SIZZLE
SIZZLE
FIZZLE
FIZZLE
FIZZLE
FIZZLE
FIZZLE

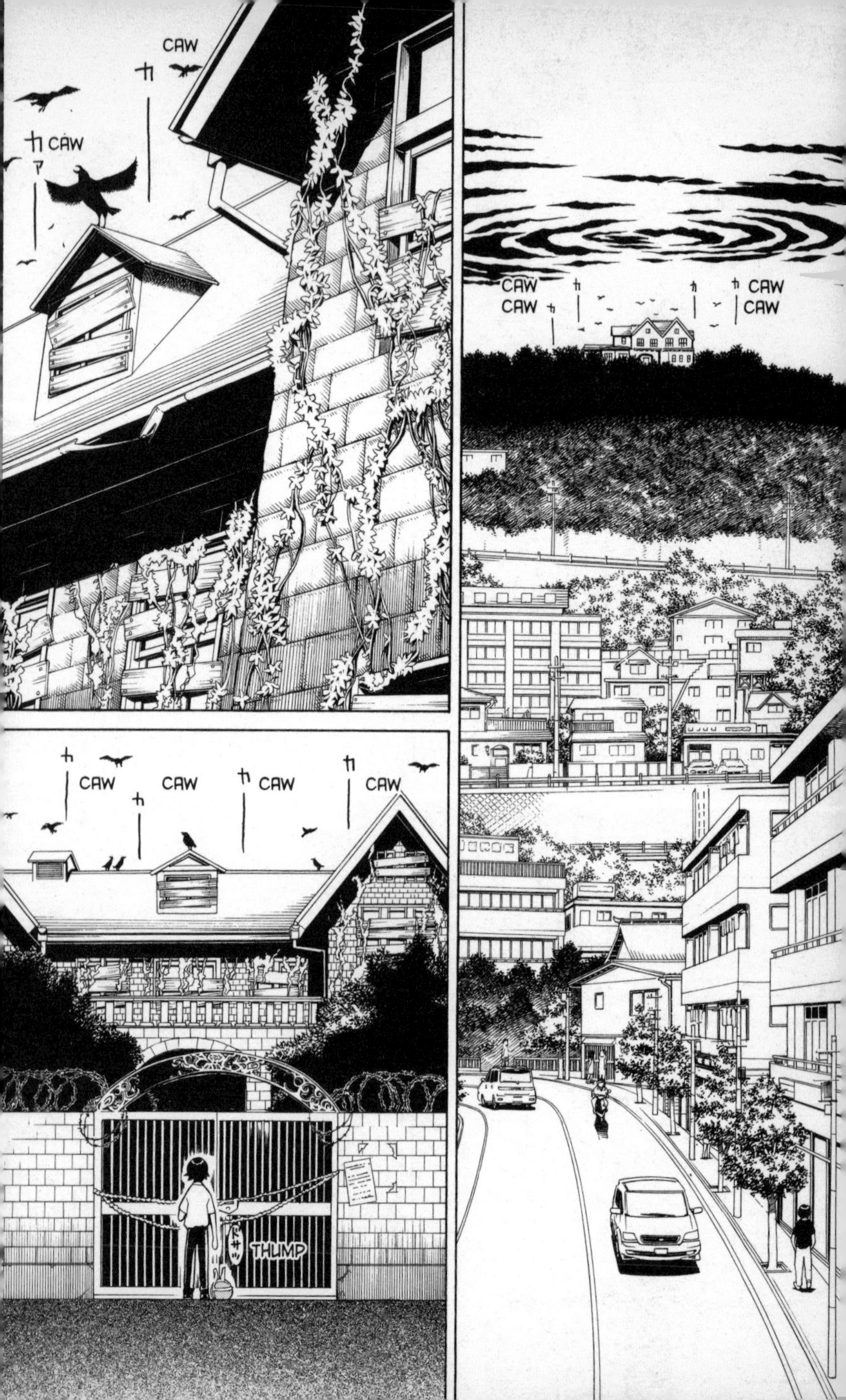
カ CAW
CAW
カ
カ
カ CAW
CAW
カ CAW
カア CAW
カ CAW
カ CAW
カ CAW
カ CAW
ドサッ THUMP

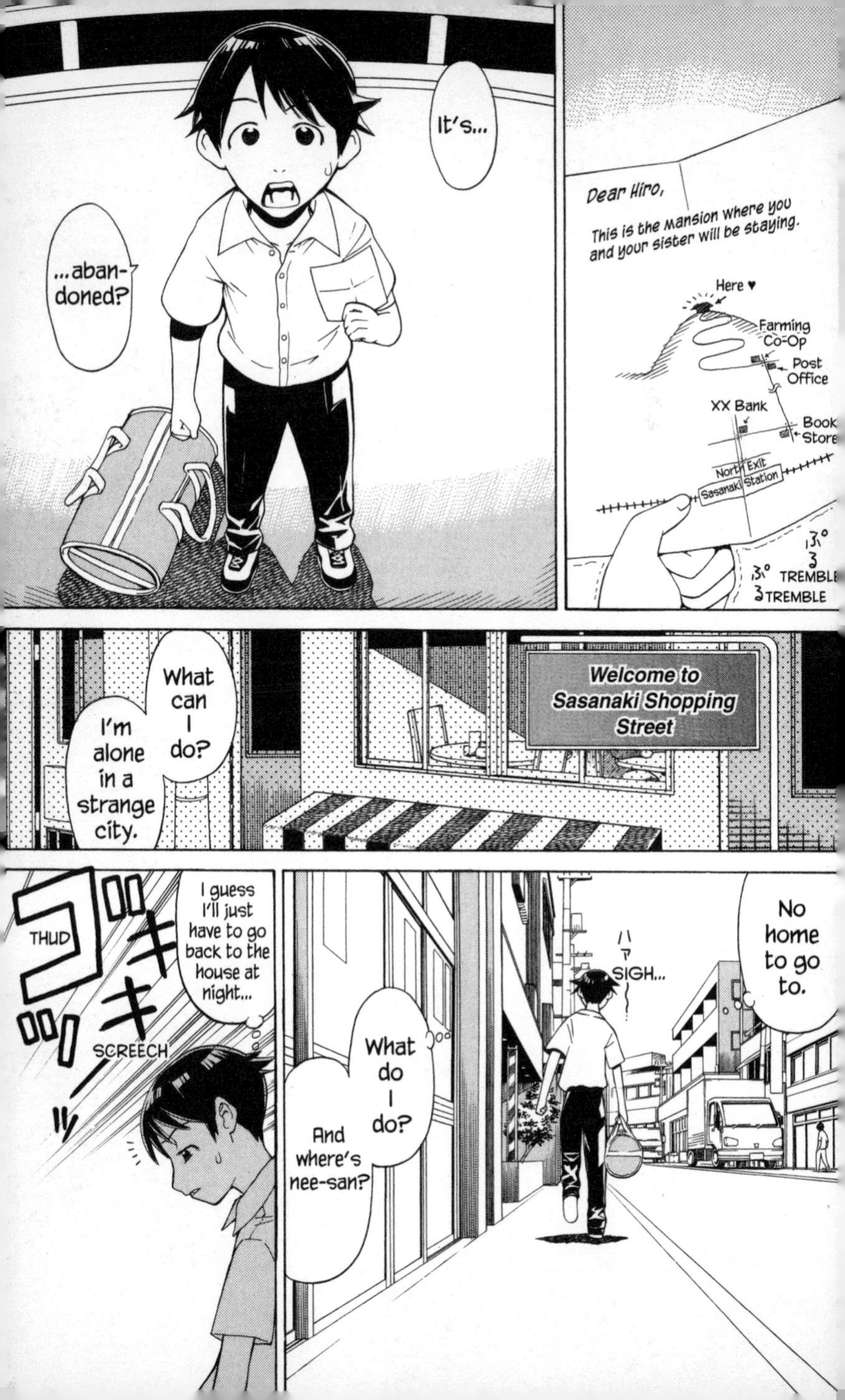
Dear Hiro,
This is the mansion where you and your sister will be staying.
Here ♥
Farming Co-Op
Post Office
XX Bank
Book Store
North Exit
Sasanaki Station
TREMBLE
TREMBLE
It's...
...aban-doned?
Welcome to Sasanaki Shopping Street
What can I do?
I'm alone in a strange city.
No home to go to.
SIGH...
What do I do?
And where's nee-san?
I guess I'll just have to go back to the house at night...
THUD
SCREECH

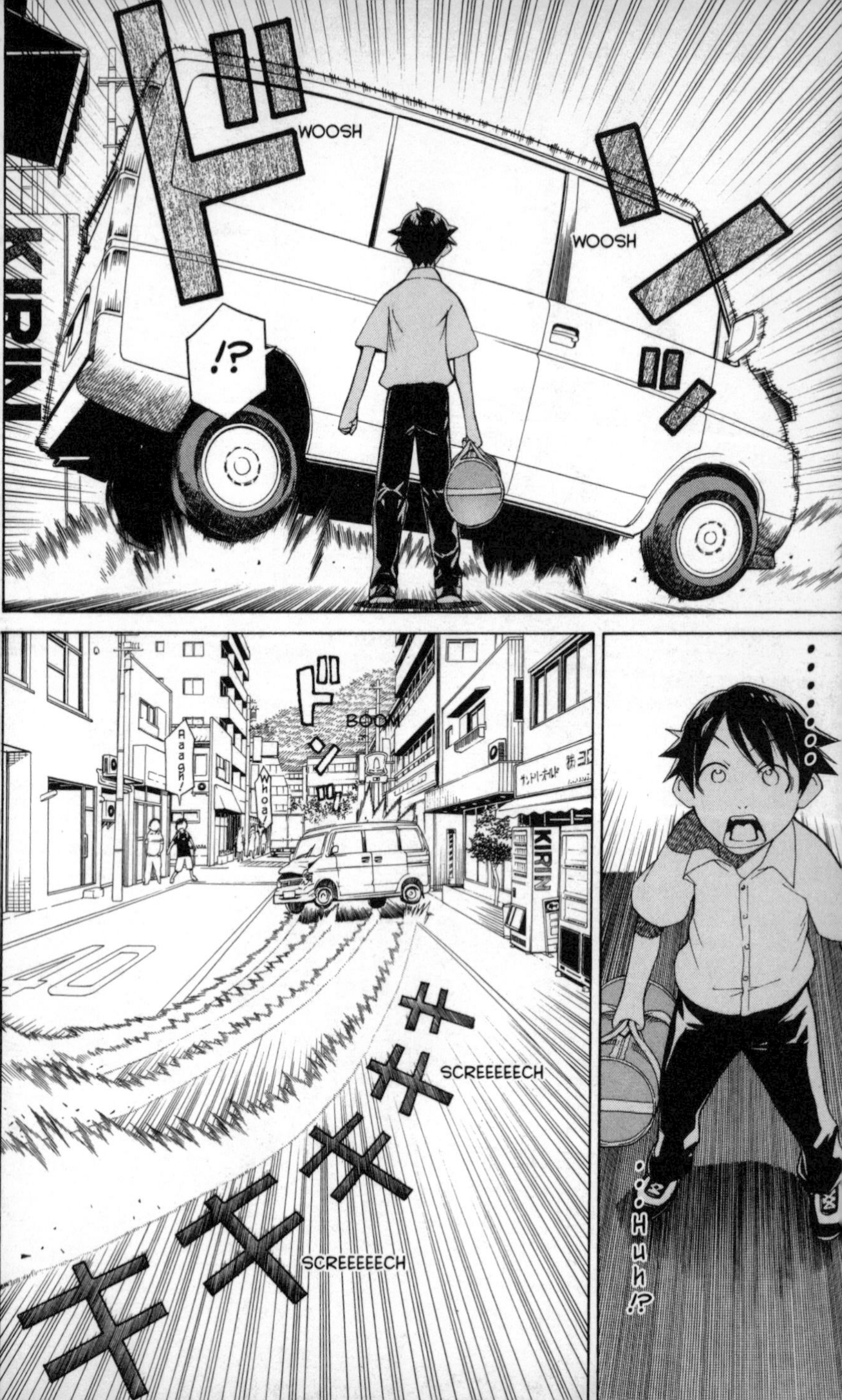
WOOSH
WOOSH
!?
KIRIN
......
Huh!?
BOOM
Raagh!
Whoa!
KIRIN
SCREEEEECH
SCREEEEECH

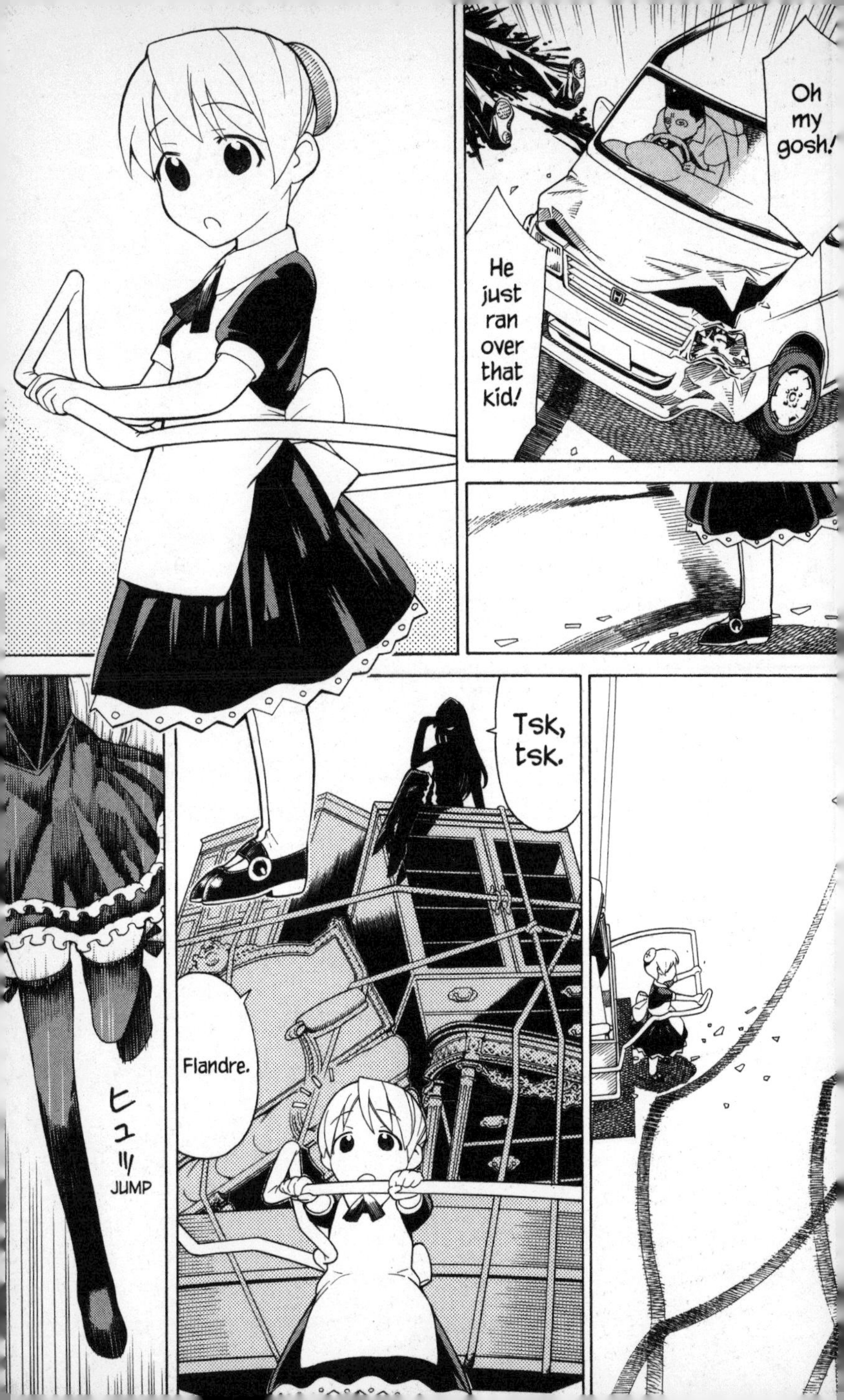
Oh my gosh!
He just ran over that kid!
Tsk, tsk.
Flandre.
ヒュッ
JUMP

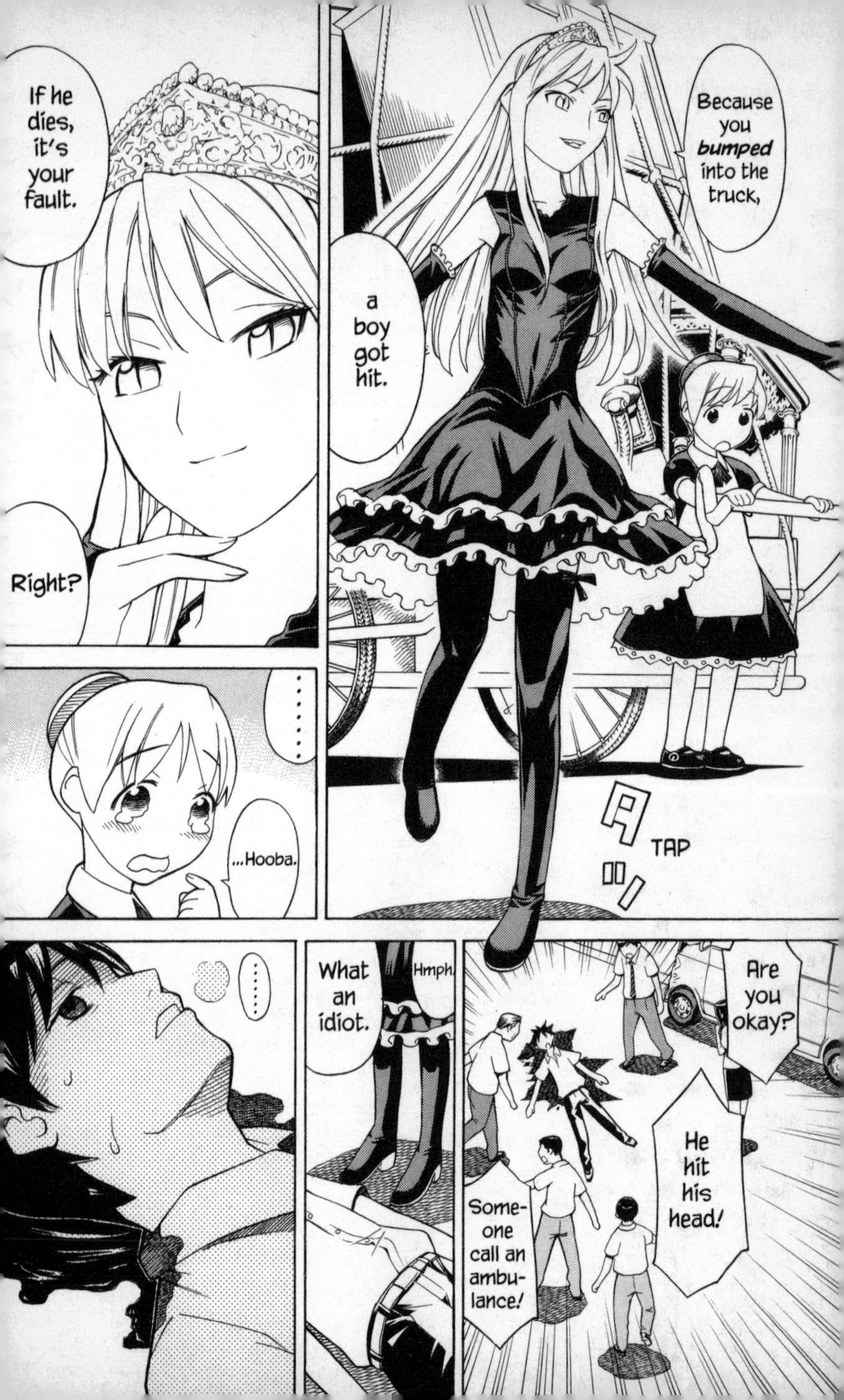
Because you *bumped* into the truck,
a boy got hit.
TAP
If he dies, it's your fault.
Right?
......
...Hooba.
Are you okay?
He hit his head!
Someone call an ambulance!
Hmph.
What an idiot.
......

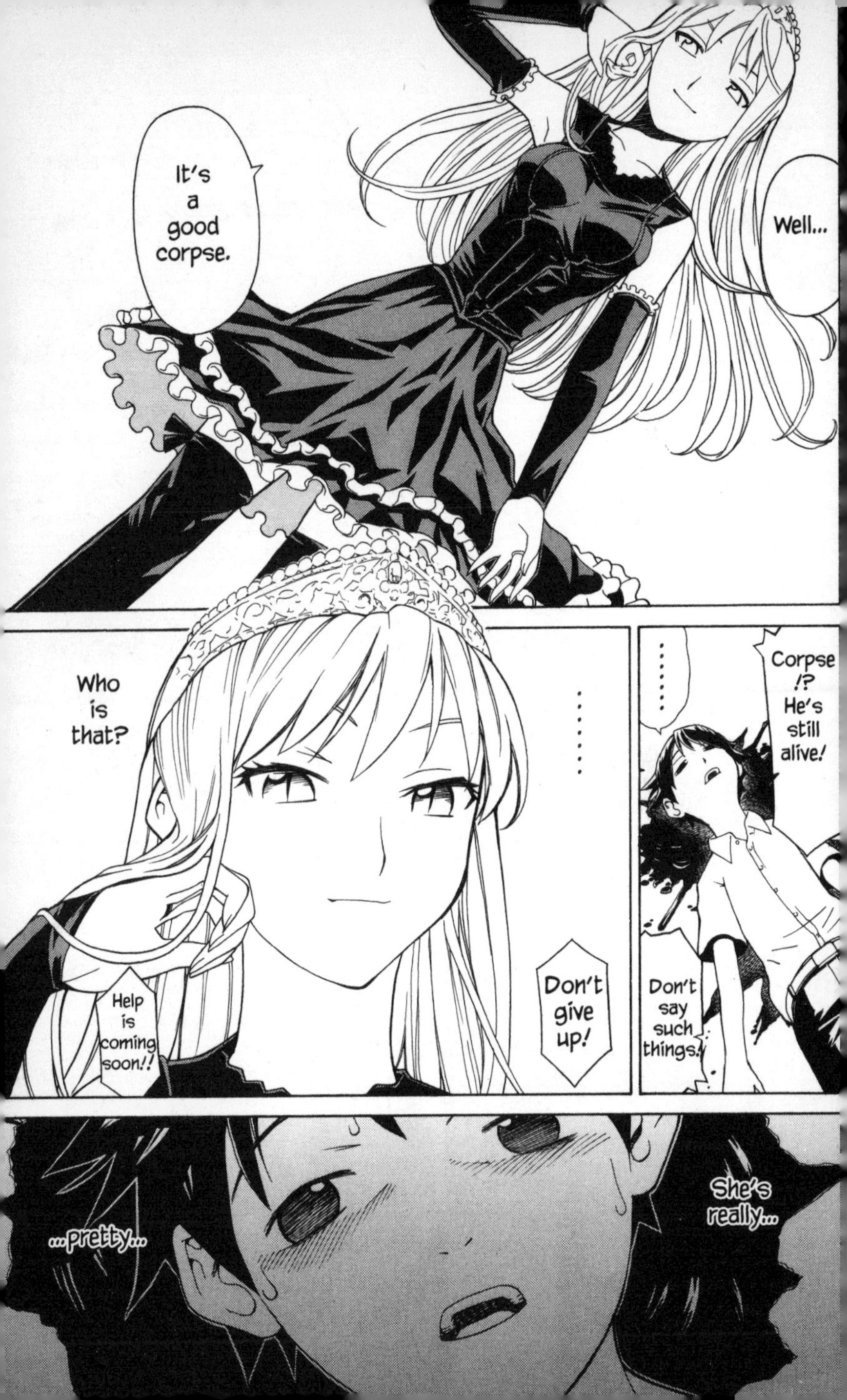
Well...
It's a good corpse.
Corpse!? He's still alive!
......
Don't say such things!
......
Who is that?
Don't give up!
Help is coming soon!!
She's really...
...pretty...

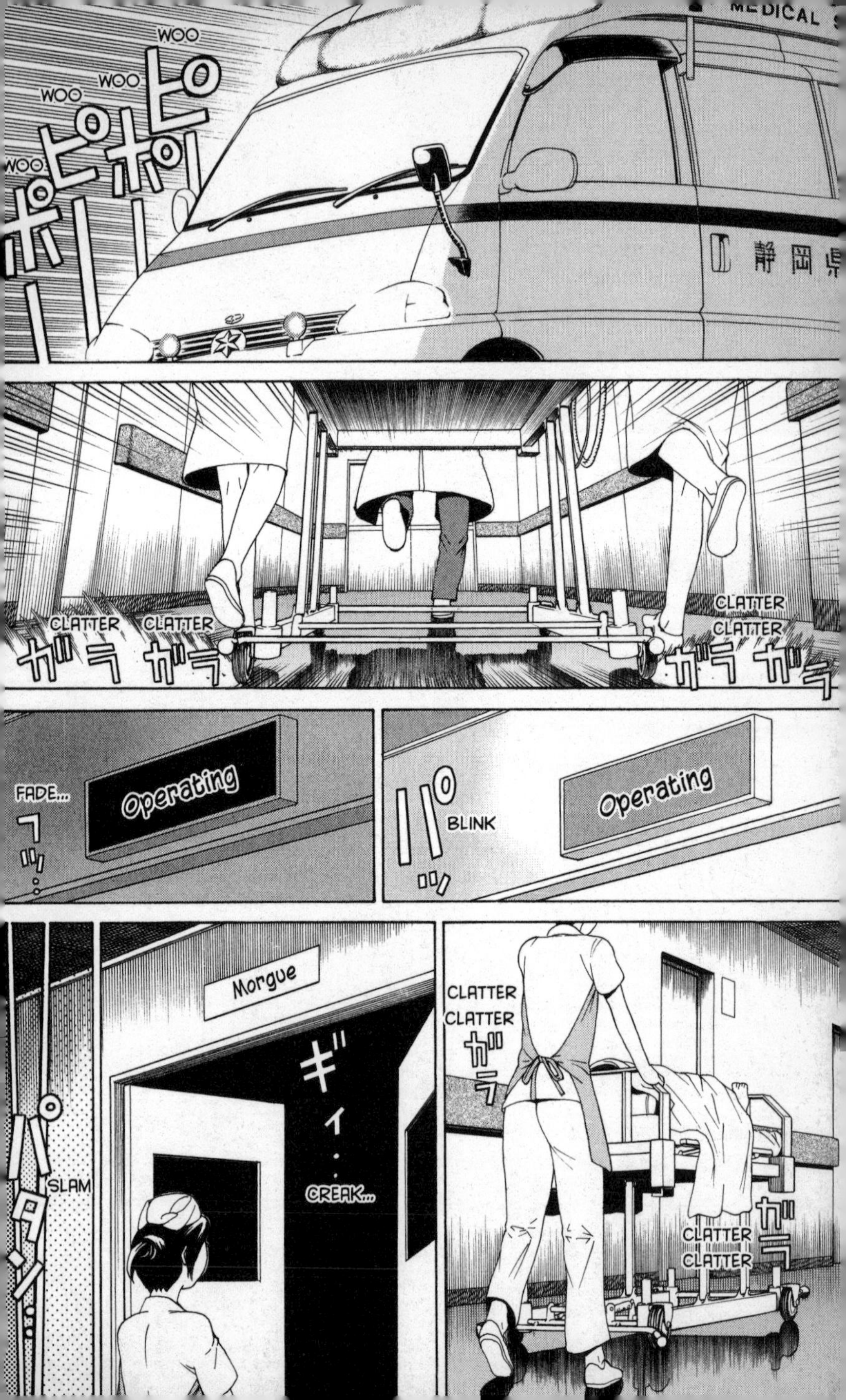
MEDICAL
静岡県
ピーポーピーポー
WOO
WOO
WOO
WOO
CLATTER
CLATTER
ガラガラ
CLATTER
CLATTER
ガラガラ
パッ
BLINK
Operating
Operating
FADE...
フッ…
CLATTER
CLATTER
ガラ
CLATTER
CLATTER
ガラ
Morgue
ギィ・・
CREAK...
パタン…
SLAM

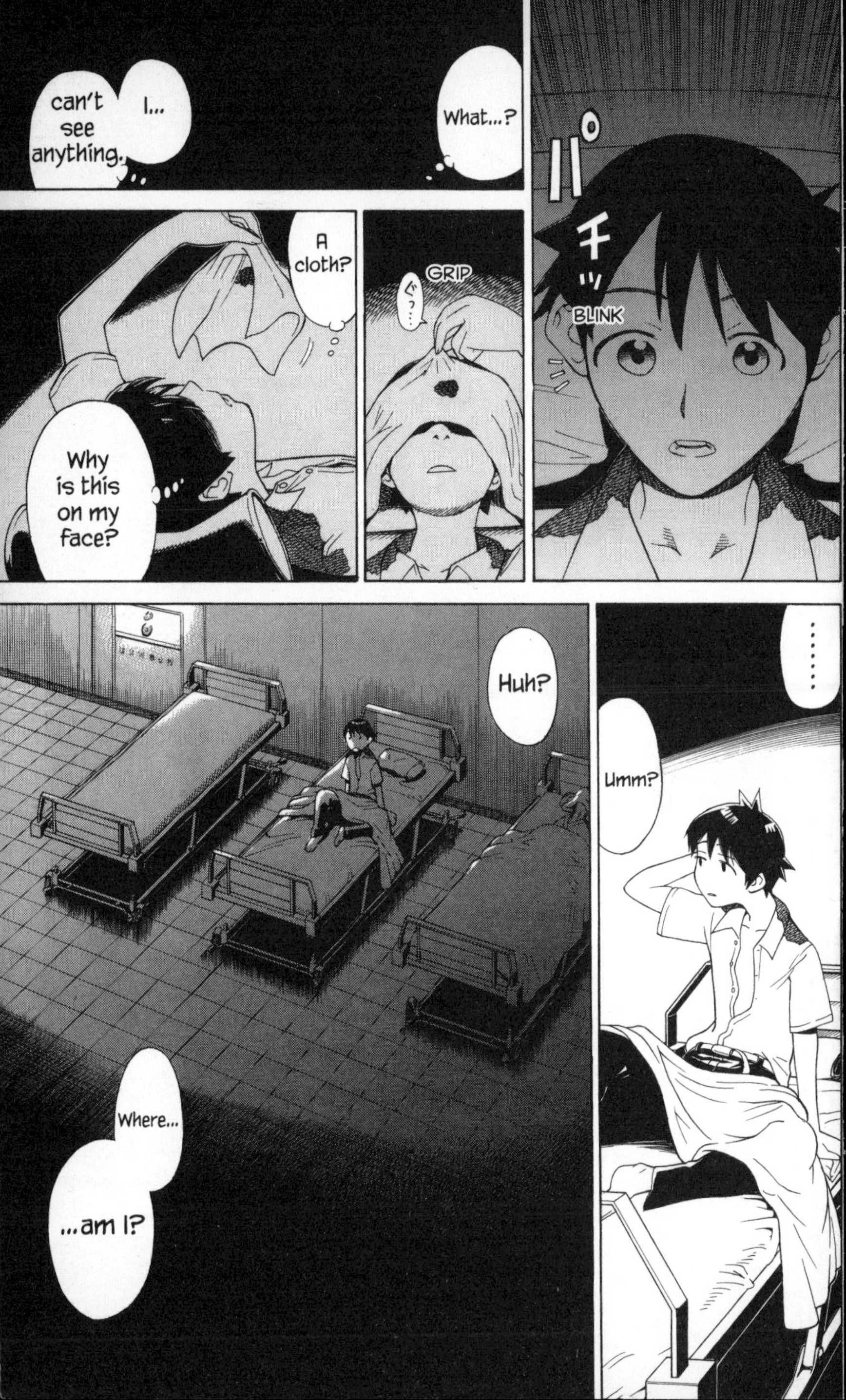
パチッ
BLINK
What...?
I...
can't see anything.
GRIP
ぐっ…
A cloth?
Why is this on my face?
....
Umm?
Huh?
Where...
...am I?

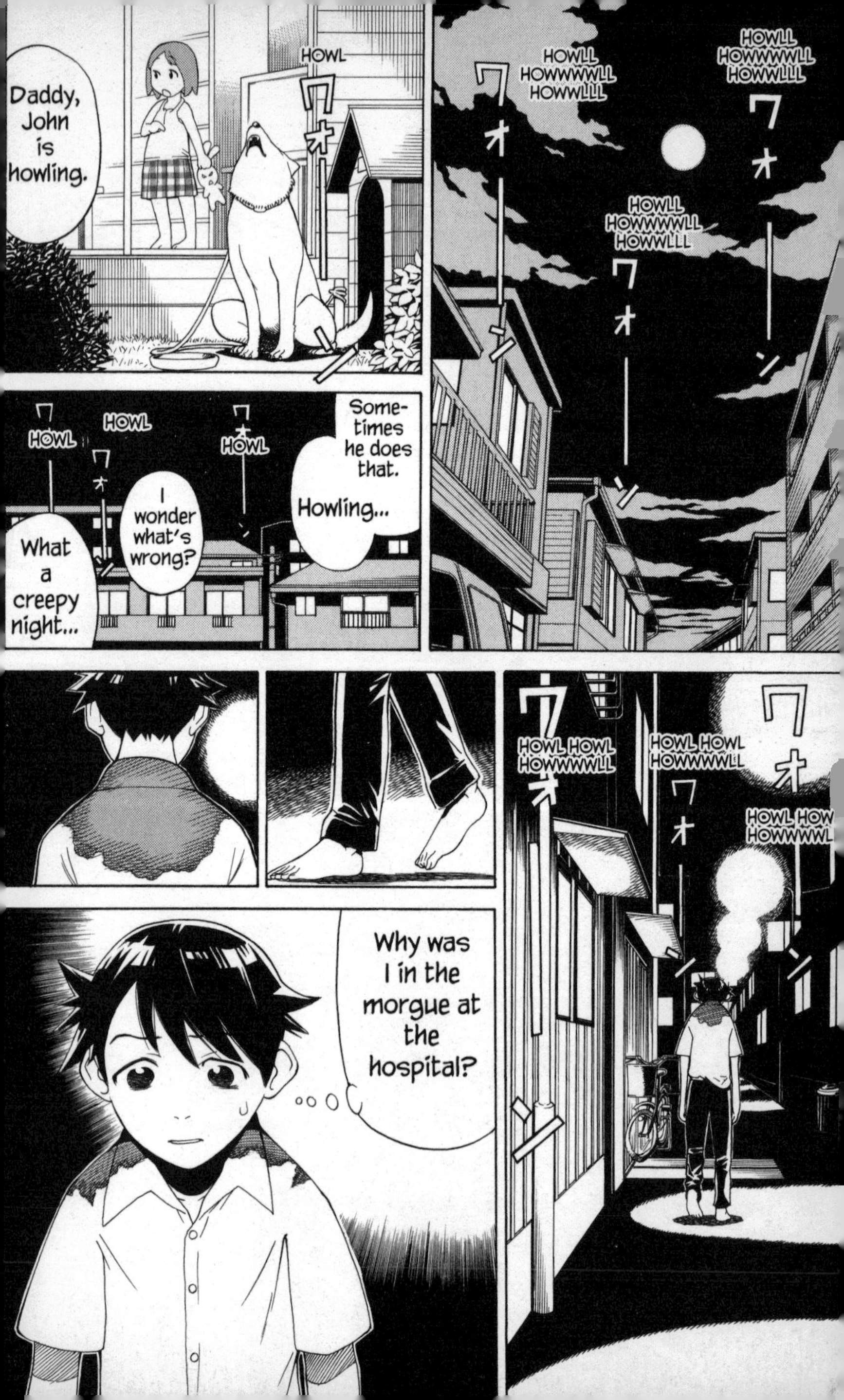
HOWLL
HOWWWWLL
HOWWLLL
HOWLL
HOWWWWLL
HOWWLLL
HOWLL
HOWWWWLL
HOWWLLL
HOWL
Daddy, John is howling.
Some-times he does that.
Howling...
HOWL
I wonder what's wrong?
HOWL
HOWL
What a creepy night...
HOWL HOW
HOWWWWL
HOWL HOWL
HOWWWWL
HOWL HOWL
HOWWWWLL
Why was I in the morgue at the hospital?

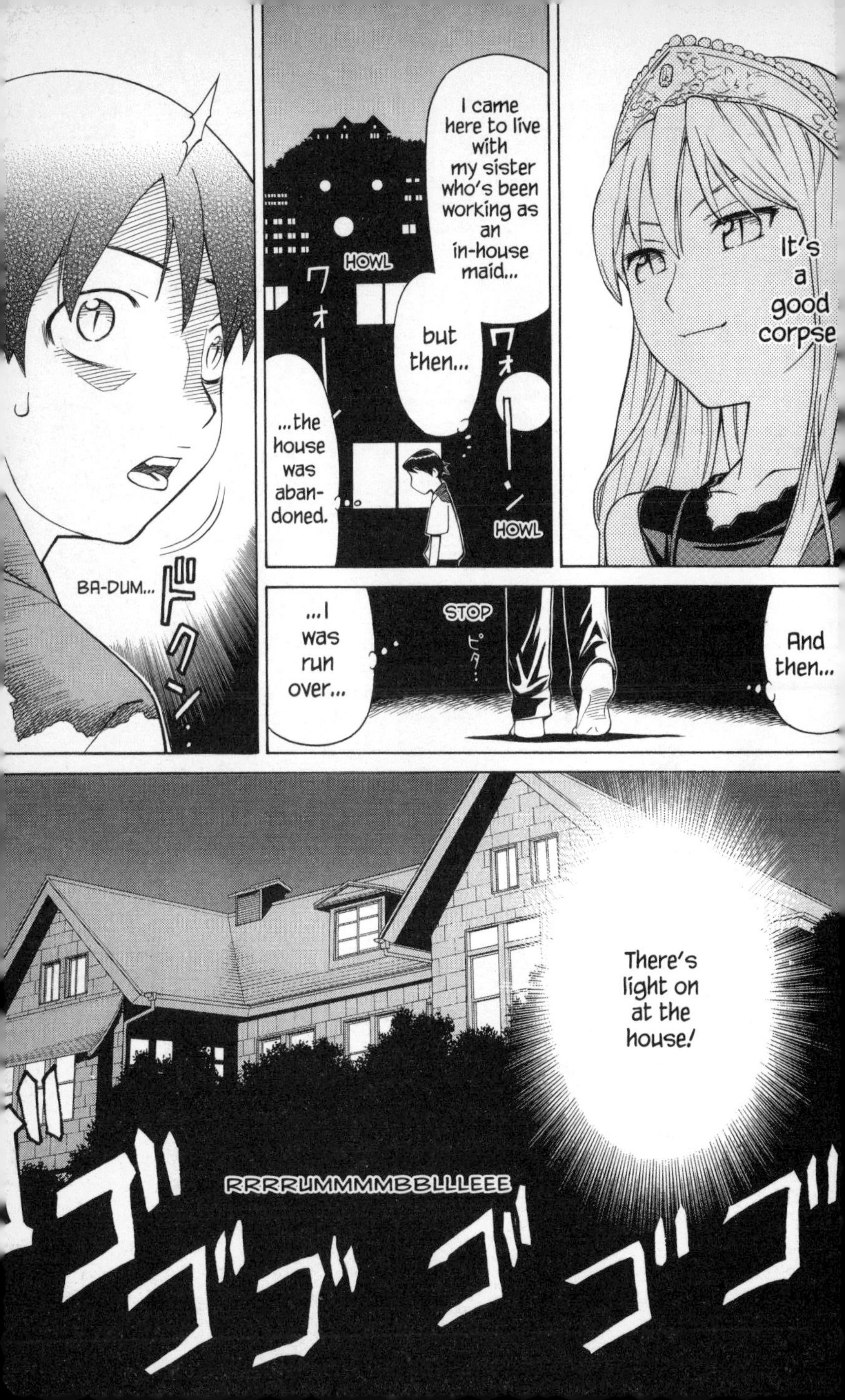
It's a good corpse
I came here to live with my sister who's been working as an in-house maid...
HOWL
but then...
...the house was abandoned.
HOWL
And then...
STOP
...I was run over...
BA-DUM...
There's light on at the house!
RRRRUMMMMBBLLLEEE

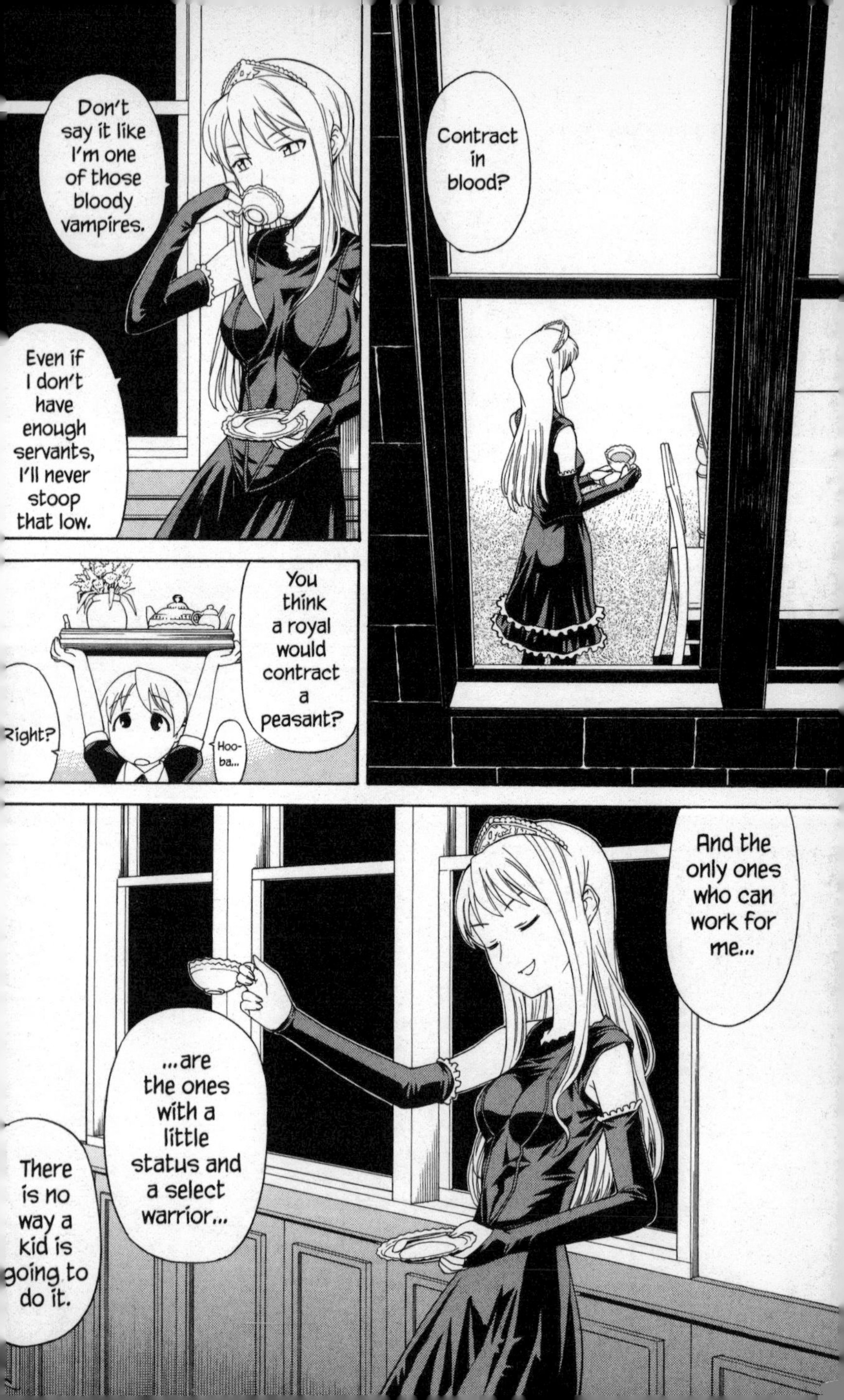
Contract in blood?
Don't say it like I'm one of those bloody vampires.
Even if I don't have enough servants, I'll never stoop that low.
You think a royal would contract a peasant?
Hoo-ba...
Right?
And the only ones who can work for me...
...are the ones with a little status and a select warrior...
There is no way a kid is going to do it.

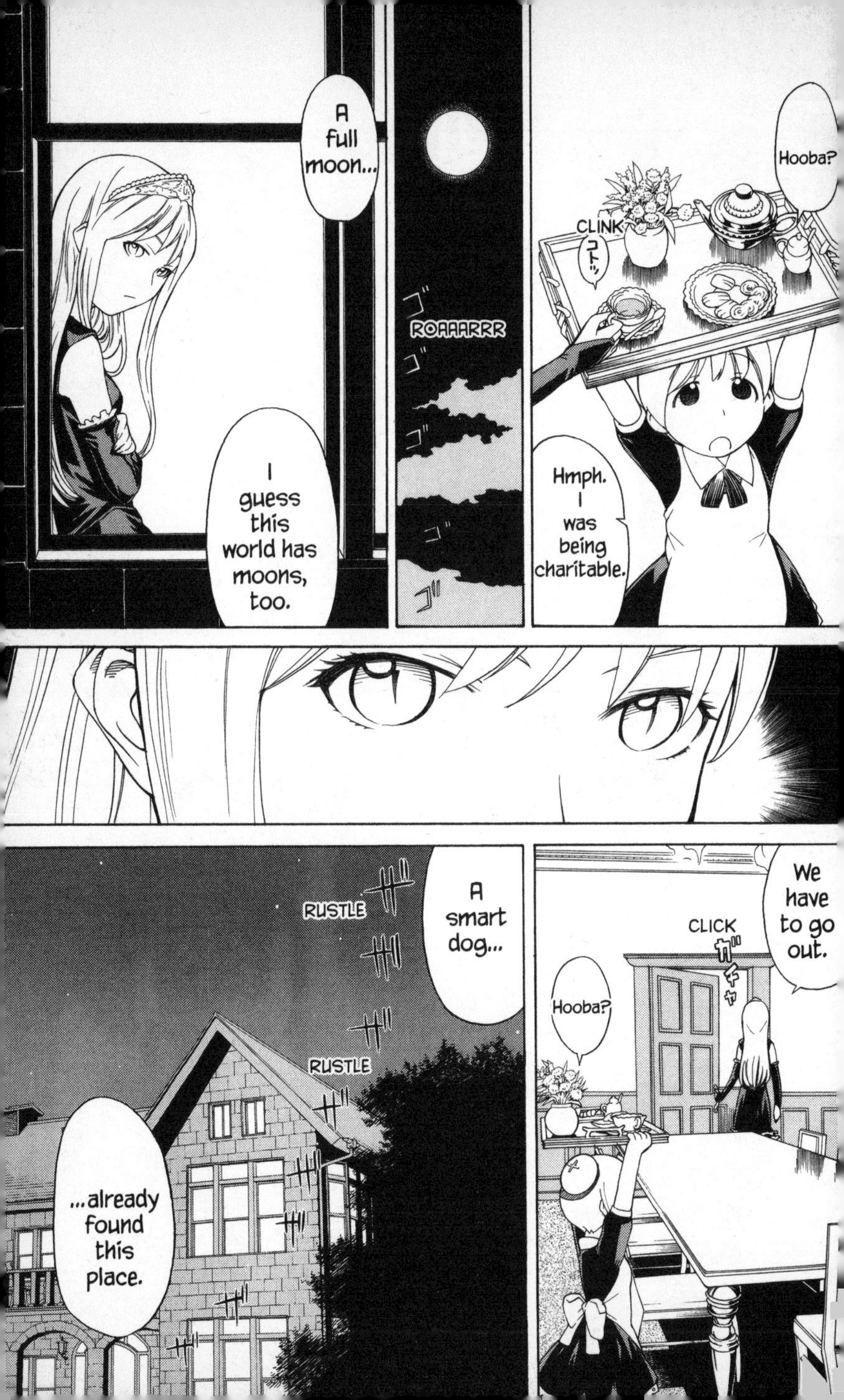
Hooba?
CLINK
コトッ
Hmph. I was being charitable.
ゴ
ROAAARRR
ゴゴゴゴ
A full moon...
I guess this world has moons, too.
We have to go out.
CLICK
ガチャ
Hooba?
A smart dog...
RUSTLE
RUSTLE
...already found this place.

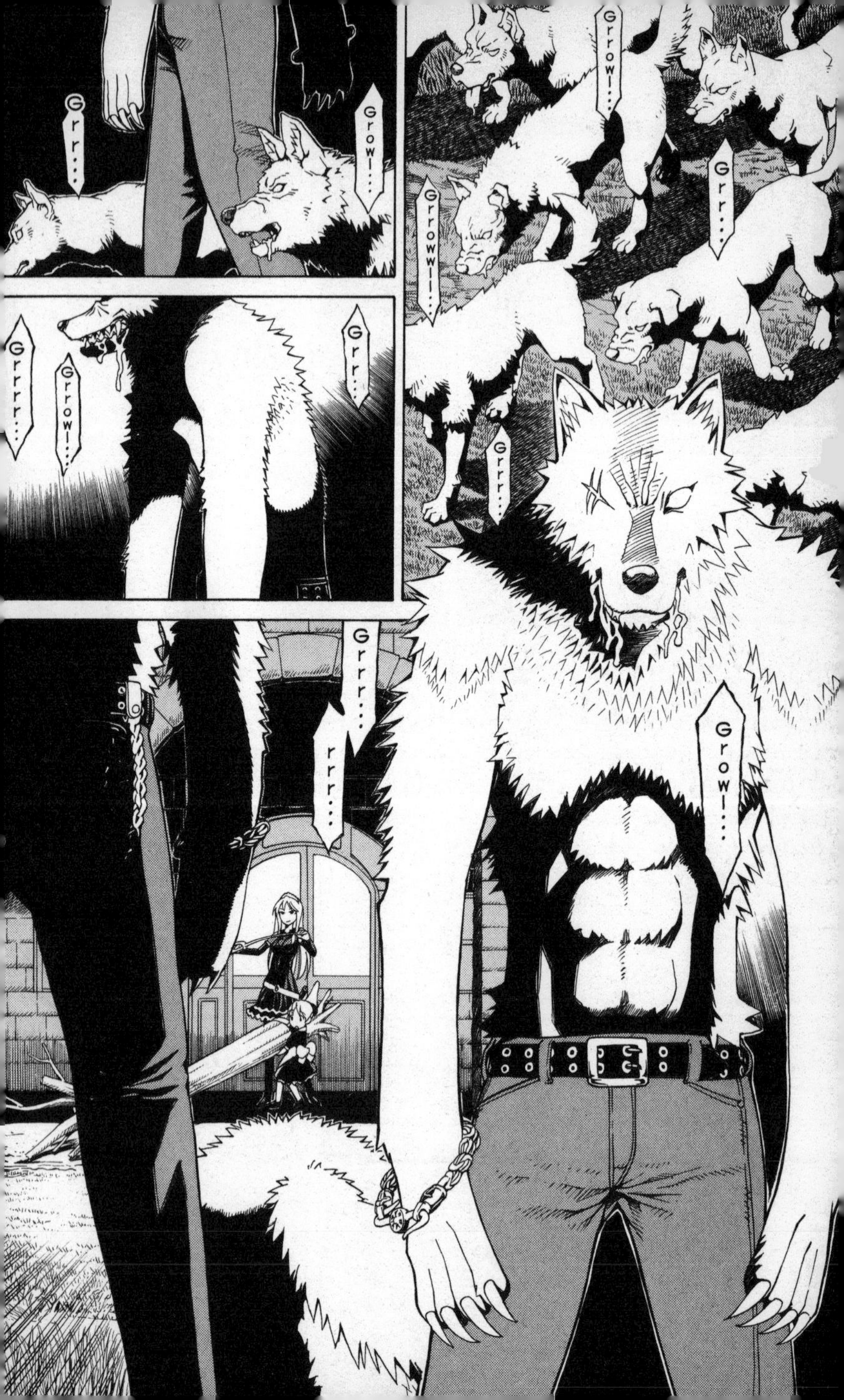
Grr...
Grrowl...
Grrowwl...
Grr...
Growl...
Grr...
Grr...
Grrowl...
Grrrr...
Growl...
Grrr...
rrr...

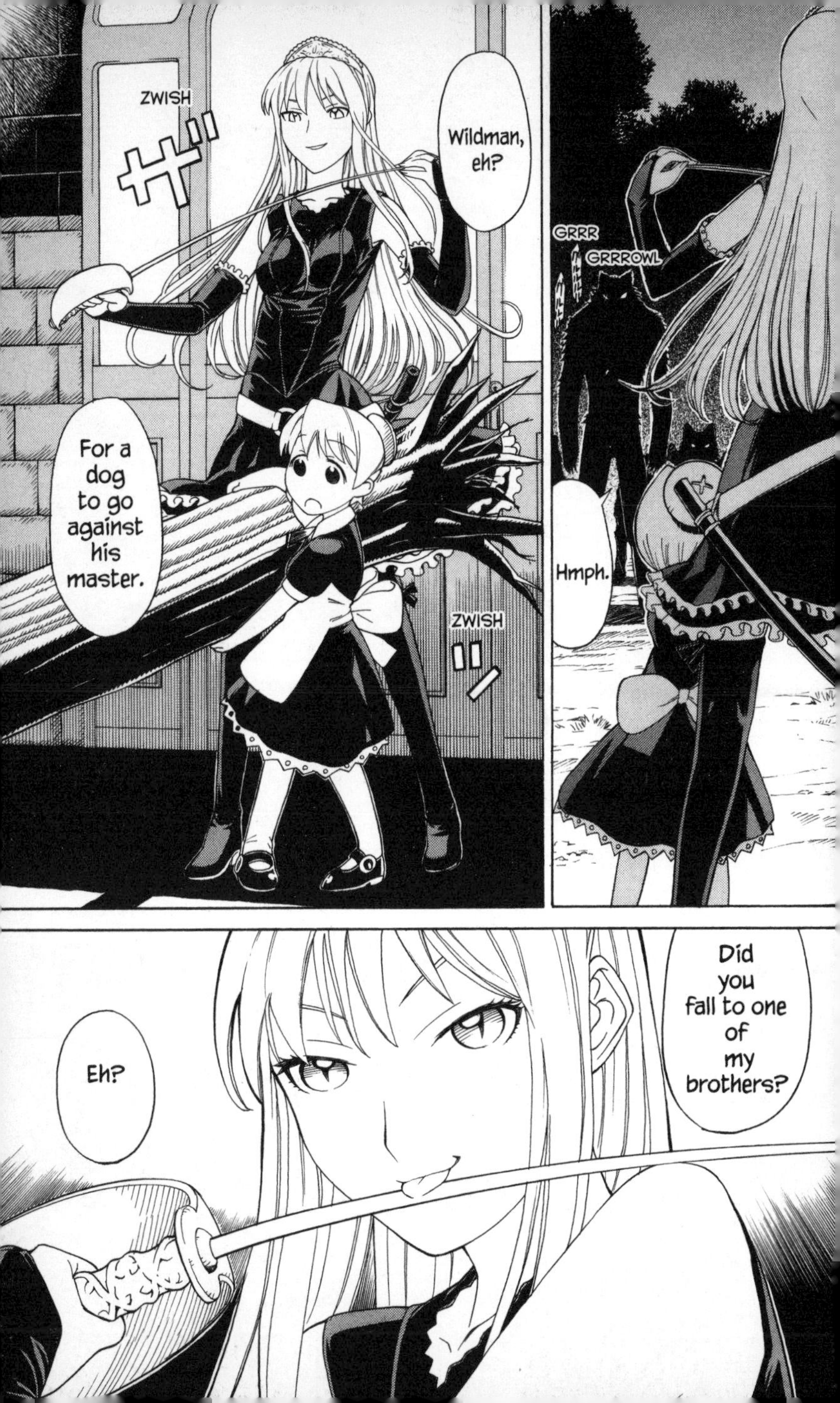
GRRR
GRRROWL
Hmph.
Wildman, eh?
ZWISH
For a dog to go against his master.
ZWISH
Did you fall to one of my brothers?
Eh?

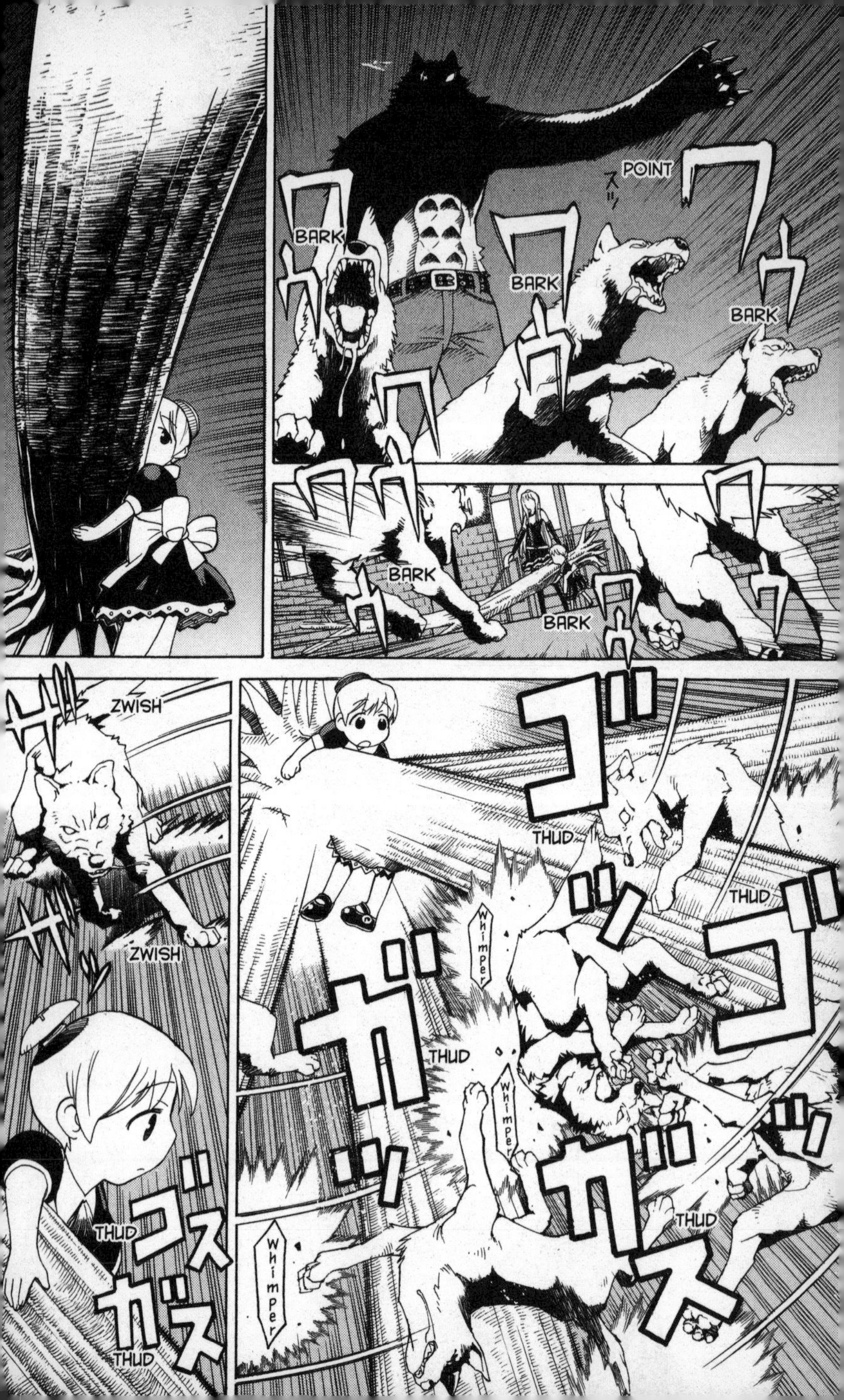
POINT
BARK
BARK
BARK
BARK
BARK
THUD
THUD
Whimper
THUD
Whimper
THUD
Whimper
ZWISH
ZWISH
THUD
THUD

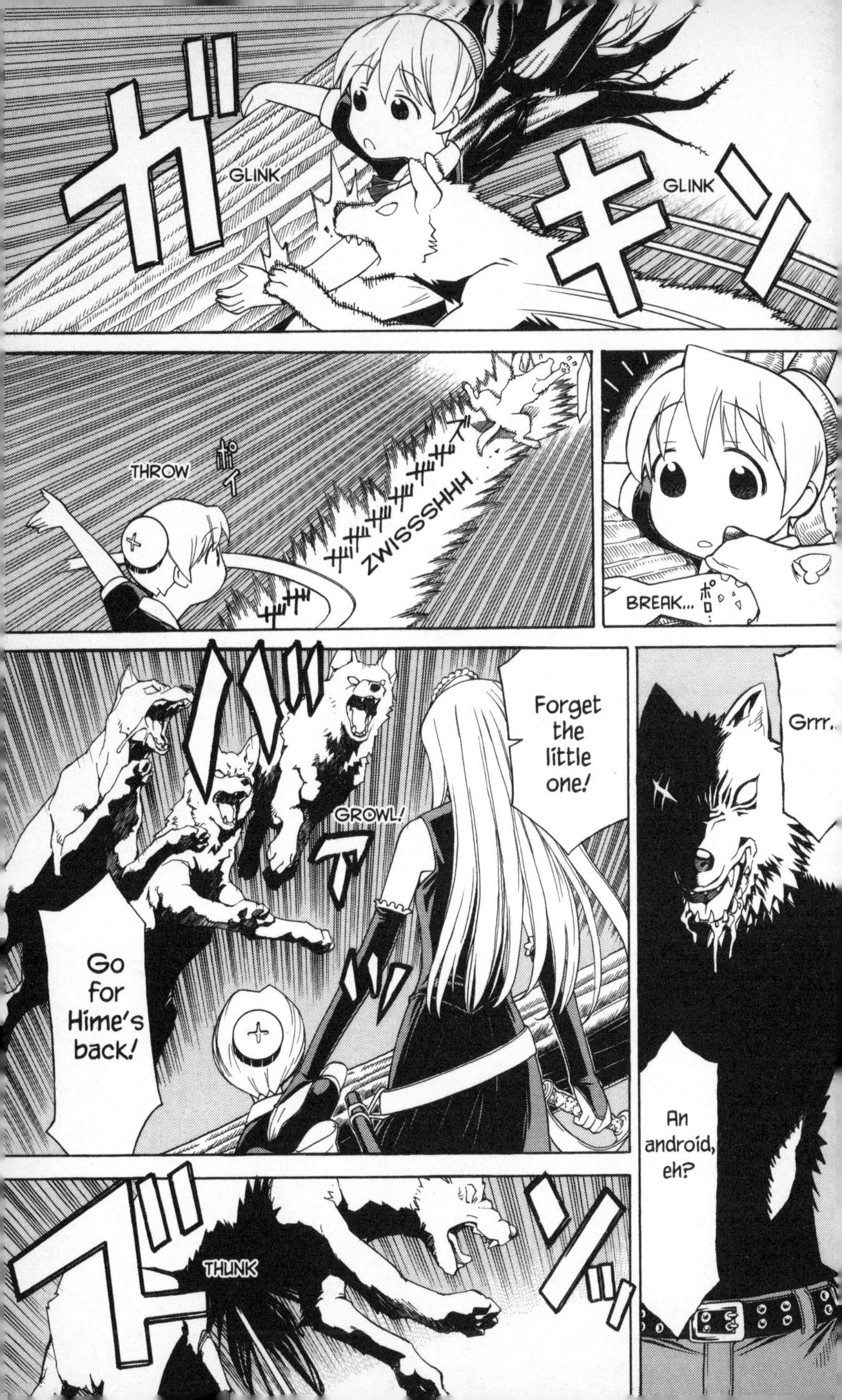
ガキン
GLINK
GLINK
BREAK...
ポロ
ZWISSSHHH
ギギギギギギズ
THROW
ポイ
ギギ
Grrr..
An android, eh?
Forget the little one!
GROWL!
Go for Hime's back!
ズドン
THUNK

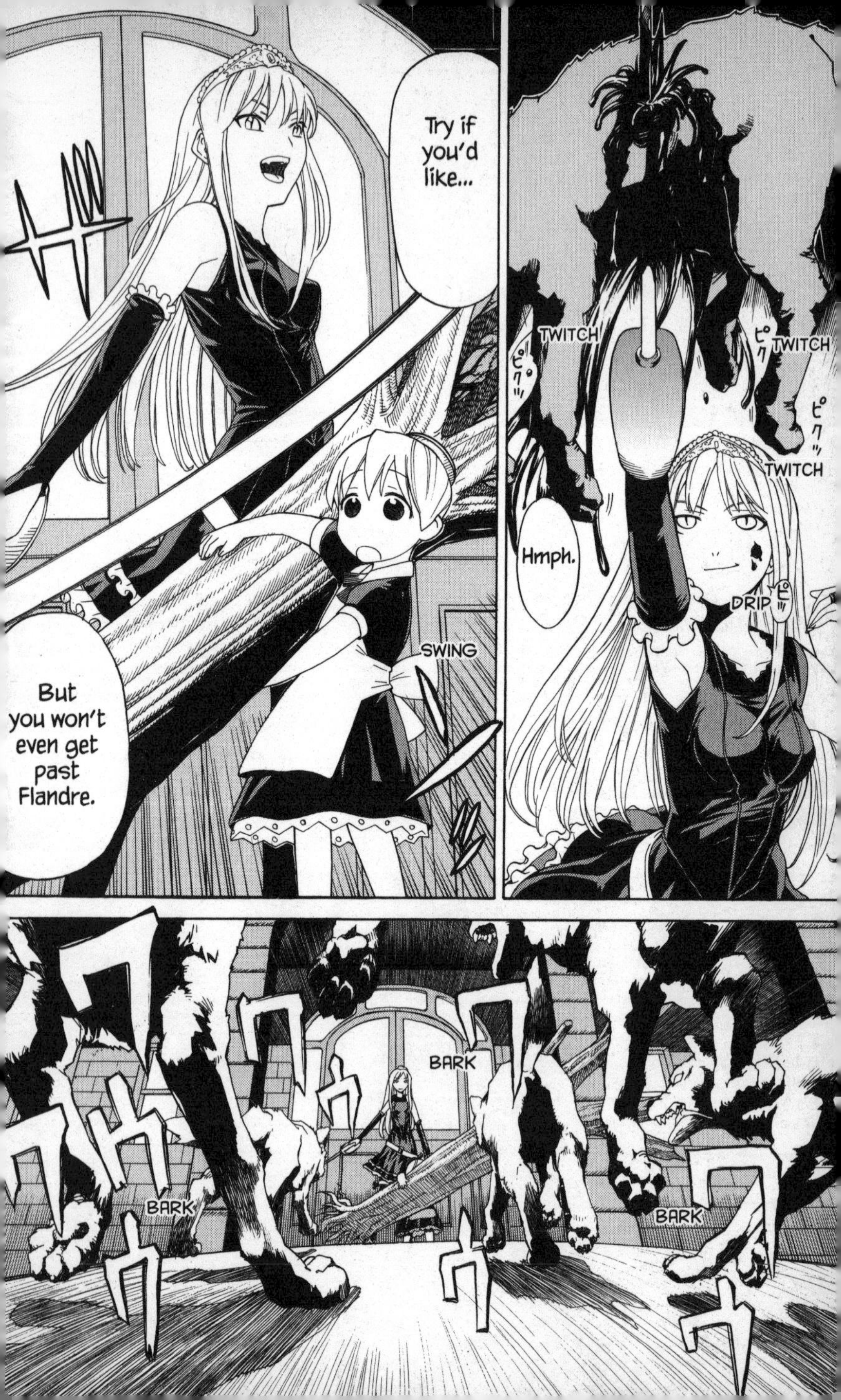

TWITCH
ピクッ
TWITCH
ピクッ
TWITCH
Hmph.
DRIP
Try if you'd like...
But you won't even get past Flandre.
SWING
BARK
BARK
BARK

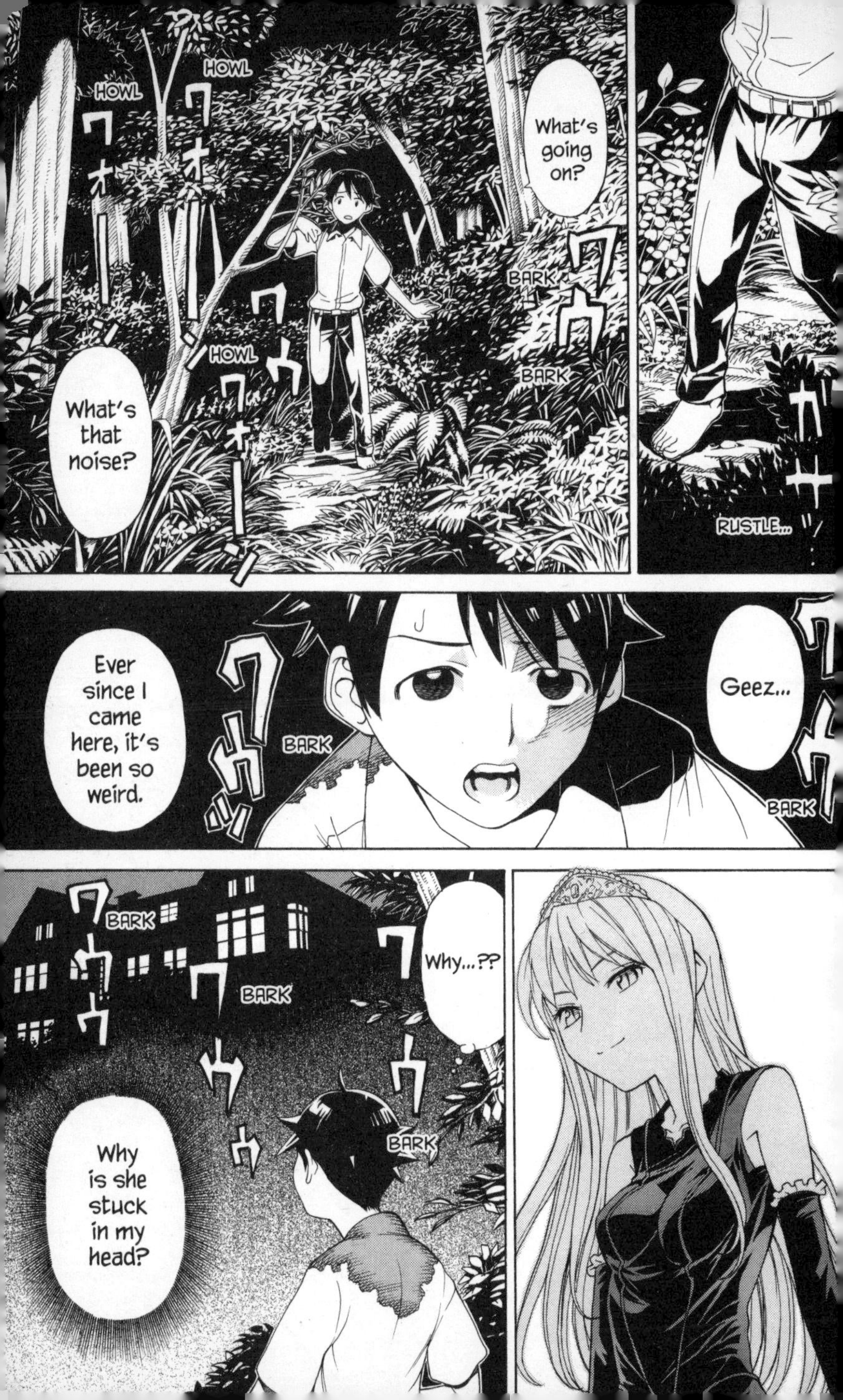
RUSTLE...
What's going on?
HOWL
HOWL
BARK
HOWL
BARK
What's that noise?
Geez...
BARK
BARK
Ever since I came here, it's been so weird.
Why...??
BARK
BARK
BARK
Why is she stuck in my head?

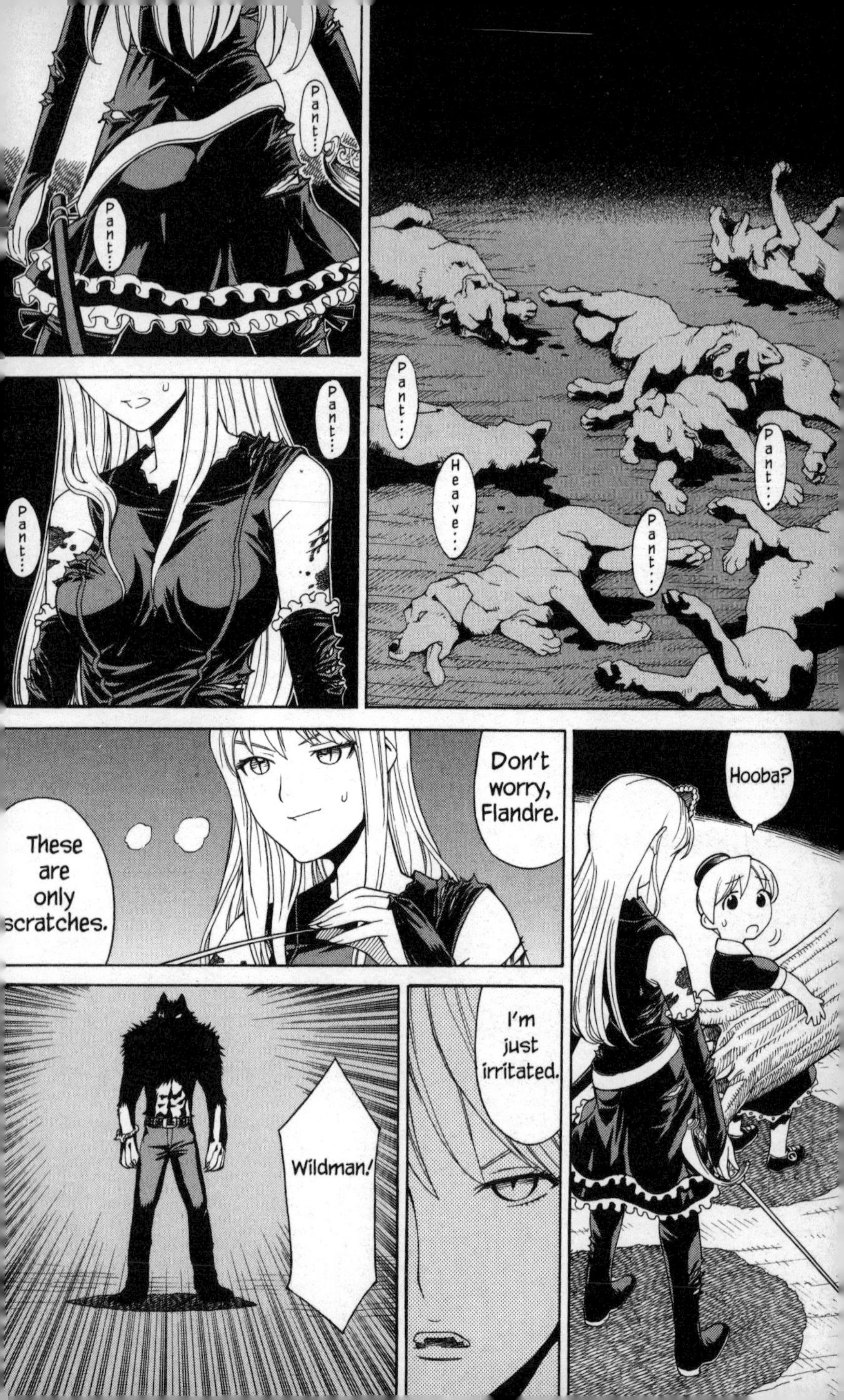

Pant...
Pant...
Pant...
Heave...
Pant...
Pant...
Pant...
Pant...
Hooba?
Don't worry, Flandre.
These are only scratches.
I'm just irritated.
Wildman!

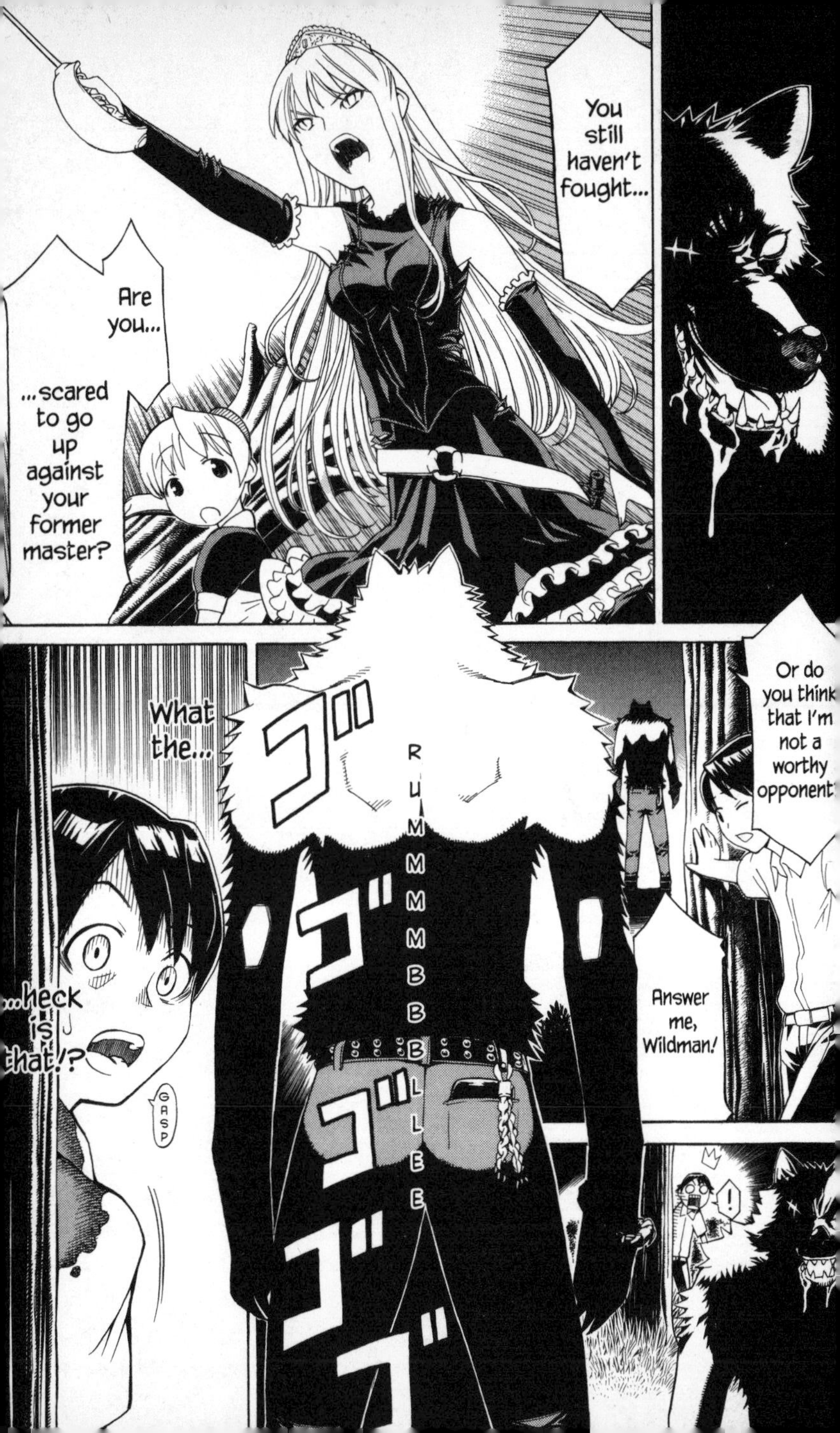
You still haven't fought...
Are you...
...scared to go up against your former master?
Or do you think that I'm not a worthy opponent
Answer me, Wildman!
!
What the...
...heck is that!?
GASP
RUMMMMMBBBLLEE

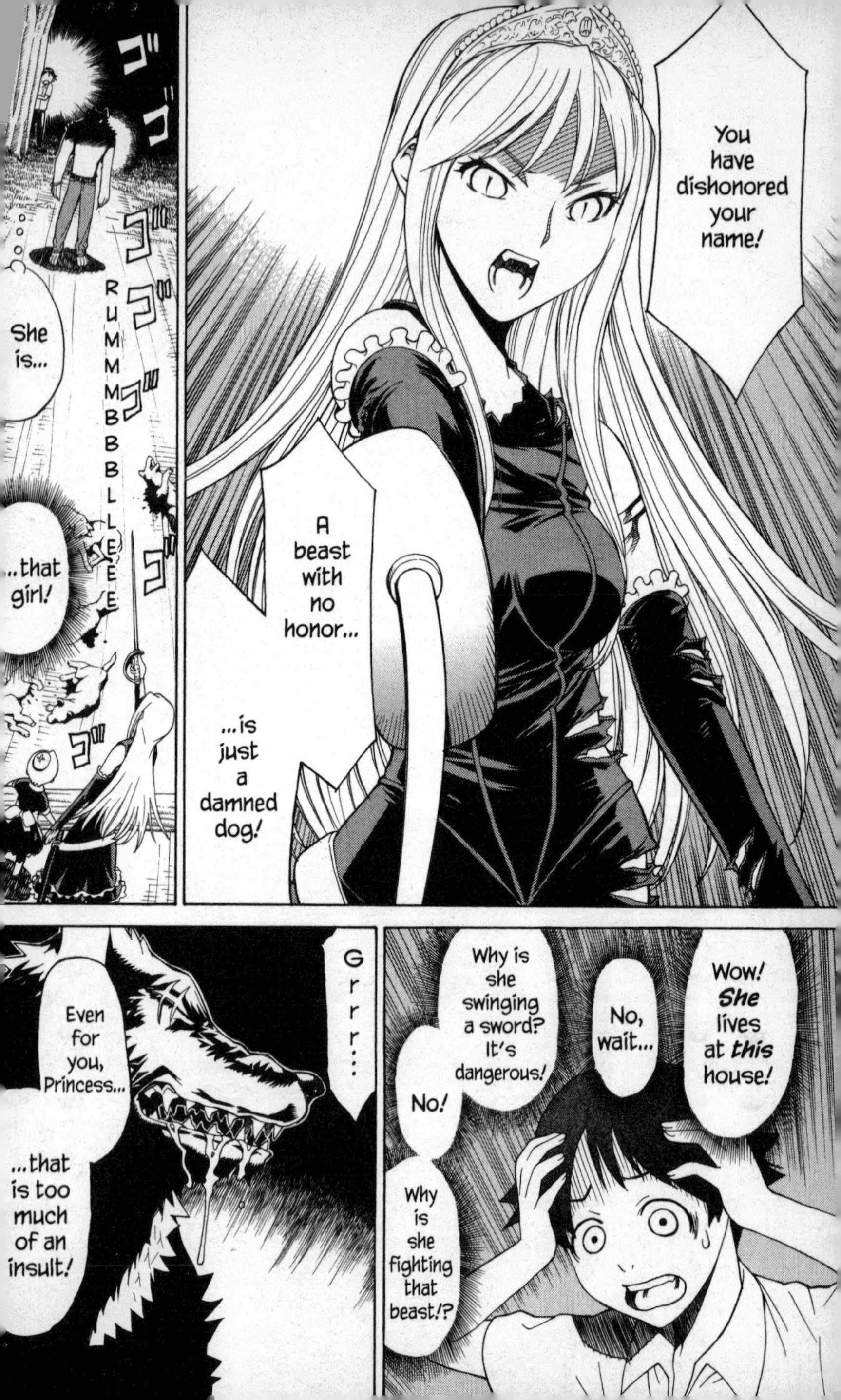
You have dishonored your name!
A beast with no honor...
...is just a damned dog!
She is...
RUMMMBBBLLEEE
...that girl!
Wow! *She* lives at *this* house!
No, wait...
Why is she swinging a sword? It's dangerous!
No!
Why is she fighting that beast!?
Grrr...
Even for you, Princess...
...that is too much of an insult!

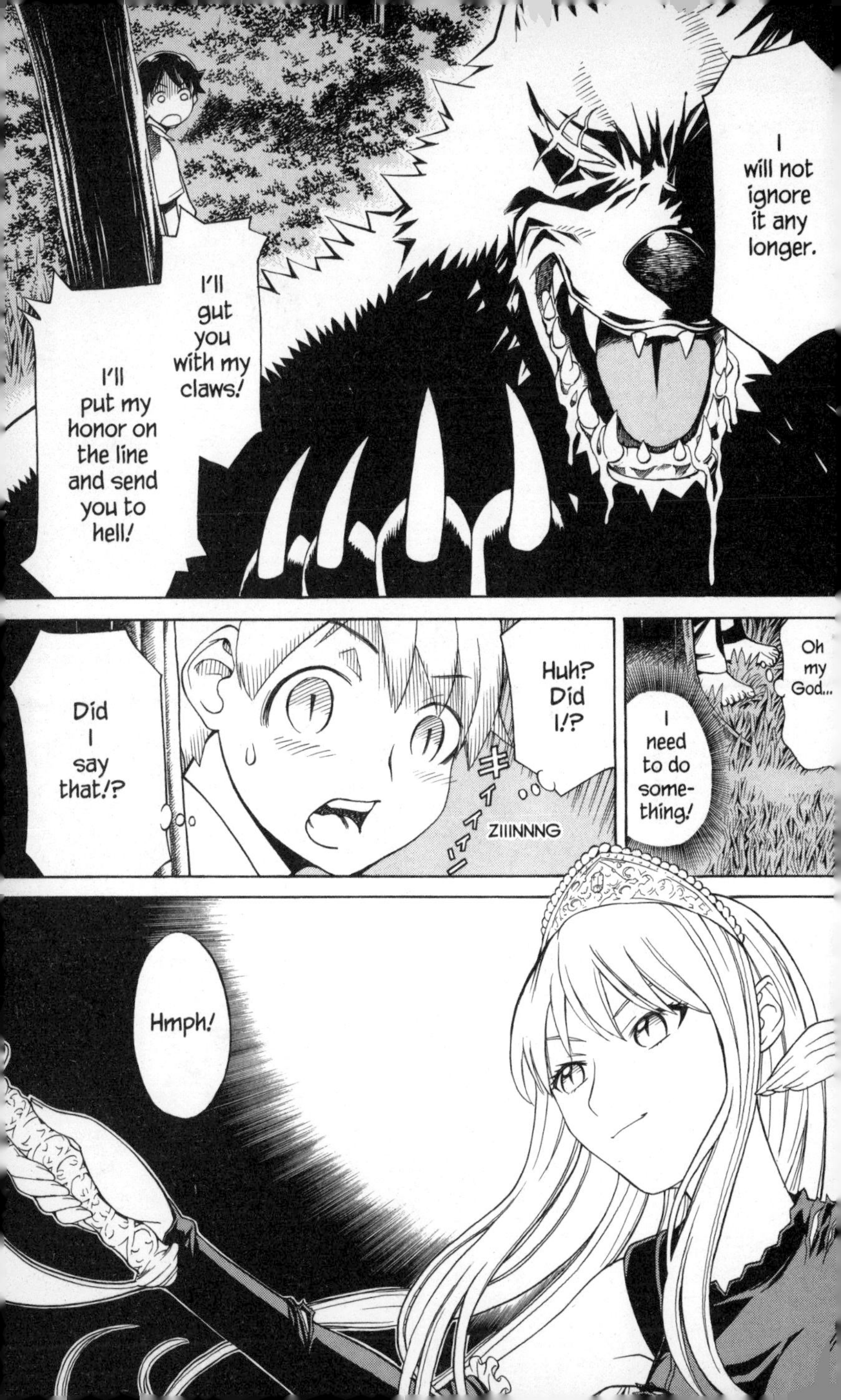
I will not ignore it any longer.
I'll gut you with my claws!
I'll put my honor on the line and send you to hell!
Oh my God...
I need to do something!
Huh? Did I!?
ZIIINNNG
Did I say that!?
Hmph!

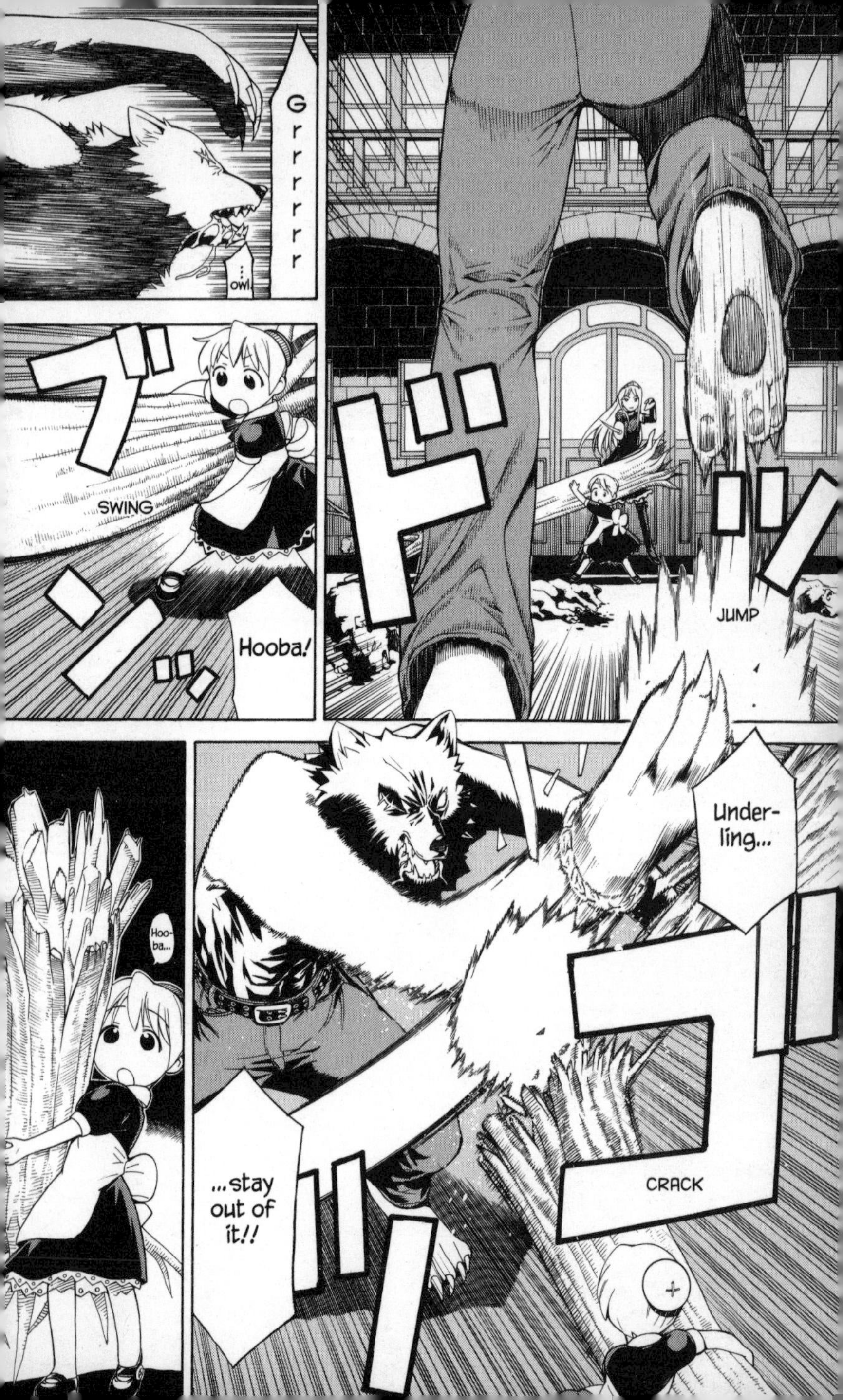

ドン
JUMP
Grrrrrr
...ow!
ブン
SWING
Hooba!
Under-ling...
...stay out of it!!
ゴン
CRACK
Hoo-ba...

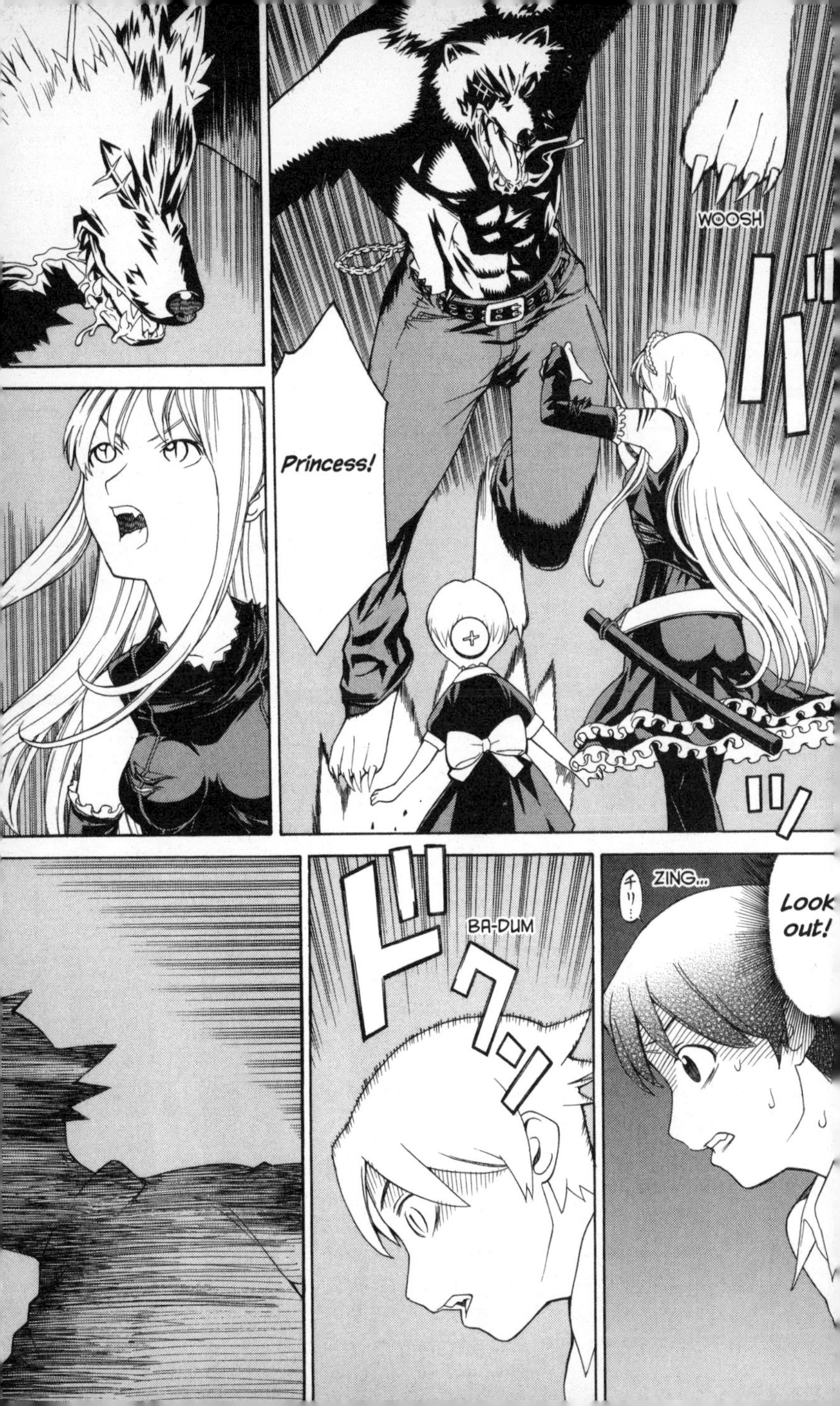
WOOSH
Princess!
Look out!
ZING...
チリ…
BA-DUM

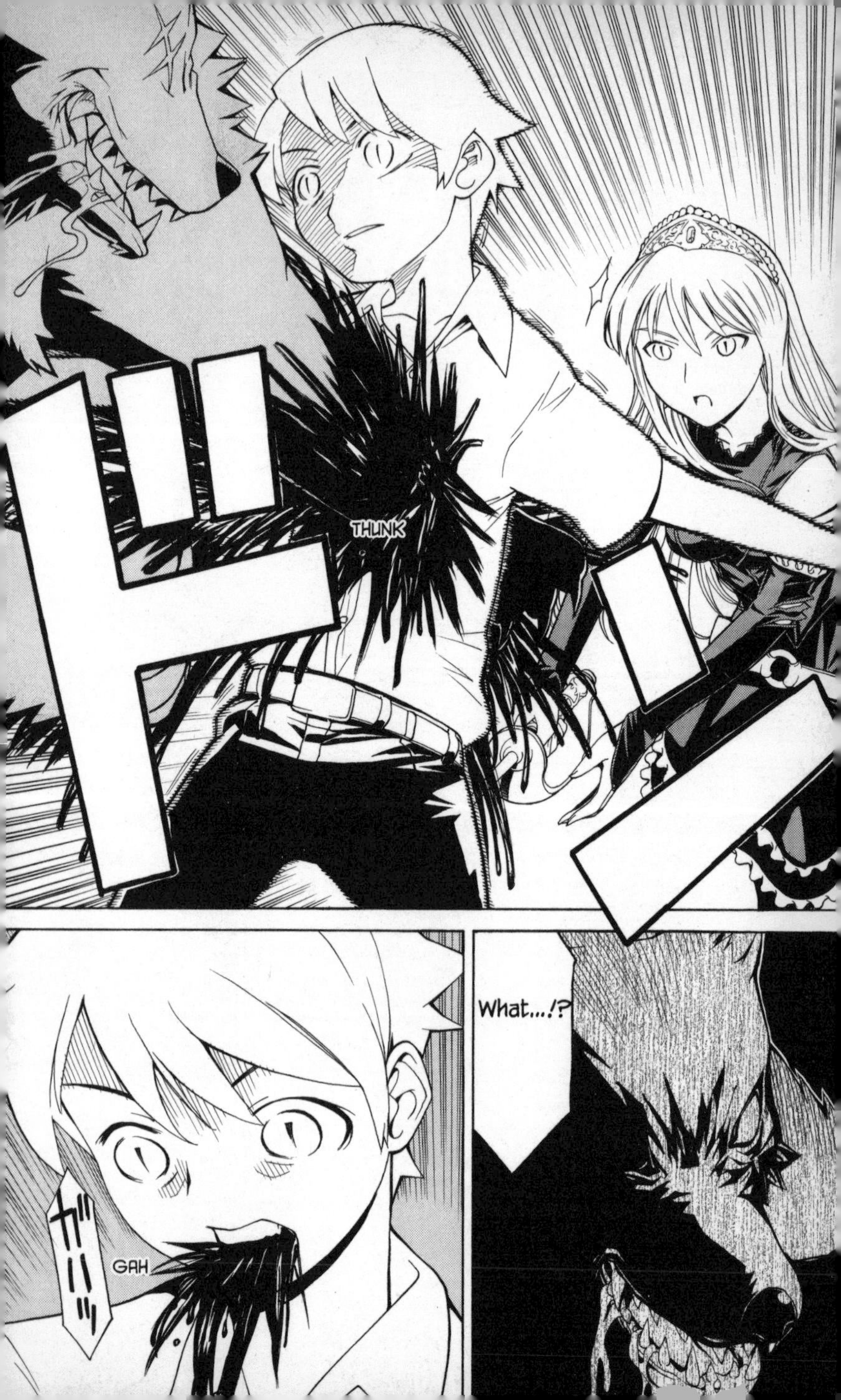
THUNK
What...!?
ガハッ
GAH

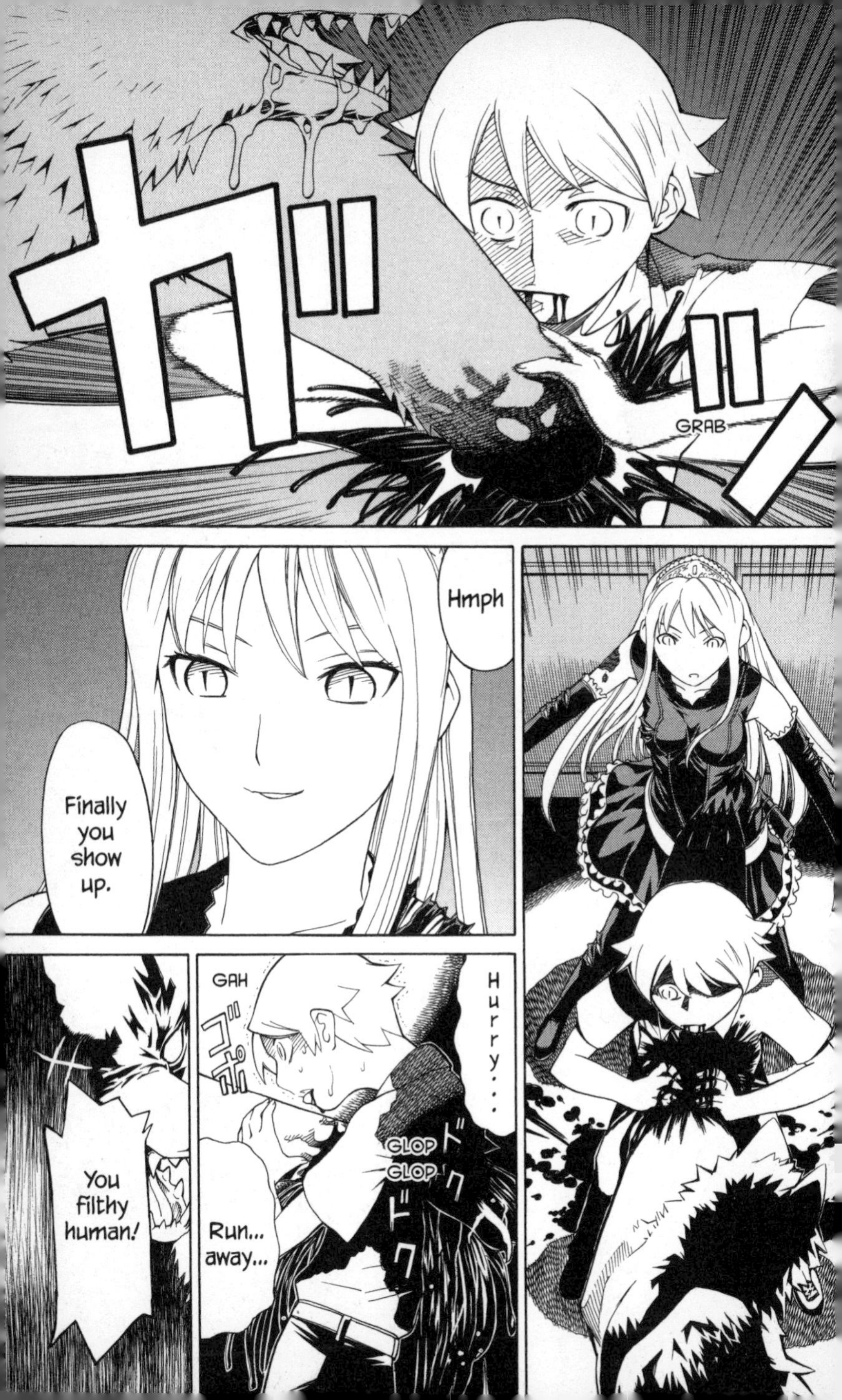

ガッ
GRAB
Hmph
Finally you show up.
Hurry...
GAH
ゴポッ
GLOP GLOP
ドクドク
Run... away...
You filthy human!

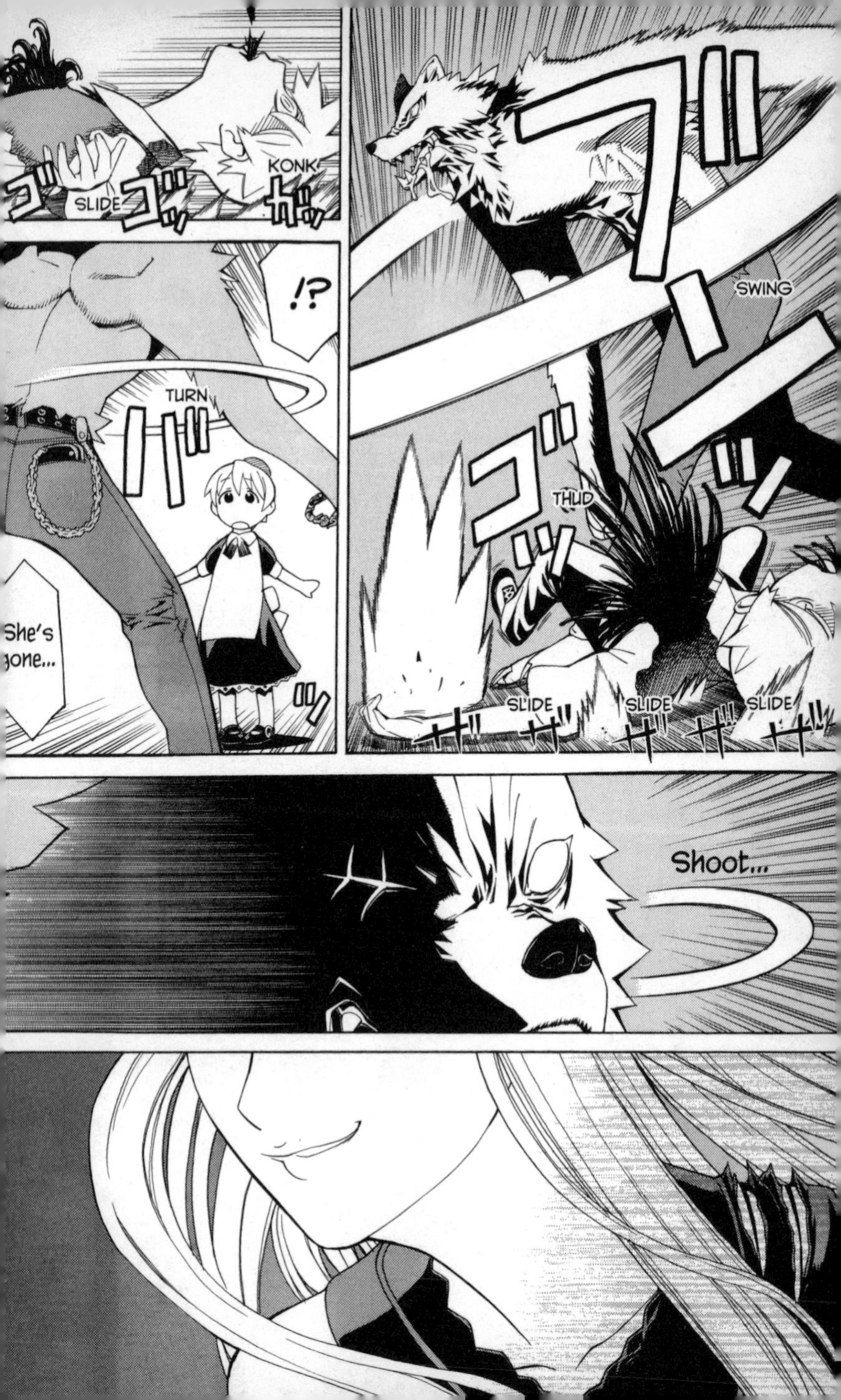
SWING
THUD
SLIDE
SLIDE
SLIDE
KONK
SLIDE
!?
TURN
She's gone...
Shoot...

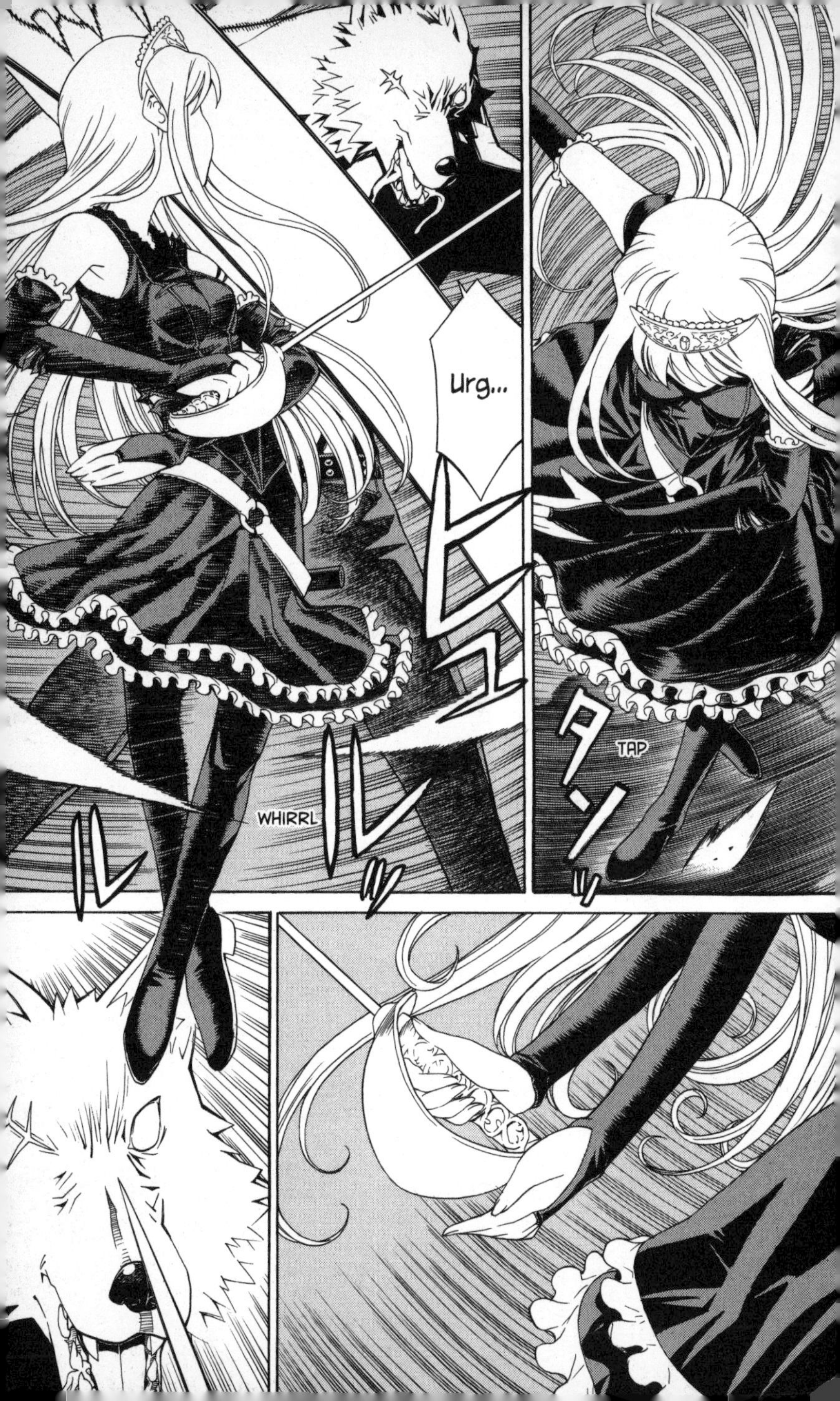
TAP
Urg...
WHIRRL

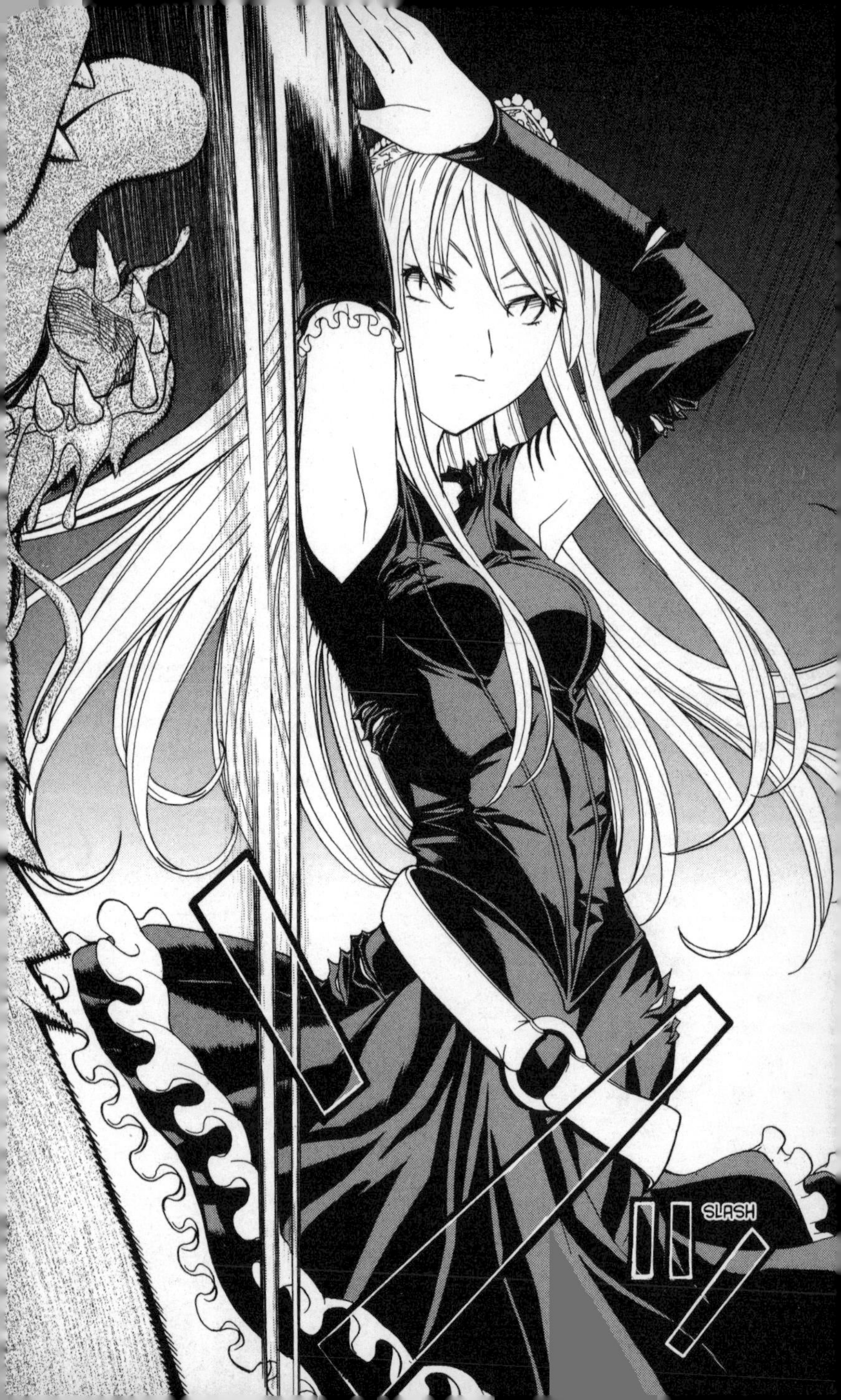
SLASH

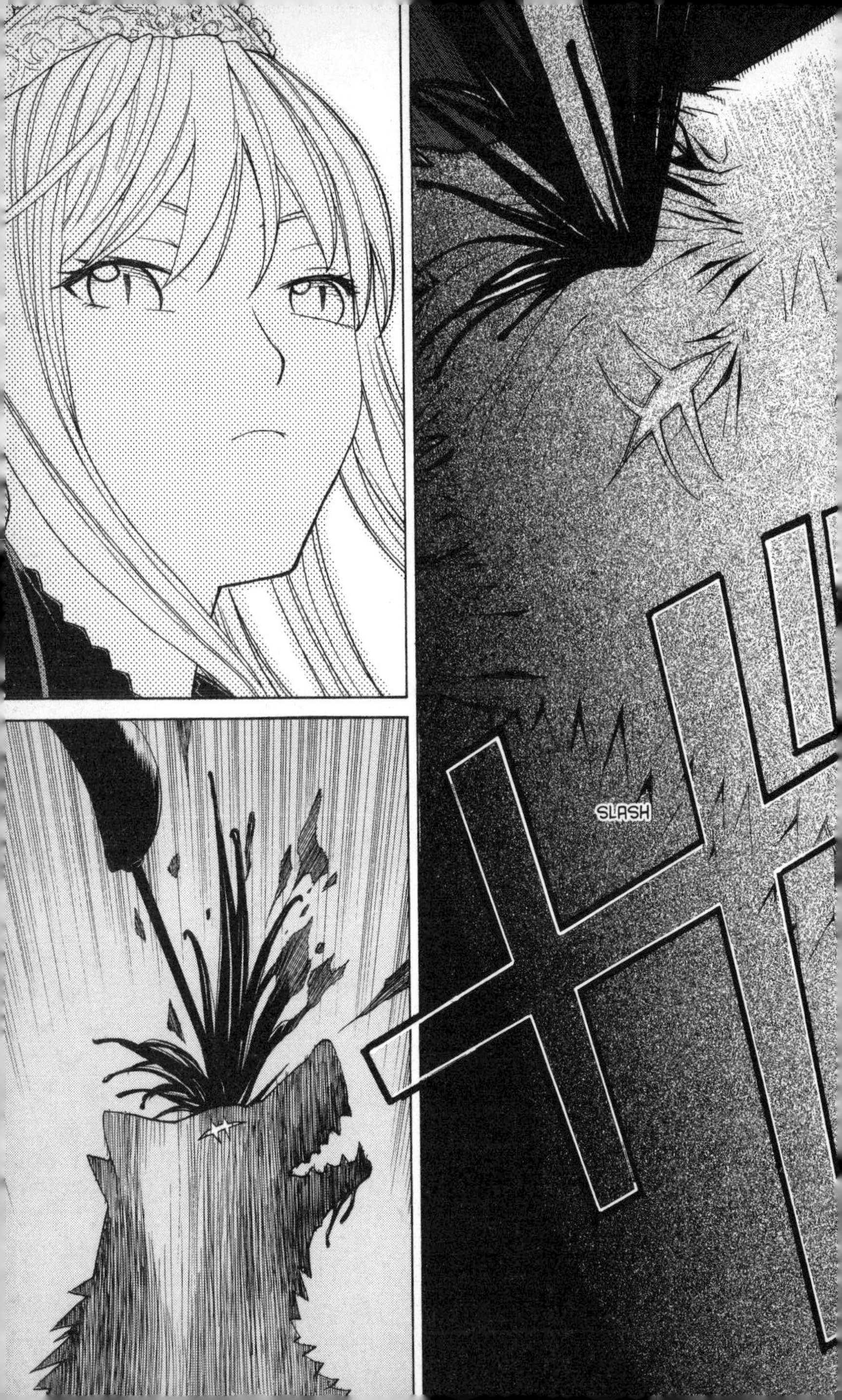
SLASH

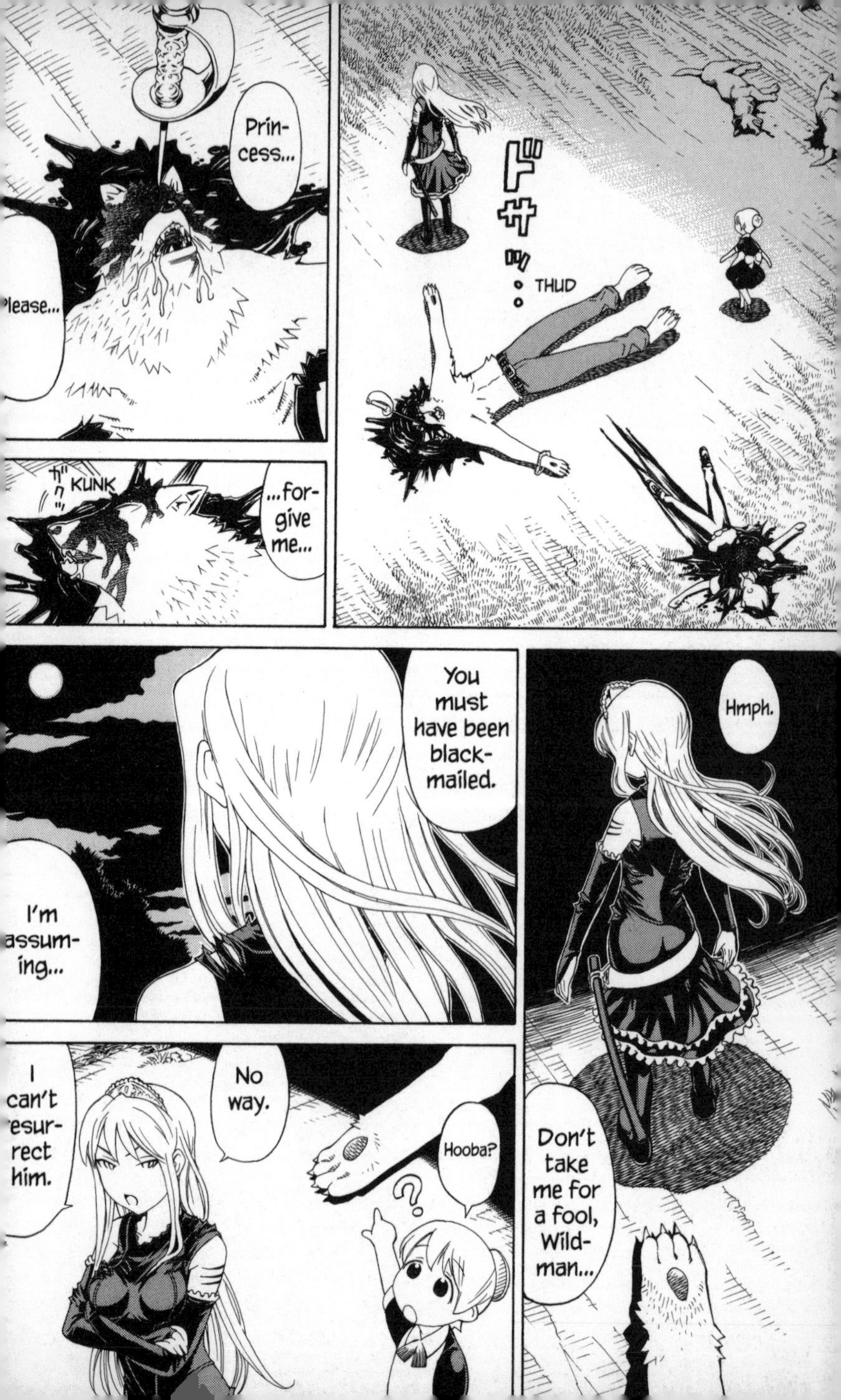

ドサッ
THUD
Prin-cess...
Please...
...for-give me...
ガクッ
KUNK
Hmph.
Don't take me for a fool, Wild-man...
You must have been black-mailed.
I'm assuming...
Hooba?
No way.
I can't resurrect him.

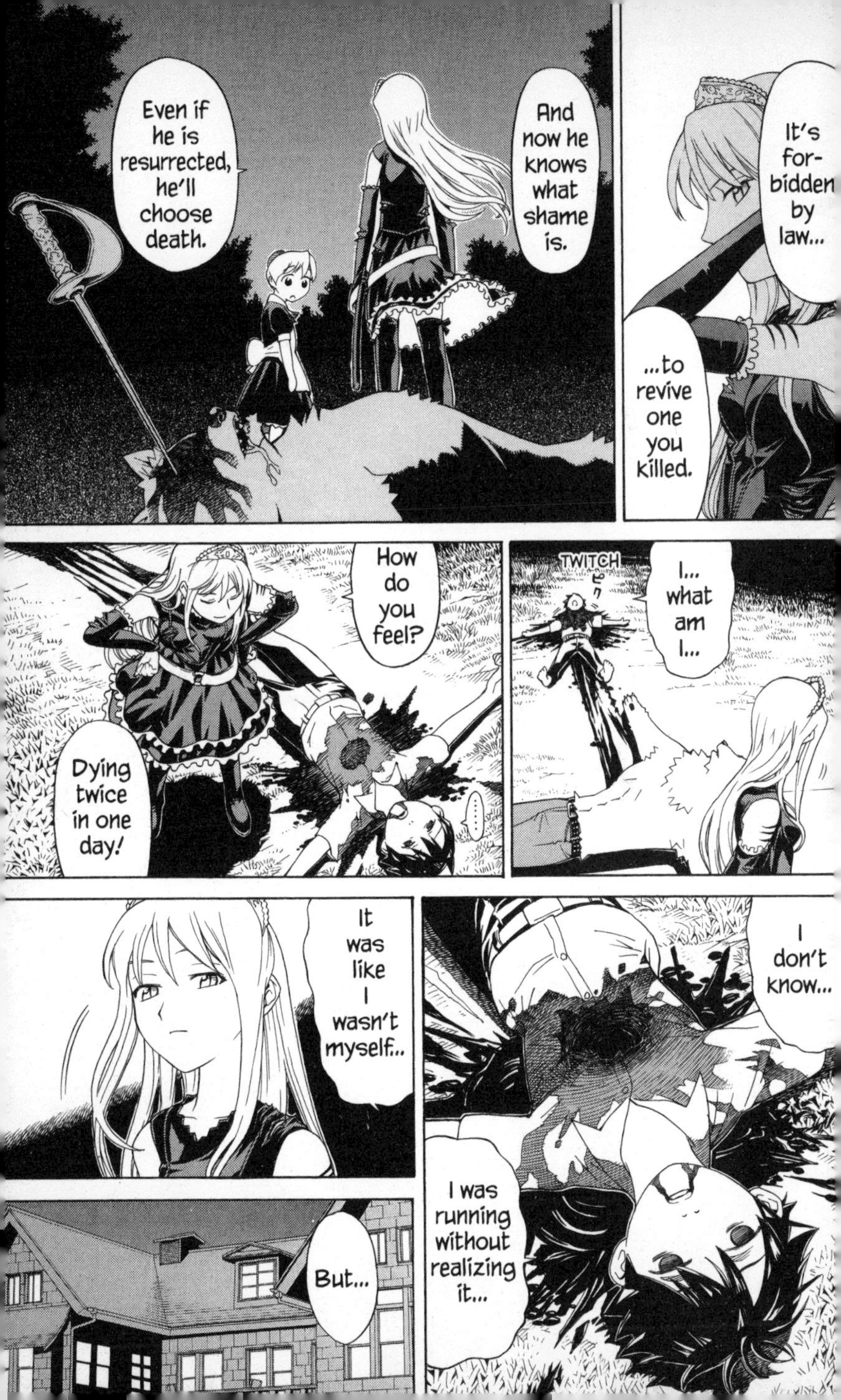

It's forbidden by law...
...to revive one you killed.
And now he knows what shame is.
Even if he is resurrected, he'll choose death.
TWITCH
ピク
I... what am I...
How do you feel?
...
Dying twice in one day!
I don't know...
I was running without realizing it...
It was like I wasn't myself...
But...

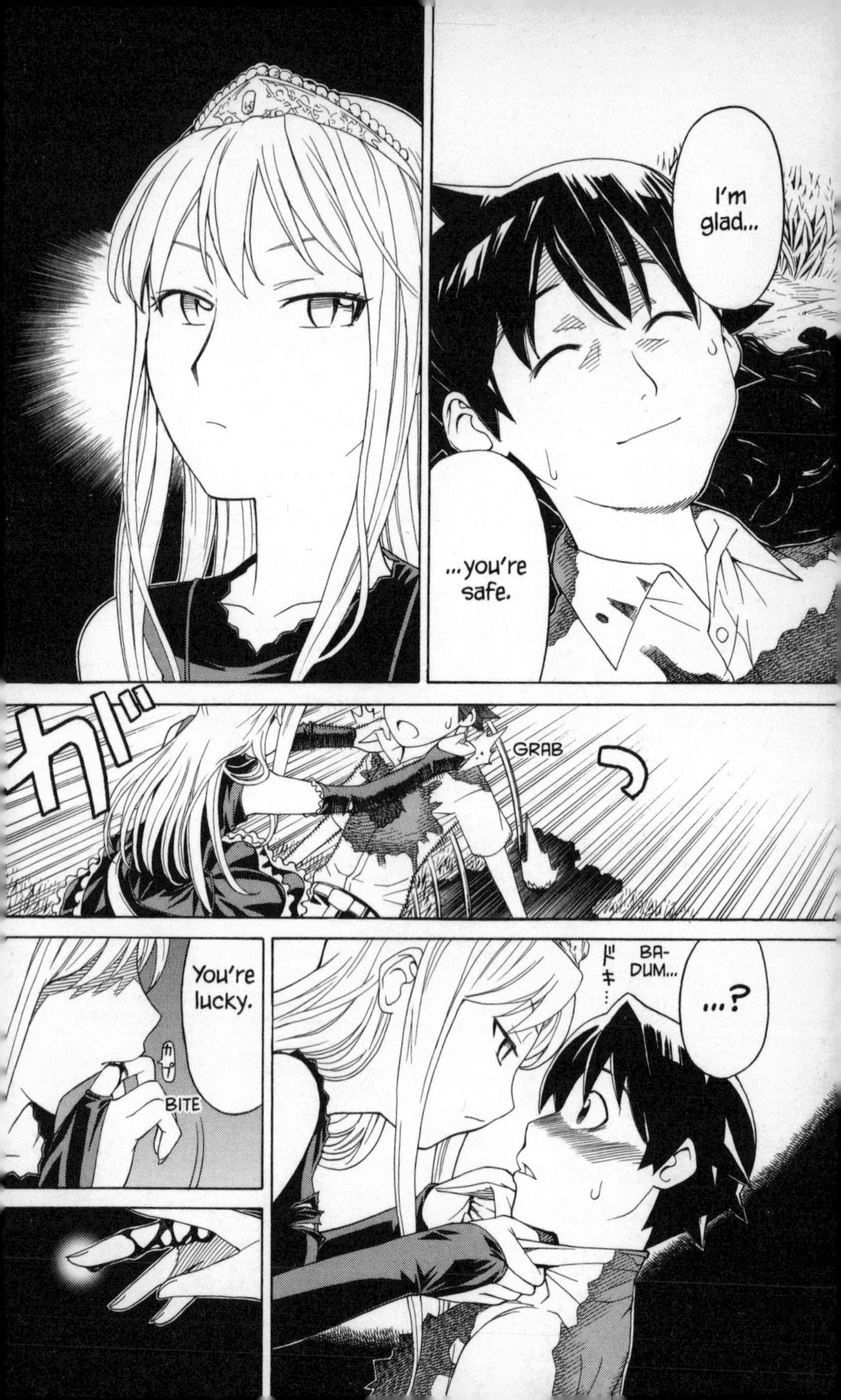
I'm glad...
...you're safe.
GRAB
...?
BA-DUM...
You're lucky.
BITE

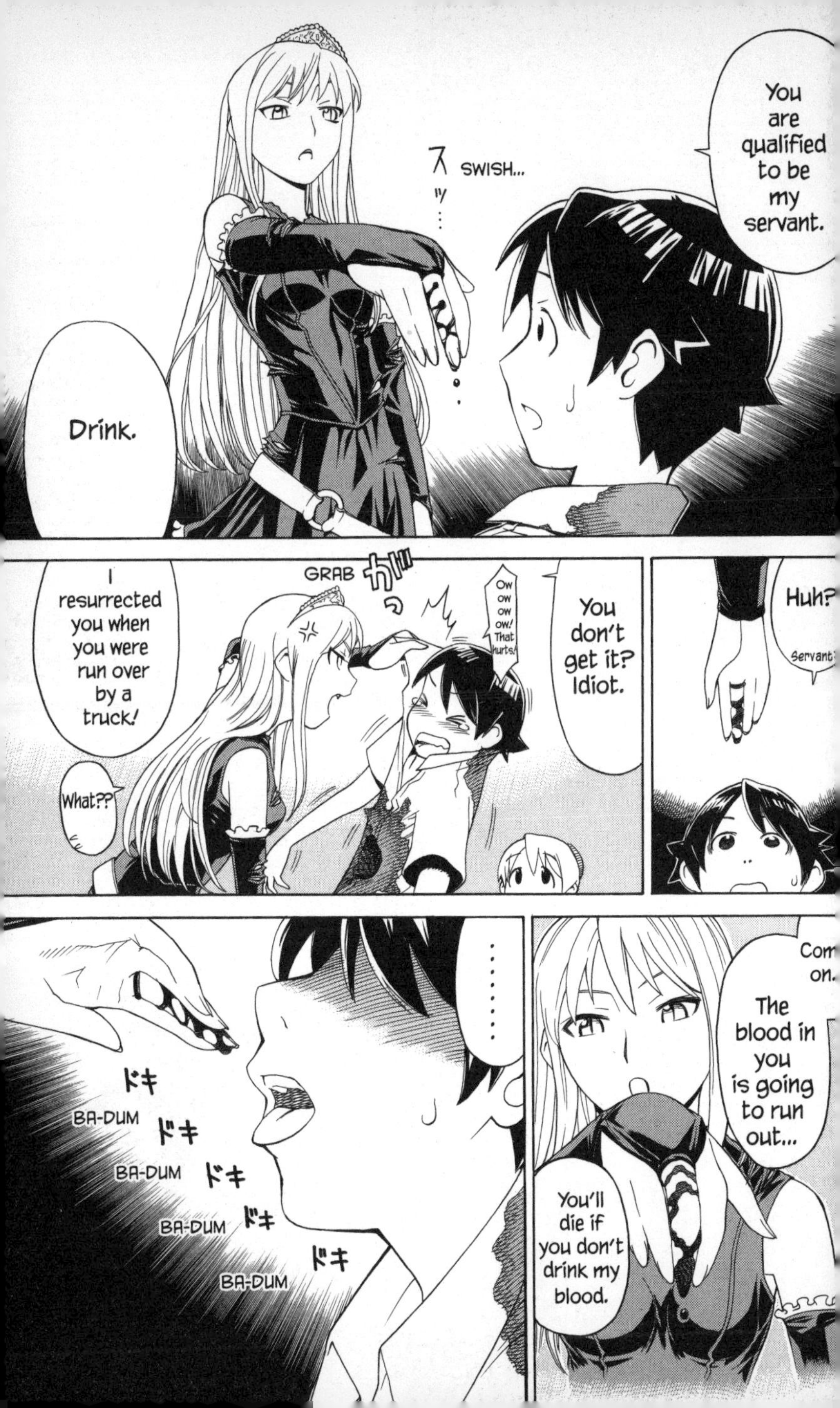

You are qualified to be my servant.
スッ…
SWISH...
Drink.
Huh?
Servant?
You don't get it? Idiot.
がっ
GRAB
Ow ow ow ow! That hurts!
I resurrected you when you were run over by a truck!
What??
Come on.
The blood in you is going to run out...
You'll die if you don't drink my blood.
......
ドキ
BA-DUM
ドキ
BA-DUM
ドキ
BA-DUM
ドキ
BA-DUM
ドキ

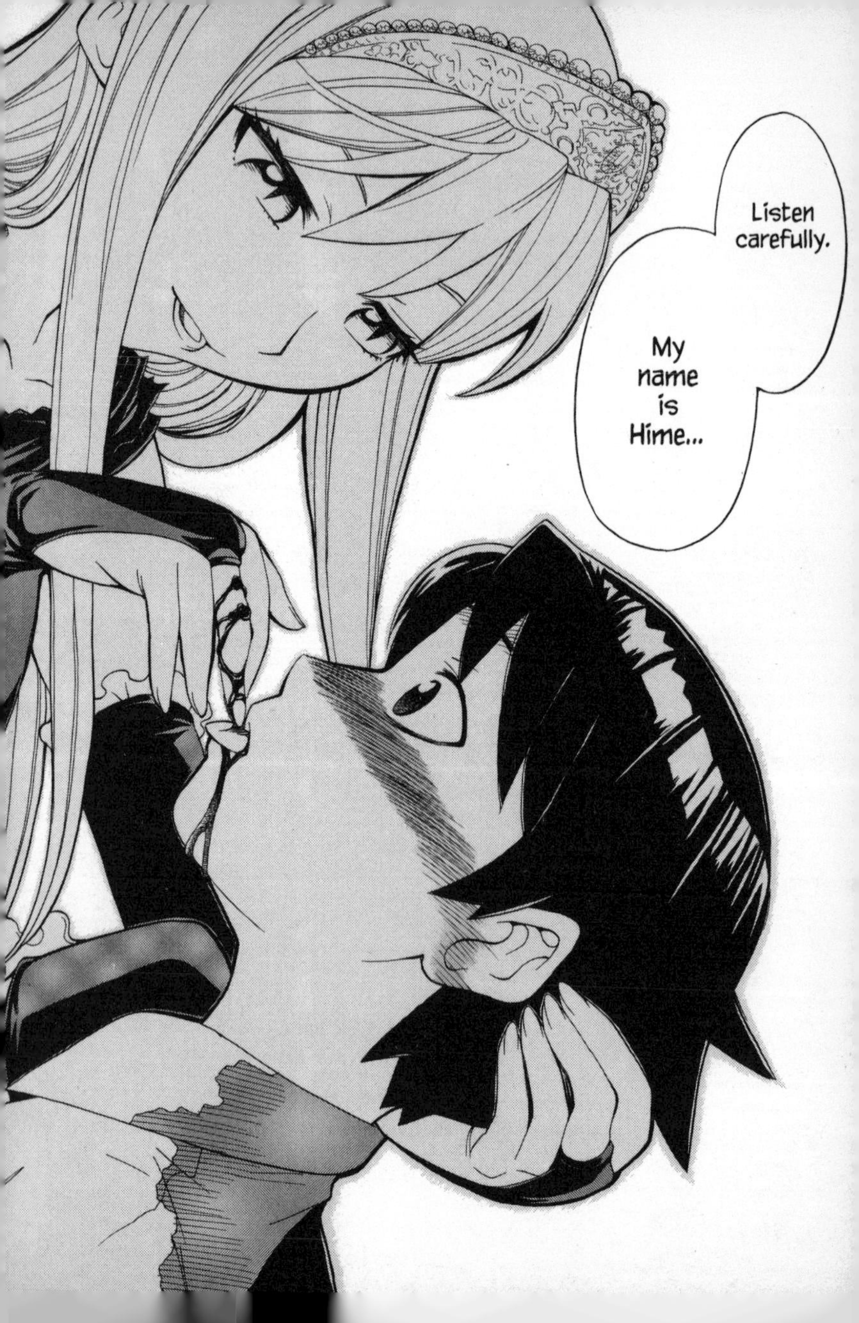
Listen carefully.
My name is Hime...

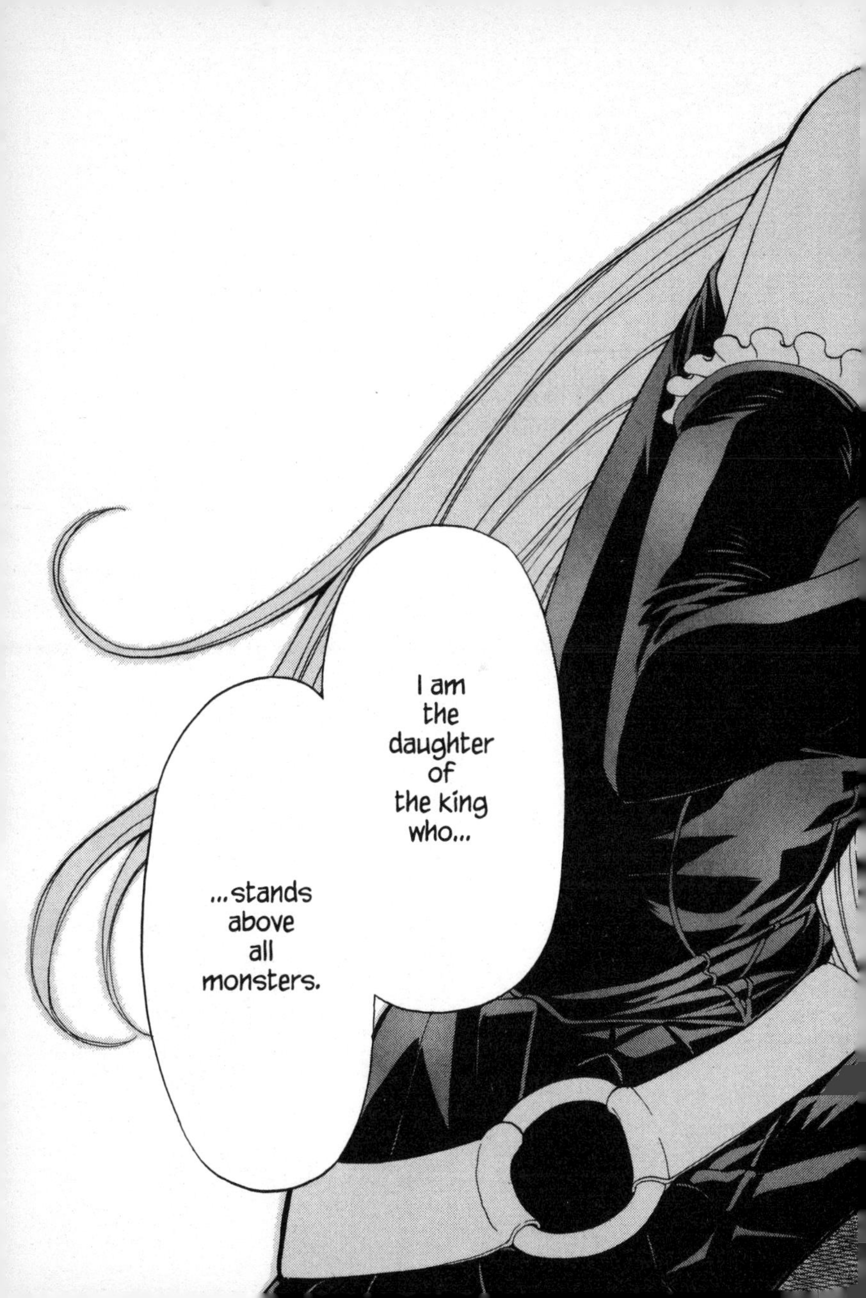
I am the daughter of the king who...
...stands above all monsters.

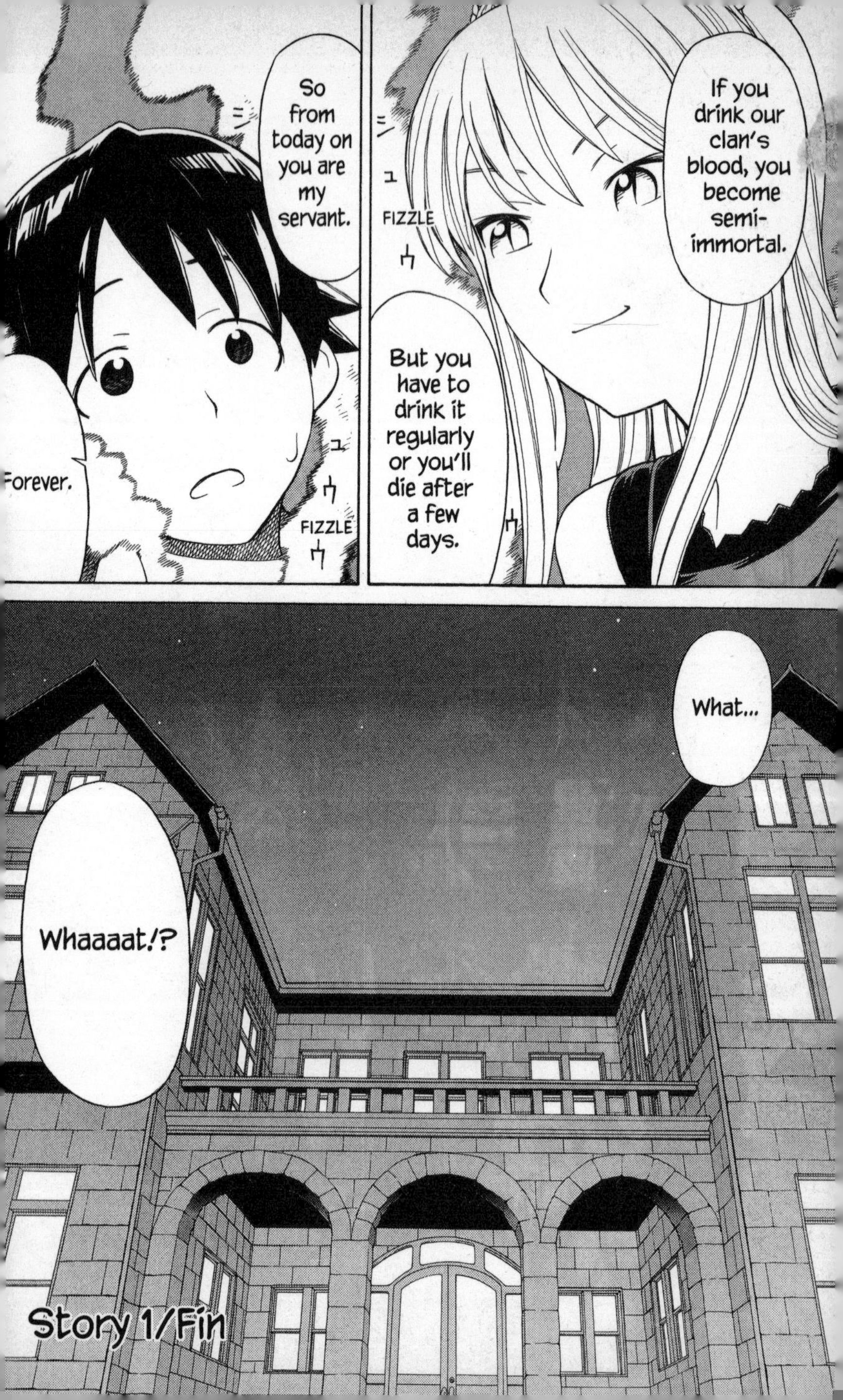
If you drink our clan's blood, you become semi-immortal.
FIZZLE
But you have to drink it regularly or you'll die after a few days.
So from today on you are my servant.
FIZZLE
Forever.
What...
Whaaaat!?
Story 1/Fin

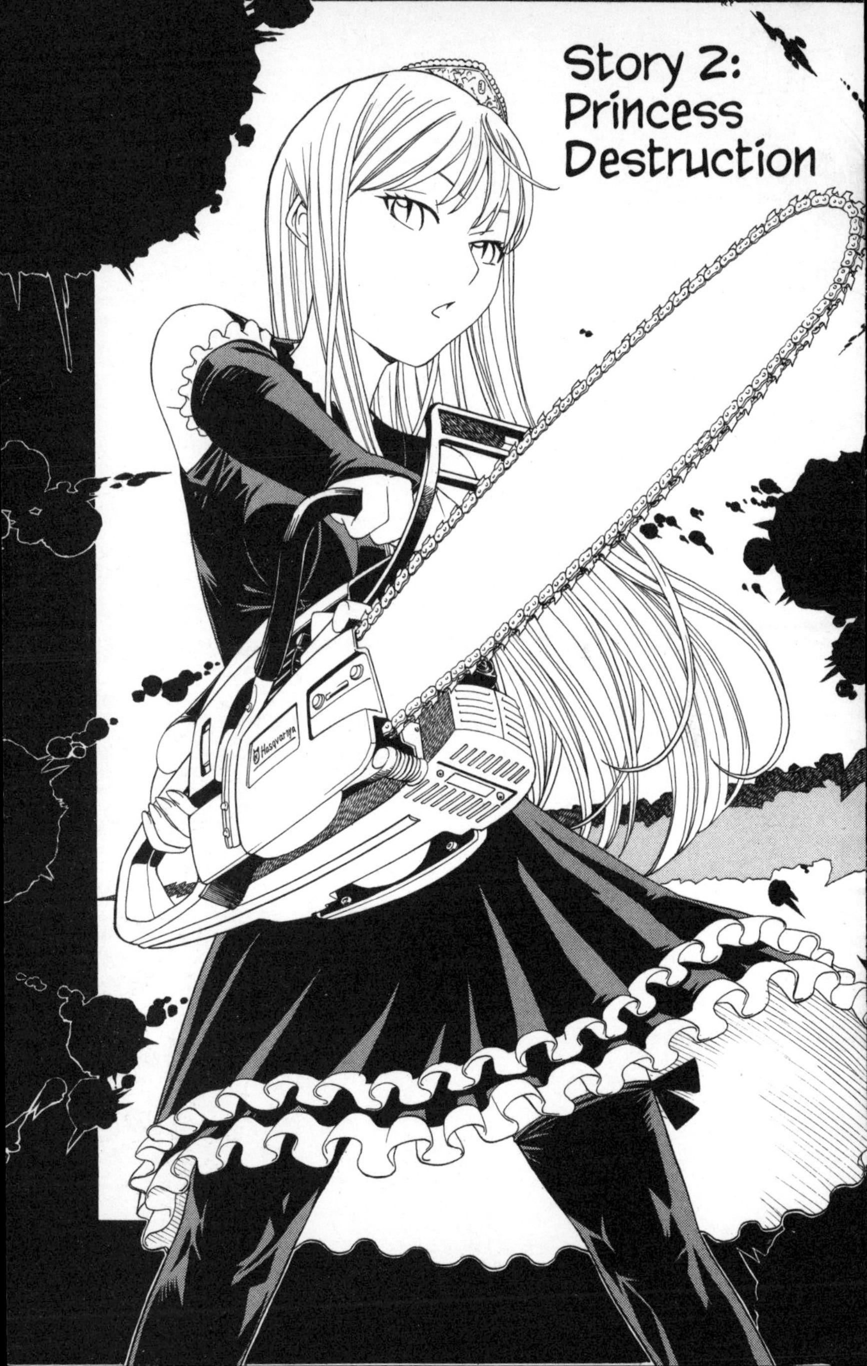
Story 2:
Princess
Destruction

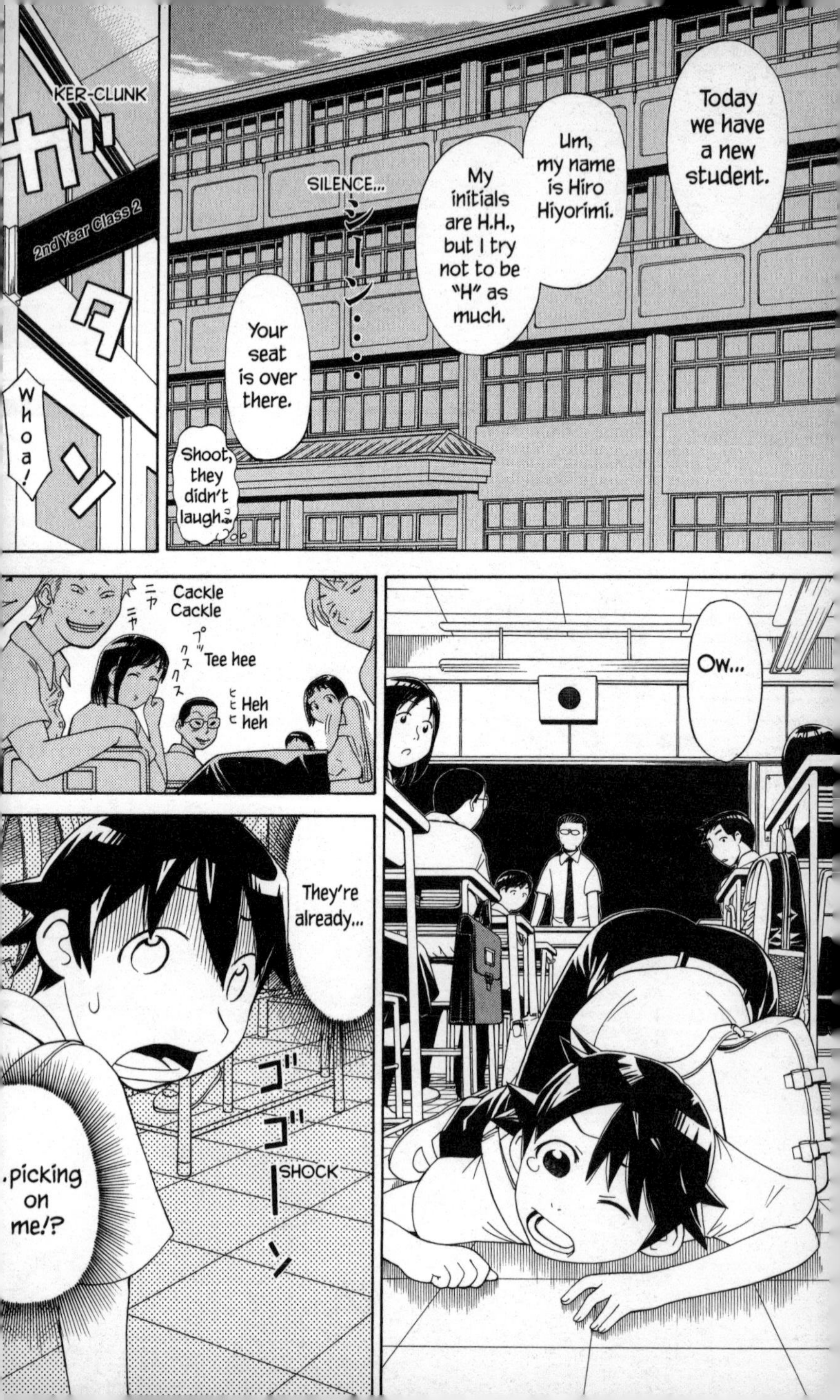
Today we have a new student.
Um, my name is Hiro Hiyorimi.
My initials are H.H., but I try not to be "H" as much.
SILENCE...
Your seat is over there.
Shoot, they didn't laugh...
KER-CLUNK
2nd Year Class 2
Whoa!
Ow...
Cackle Cackle
Tee hee
Heh heh
They're already...
...picking on me!?
SHOCK

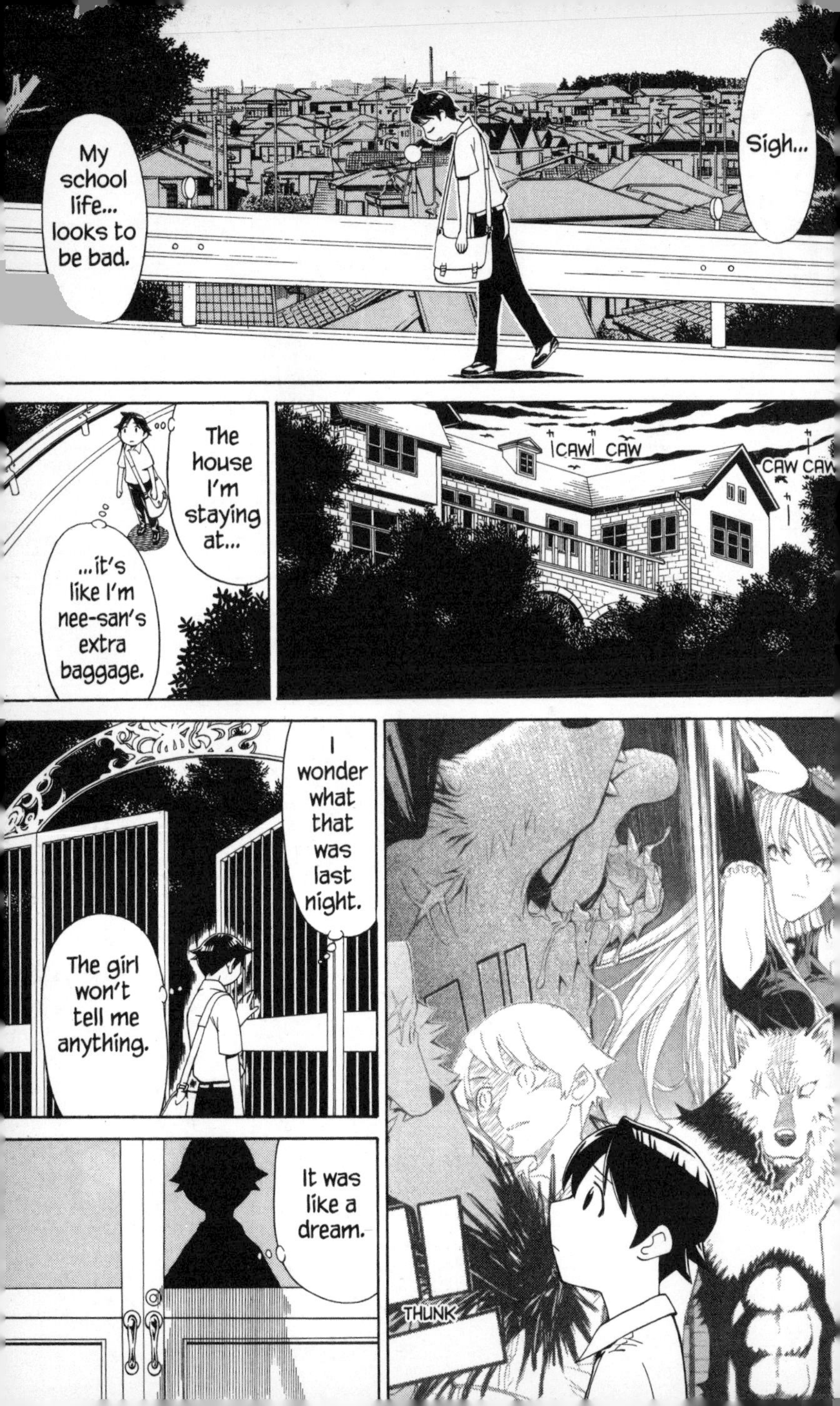
Sigh...
My school life... looks to be bad.
CAW CAW
CAW CAW
The house I'm staying at...
...it's like I'm nee-san's extra baggage.
THUNK
I wonder what that was last night.
The girl won't tell me anything.
It was like a dream.

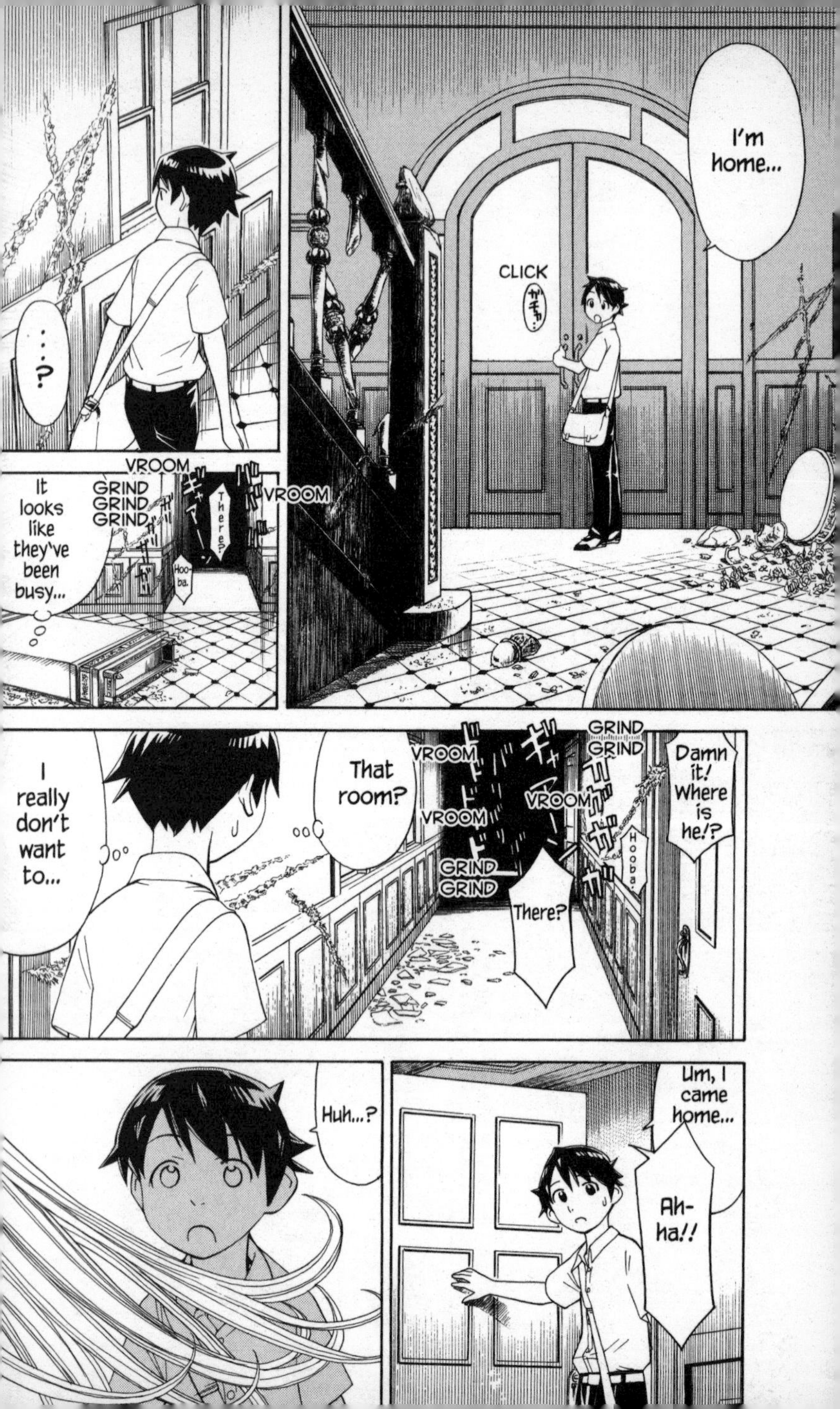
I'm home...
CLICK
...?
VROOM
GRIND GRIND GRIND
VROOM
There?
Hooba.
It looks like they've been busy...
Damn it! Where is he!?
GRIND GRIND
VROOM
Hooba.
There?
VROOM
VROOM
GRIND GRIND
That room?
I really don't want to...
Um, I came home...
Ah-ha!!
Huh...?

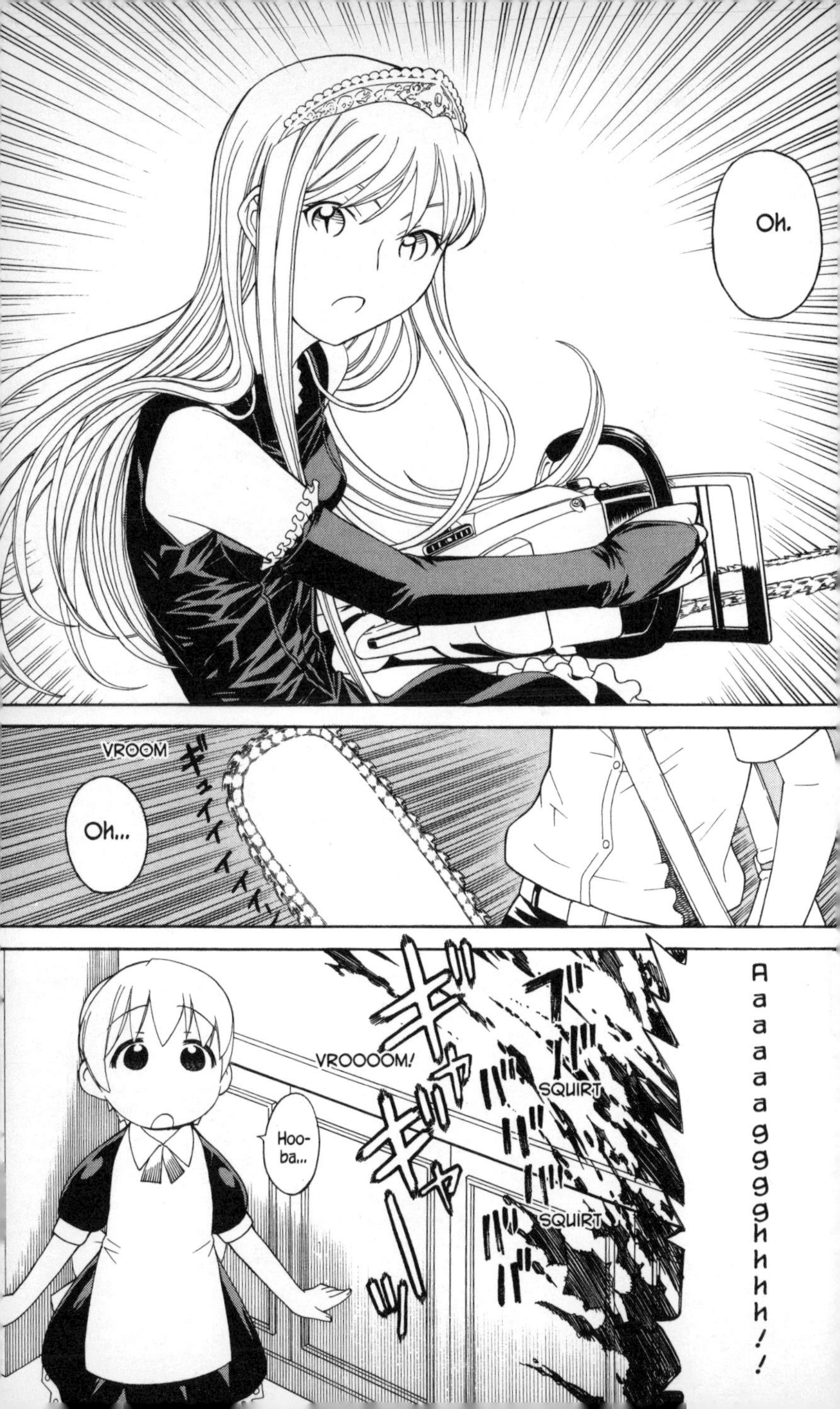
Oh.
VROOM
Oh...
Aaaaaaaggghhhhh!!
SQUIRT
SQUIRT
VROOOOM!
Hoo-ba...

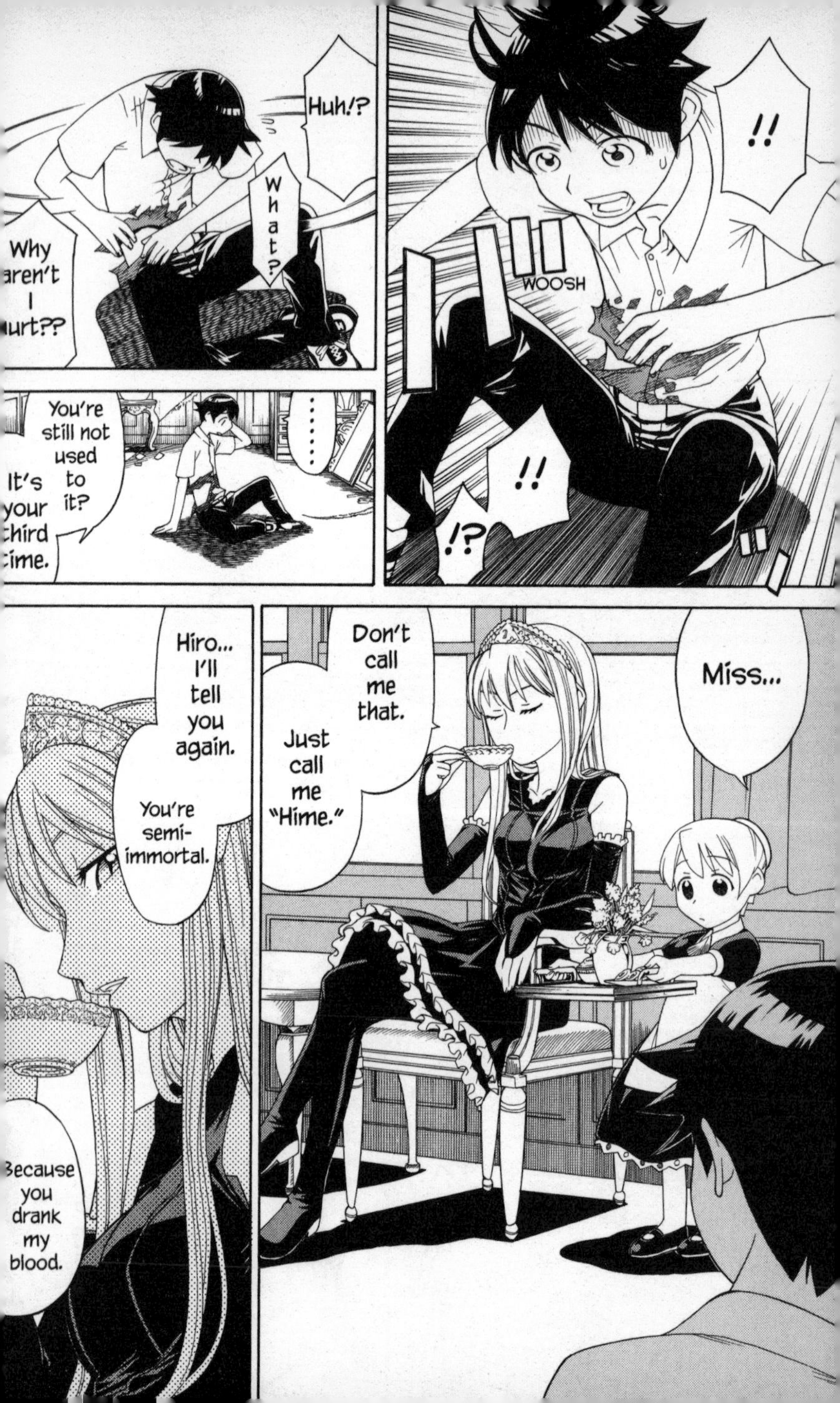
!!
WOOSH
!!
!?
Huh!?
What?
Why aren't I urt??
......
You're still not used to it?
It's your hird ime.
Miss...
Don't call me that.
Just call me "Hime."
Hiro... I'll tell you again.
You're semi-immortal.
ecause you drank my blood.

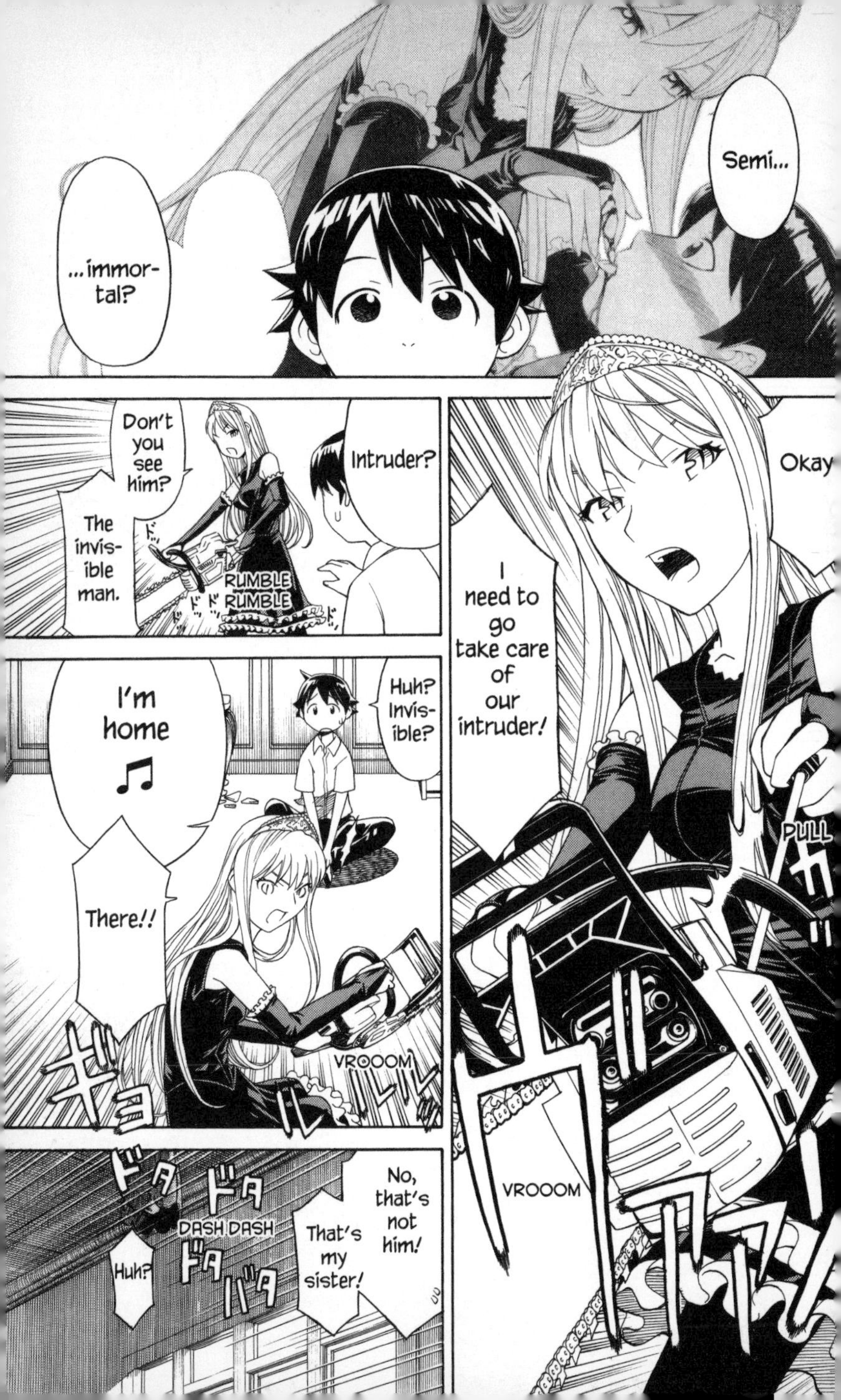

Semi...
...immor-tal?
Okay
I need to go take care of our intruder!
PULL
VROOOM
Intruder?
Don't you see him?
The invisible man.
RUMBLE RUMBLE
Huh? Invisible?
I'm home ♫
There!!
VROOOM
No, that's not him!
That's my sister!
DASH DASH
Huh?

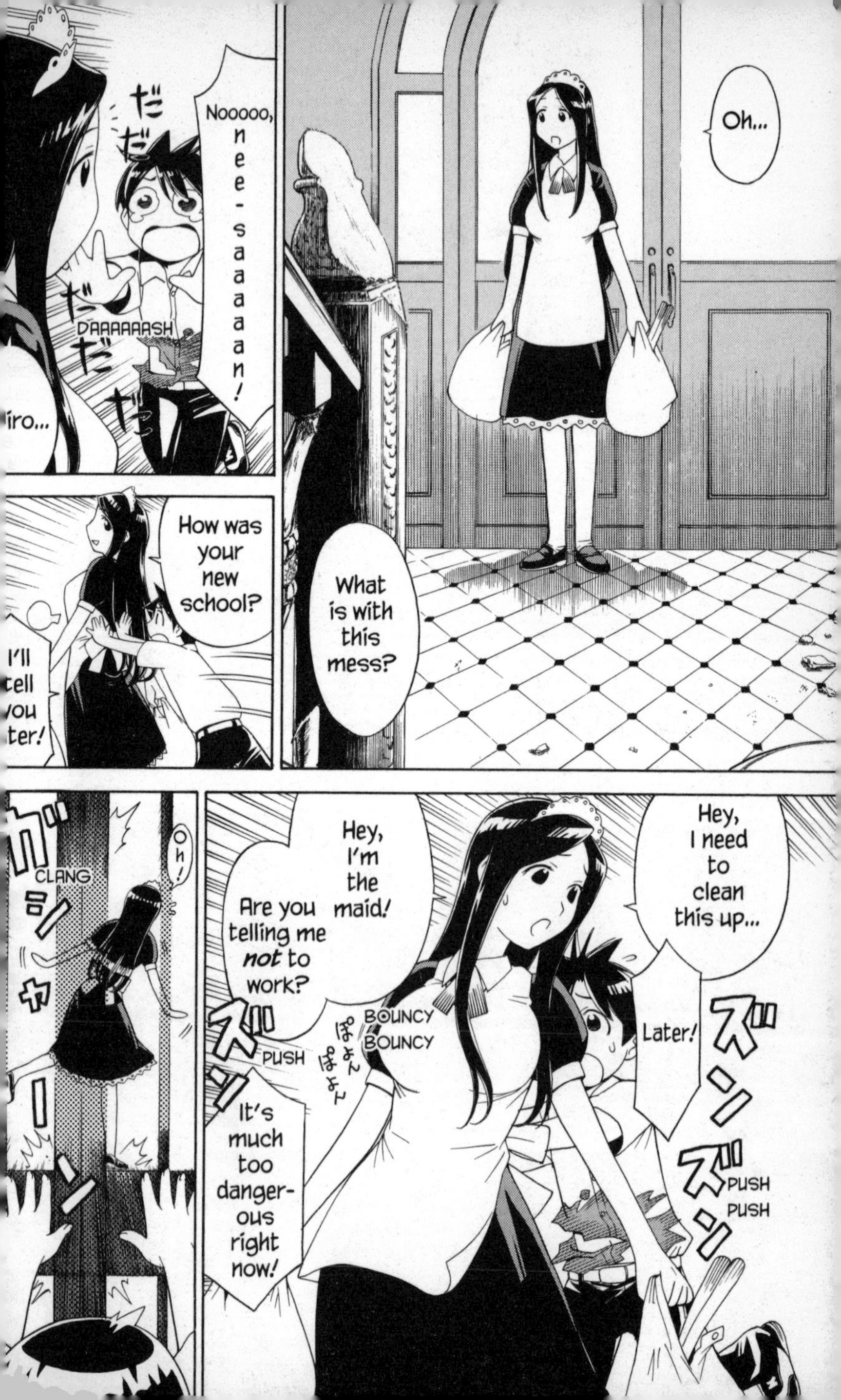
Oh...
What is with this mess?
Nooooo, nee-saaaaaan!
DAAAAAASH
iro...
How was your new school?
I'll tell you ter!
Hey, I need to clean this up...
Later!
Hey, I'm the maid!
Are you telling me *not* to work?
PUSH PUSH
BOUNCY BOUNCY
PUSH
It's much too danger-ous right now!
Oh!
CLANG

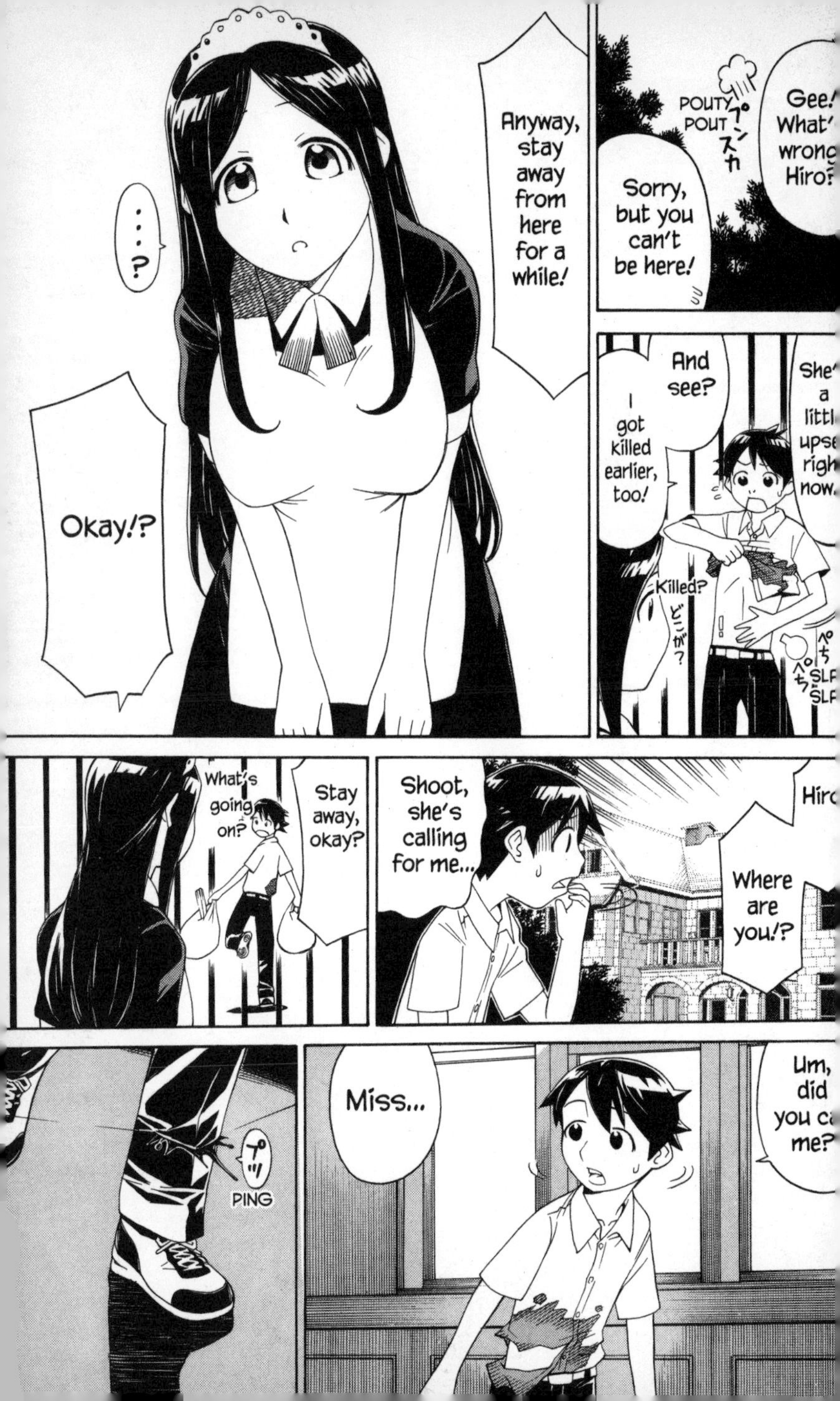
Gee! What' wrong Hiro?
POUTY POUT
プンスカ
Sorry, but you can't be here!
She' a littl upse righ now.
And see?
I got killed earlier, too!
Killed?
どこが？
ぺちぺち
SLP SLP
Anyway, stay away from here for a while!
...?
Okay!?
Hiro
Where are you!?
Shoot, she's calling for me...
Stay away, okay?
What's going on?
Um, did you ca me?
Miss...
プツ
PING

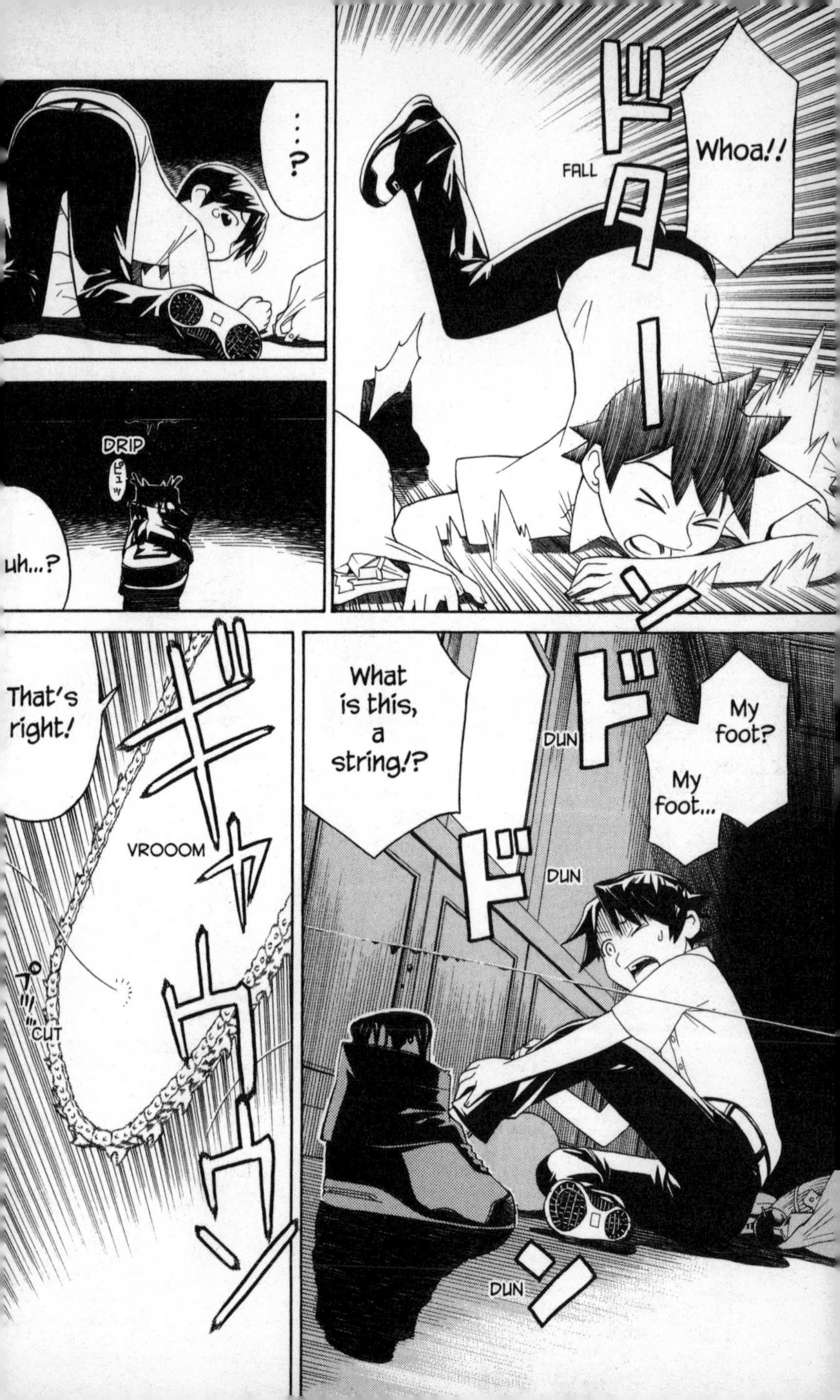
Whoa!!
FALL
...?
DRIP
uh...?
What is this, a string!?
DUN
My foot?
My foot...
DUN
DUN
That's right!
VROOOM
CUT

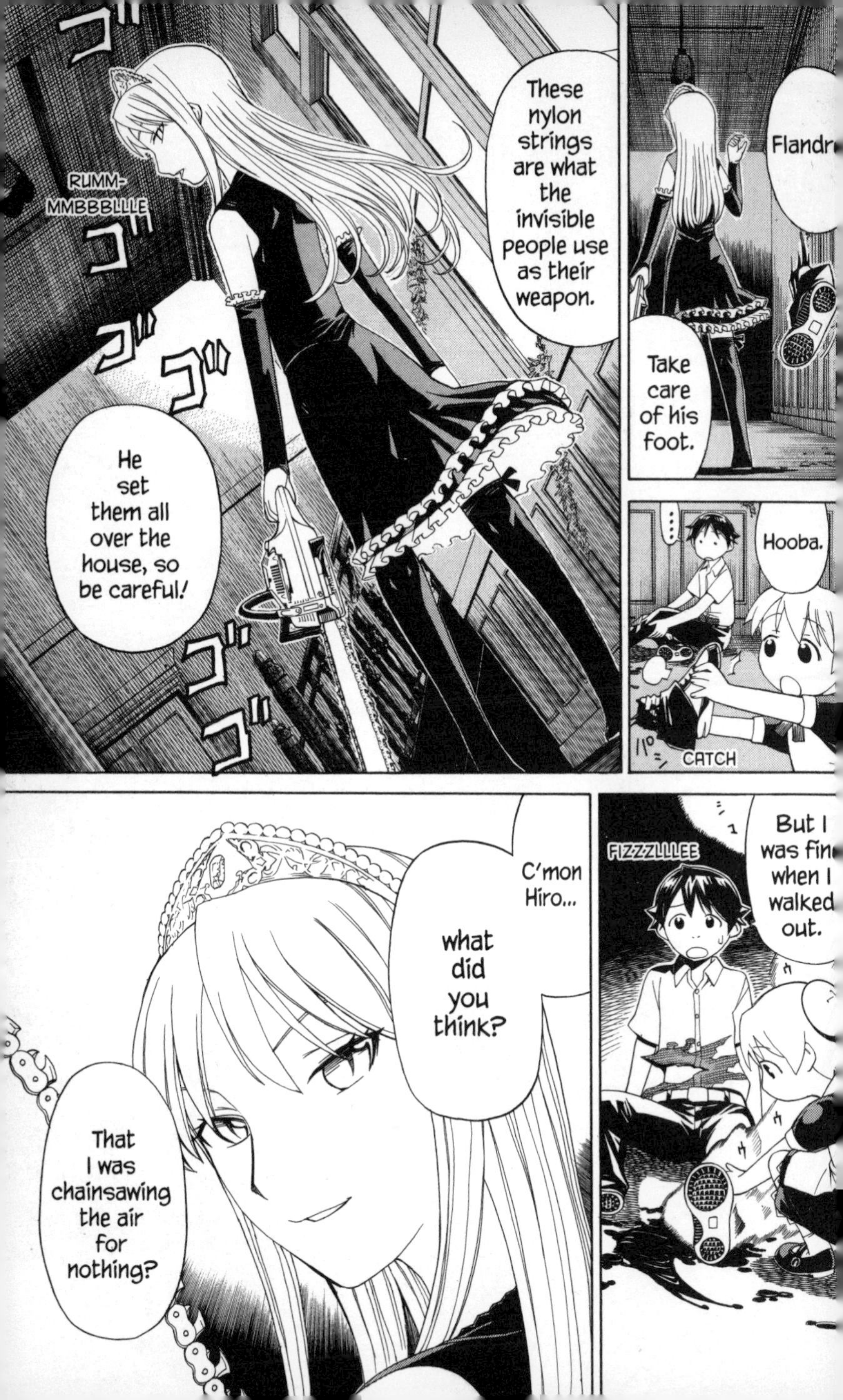
Flandr
Take care of his foot.
Hooba.
CATCH
These nylon strings are what the invisible people use as their weapon.
RUMMMMBBBLLLE
He set them all over the house, so be careful!
But I was fin when I walked out.
FIZZZLLLEE
C'mon Hiro...
what did you think?
That I was chainsawing the air for nothing?

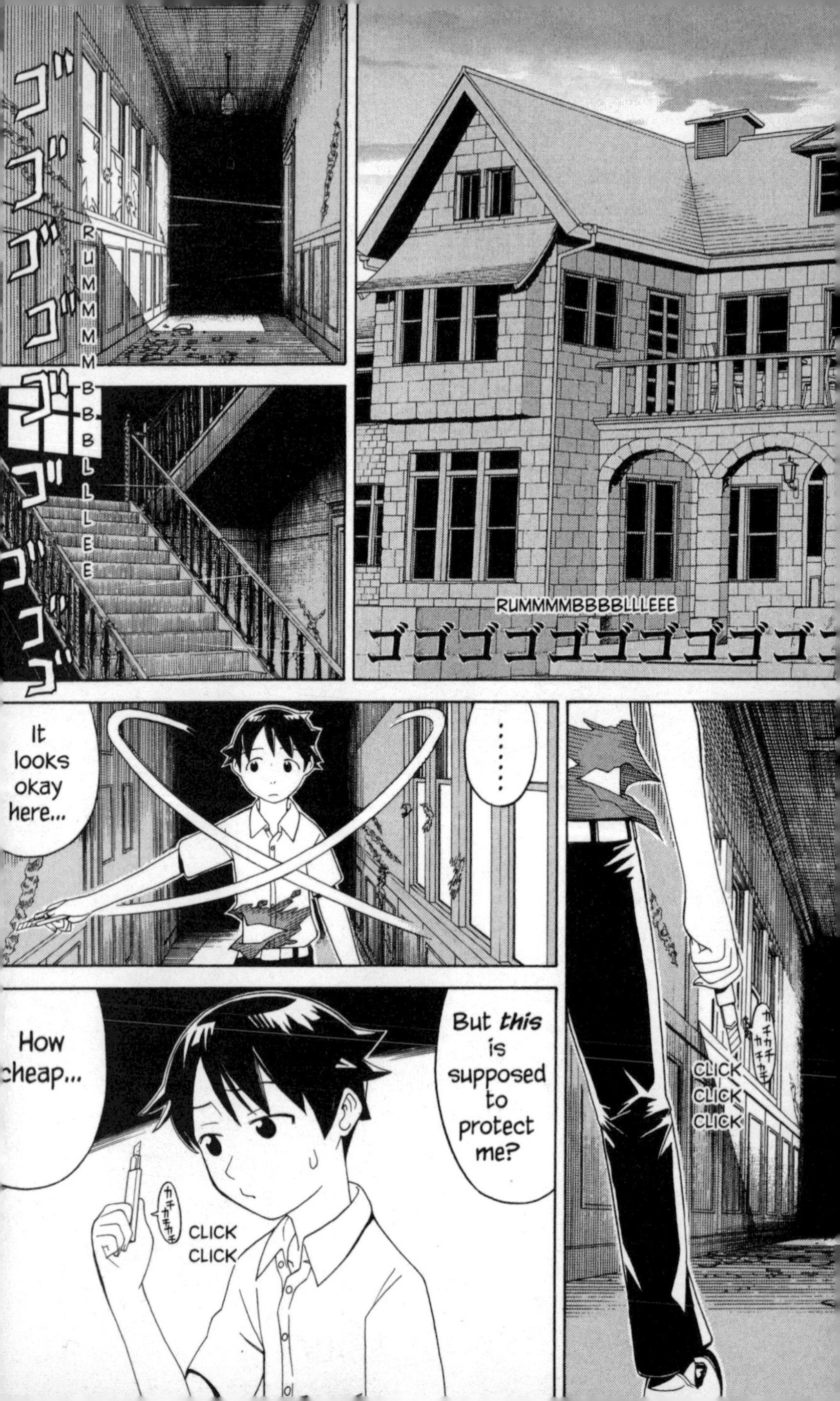
RUMMMMBBBBLLLEEE
ゴゴゴゴゴゴゴゴゴゴ
RUMMMMBBBLLLEE
ゴゴゴゴ
ゴゴゴゴ
CLICK
CLICK
CLICK
......
It looks okay here...
But this is supposed to protect me?
How cheap...
CLICK
CLICK

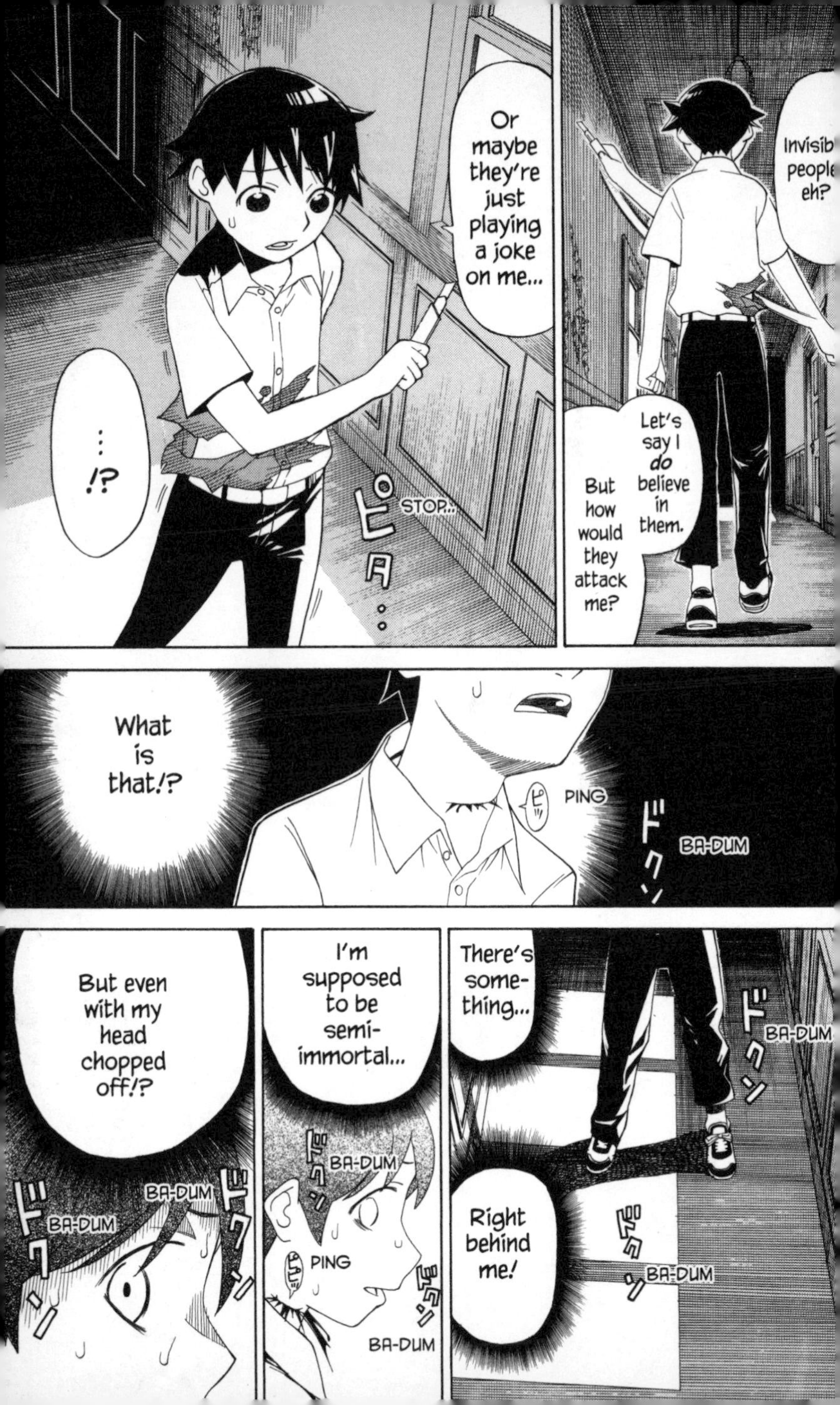
Invisib
people
eh?
Let's say I do believe in them.
But how would they attack me?
Or maybe they're just playing a joke on me...
STOP...
...!?
BA-DUM
PING
What is that!?
There's some-thing...
BA-DUM
Right behind me!
BA-DUM
I'm supposed to be semi-immortal...
BA-DUM
PING
BA-DUM
But even with my head chopped off!?
BA-DUM
BA-DUM

There's no

GUSH

Shadow!

Hooba.

THROW

ziel
"target"

freund
"friend"

ピピピッ

PEEP
PEEP

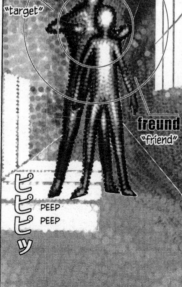

PEEK

PEEP
PEEP

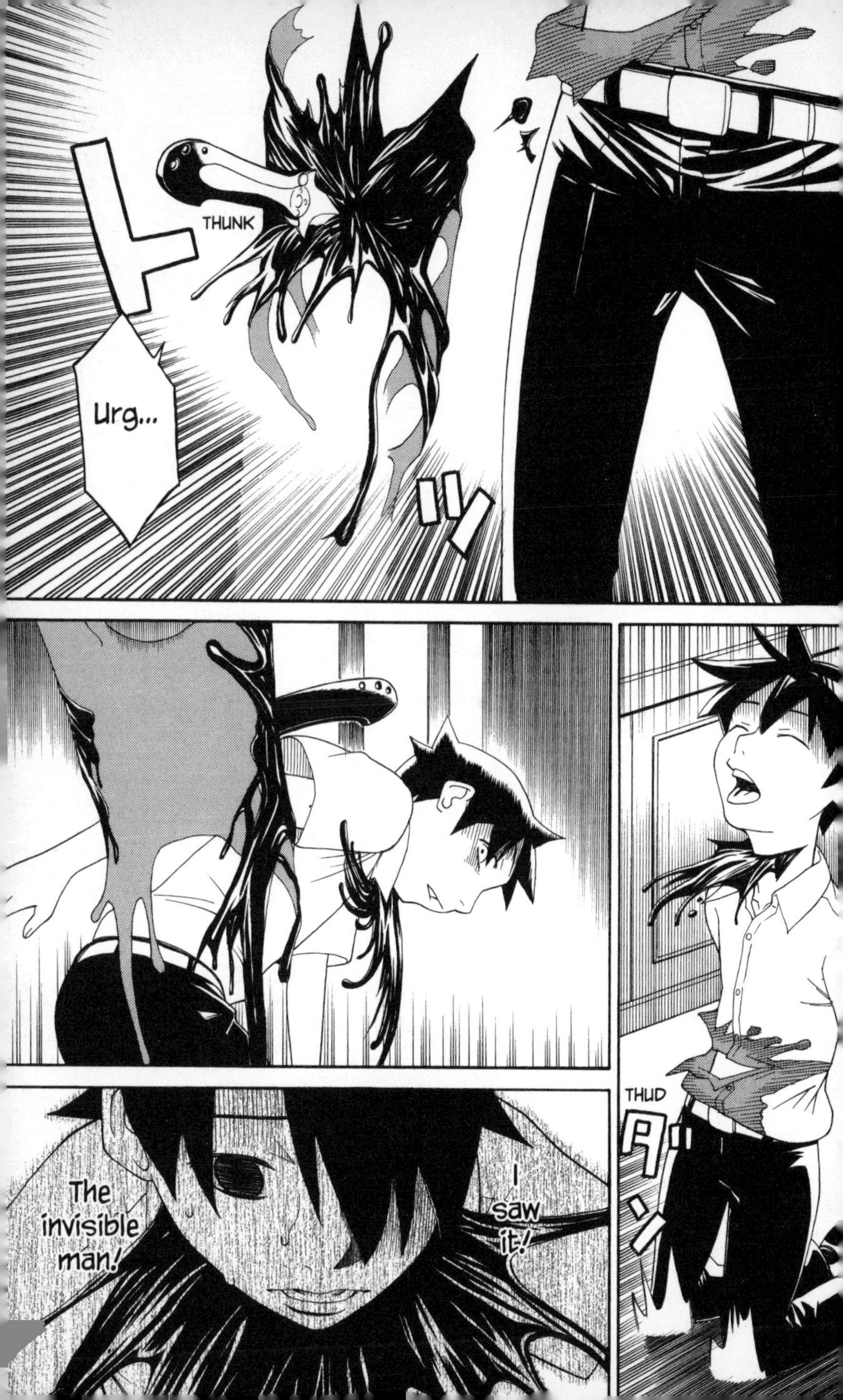
THUNK
Urg...
THUD
I saw it!
The invisible man!

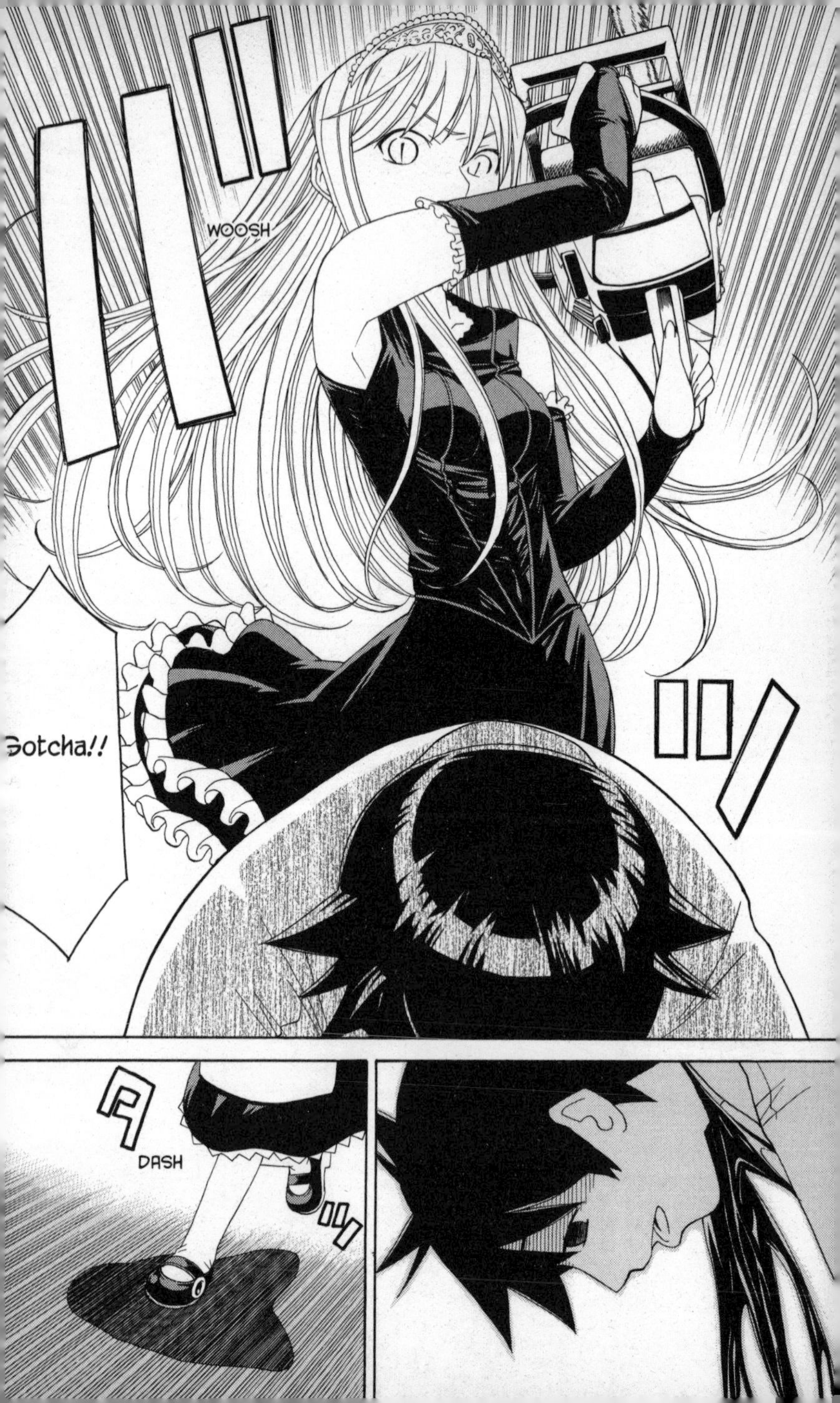
WOOSH
Gotcha!!
DASH

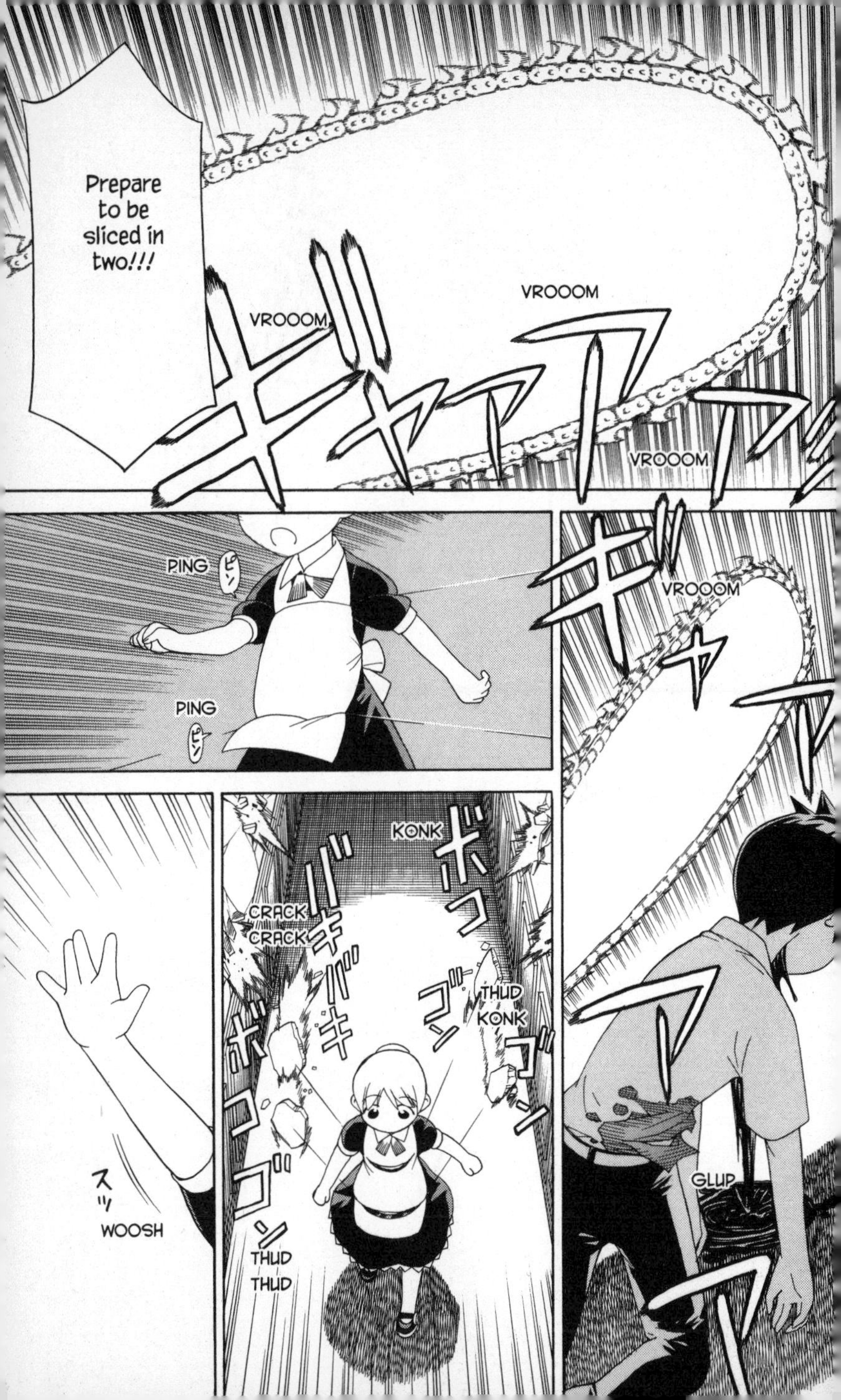

Prepare to be sliced in two!!!
VROOOM
VROOOM
VROOOM
VROOOM
GLUP
PING
ピン
PING
ピン
KONK
CRACK
CRACK
THUD
KONK
THUD
THUD
スッ
WOOSH

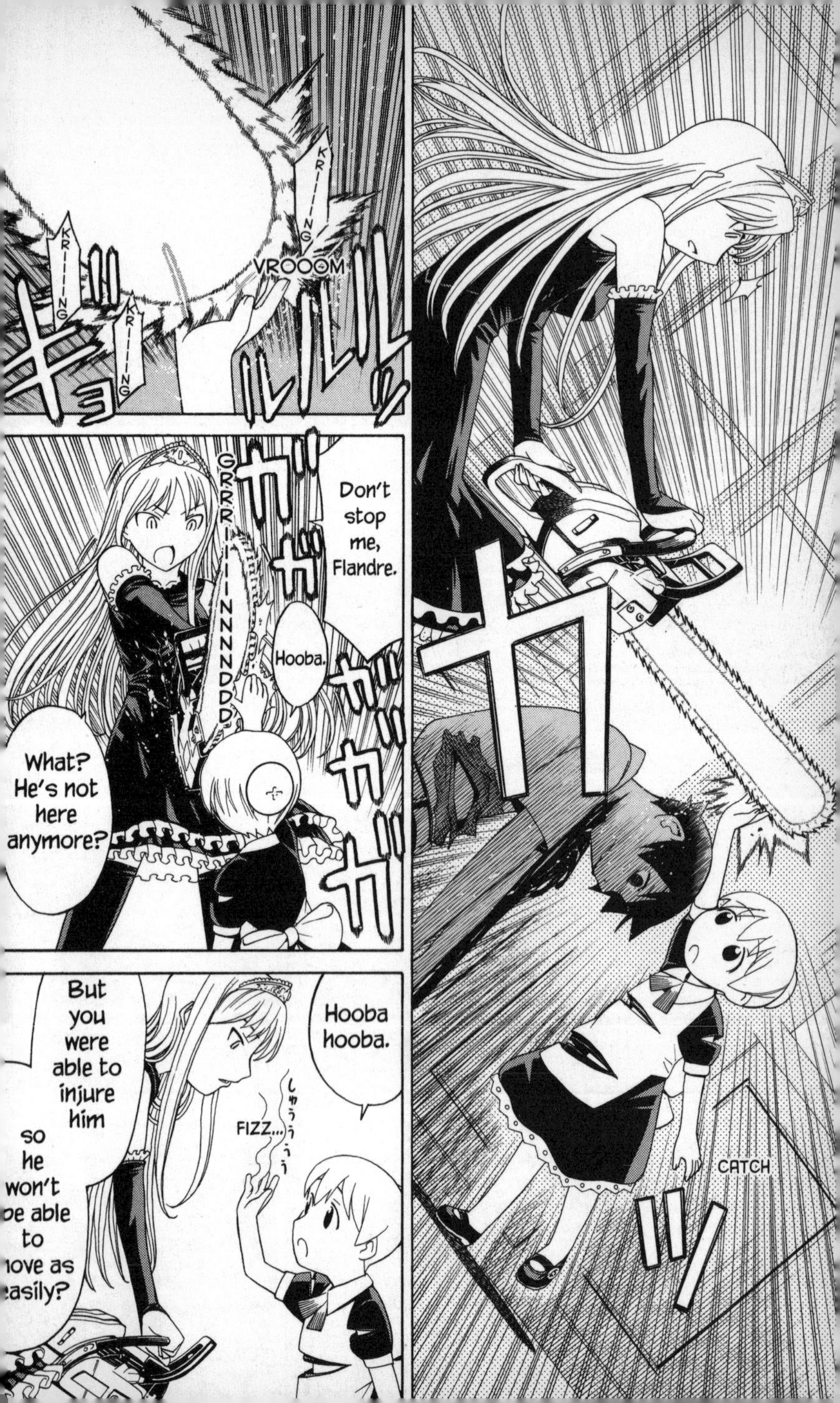
CATCH
KRIIING
VROOOM
KRIIING
KRIIING
ギョルルルッ
Don't stop me, Flandre.
GRRRIIIINNNNDDD
Hooba.
What? He's not here anymore?
Hooba hooba.
But you were able to injure him so he won't be able to move as easily?
FIZZ...
しゅううううう

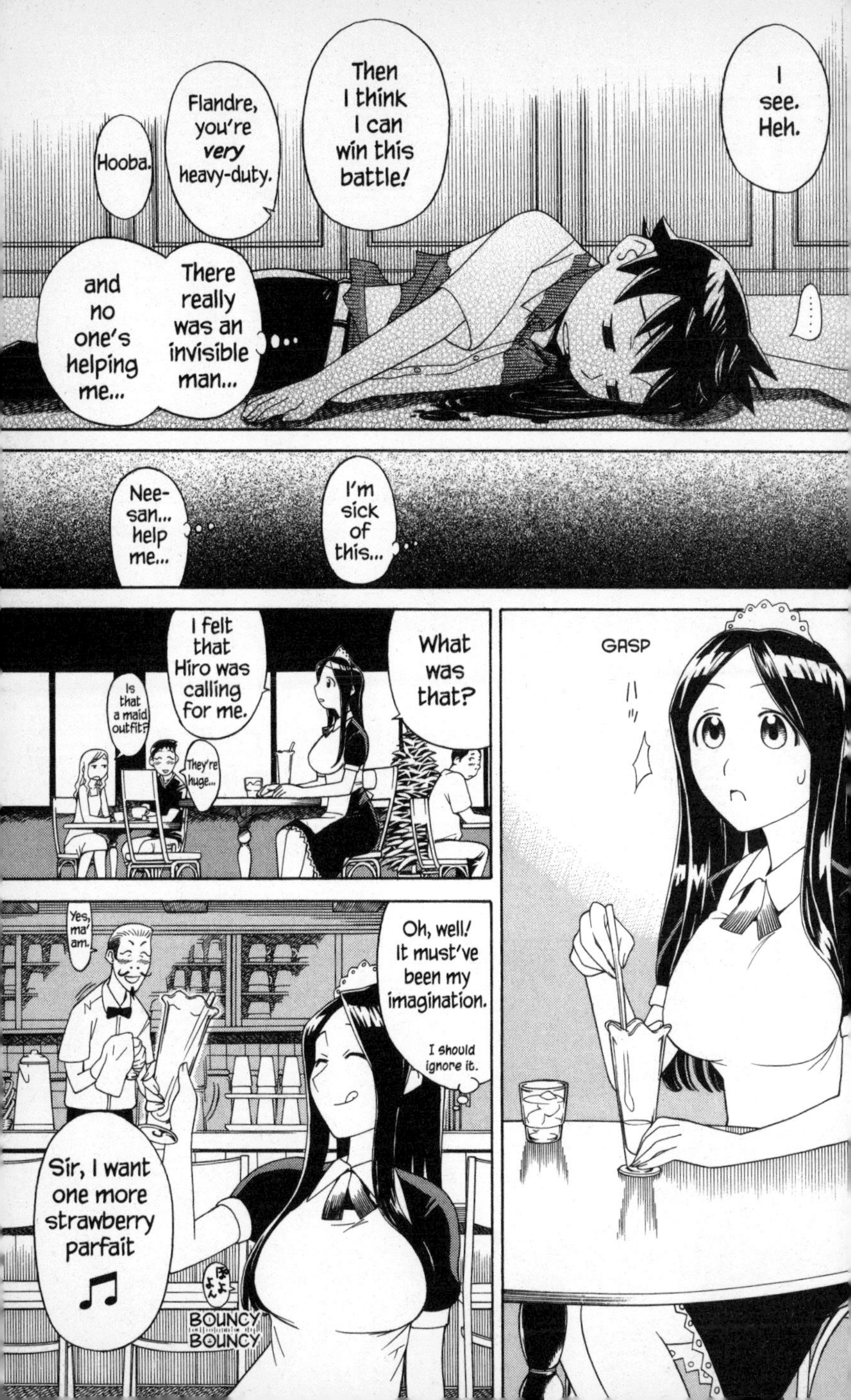
I see. Heh.
...
Then I think I can win this battle!
Flandre, you're *very* heavy-duty.
Hooba.
There really was an invisible man...
and no one's helping me...
I'm sick of this...
Nee-san... help me...
GASP
What was that?
I felt that Hiro was calling for me.
They're huge...
Is that a maid outfit?
Oh, well! It must've been my imagination.
I should ignore it.
Yes, ma' am.
Sir, I want one more strawberry parfait ♫
ぽよん
BOUNCY BOUNCY

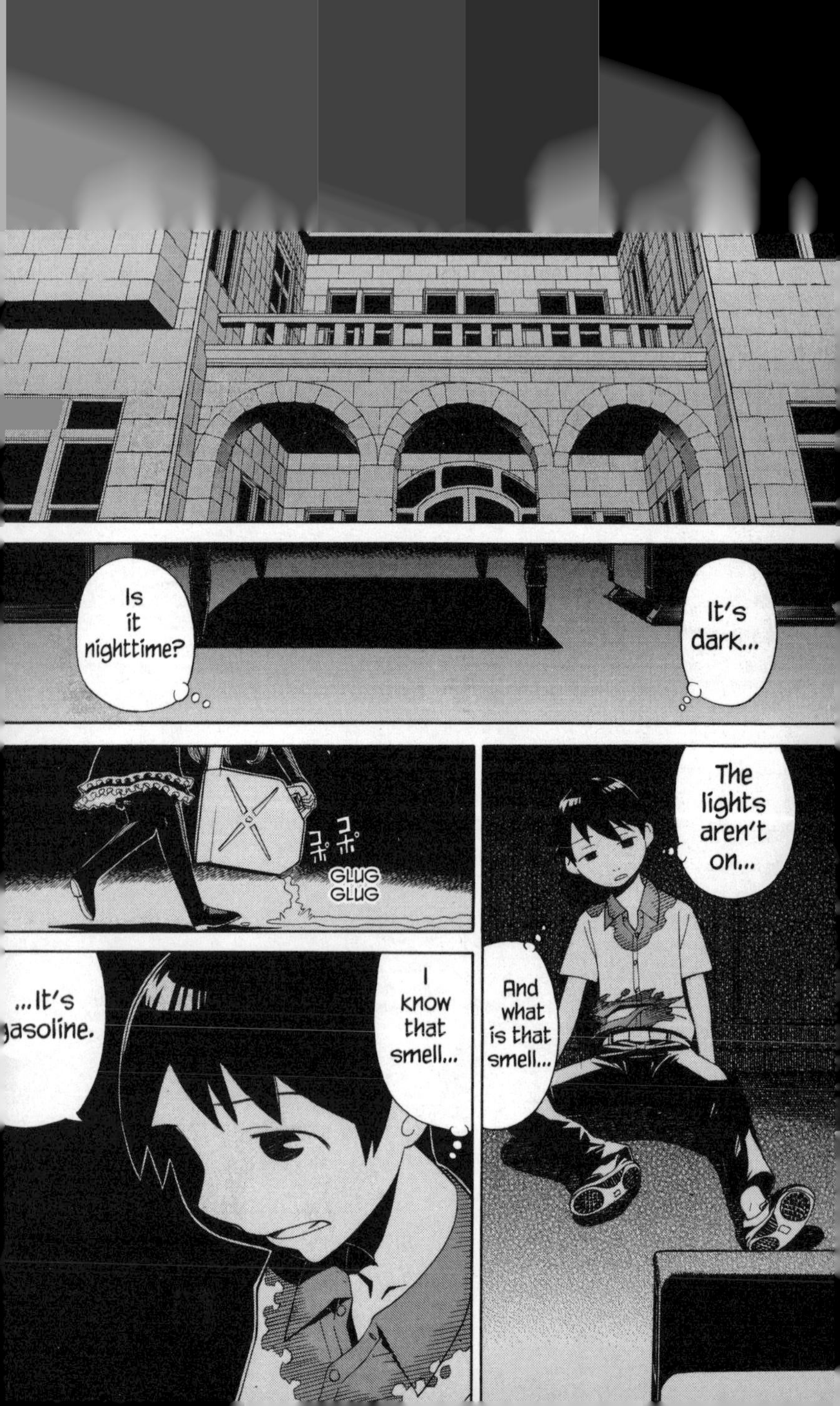
It's dark...
Is it nighttime?
The lights aren't on...
And what is that smell...
コポコポ
GLUG GLUG
I know that smell...
...It's gasoline.

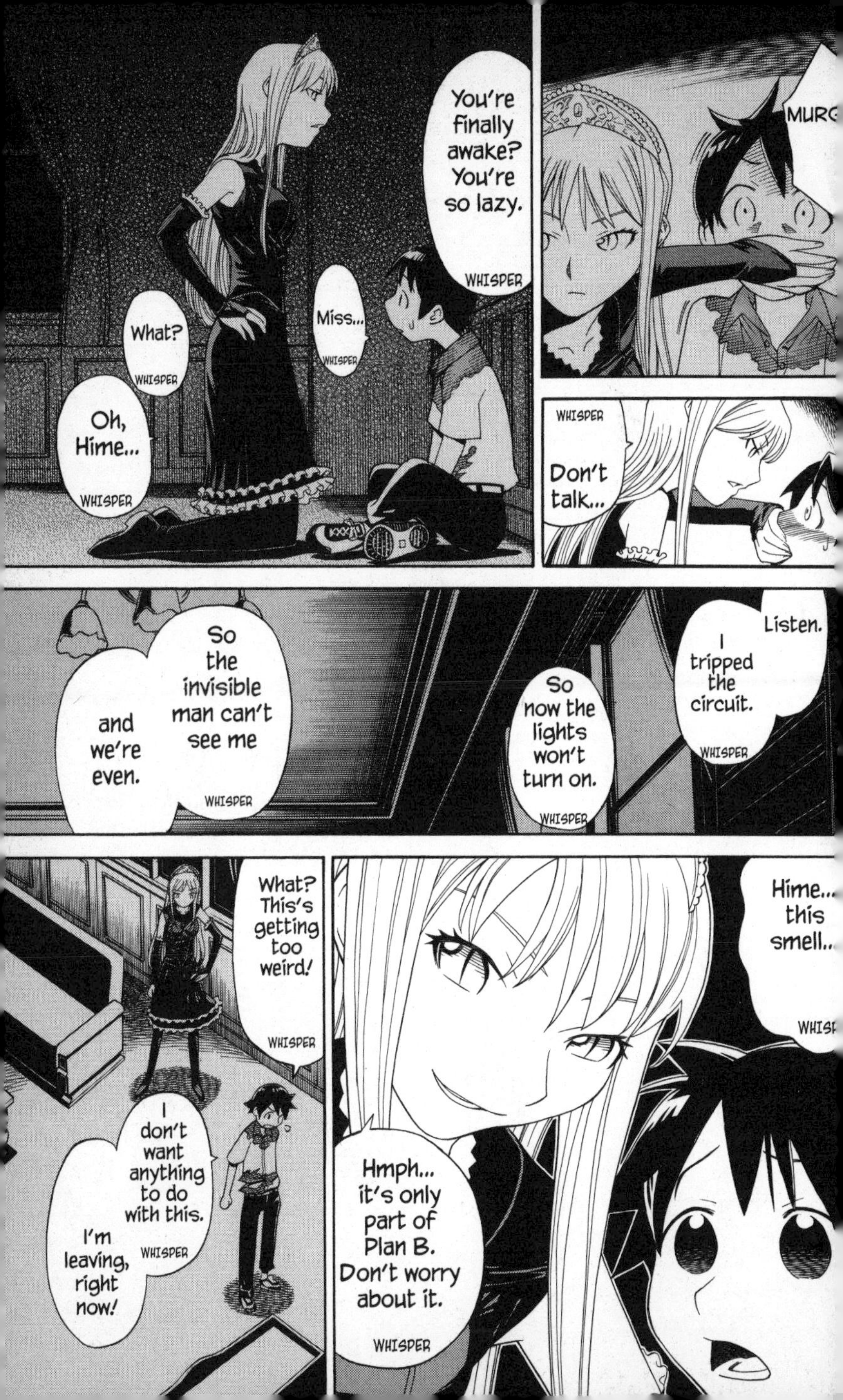
MURG
WHISPER
Don't talk...
You're finally awake? You're so lazy.
WHISPER
Miss...
WHISPER
What?
WHISPER
Oh, Hime...
WHISPER
Listen. I tripped the circuit.
WHISPER
So now the lights won't turn on.
WHISPER
So the invisible man can't see me and we're even.
WHISPER
Hime... this smell...
WHISP
Hmph... it's only part of Plan B. Don't worry about it.
WHISPER
What? This's getting too weird!
WHISPER
I don't want anything to do with this. I'm leaving, right now!
WHISPER

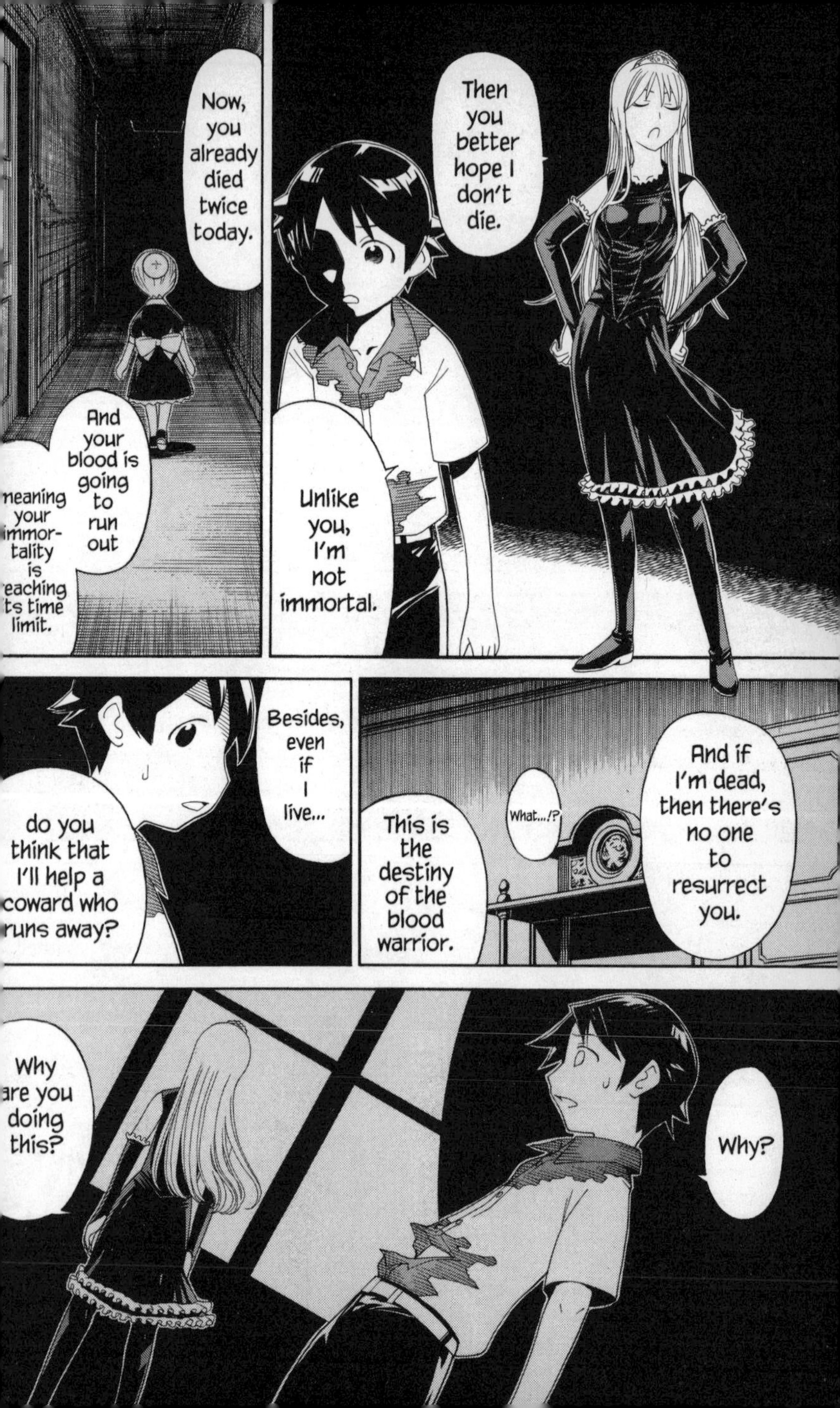
Then you better hope I don't die.
Unlike you, I'm not immortal.
Now, you already died twice today.
And your blood is going to run out
neaning your immor- tality is eaching ts time limit.
And if I'm dead, then there's no one to resurrect you.
What...!?
This is the destiny of the blood warrior.
Besides, even if I live...
do you think that I'll help a coward who runs away?
Why?
Why are you doing this?

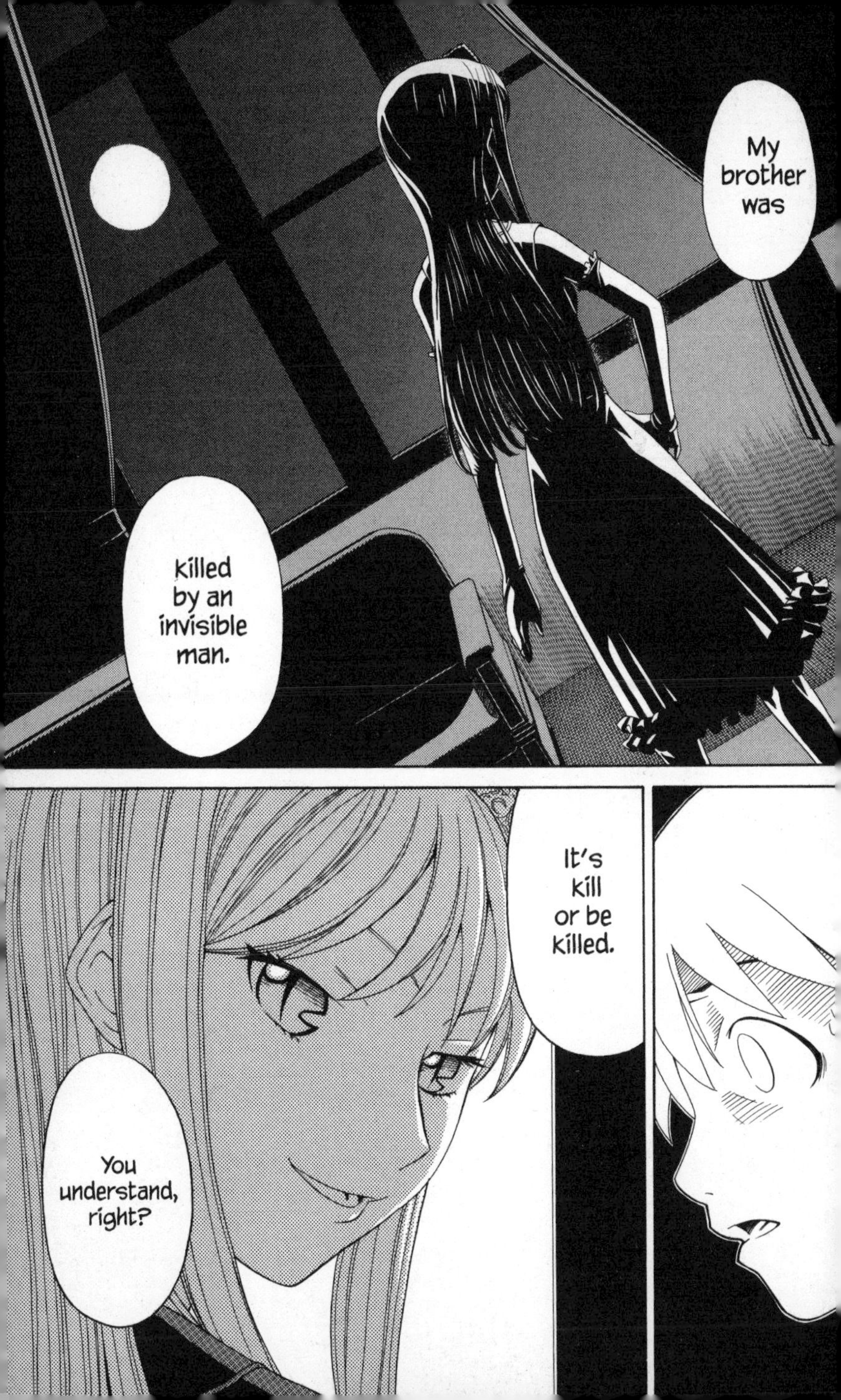
My brother was
killed by an invisible man.
It's kill or be killed.
You understand, right?

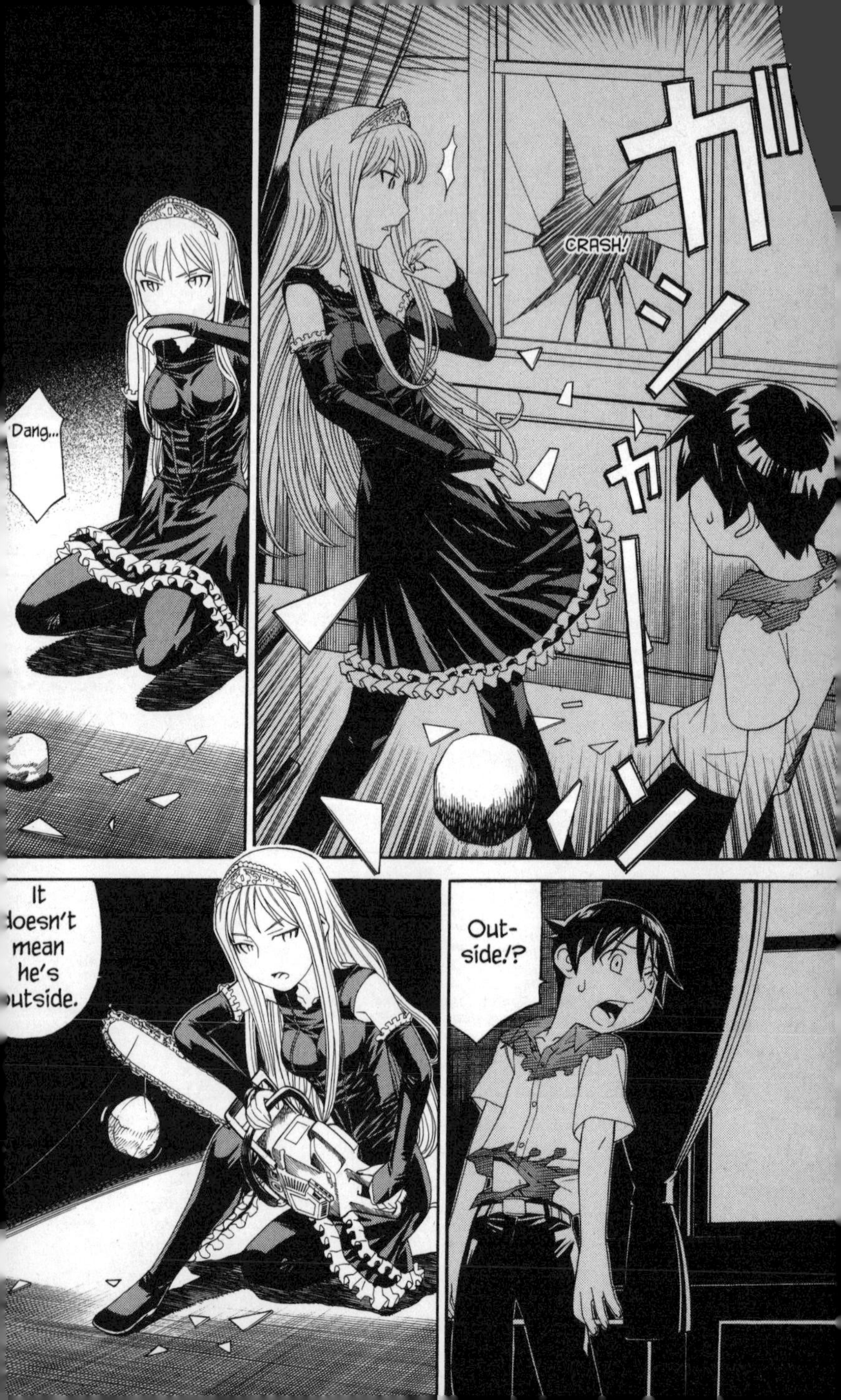
CRASH!
Dang...
Out-side!?
It doesn't mean he's outside.

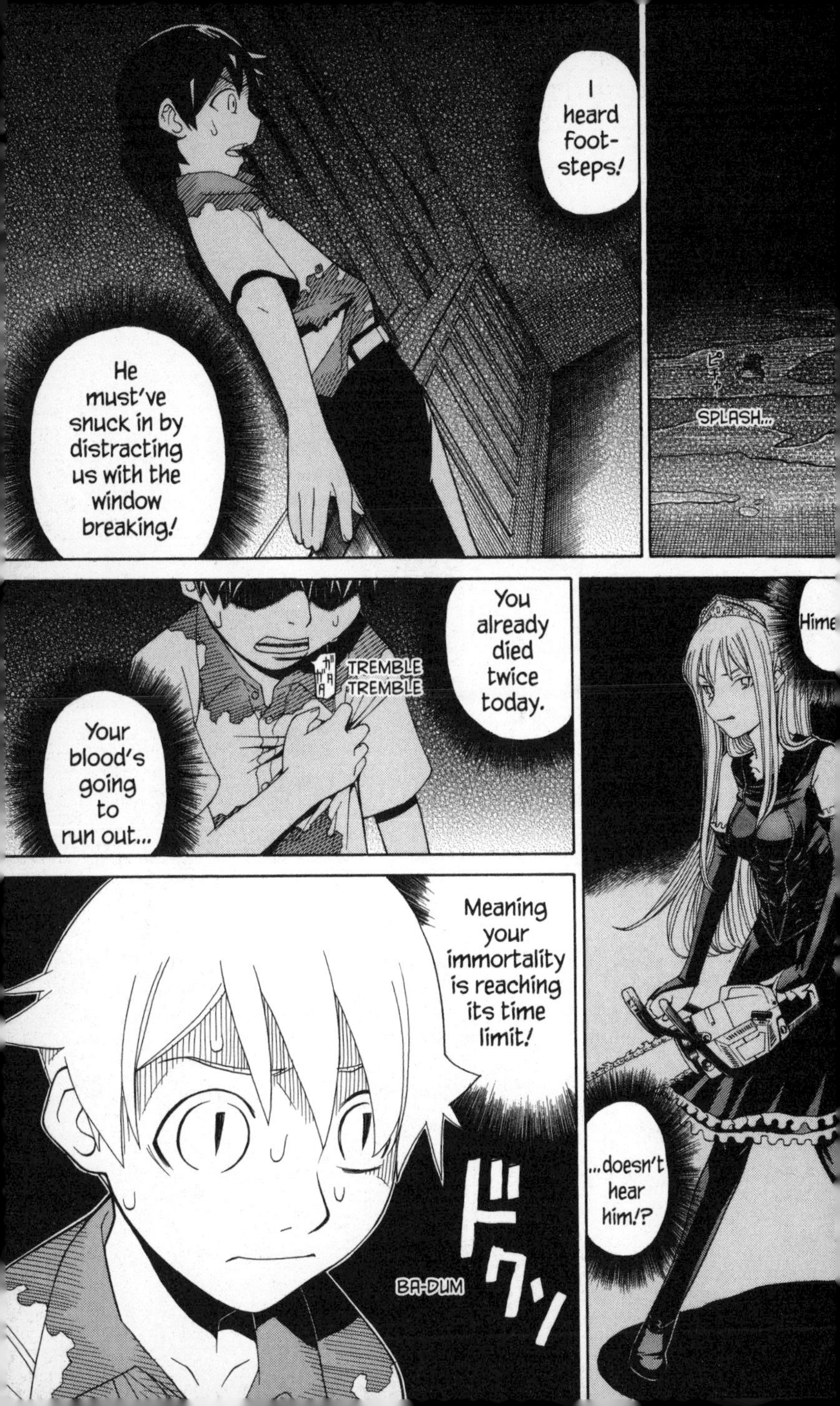
SPLASH...
I heard foot-steps!
He must've snuck in by distracting us with the window breaking!
Hime
...doesn't hear him!?
You already died twice today.
TREMBLE TREMBLE
Your blood's going to run out...
Meaning your immortality is reaching its time limit!
ドクッ
BA-DUM

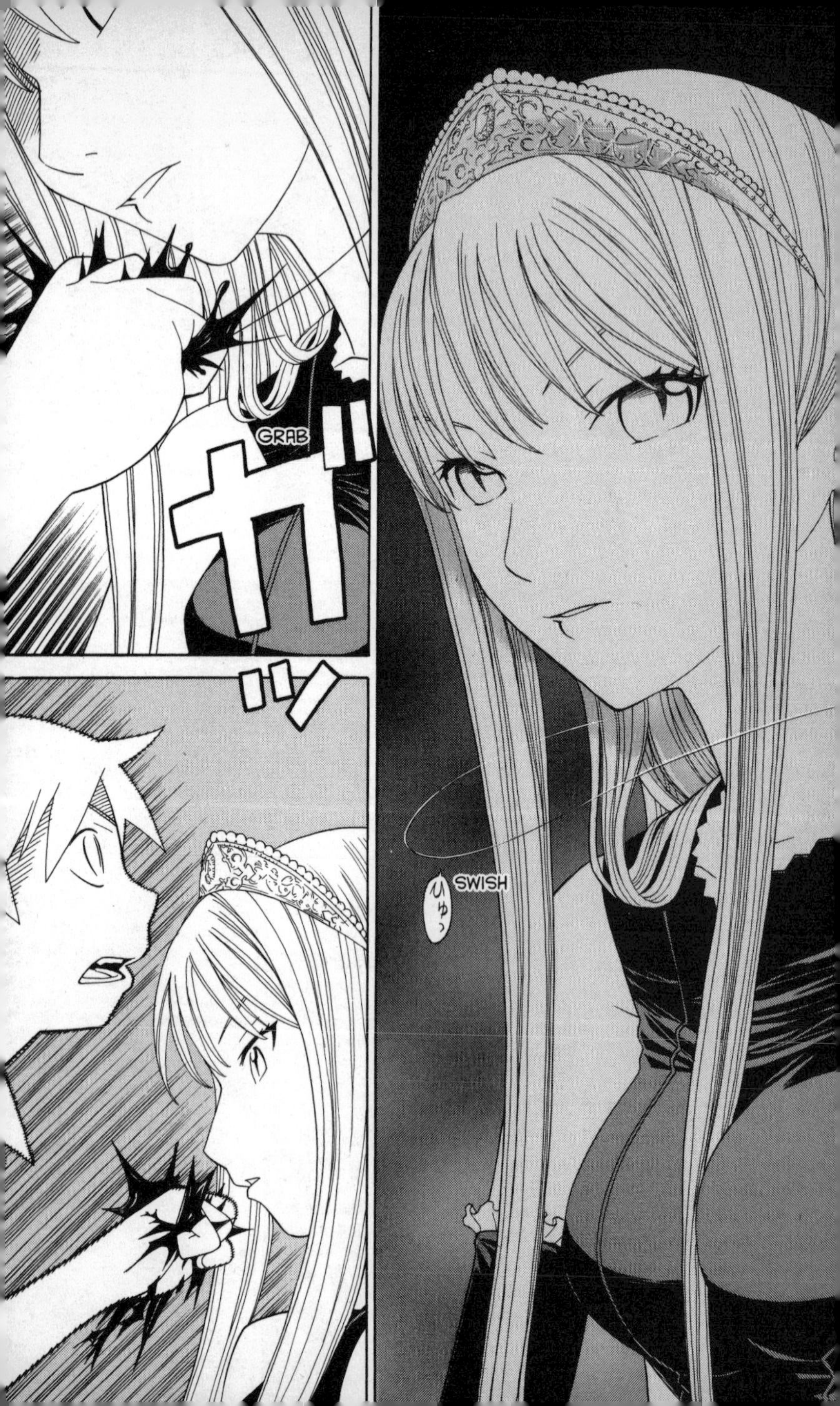
ひゅっ
SWISH
ガッ
GRAB

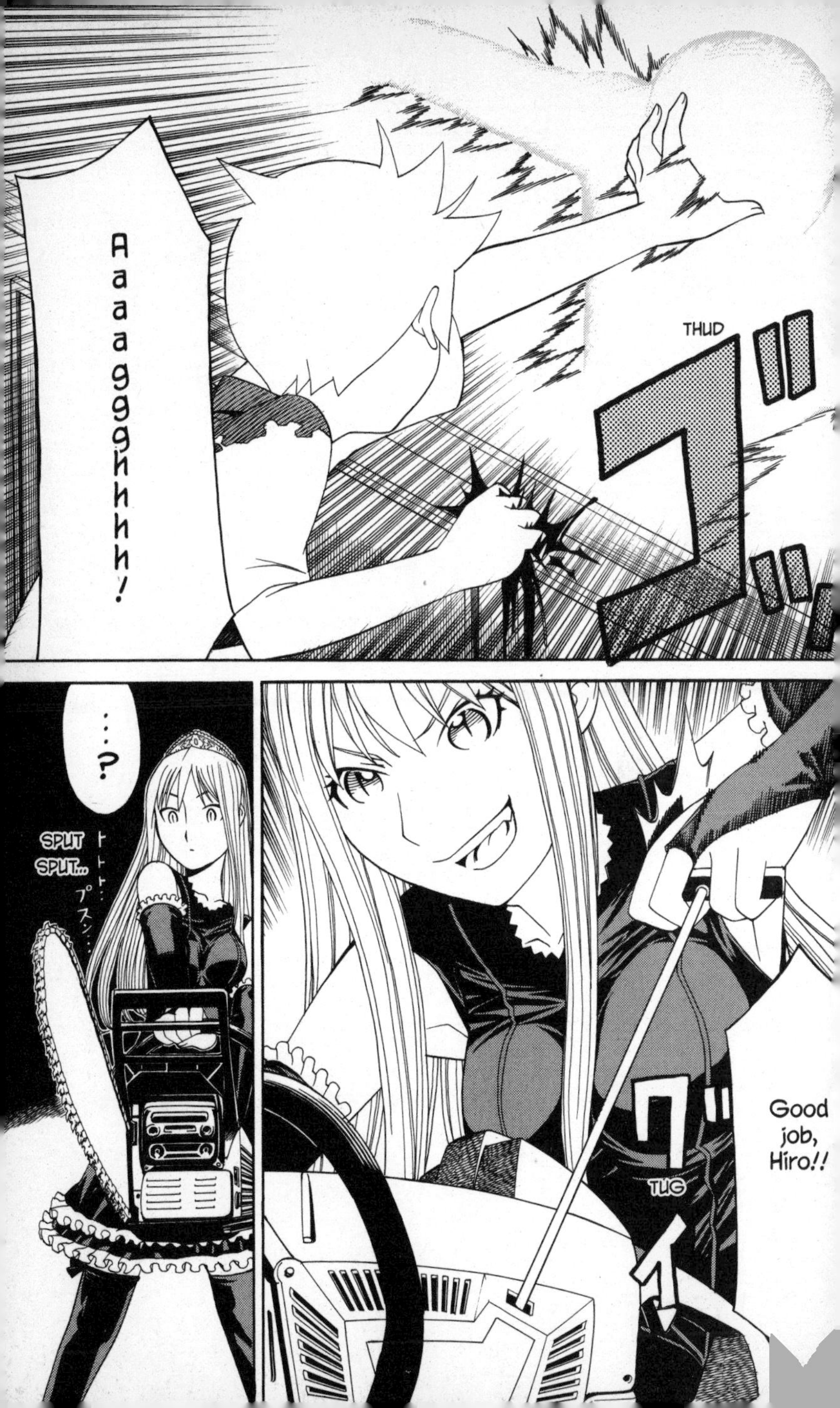

Aaaagghhhhh!
THUD
Good job, Hiro!!
TUG
...?
SPLUT SPLUT...
トトト… プスン…

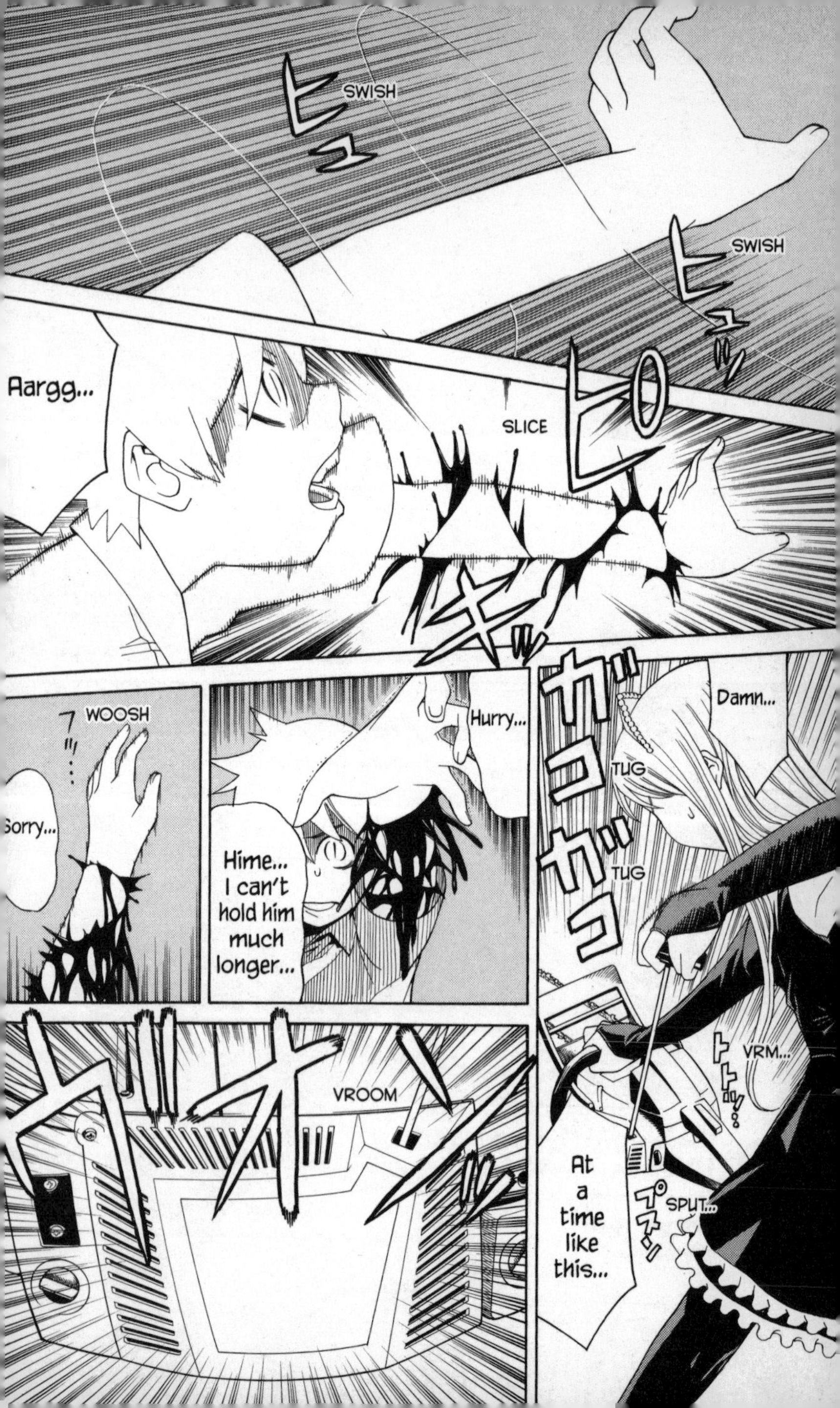
SWISH
SWISH
SLICE
Aargg...
Damn...
TUG
TUG
VRM...
At a time like this...
SPUT...
Hurry...
Hime... I can't hold him much longer...
WOOSH
Sorry...
VROOM

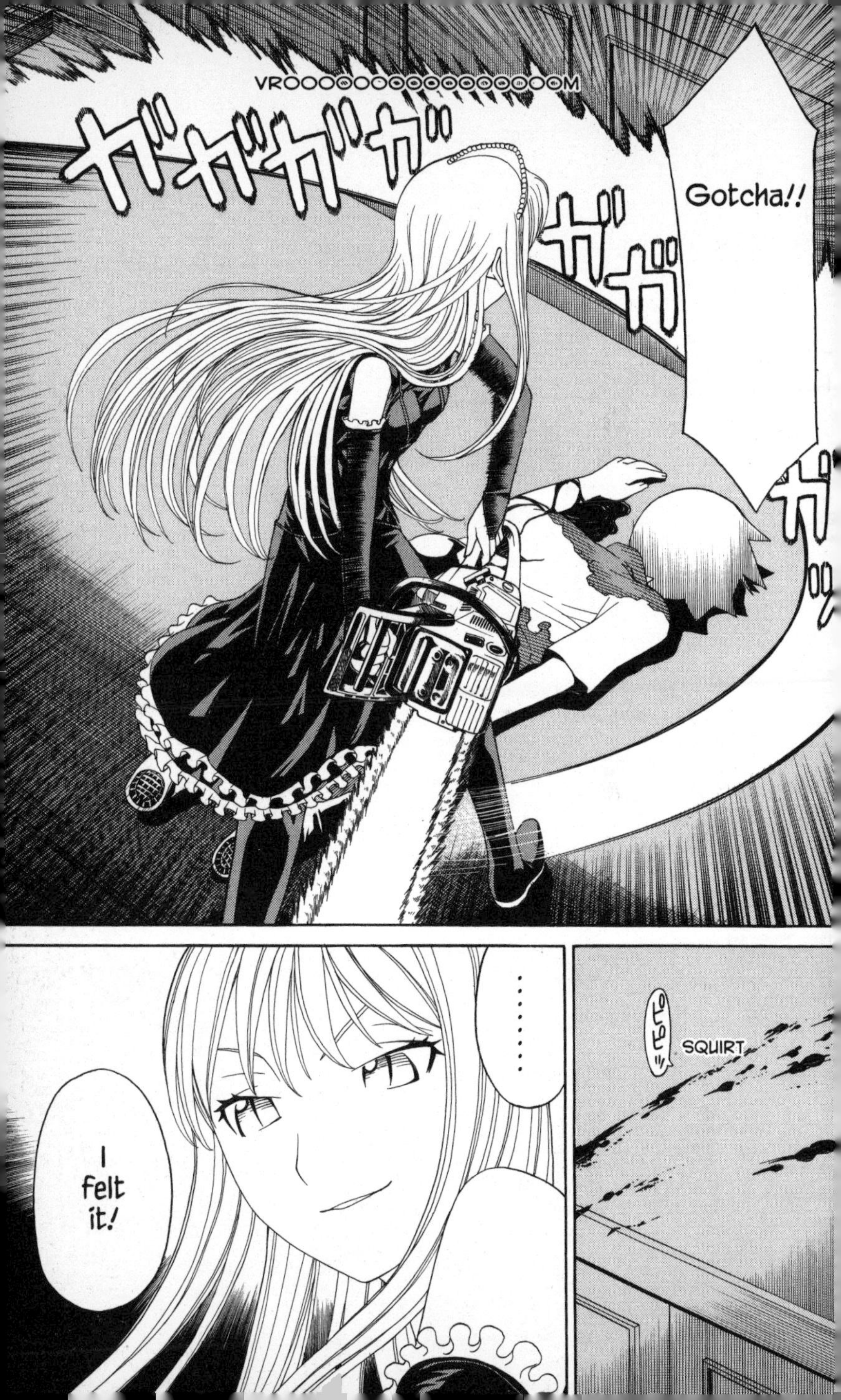
VROOOOOOOOOOOOOOOOOM
Gotcha!!
SQUIRT
......
I felt it!

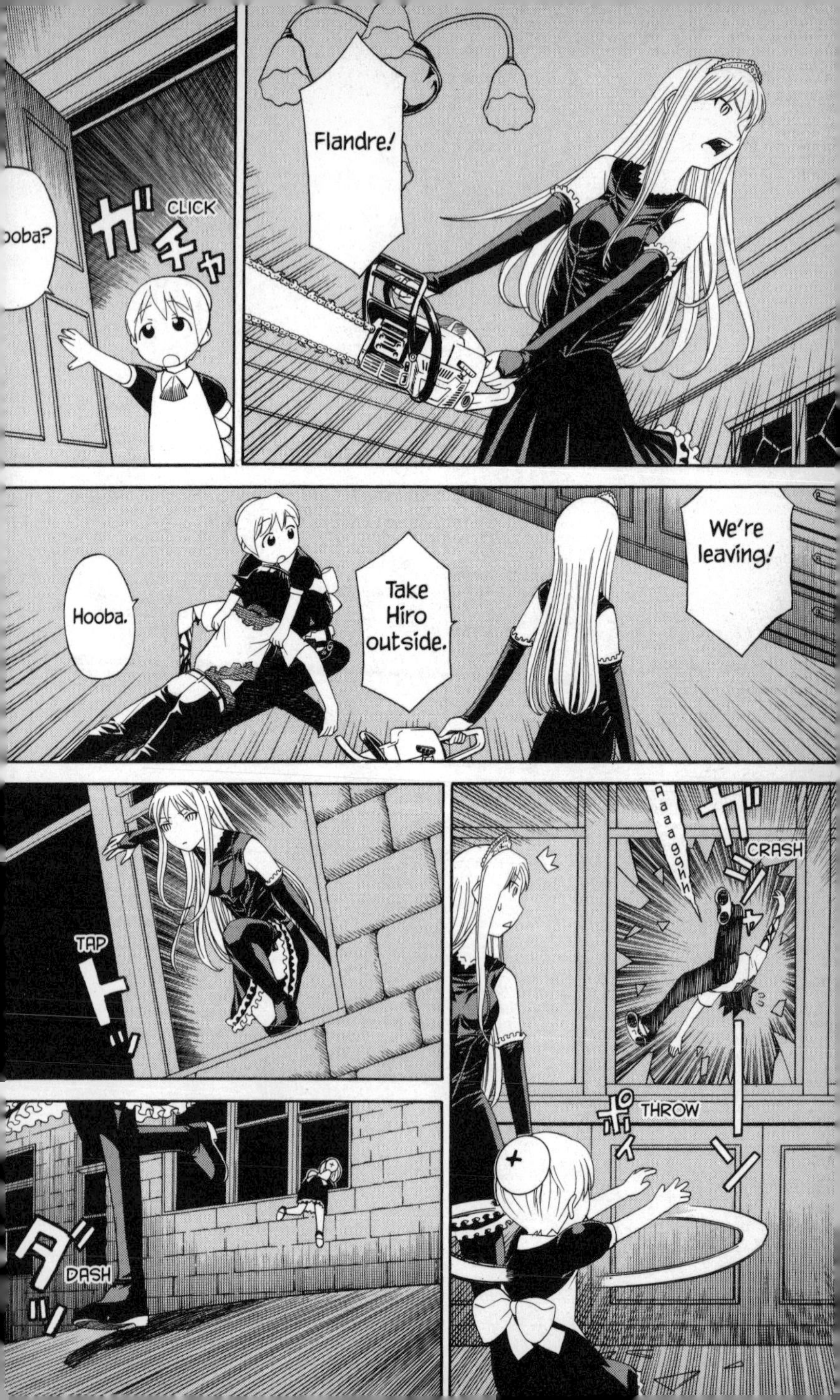
Flandre!
ooba?
ガチャ
CLICK
We're leaving!
Take Hiro outside.
Hooba.
Aaaagghh
CRASH
THROW
TAP
DASH

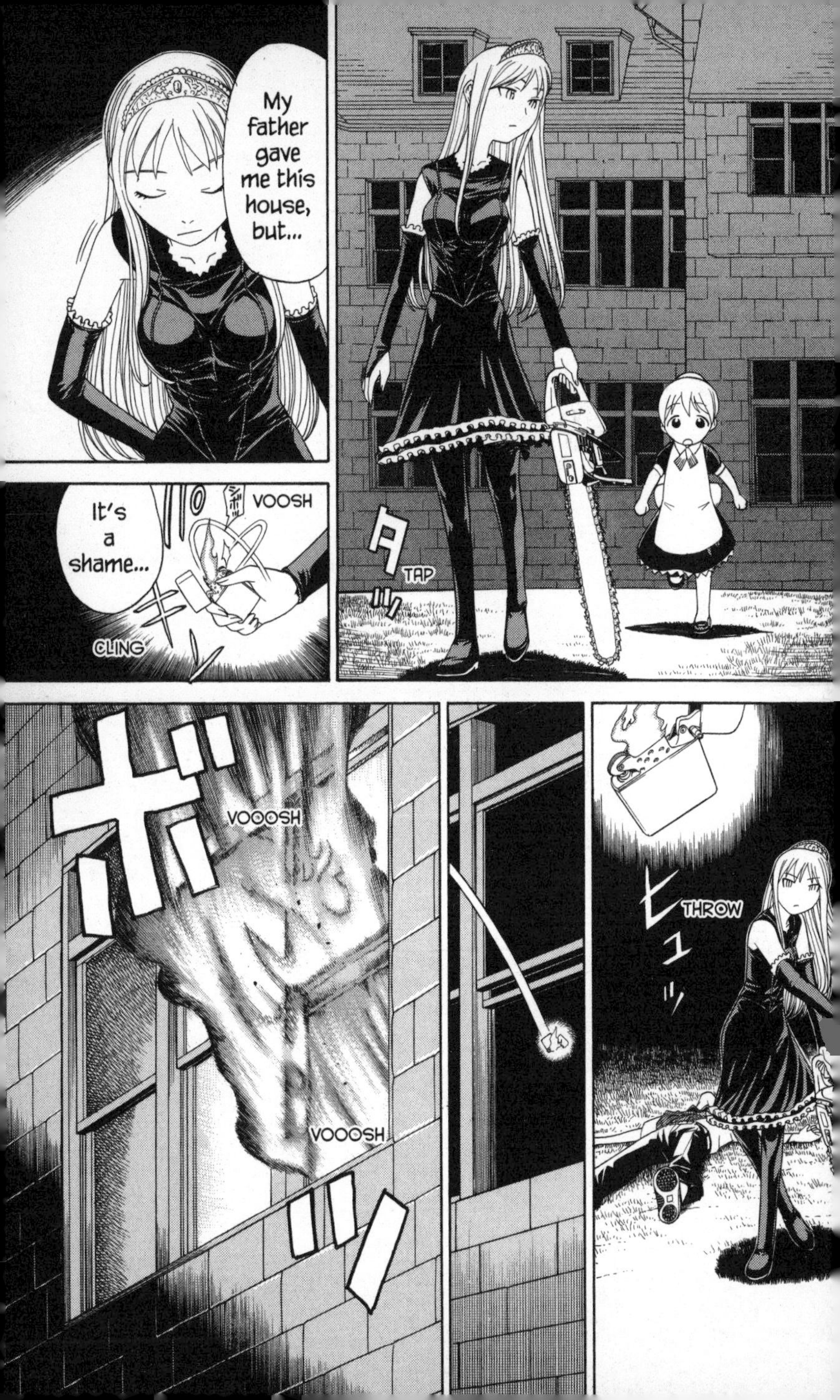

タッ
TAP
My father gave me this house, but...
It's a shame...
VOOSH
CLING
ヒュッ
THROW
VOOOSH
VOOOSH

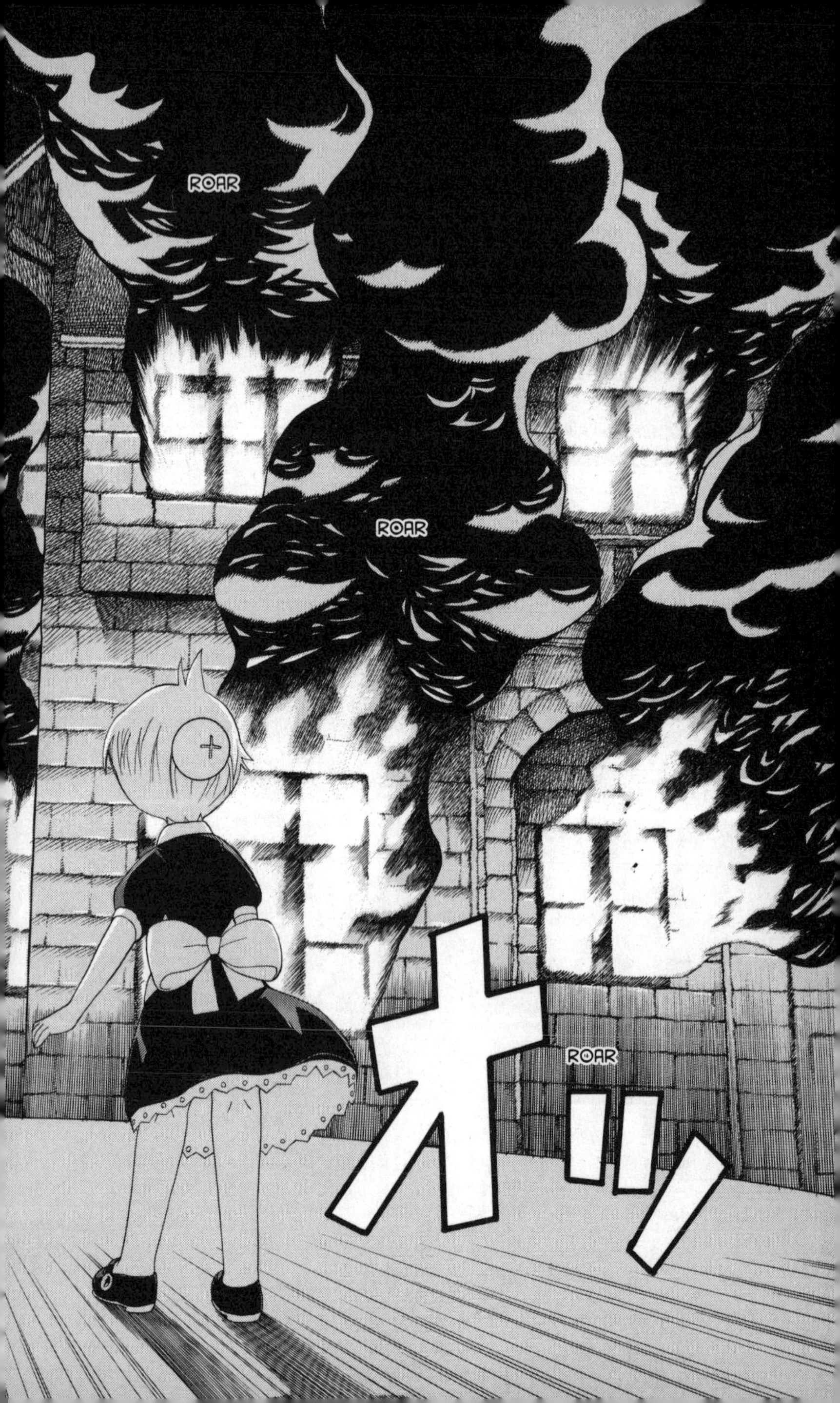
ROAR
ROAR
ROAR
オッ

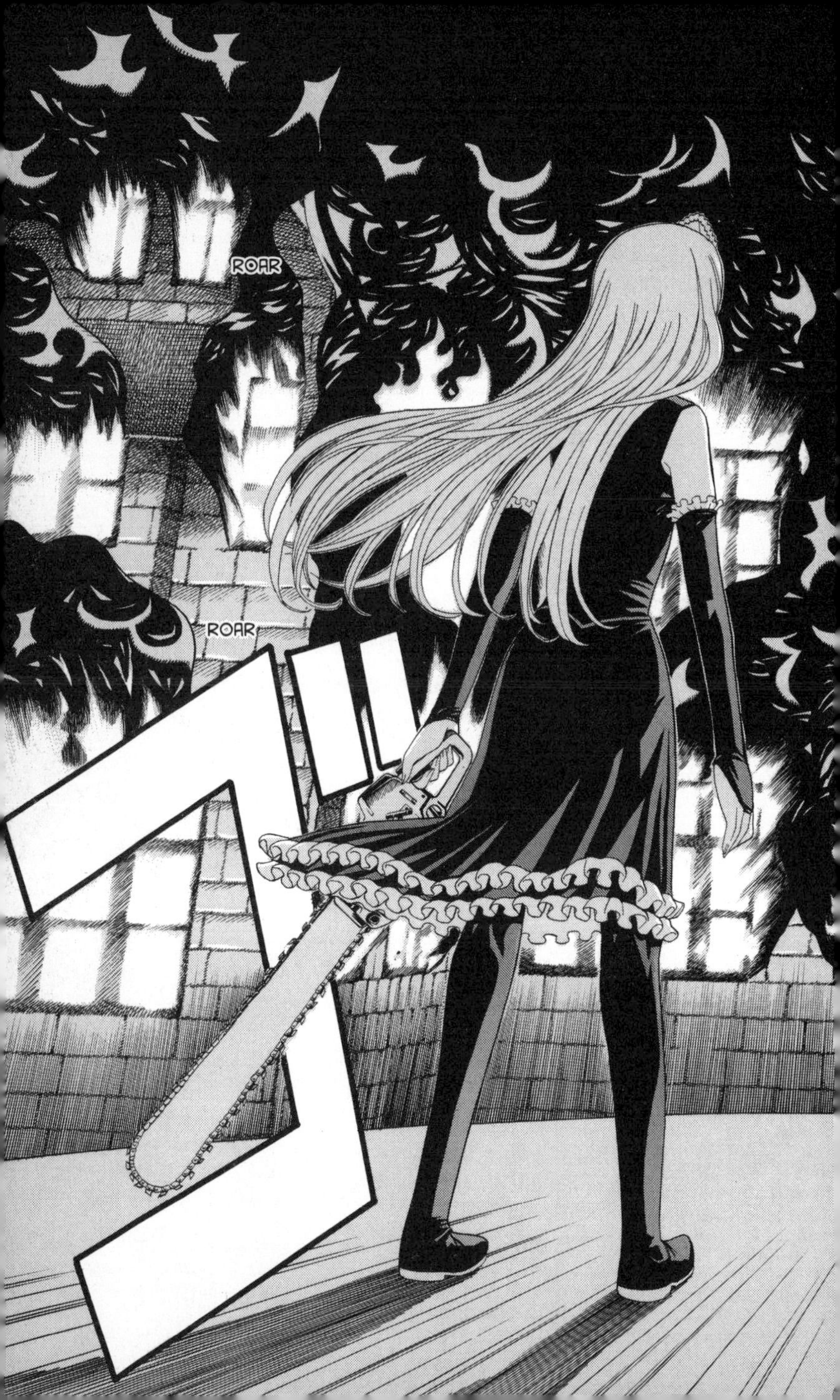
ROAR
ROAR
ズ

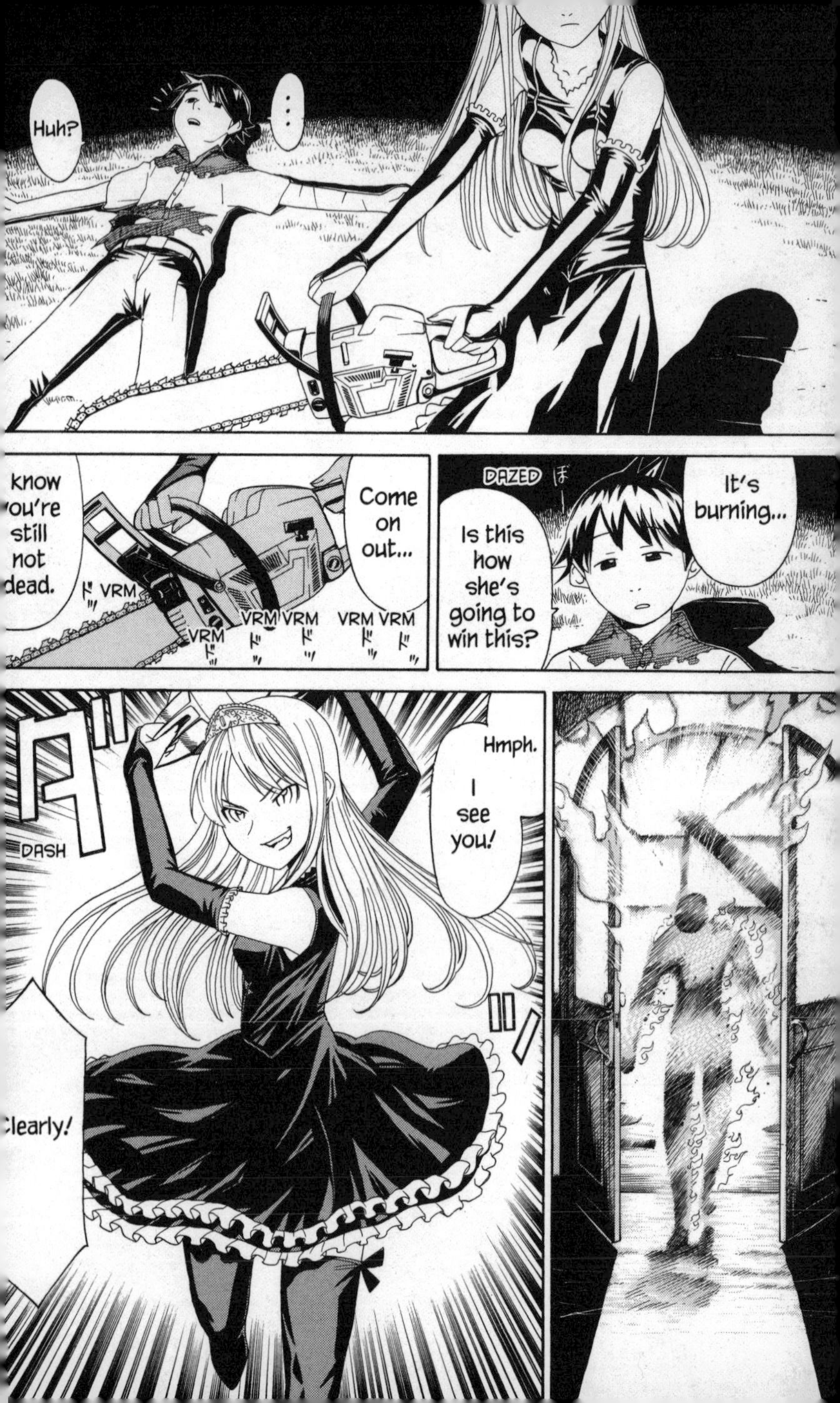

...
Huh?
It's burning...
DAZED ぼー
Is this how she's going to win this?
Come on out...
know ou're still not dead.
VRM VRM VRM VRM VRM VRM
ドドドドドド
Hmph.
I see you!
DASH ダッ
learly!

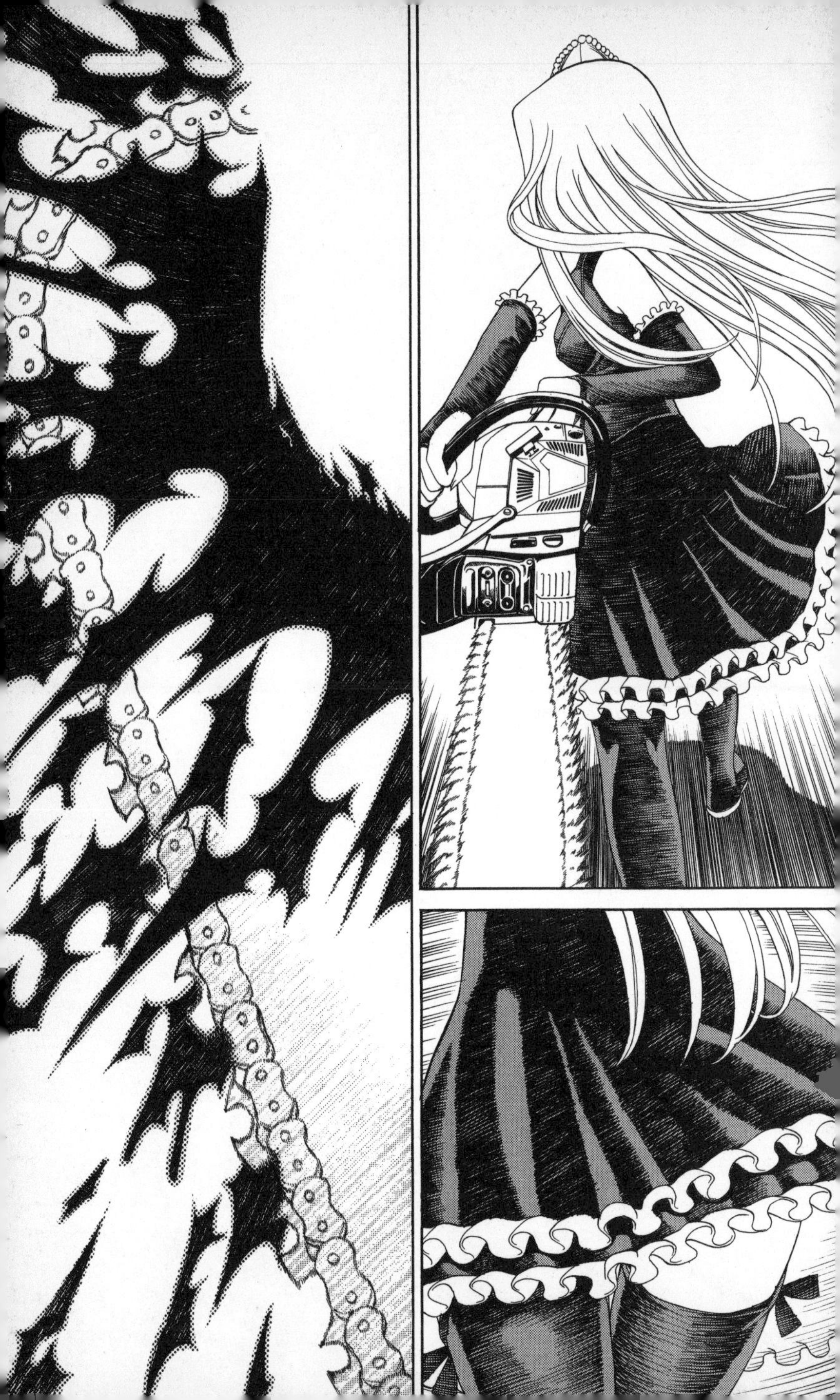

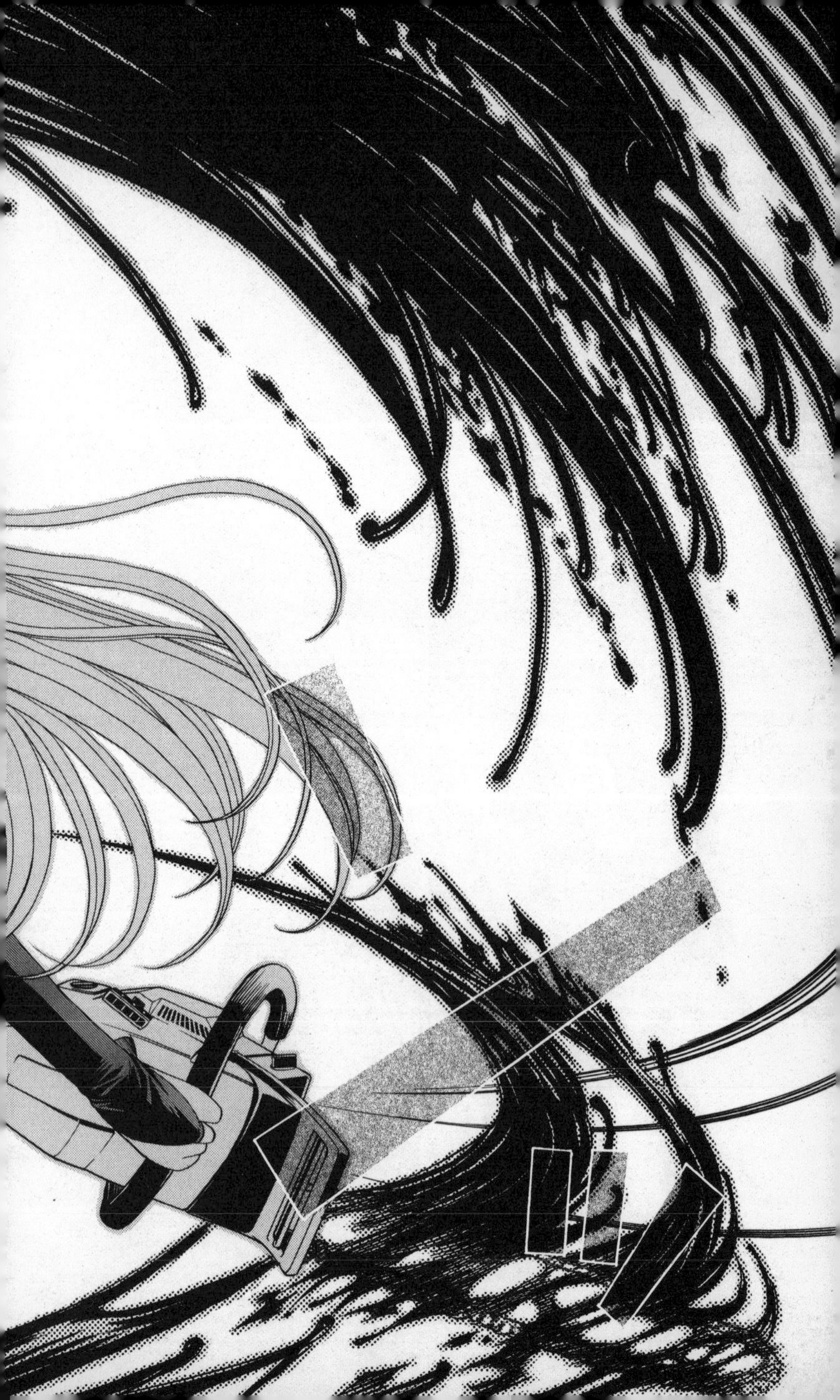

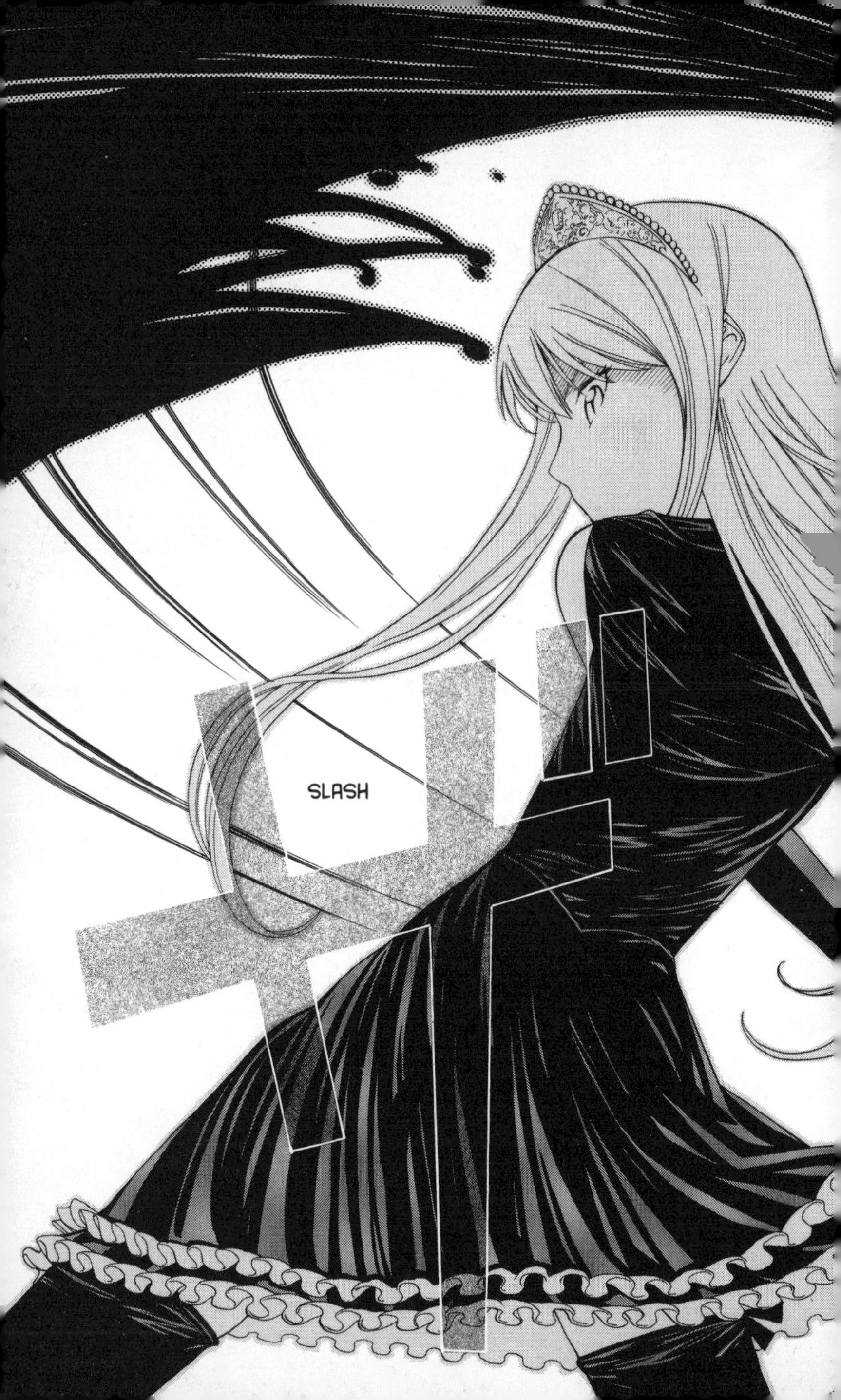
SLASH

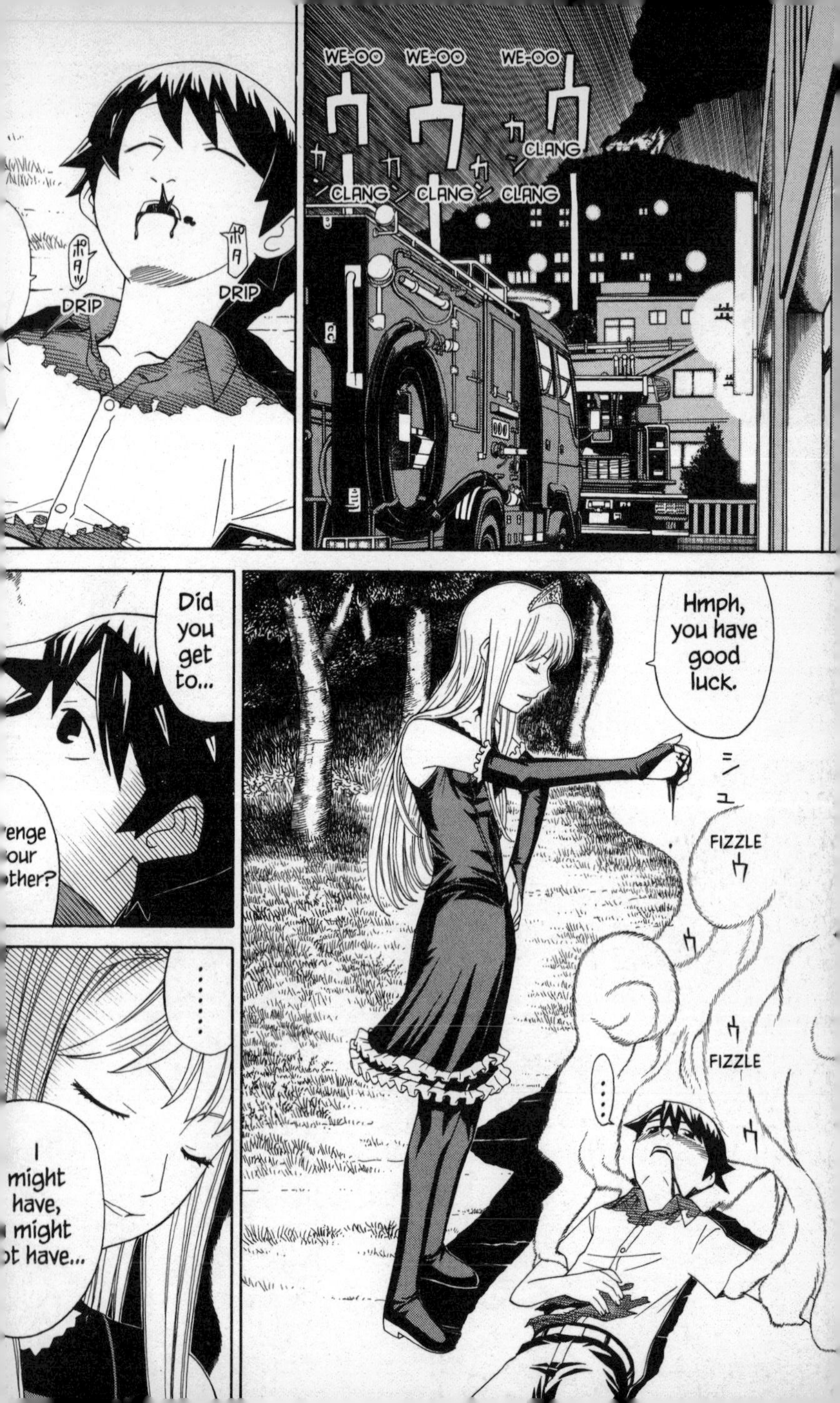
WE-OO WE-OO WE-OO
ウ ウ ウ
カン カン カン カン
CLANG
CLANG CLANG CLANG
ポタ
DRIP
ポタッ
DRIP
Hmph, you have good luck.
シュ
FIZZLE
ウ
ウ
ウ
FIZZLE
ウ
.....
Did you get to...
venge our ther?
......
I might have, might ot have...

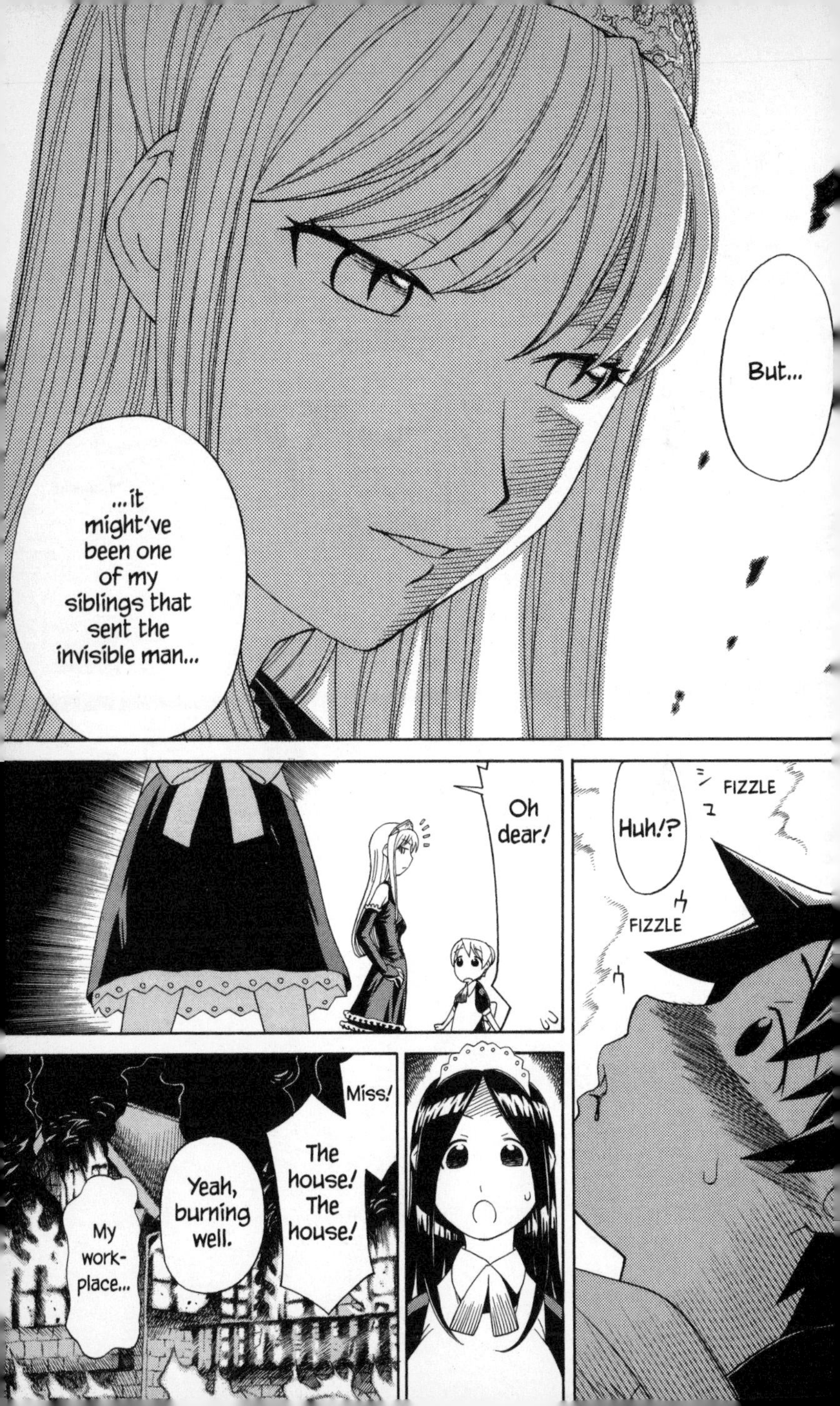
But...
...it might've been one of my siblings that sent the invisible man...
Huh!?
FIZZLE
FIZZLE
Oh dear!
Miss!
The house! The house!
Yeah, burning well.
My work-place...

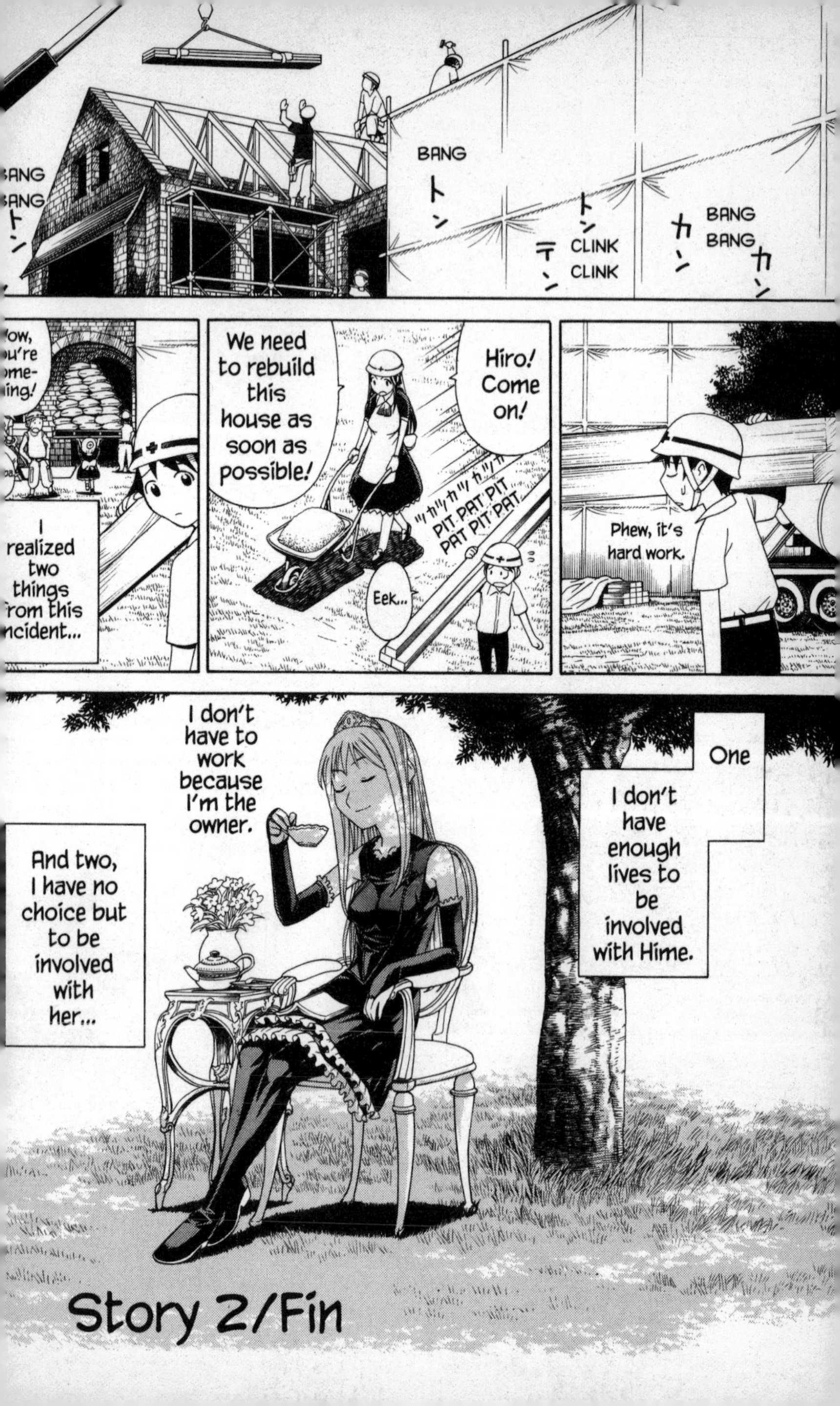
BANG BANG カン
カン
CLINK CLINK テン
トン
BANG トン
BANG BANG トン
Phew, it's hard work.
Hiro! Come on!
We need to rebuild this house as soon as possible!
ツカツカツカツカ PIT PAT PIT PAT PIT PAT
Eek...
I realized two things rom this ncident...
One
I don't have enough lives to be involved with Hime.
I don't have to work because I'm the owner.
And two, I have no choice but to be involved with her...
Story 2/Fin

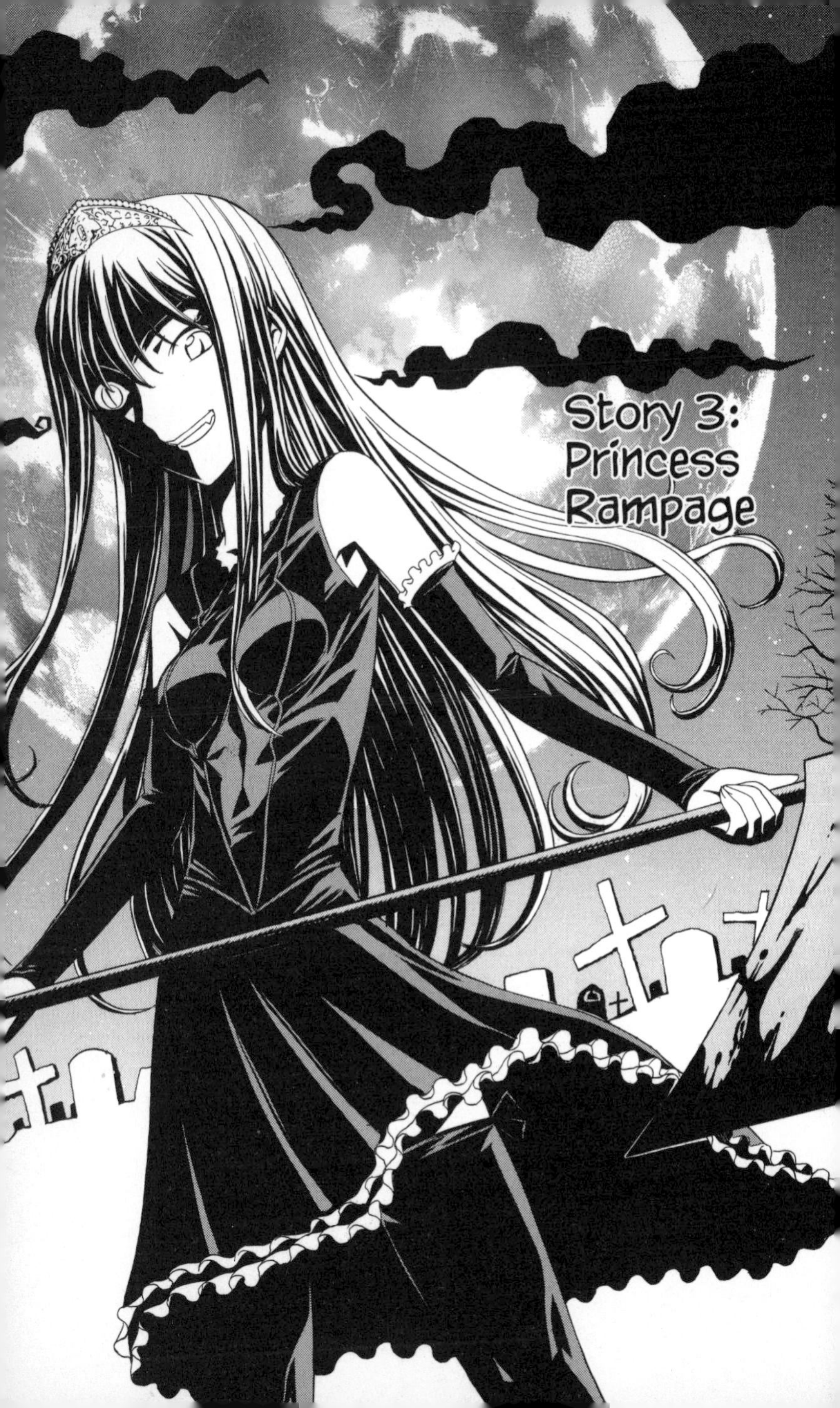
Story 3:
Princess
Rampage

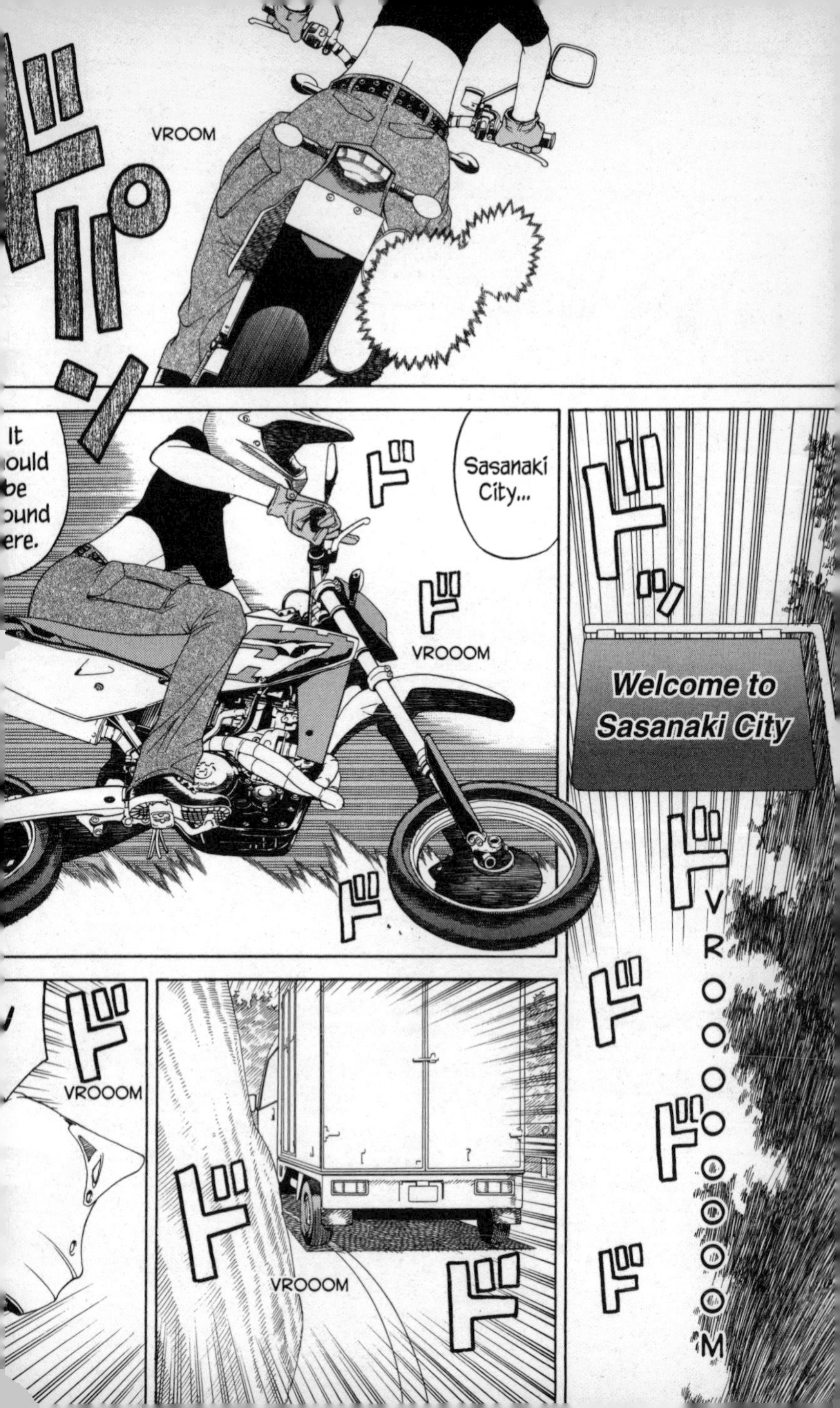

ドドッ
VROOM
ドドッ
Welcome to Sasanaki City
ド
VROOOOOOOOM
ド
ド
ド
Sasanaki City...
ド
ド
VROOOM
ド
It ould be ound ere.
ド
VROOOM
ド
ド
VROOOM

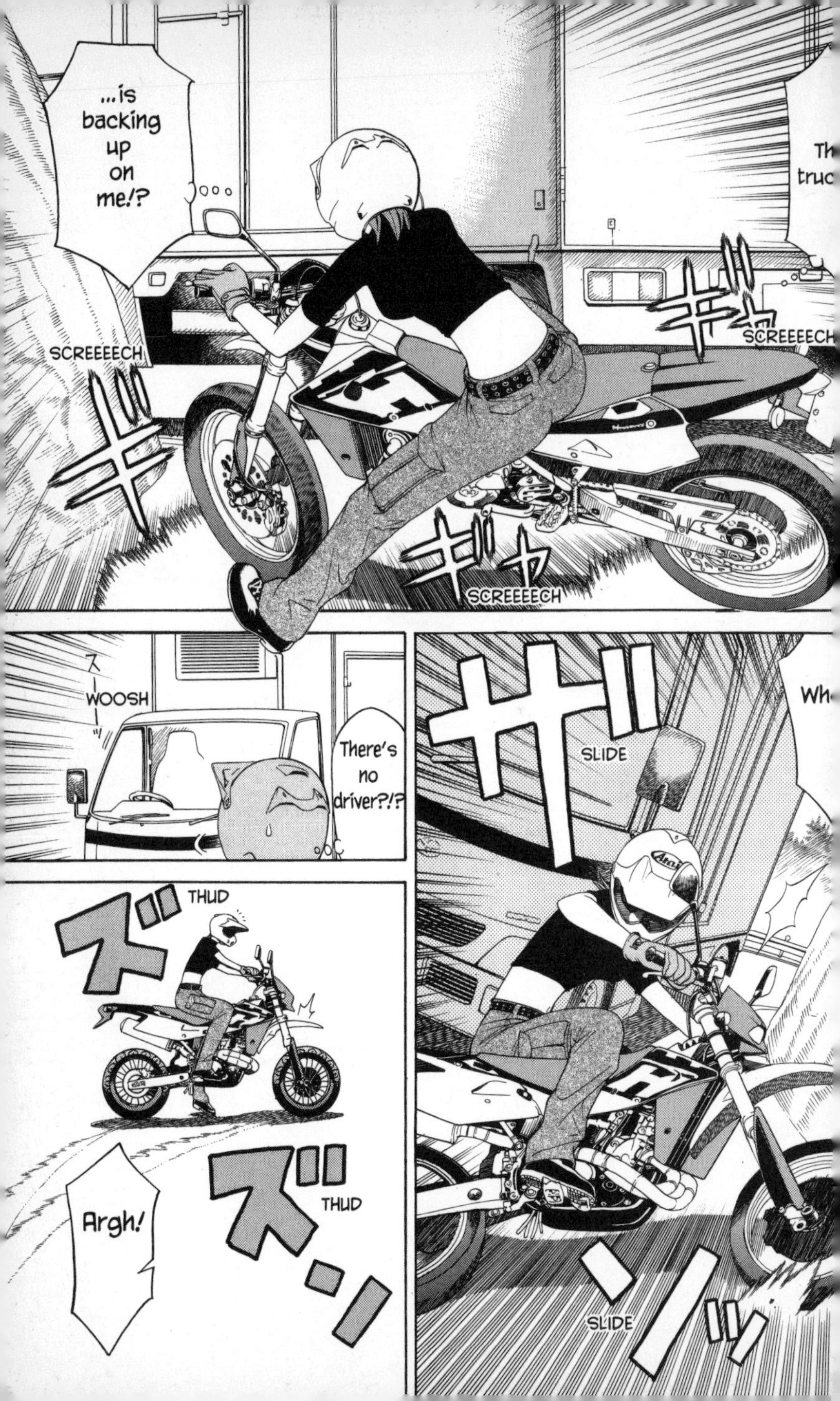

Th truc
...is backing up on me!?
SCREEEECH
SCREEEECH
SCREEEECH
Wh
SLIDE
SLIDE
WOOSH
There's no driver?!?
THUD
THUD
Argh!

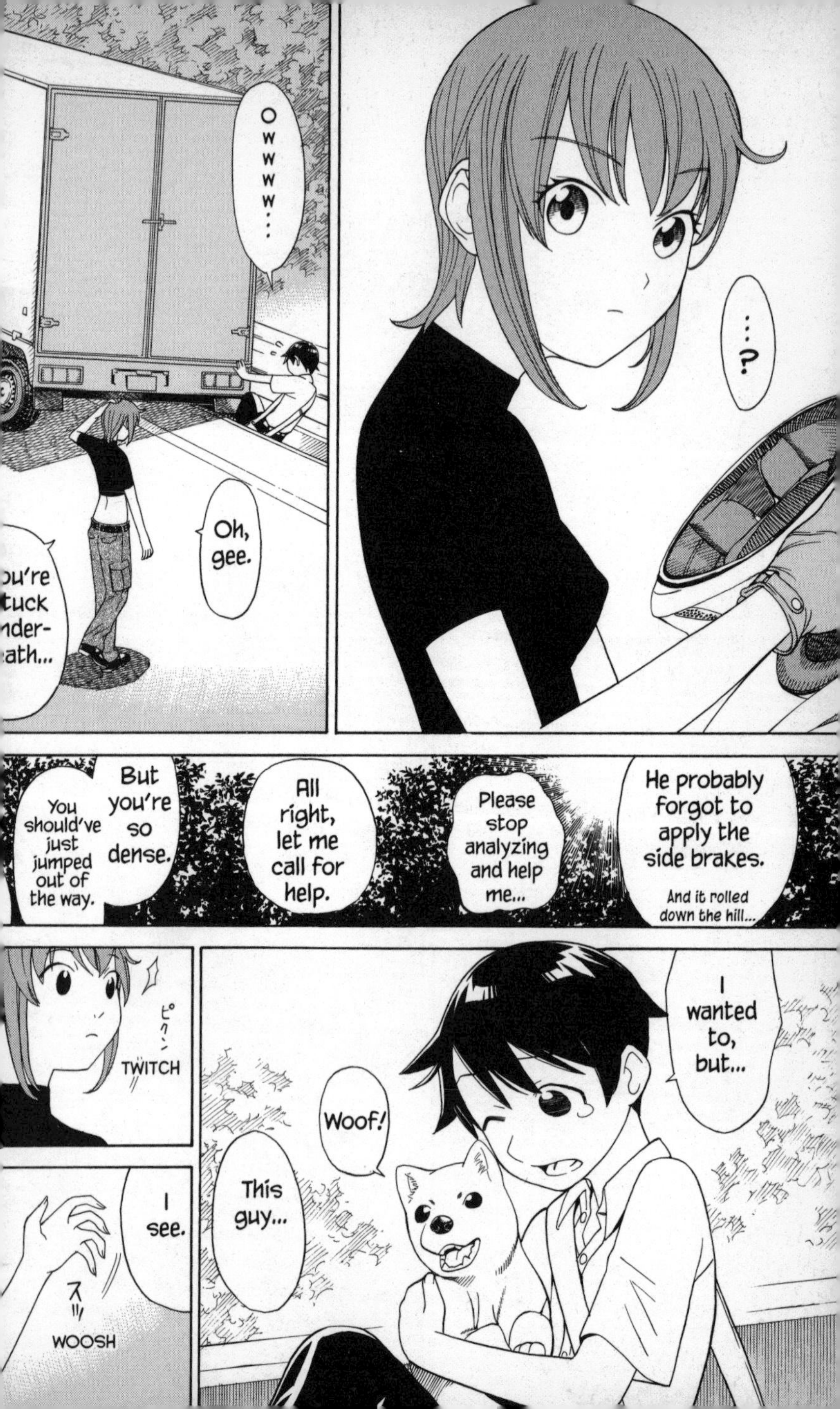
...?
Owwww...
Oh, gee.
ou're
tuck
nder-
ath...
He probably forgot to apply the side brakes.
And it rolled down the hill...
Please stop analyzing and help me...
All right, let me call for help.
But you're so dense.
You should've just jumped out of the way.
I wanted to, but...
Woof!
This guy...
ピクン
TWITCH
I see.
スッ
WOOSH

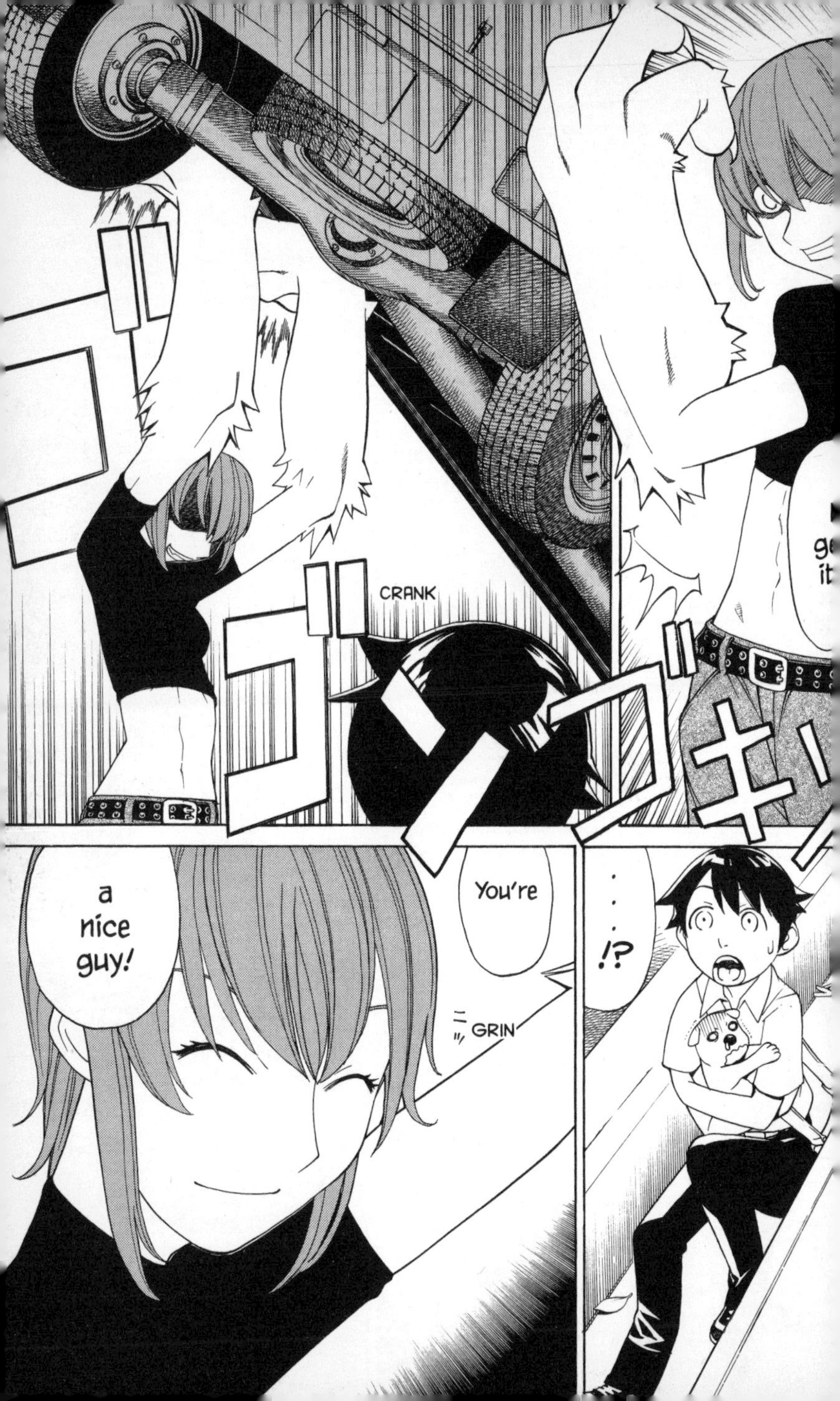

ge
it
CRANK
. . . !?
You're
a nice guy!
GRIN

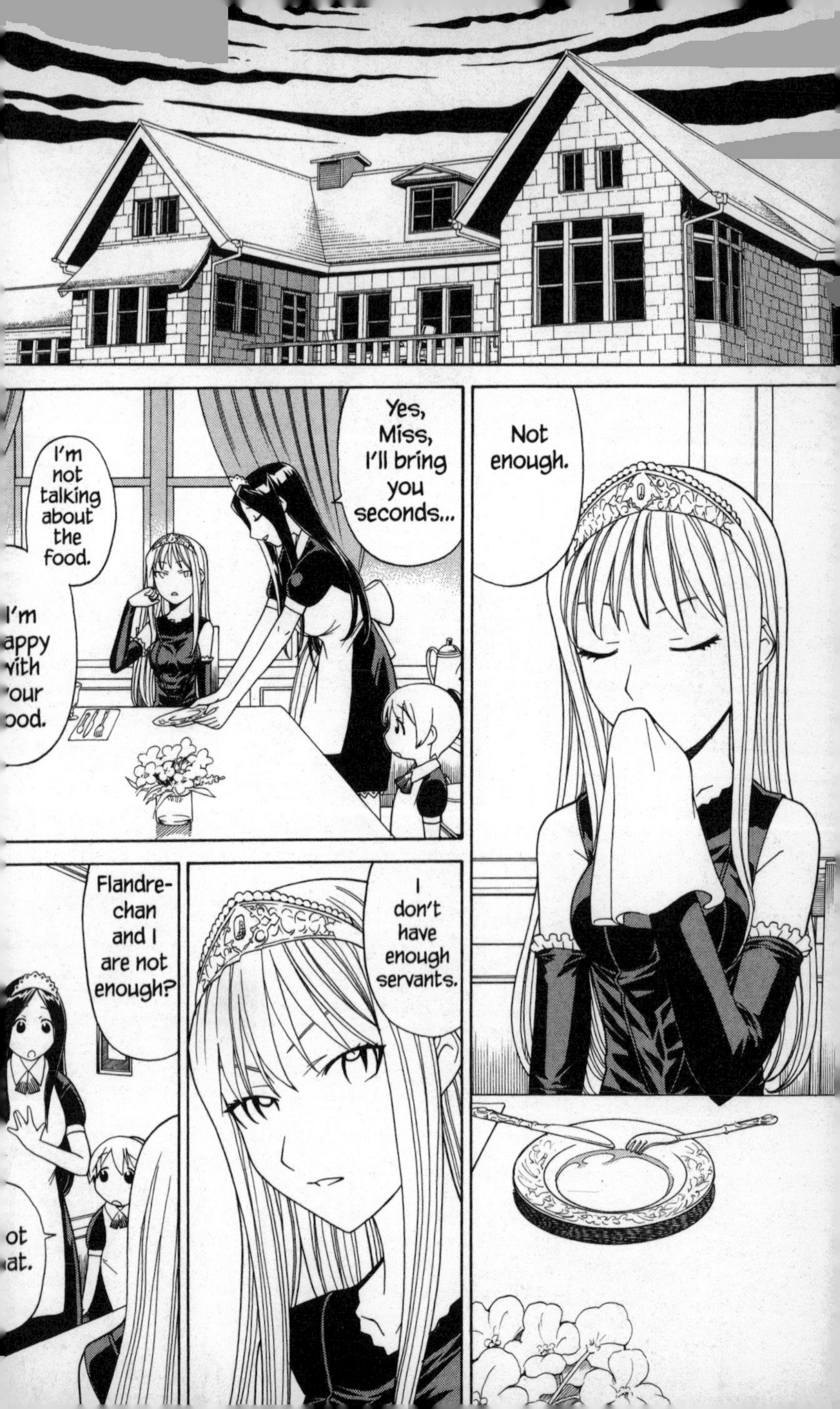

Not enough.
Yes, Miss, I'll bring you seconds...
I'm not talking about the food.
I'm appy vith our ood.
I don't have enough servants.
Flandre-chan and I are not enough?
ot at.

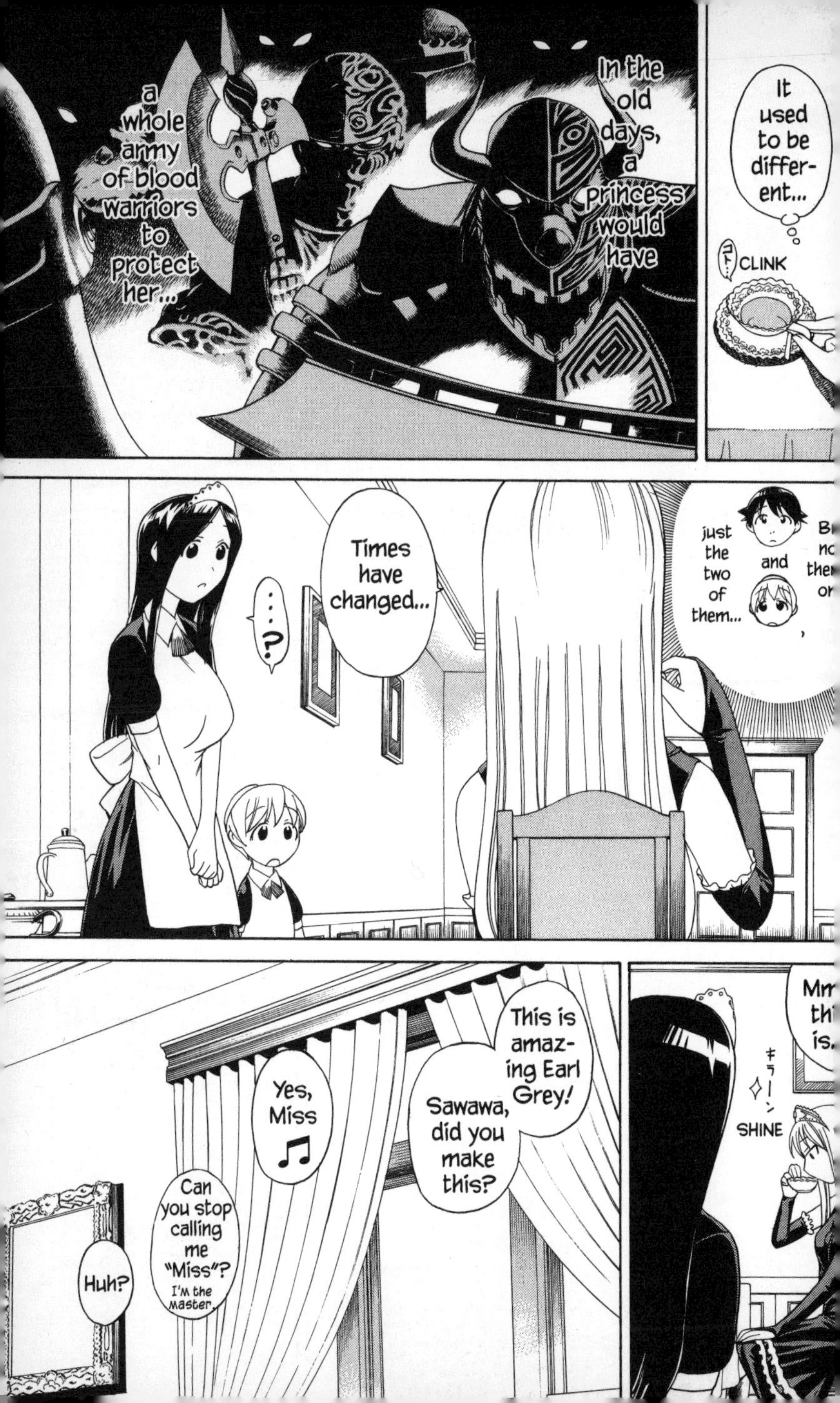

It used to be differ-ent...
コト…
CLINK
In the old days, a Princess would have
a whole army of blood warriors to protect her...
just the two of them...
and
Times have changed...
...?
キラーン
SHINE
This is amaz-ing Earl Grey!
Sawawa, did you make this?
Yes, Miss ♫
Can you stop calling me "Miss"? I'm the Master.
Huh?

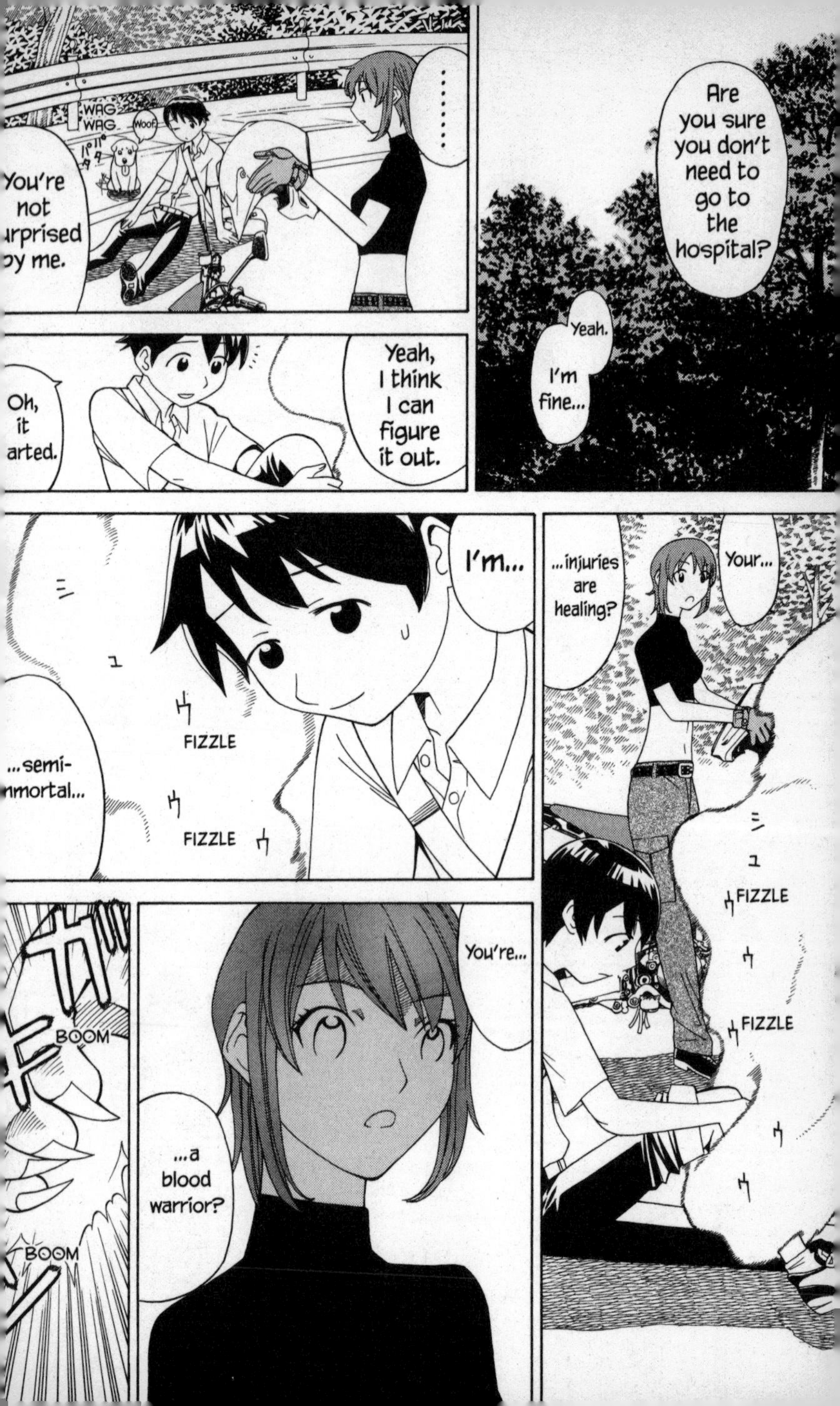
Are you sure you don't need to go to the hospital?
Yeah.
I'm fine...
......
WAG WAG
Woof
You're not
urprised
y me.
Yeah, I think I can figure it out.
Oh, it
arted.
Your...
...injuries are healing?
FIZZLE
FIZZLE
I'm...
...semi-
mmortal...
FIZZLE
FIZZLE
You're...
...a blood warrior?
BOOM
BOOM

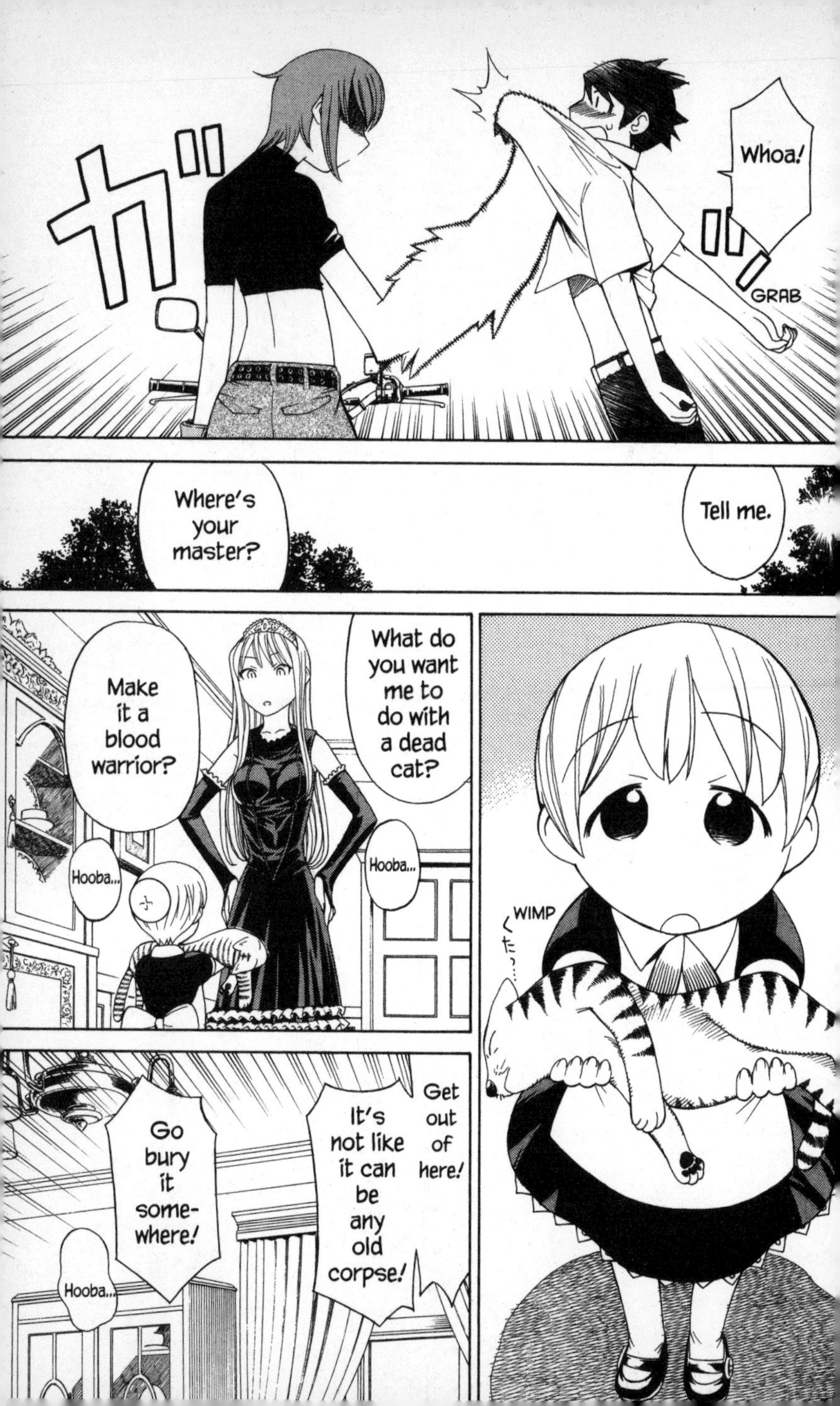
Whoa!
GRAB
ガッ
Tell me.
Where's your master?
WIMP
くたっ…
What do you want me to do with a dead cat?
Make it a blood warrior?
Hooba...
Hooba...
Get out of here!
It's not like it can be any old corpse!
Go bury it somewhere!
Hooba...

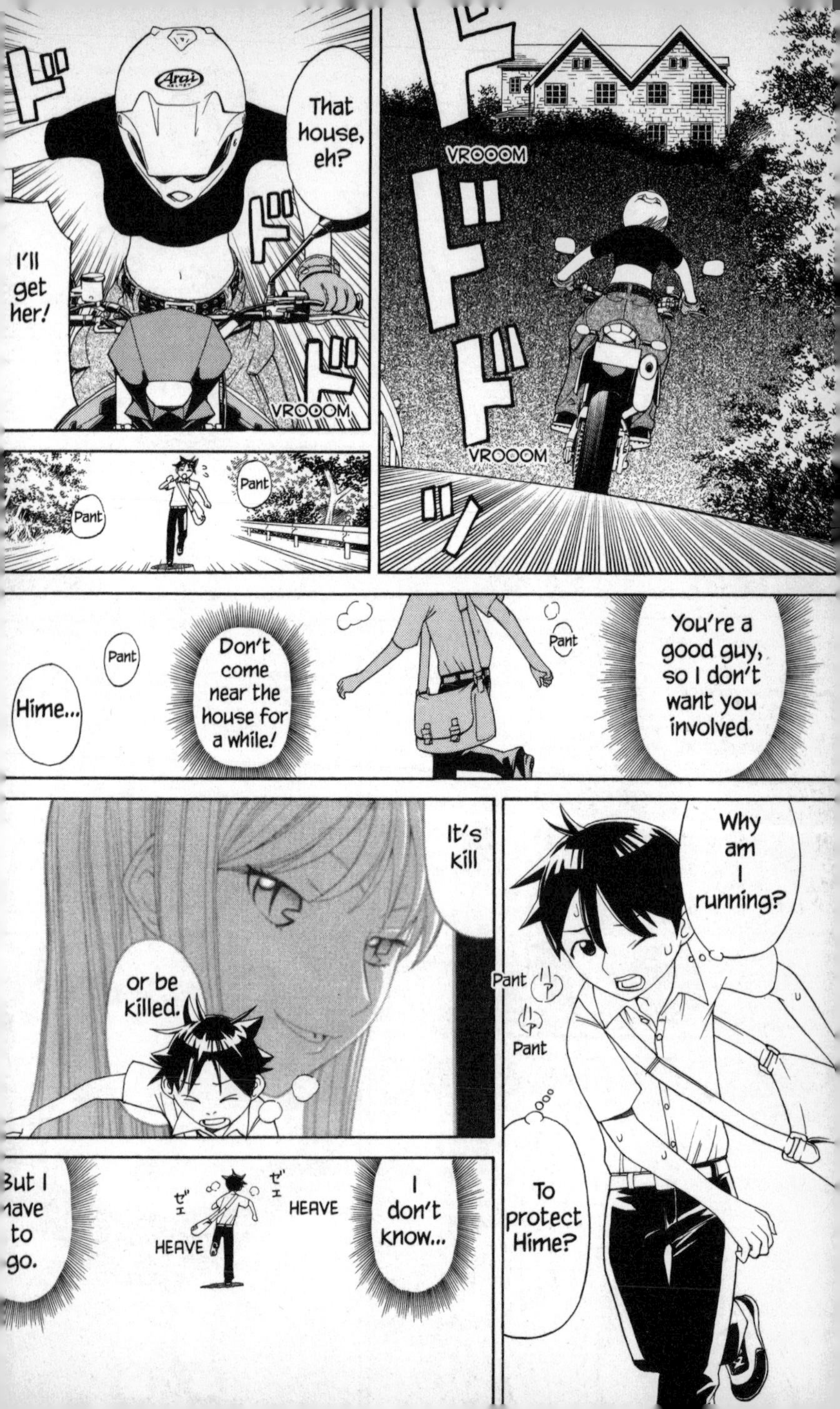

VROOOM
VROOOM
That house, eh?
I'll get her!
VROOOM
Pant
Pant
You're a good guy, so I don't want you involved.
Pant
Don't come near the house for a while!
Pant
Hime...
Why am I running?
Pant
Pant
To protect Hime?
It's kill
or be killed.
I don't know...
HEAVE
HEAVE
But I have to go.

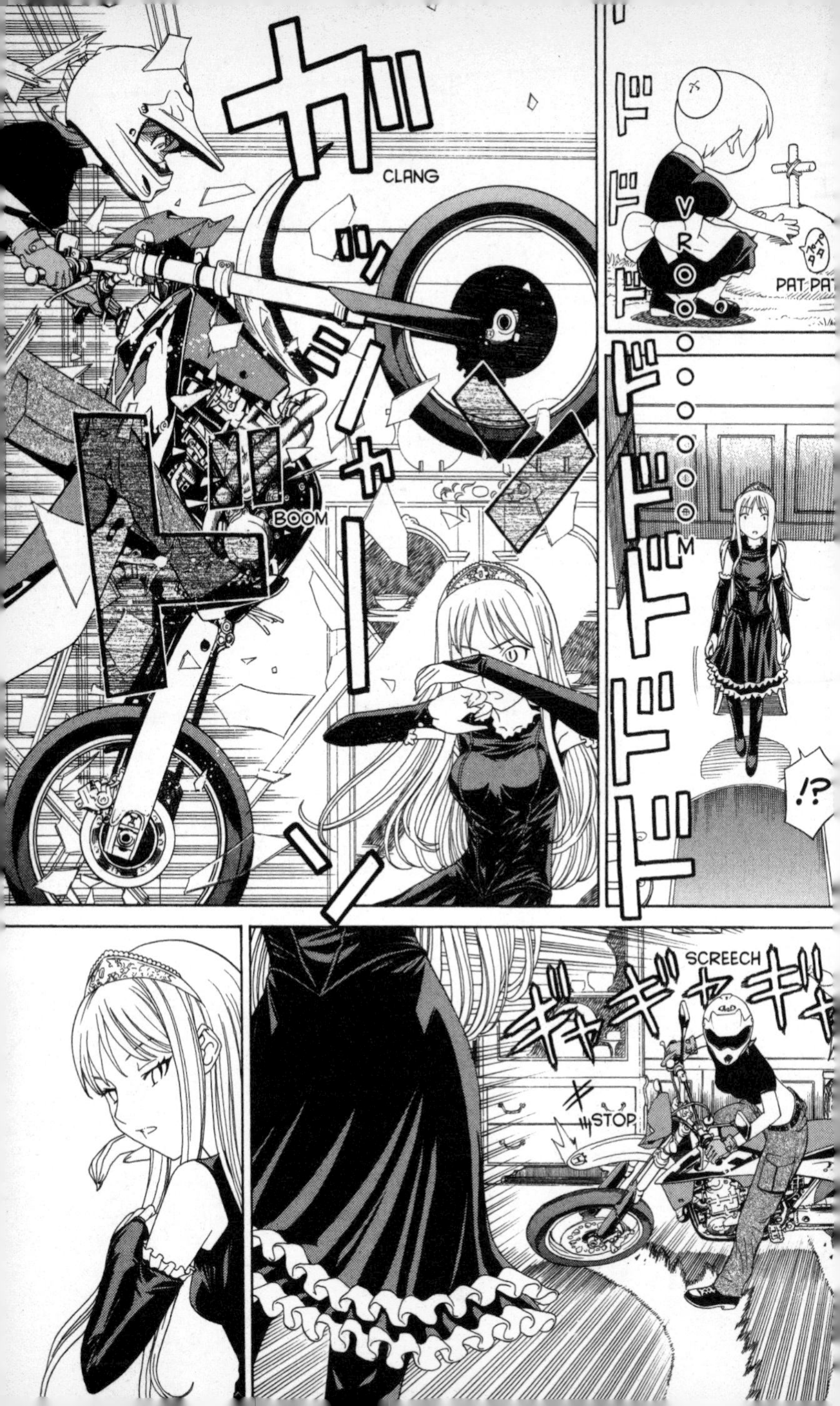
VROOOOOOOOM
PAT PAT
!?
CLANG
BOOM
SCREECH
STOP

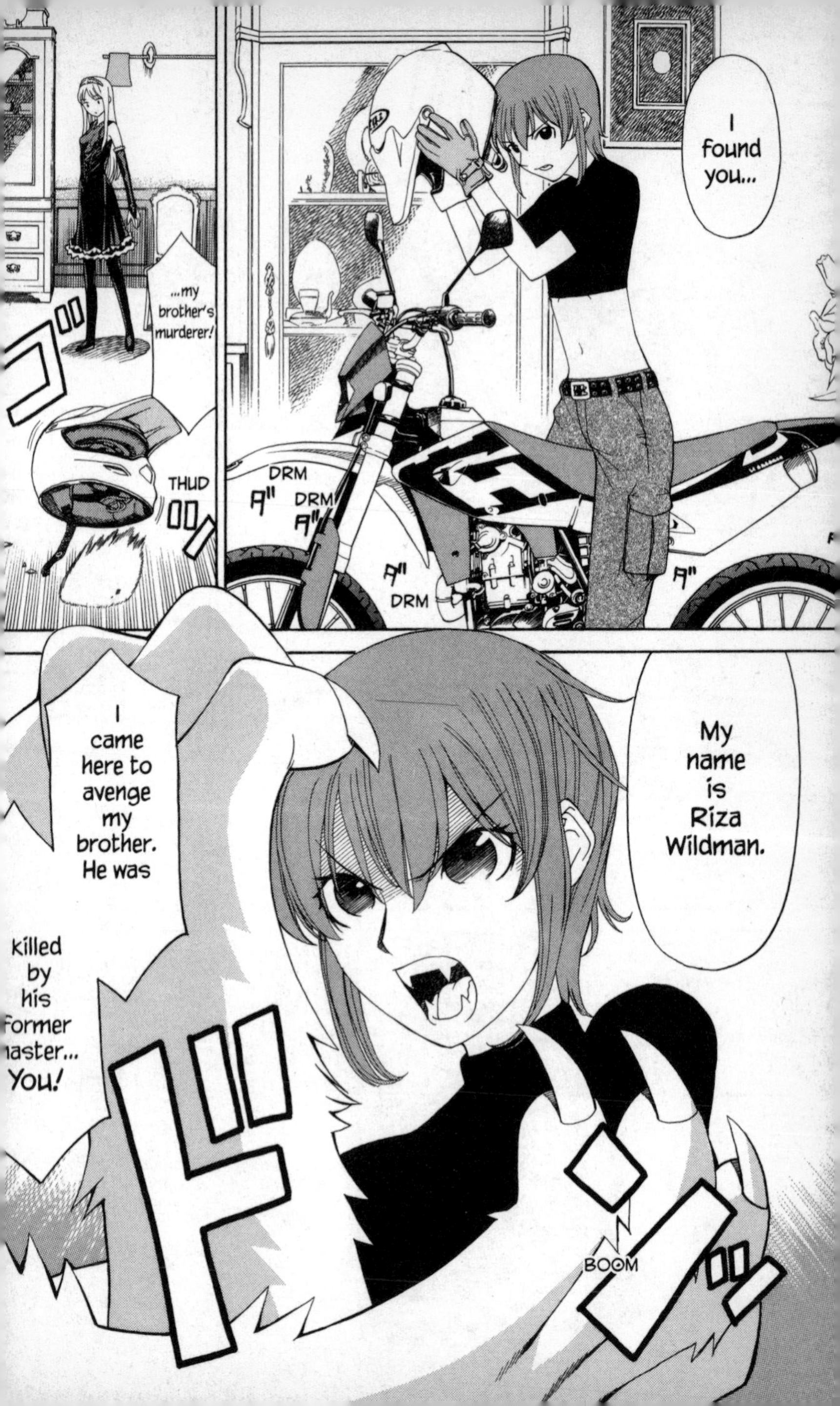

I found you...
DRM
DRM
DRM
...my brother's murderer!
THUD
My name is Riza Wildman.
I came here to avenge my brother. He was
killed by his former master... You!
BOOM

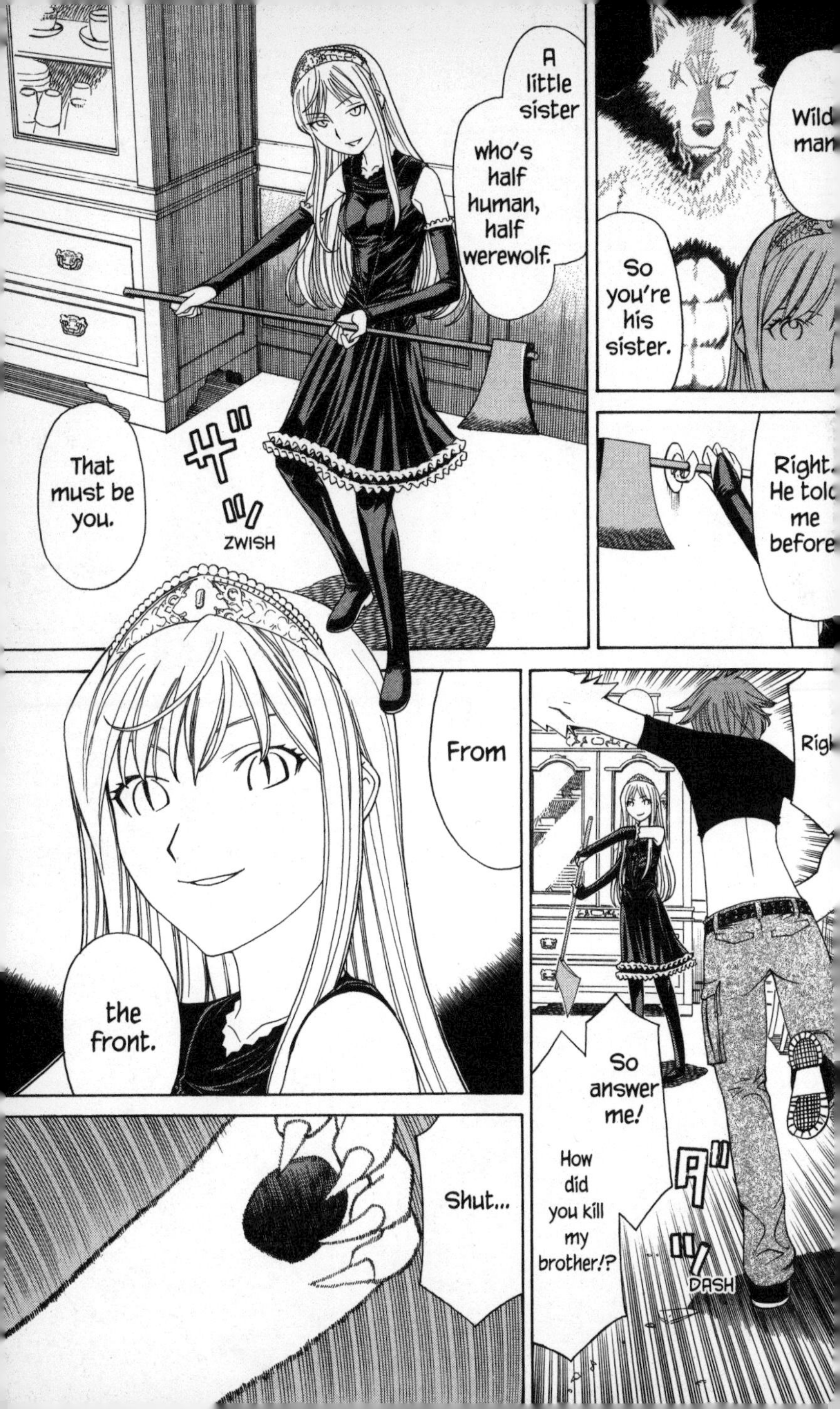

Wild man
So you're his sister.
Right. He told me before
A little sister who's half human, half werewolf.
That must be you.
ZWISH
Righ
So answer me!
How did you kill my brother!?
DASH
From
the front.
Shut...

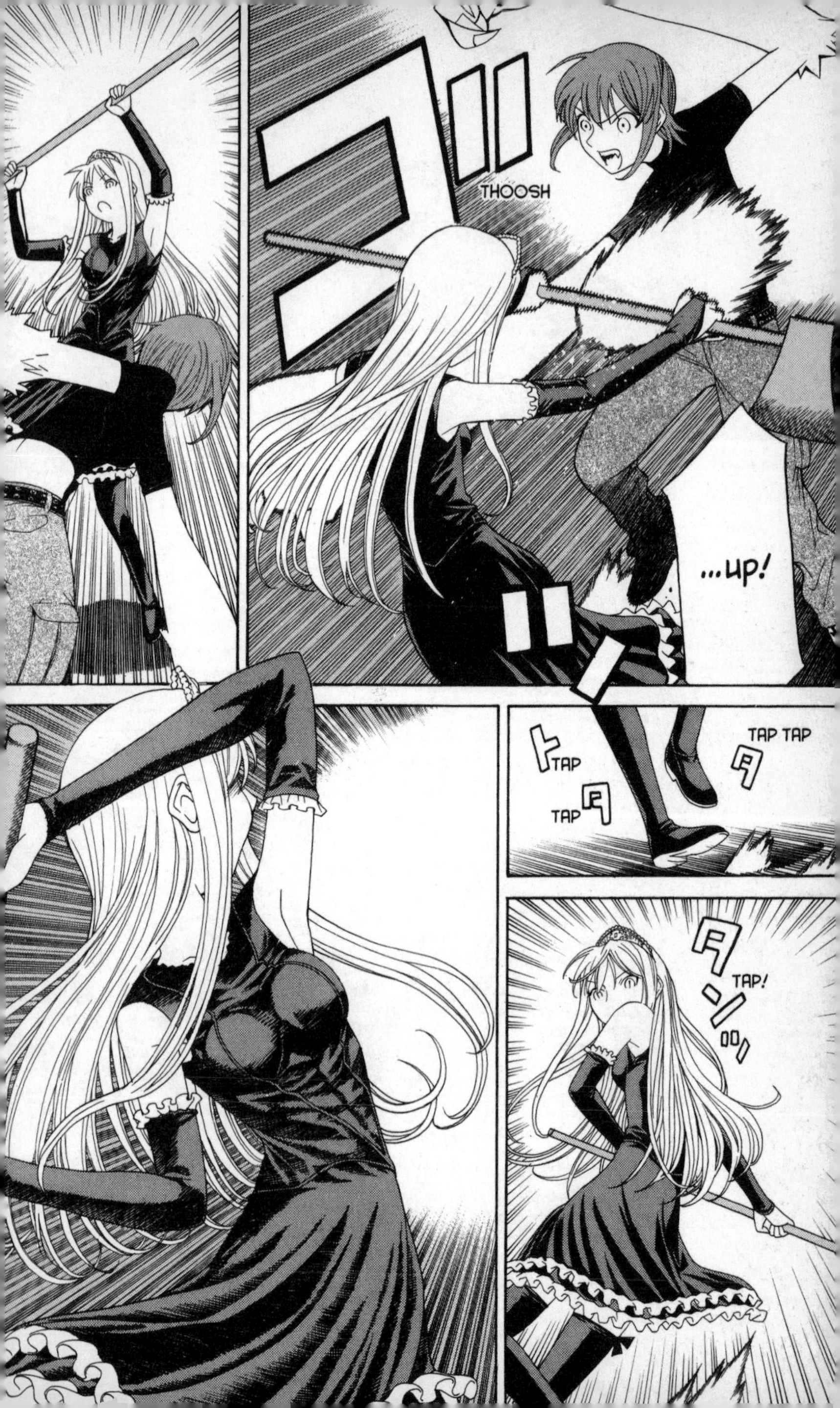

THOOSH
...up!
TAP TAP
TAP
TAP
TAP!

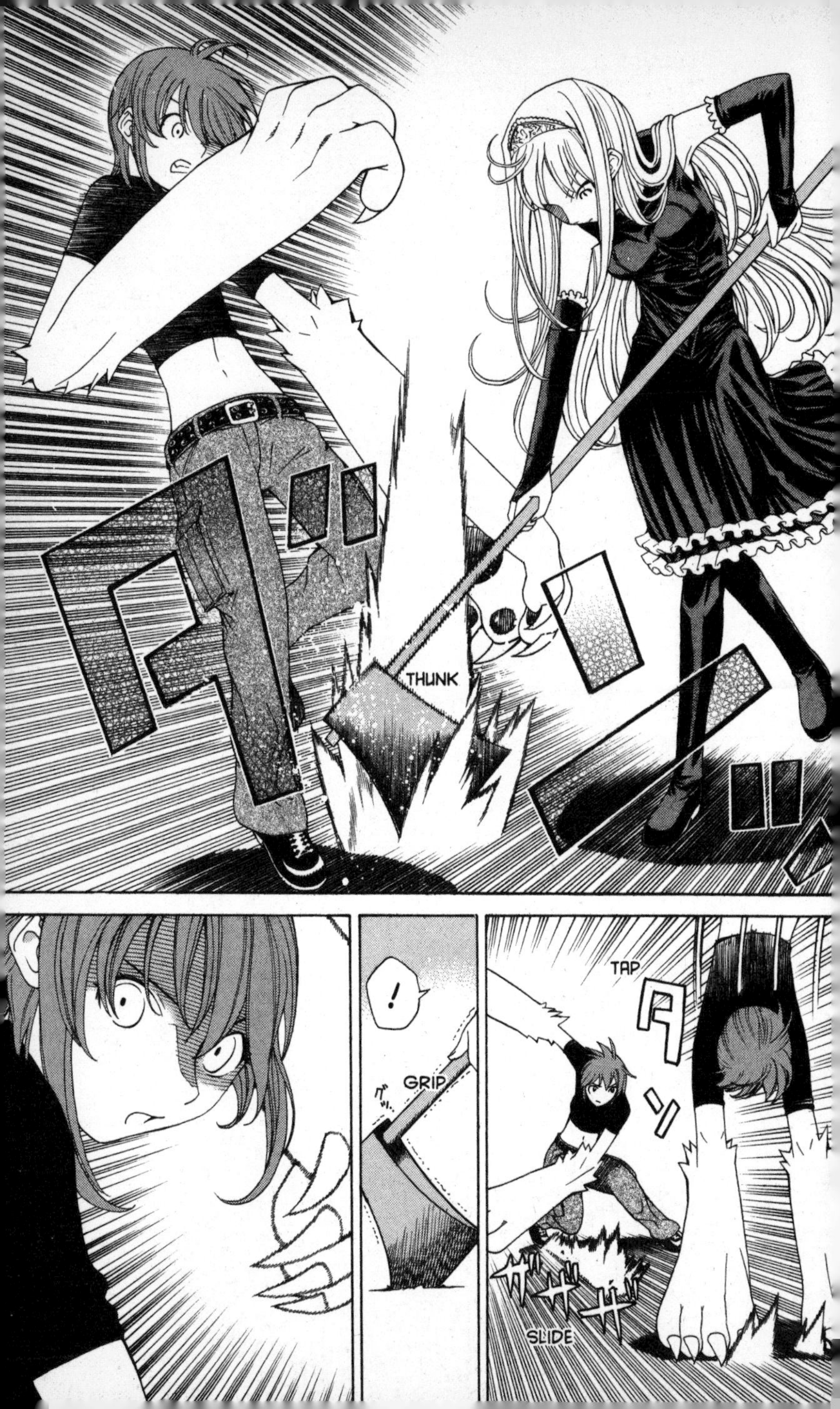
THUNK
TAP
SLIDE
!
GRIP

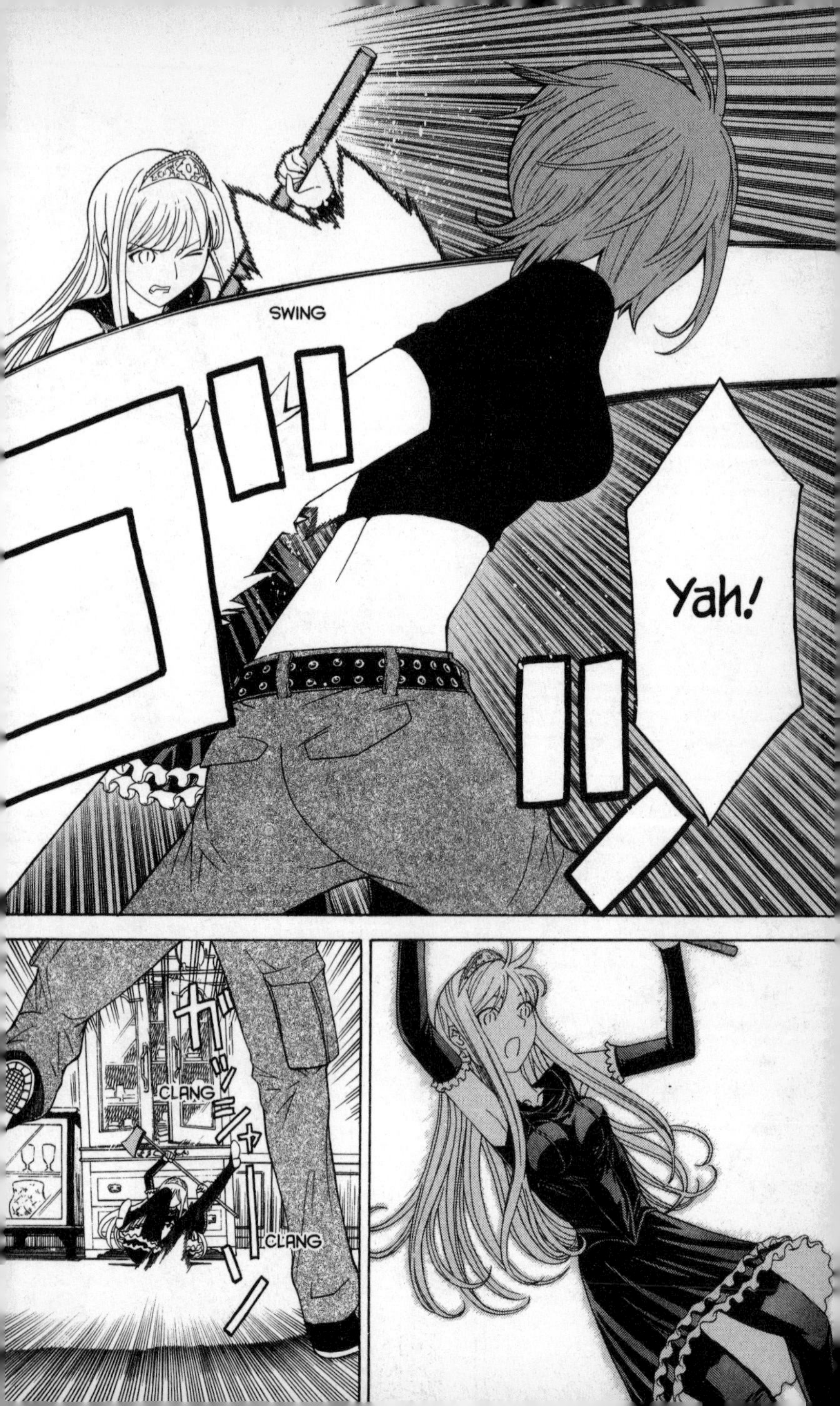
Yah!
SWING
CLANG
CLANG

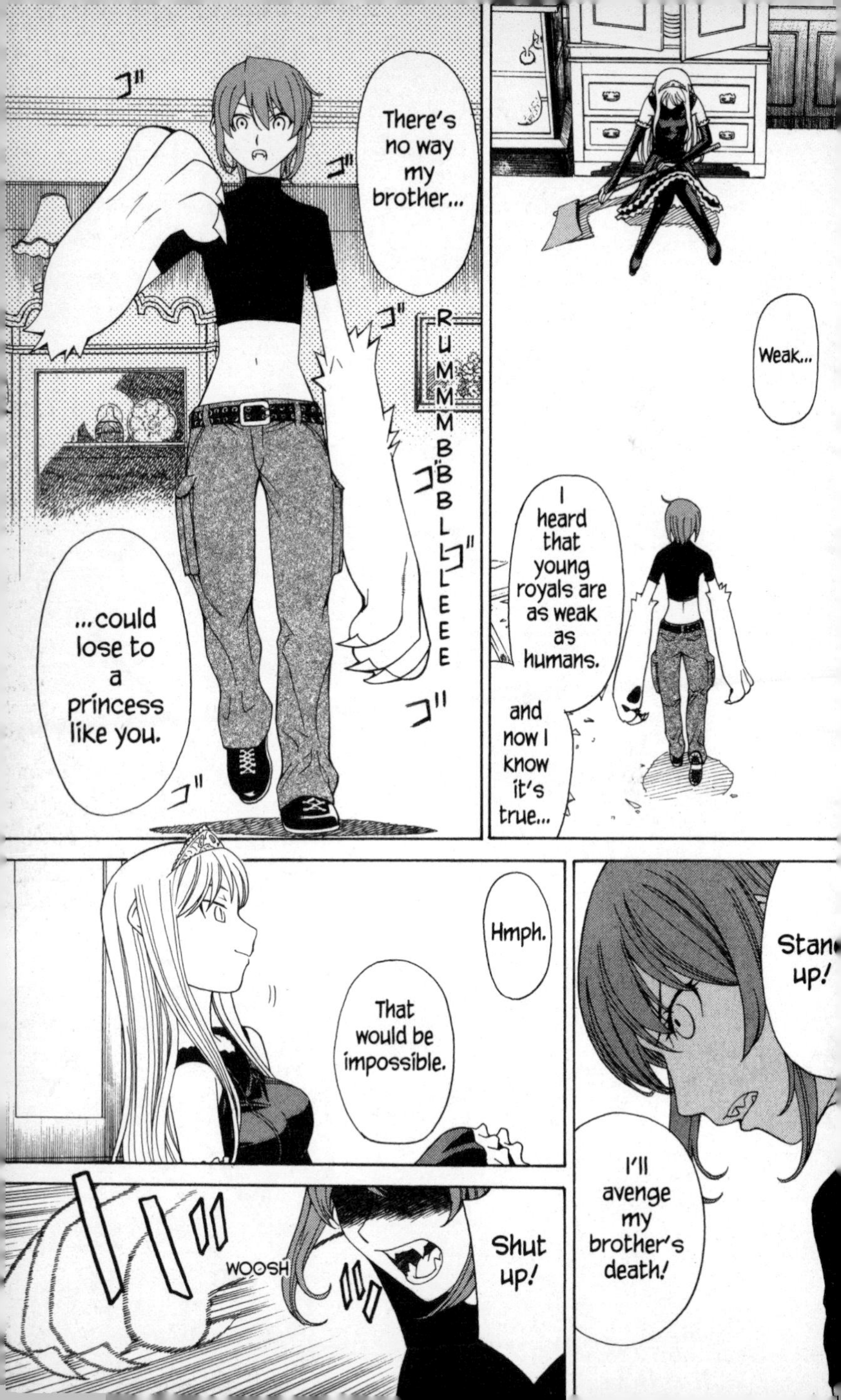

Weak...
I heard that young royals are as weak as humans.
and now I know it's true...
There's no way my brother...
RUMMBBLLEEE
...could lose to a princess like you.
Stan up!
I'll avenge my brother's death!
Hmph.
That would be impossible.
Shut up!
WOOSH

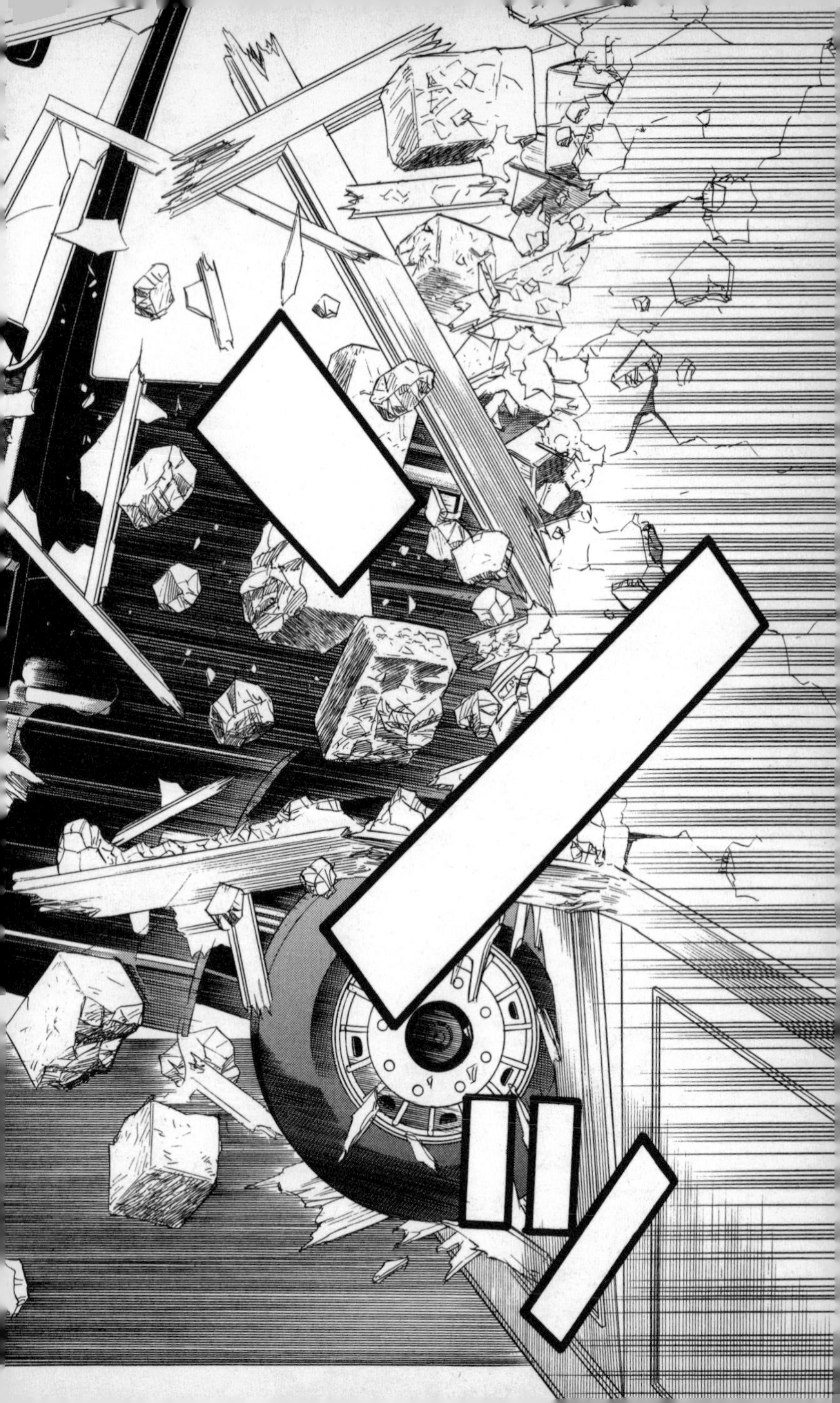

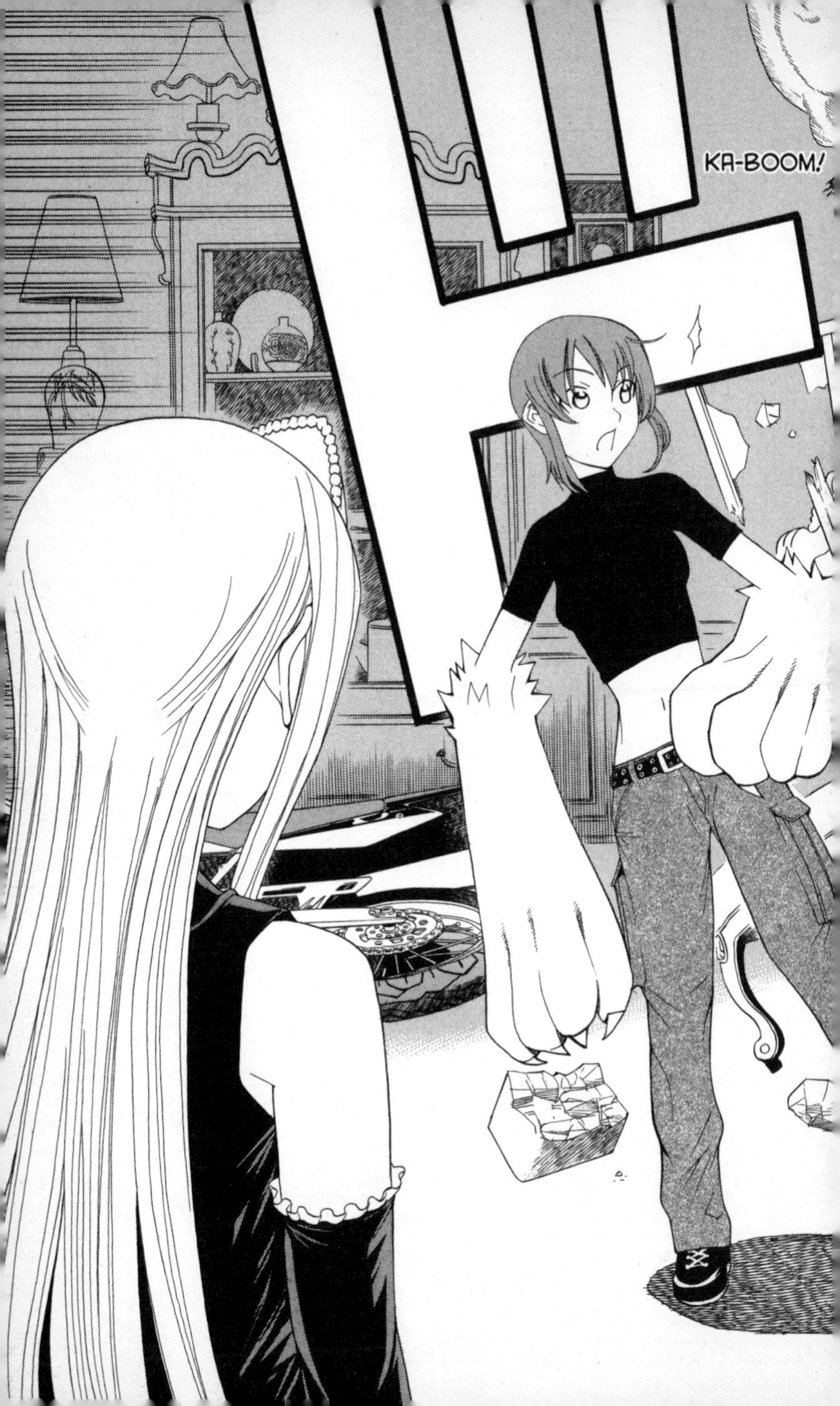
KA-BOOM!

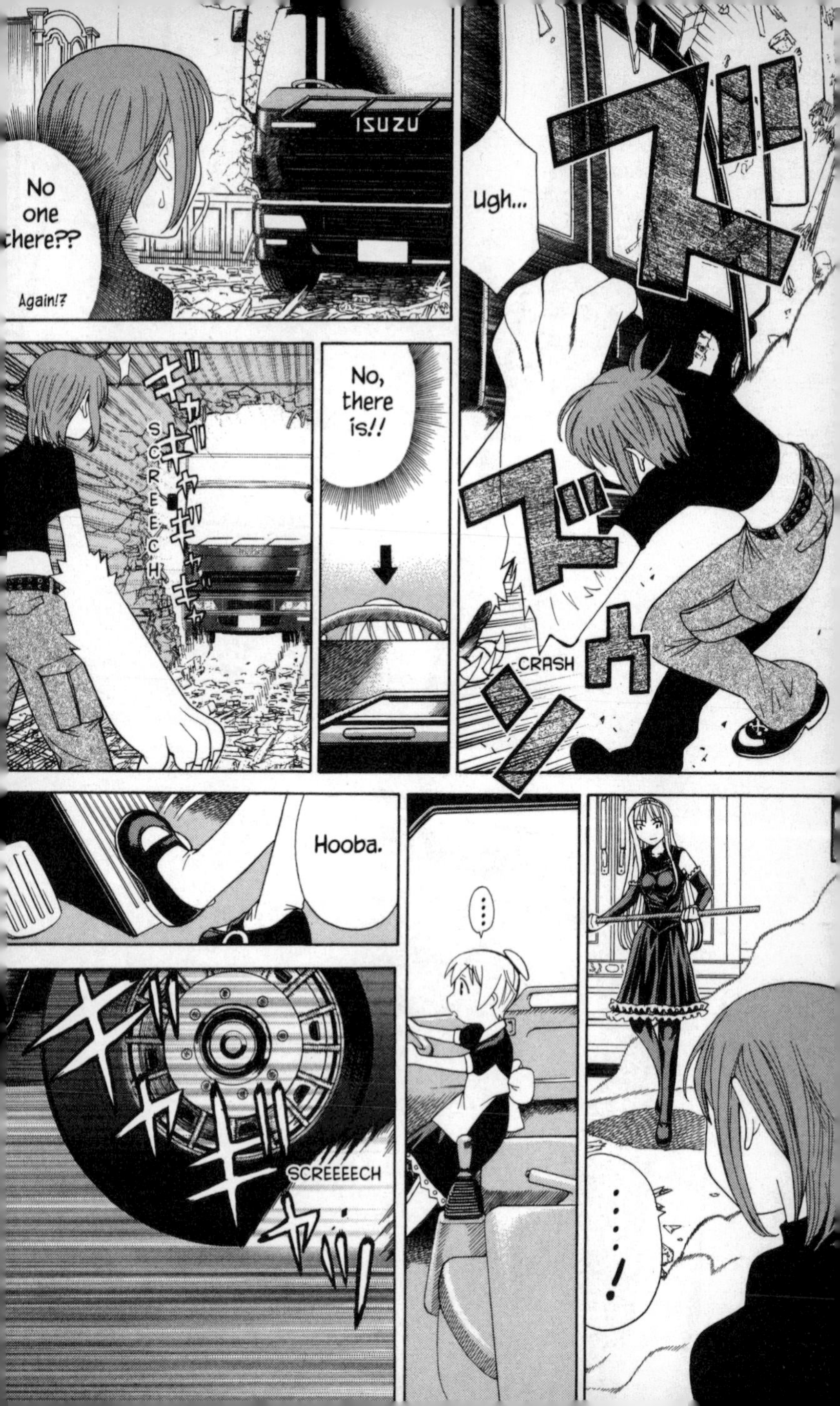

Ugh...
CRASH
No one there??
Again!?
No, there is!!
SCREECH
....!
....
Hooba.
SCREEEECH

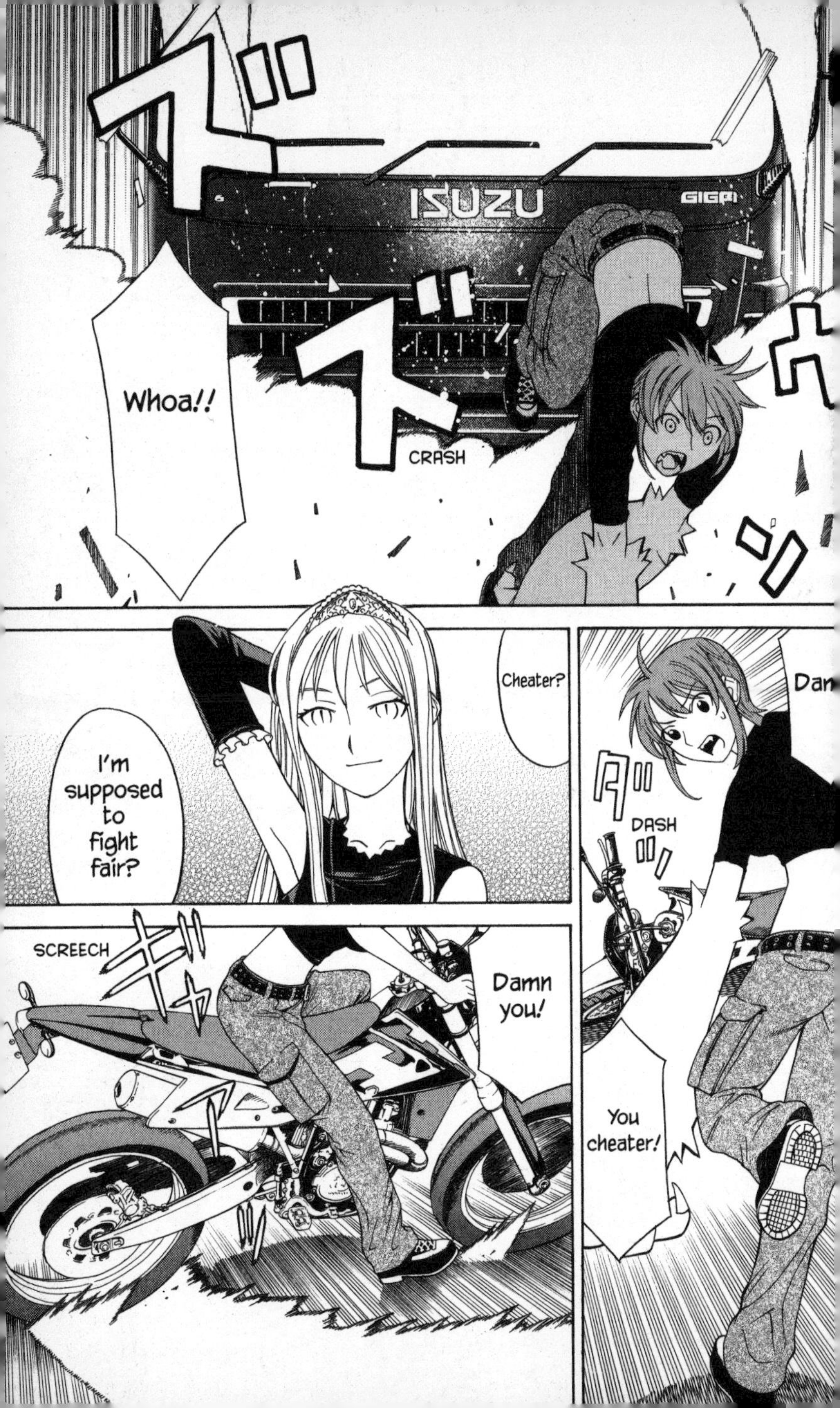

Whoa!!
CRASH
Dan
DASH
You cheater!
Cheater?
I'm supposed to fight fair?
SCREECH
Damn you!

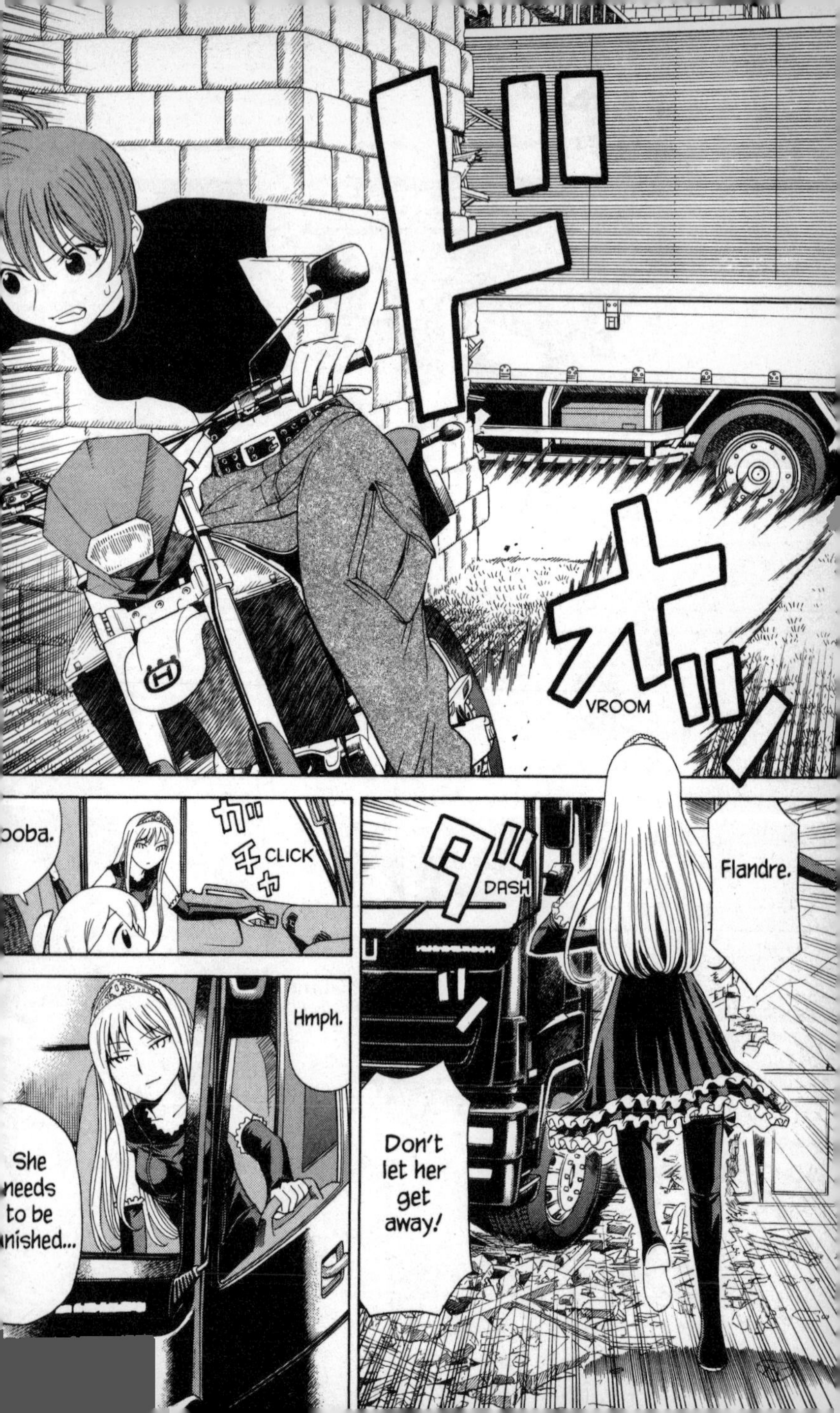
VROOM
Flandre.
ダッ
DASH
Don't let her get away!
ooba.
ガチャ
CLICK
Hmph.
She needs to be nished...

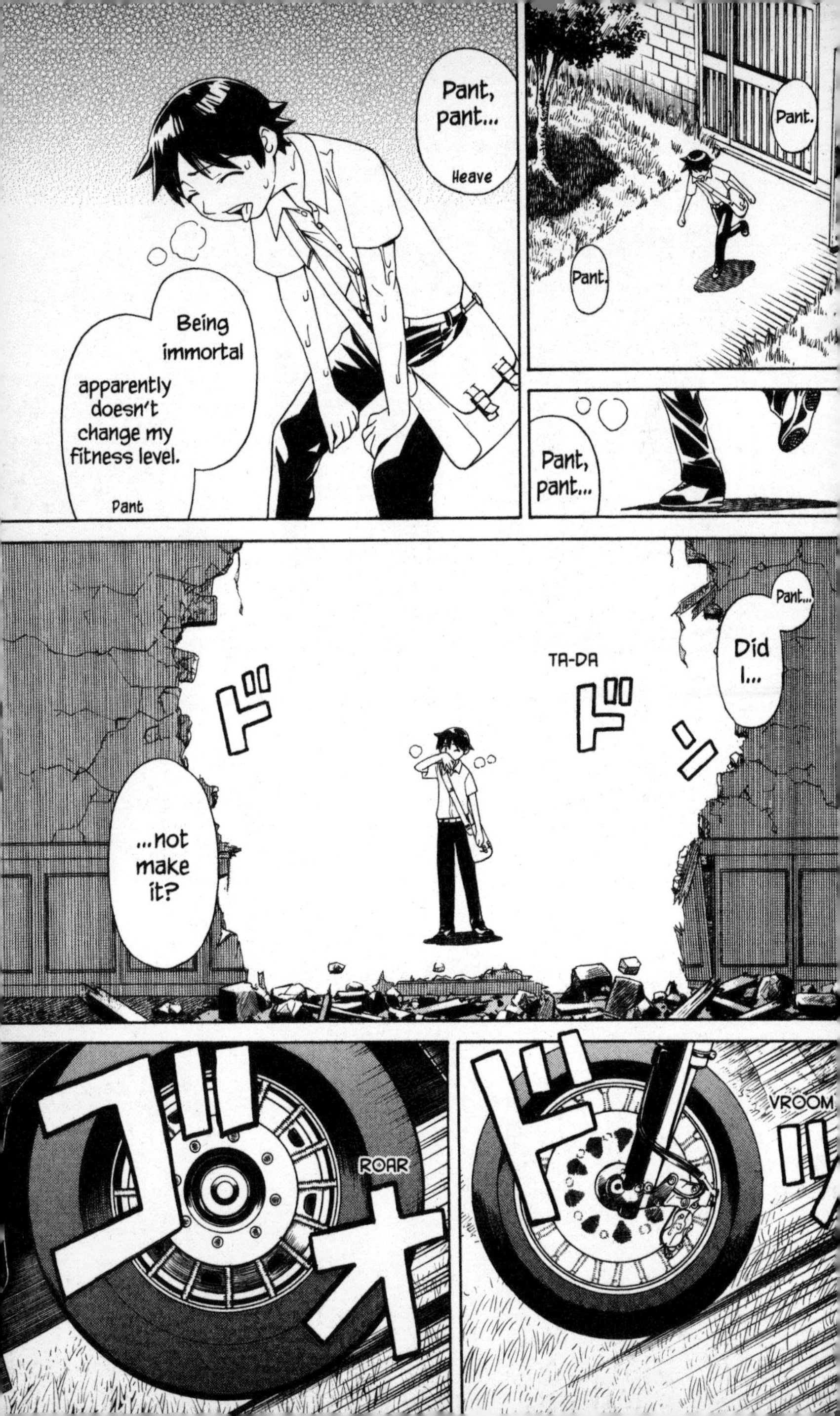
Pant.
Pant.
Pant, pant...
Pant, pant...
Heave
Being immortal
apparently doesn't change my fitness level.
Pant
Pant...
Did I...
TA-DA
ドドン
...not make it?
ドッ
VROOM
ゴォ
ROAR

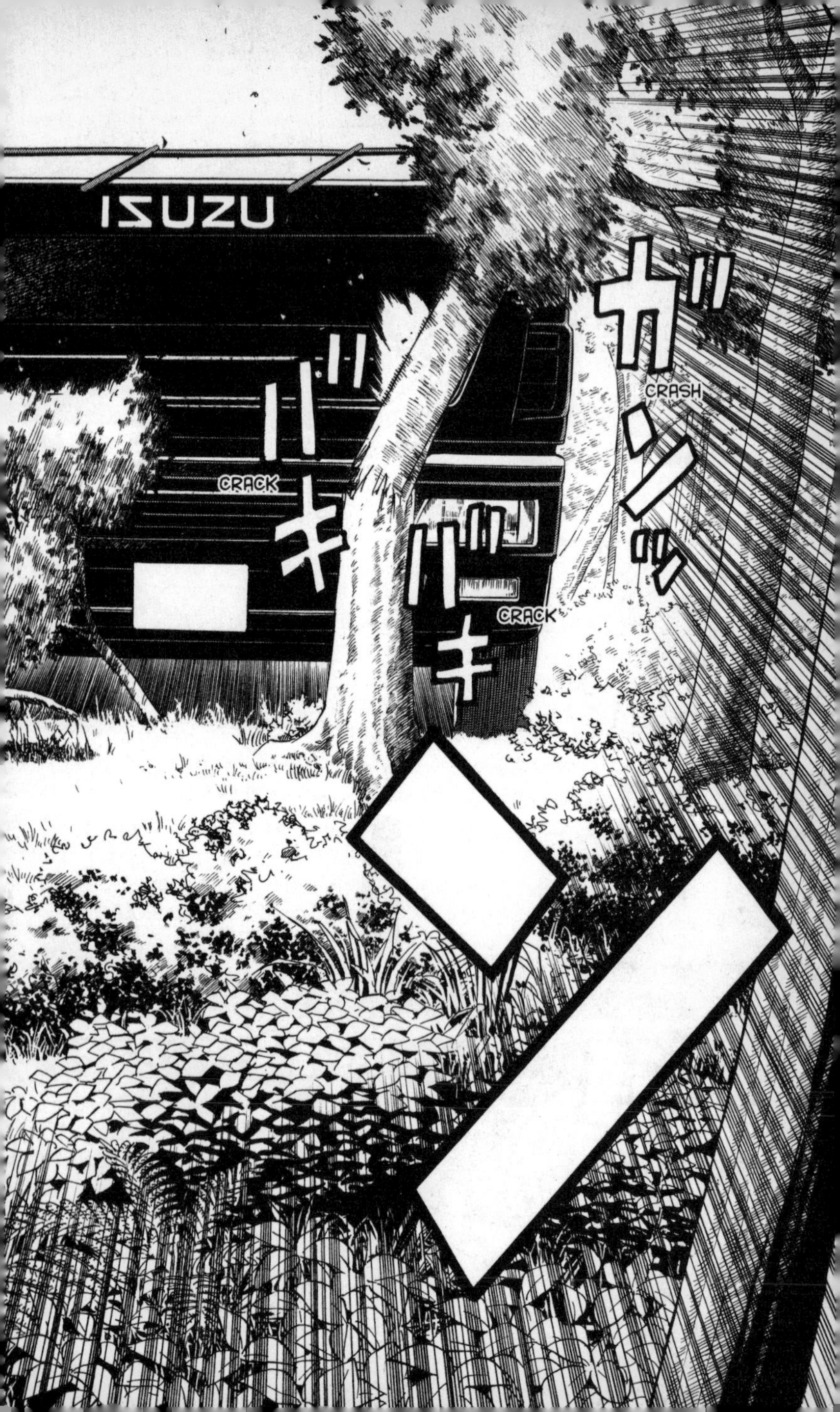

ガン
CRASH
バキ
CRACK
バキ
CRACK
ISUZU

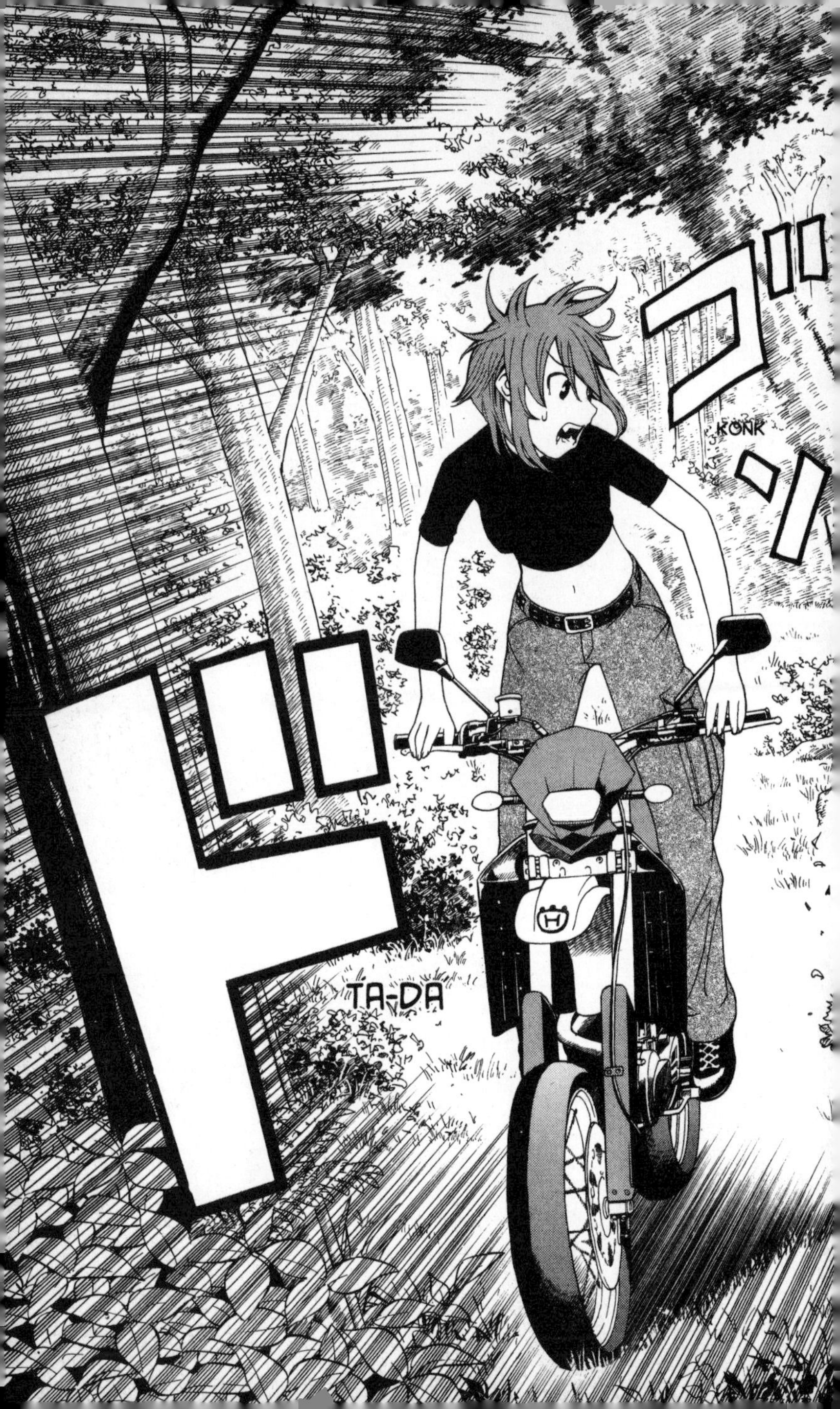
KONK
TA-DA

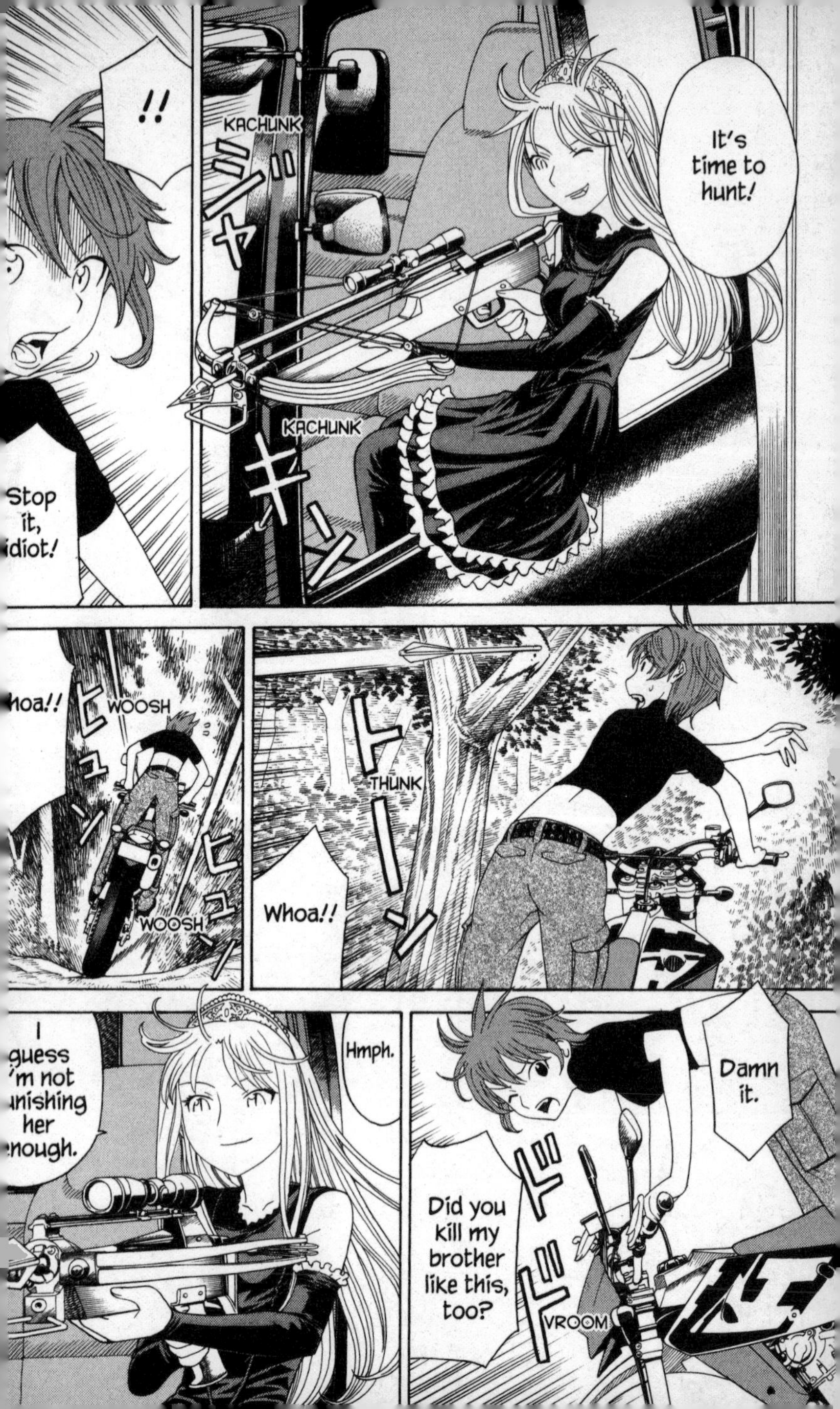
It's time to hunt!
KACHUNK
KACHUNK
!!
Stop it, idiot!
THUNK
Whoa!!
hoa!!
WOOSH
WOOSH
Damn it.
Did you kill my brother like this, too?
VROOM
Hmph.
I guess 'm not unishing her nough.

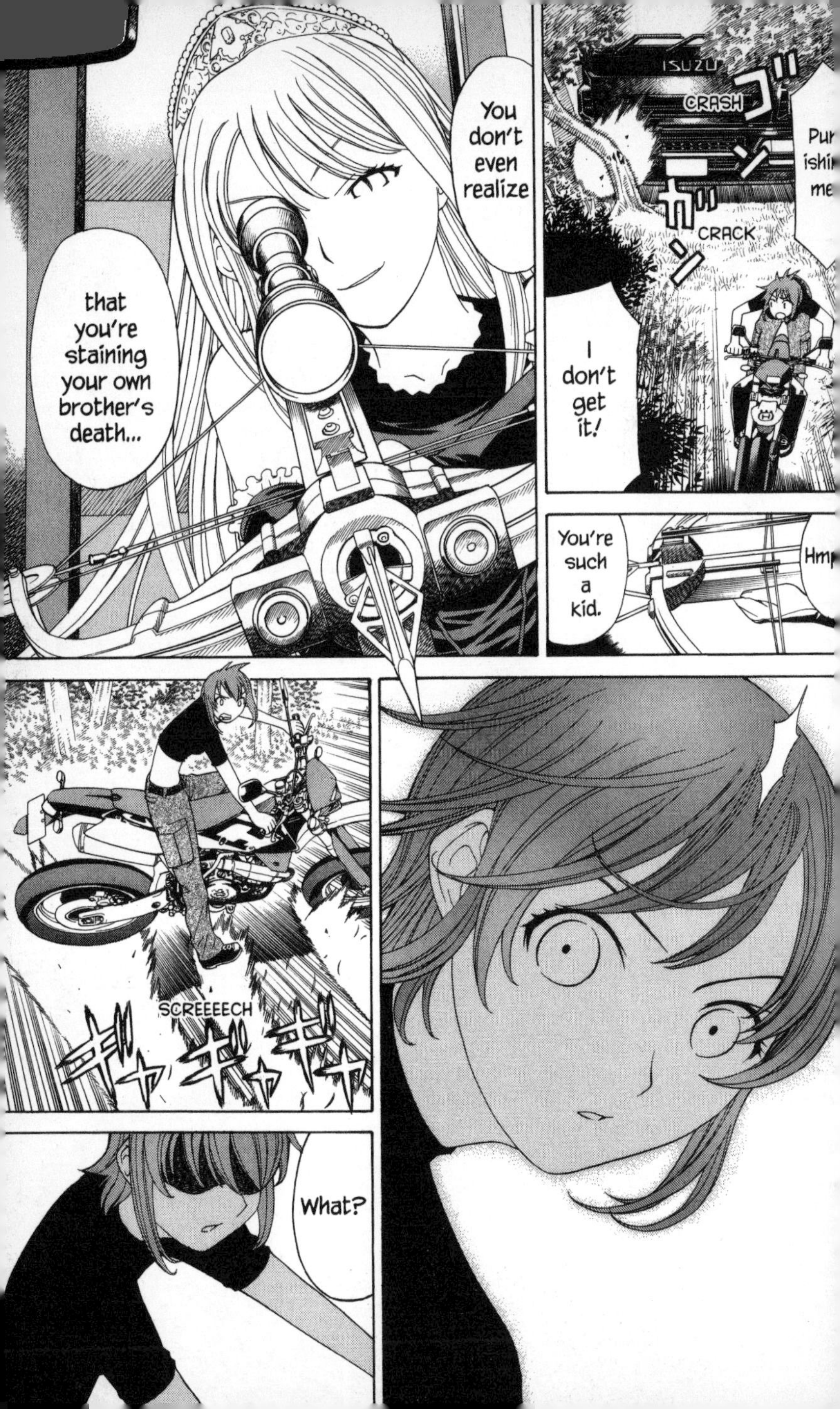
ISUZU
CRASH
CRACK
I don't get it!
Hmp
You're such a kid.
You don't even realize
that you're staining your own brother's death...
SCREEEECH
What?

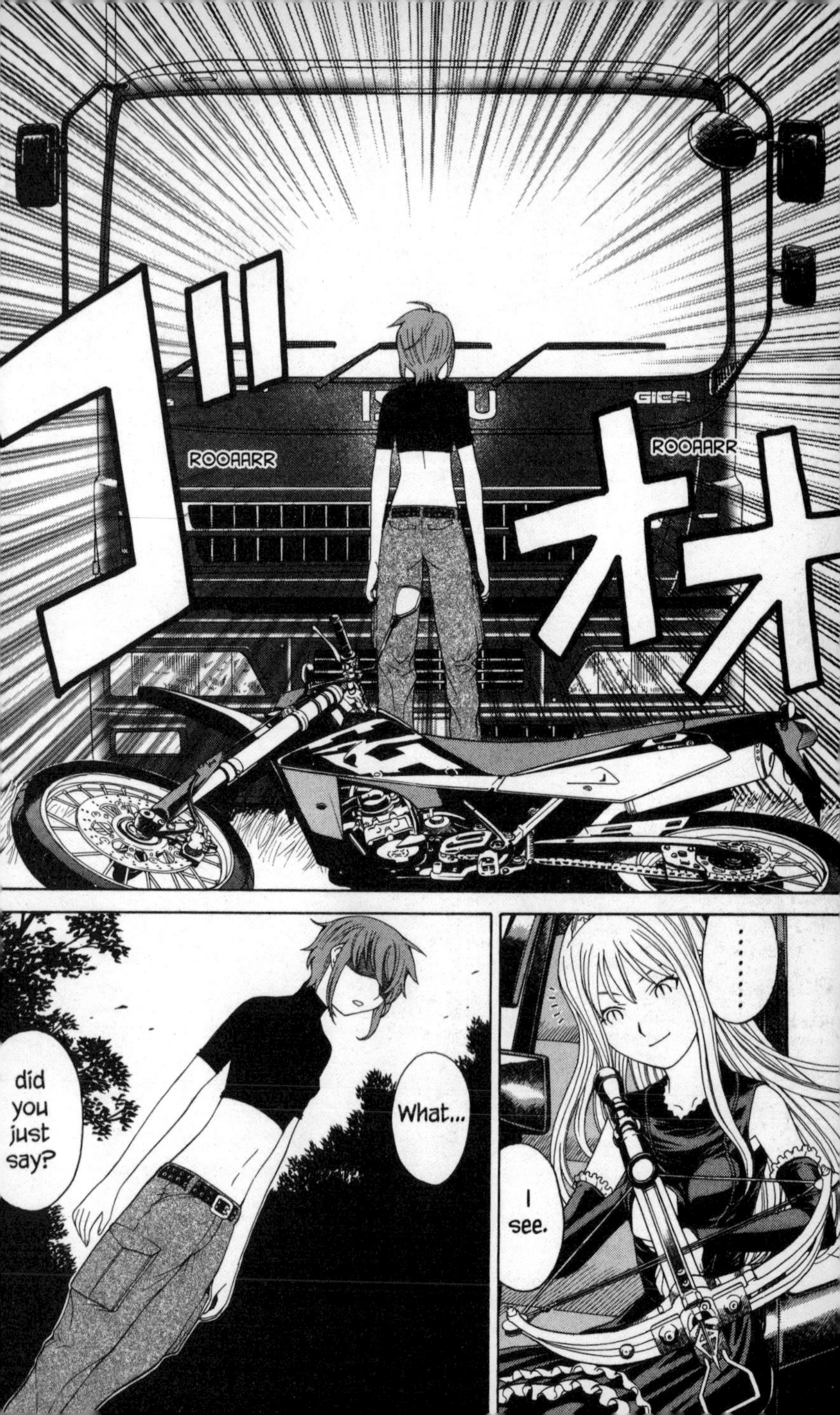
ROOAARR
ROOAARR
......
I see.
What...
did you just say?

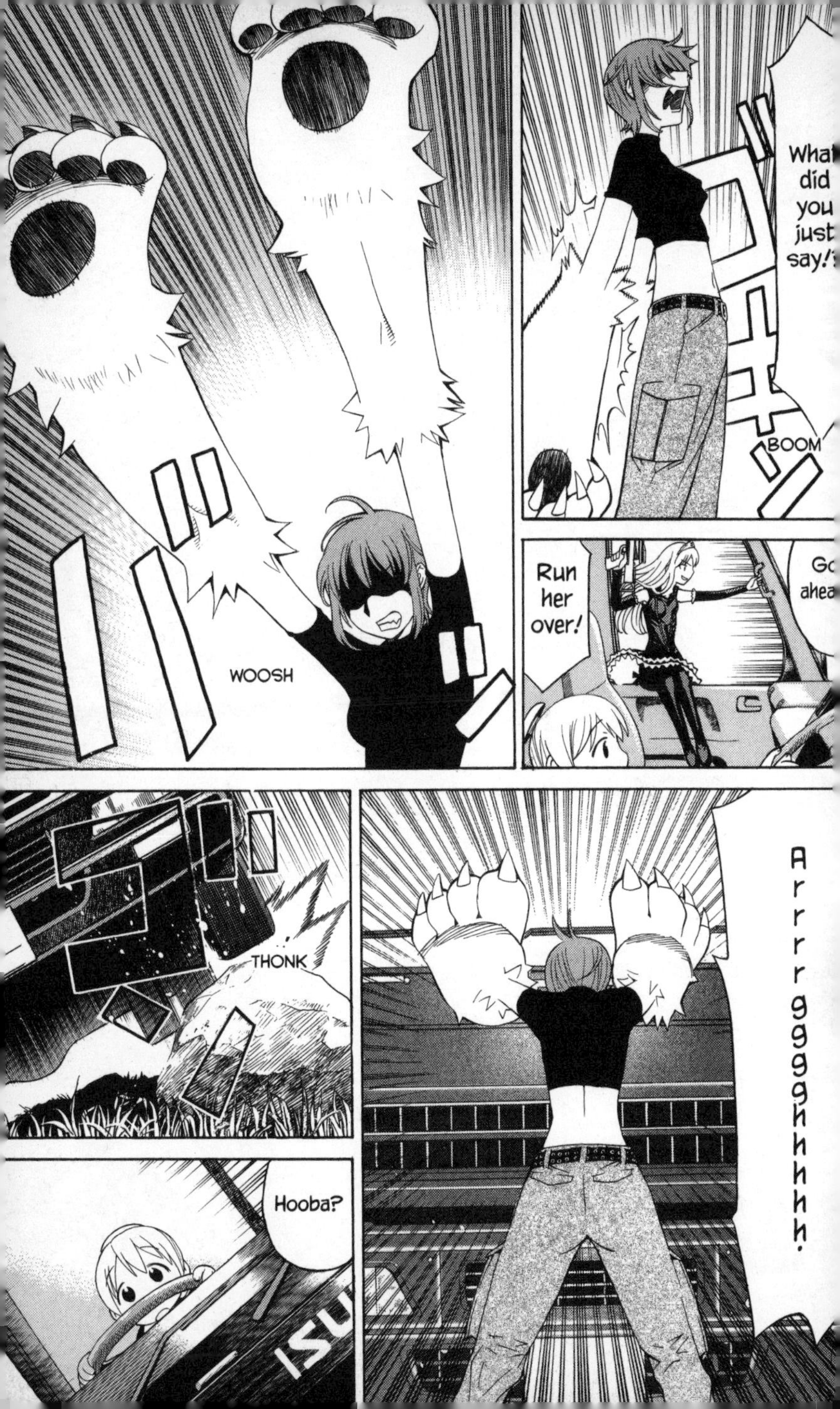

Wha did you just say!?
BOOM
Go ahea
Run her over!
WOOSH
Arrrrggggghhhhh!
THONK
Hooba?

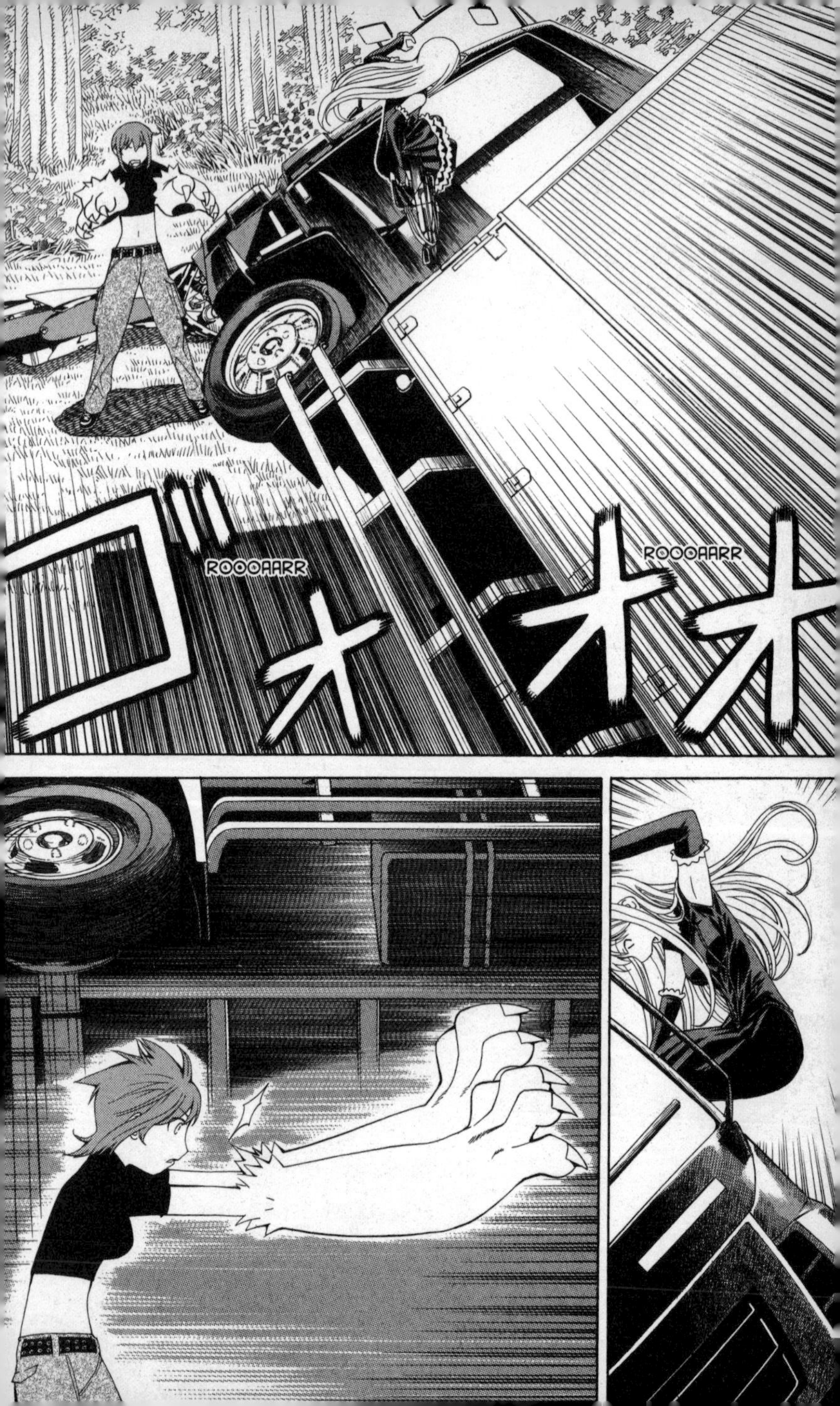
ゴオオ
ROOOAARR
ROOOAARR

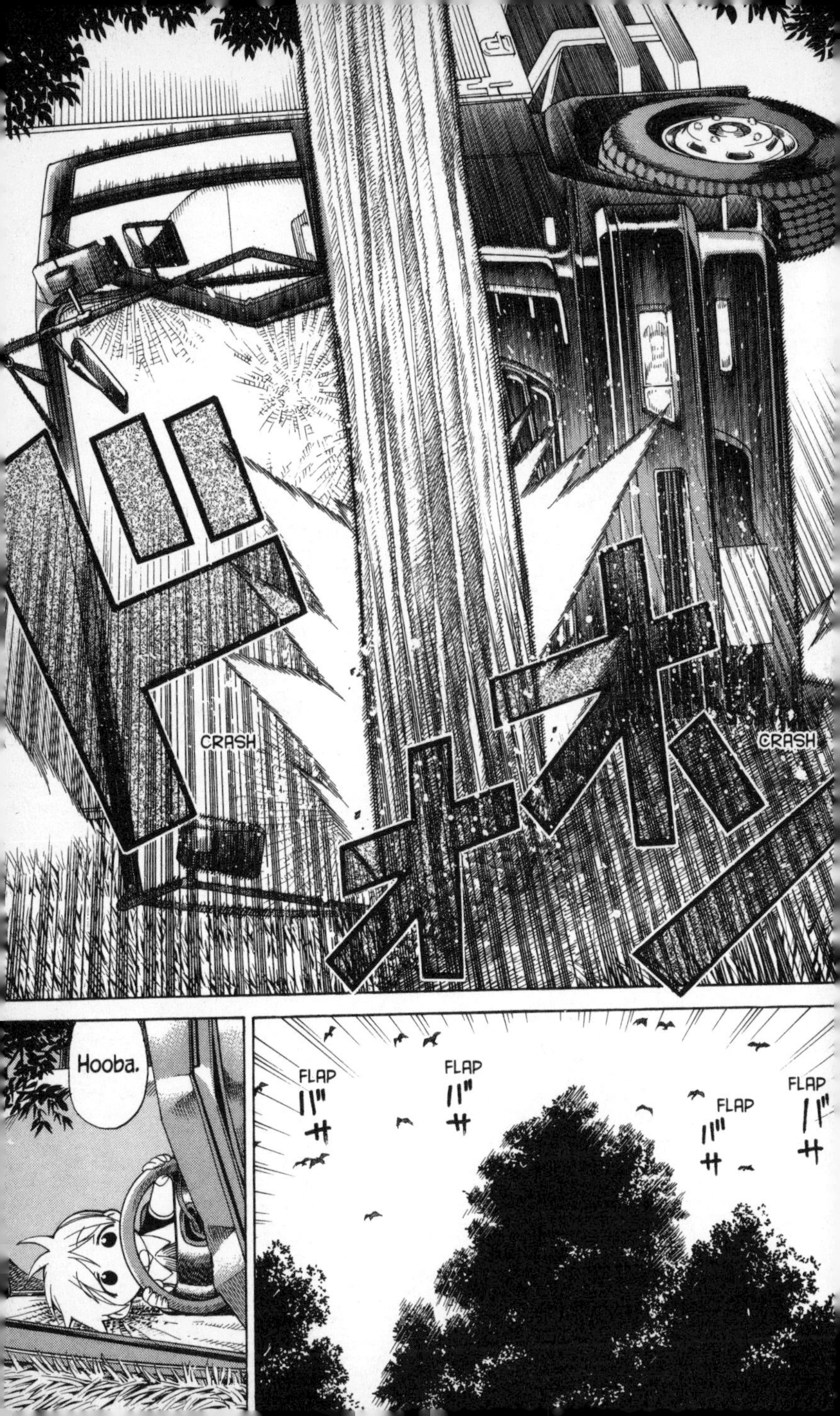
CRASH
CRASH
FLAP
FLAP
FLAP
FLAP
Hooba.

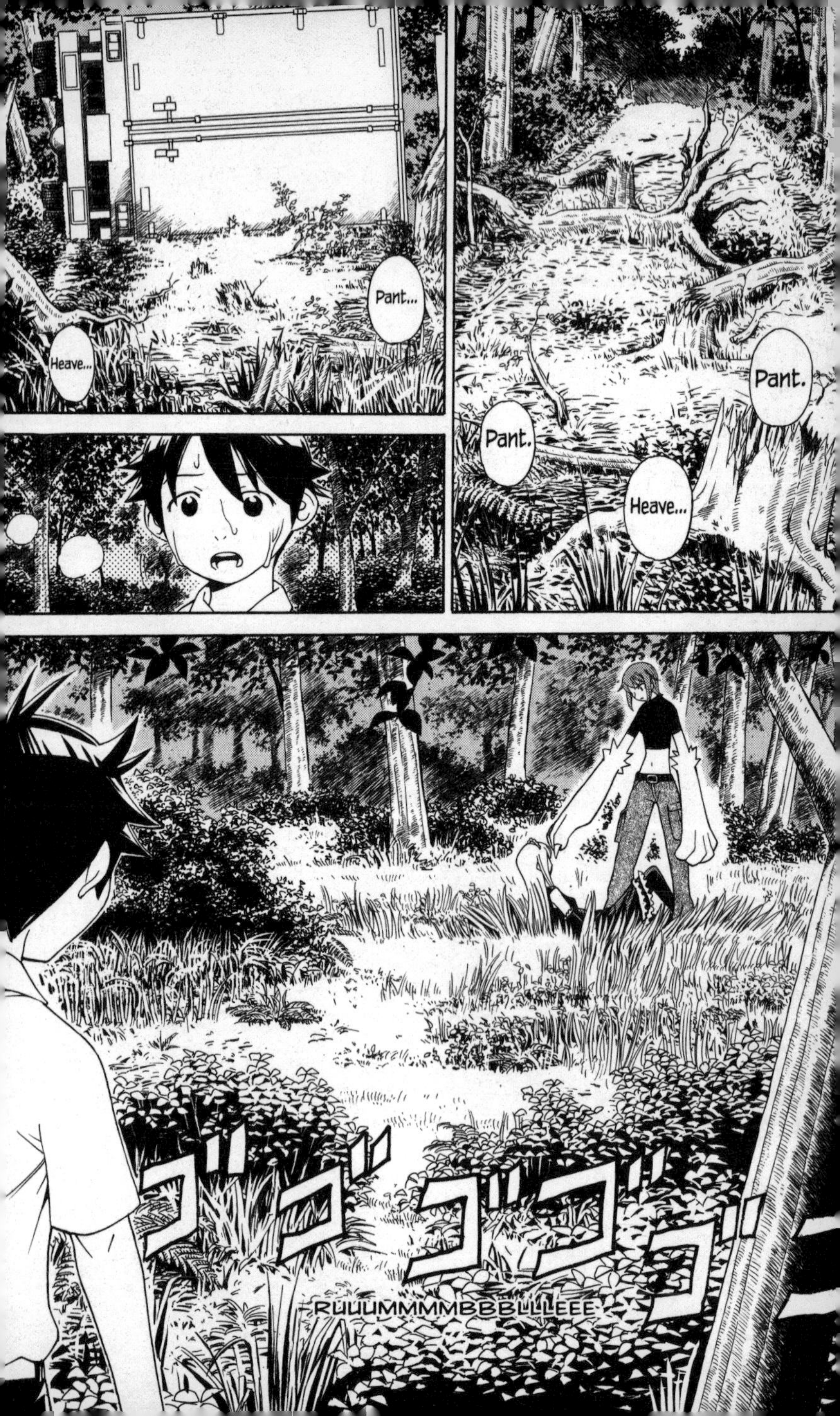
Pant.
Pant.
Heave...
Pant...
Heave...
ゴゴゴゴゴ
RUUUMMMMBBBLLLEEE

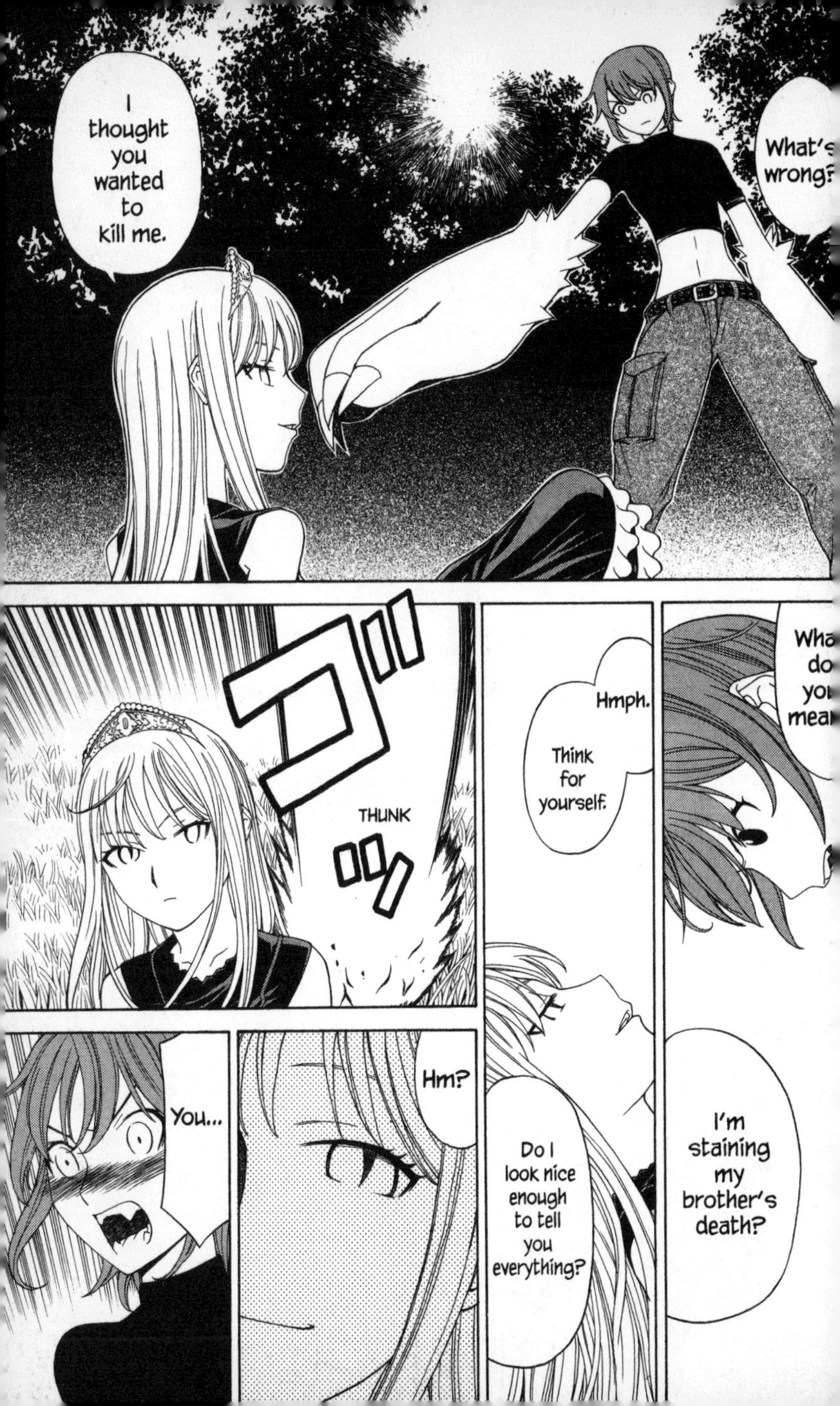
What's wrong?
I thought you wanted to kill me.
Wha do yo mea
Hmph.
Think for yourself.
THUNK
I'm staining my brother's death?
Do I look nice enough to tell you everything?
Hm?
You...

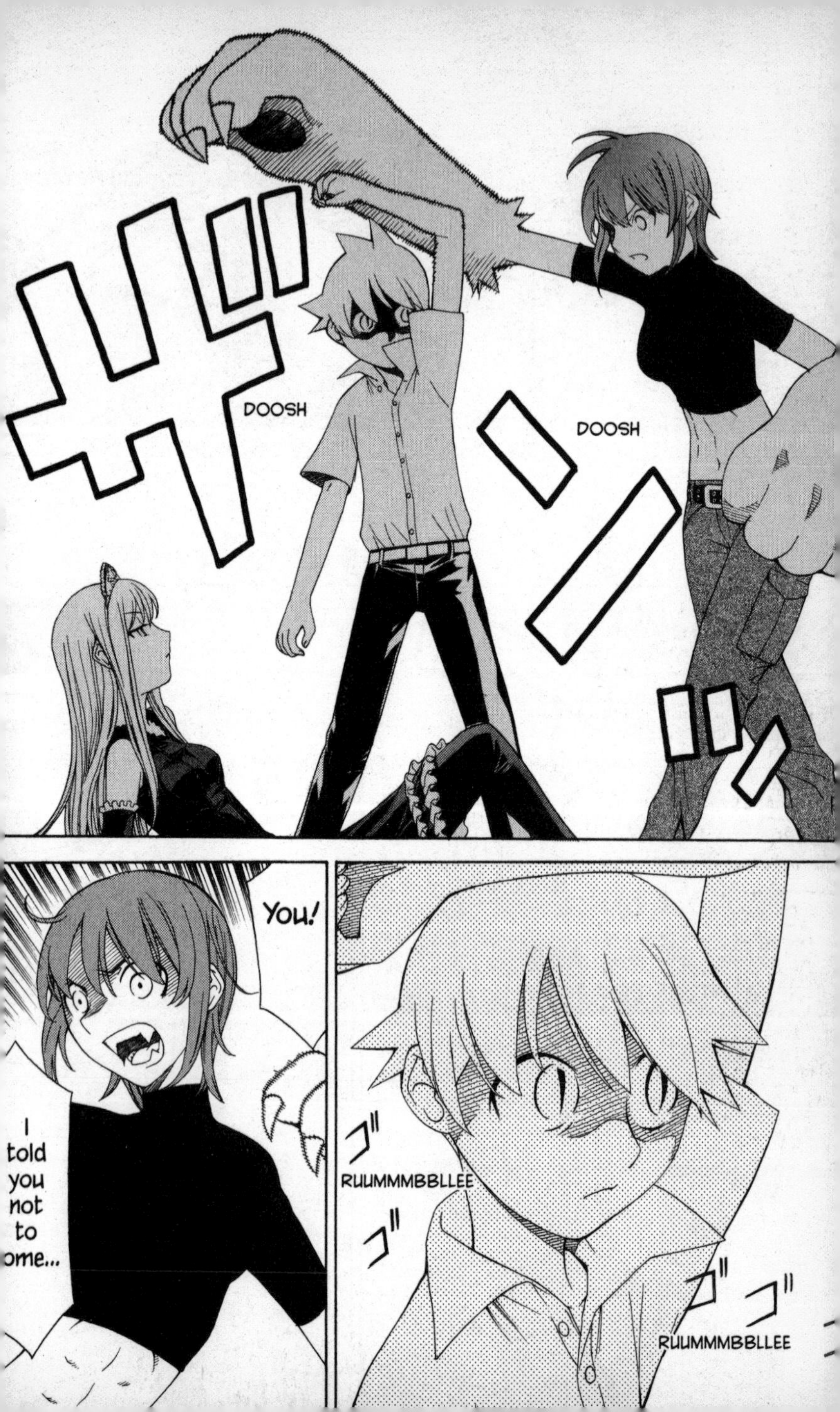
DOOSH
DOOSH
ゴ
RUUMMMBBLLEE
ゴ
ゴ ゴ
RUUMMMBBLLEE
You!
I told you not to ome...

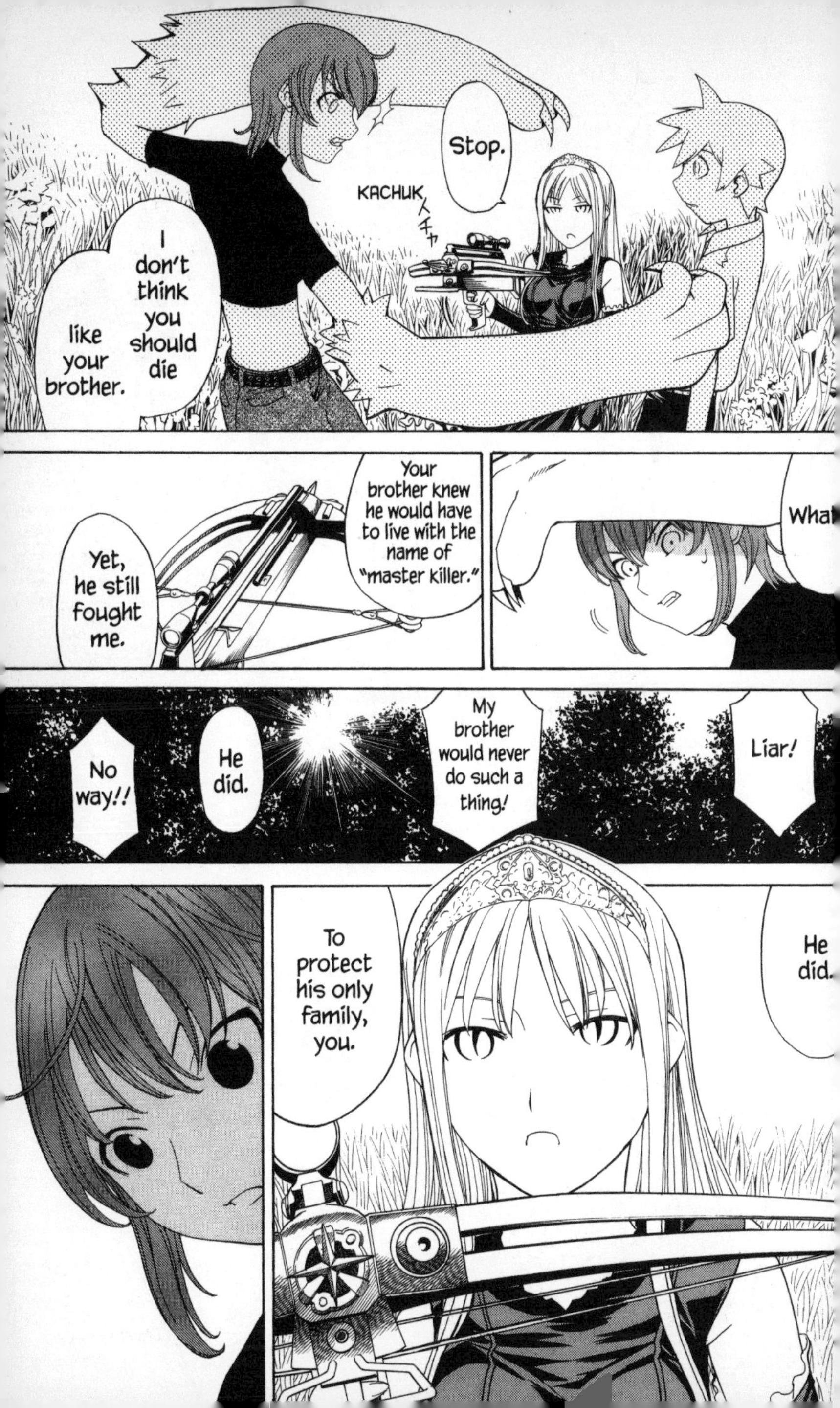
Stop.
KACHUK
I don't think you should die like your brother.
What
Your brother knew he would have to live with the name of "master killer."
Yet, he still fought me.
Liar!
My brother would never do such a thing!
He did.
No way!!
He did.
To protect his only family, you.

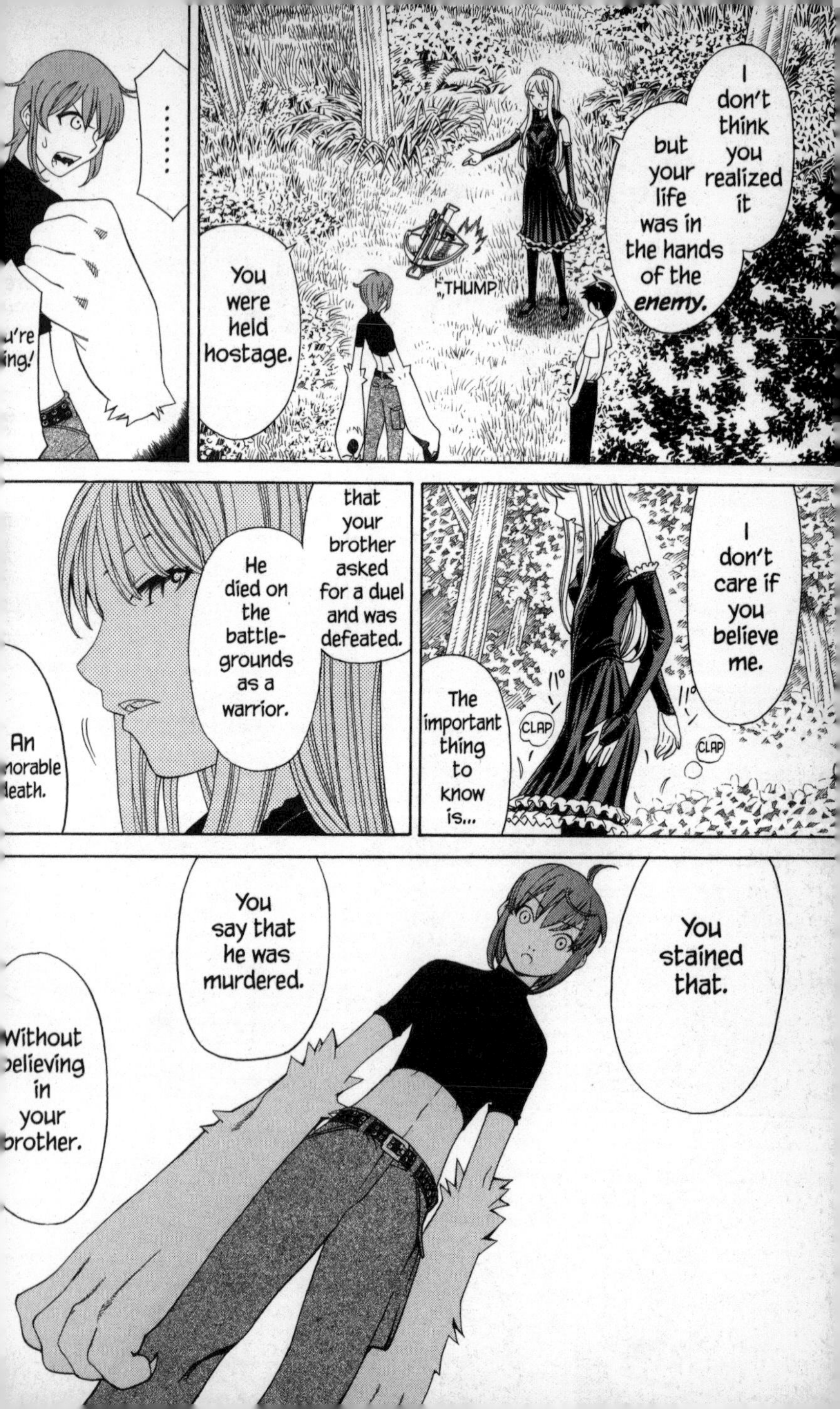

I don't think you realized it
but your life was in the hands of the *enemy.*
THUMP
You were held hostage.
......
I don't care if you believe me.
The important thing to know is...
CLAP
CLAP
that your brother asked for a duel and was defeated.
He died on the battlegrounds as a warrior.
You stained that.
You say that he was murdered.

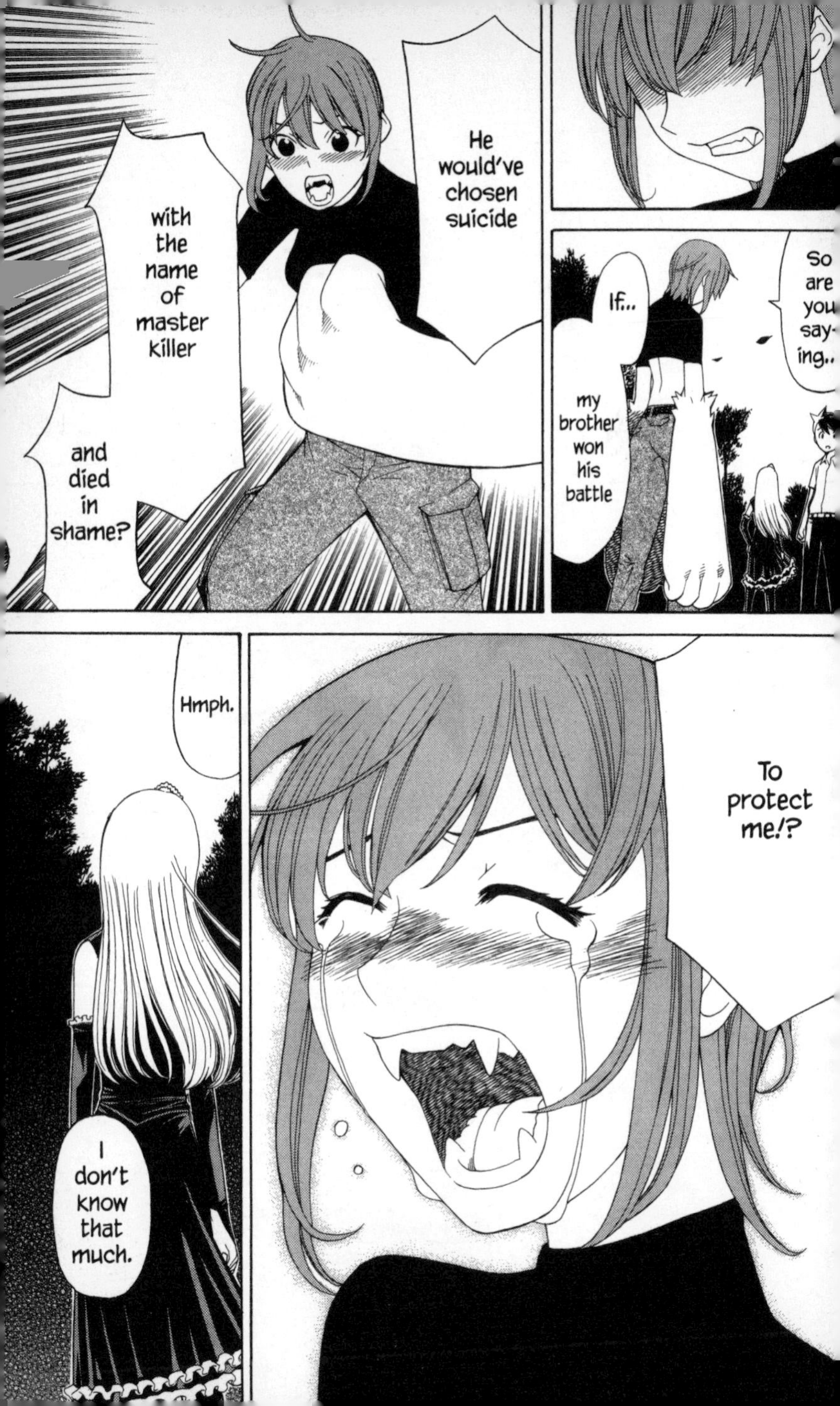
So are you say-ing..
If..
my brother won his battle
He would've chosen suicide
with the name of master killer
and died in shame?
To protect me!?
Hmph.
I don't know that much.

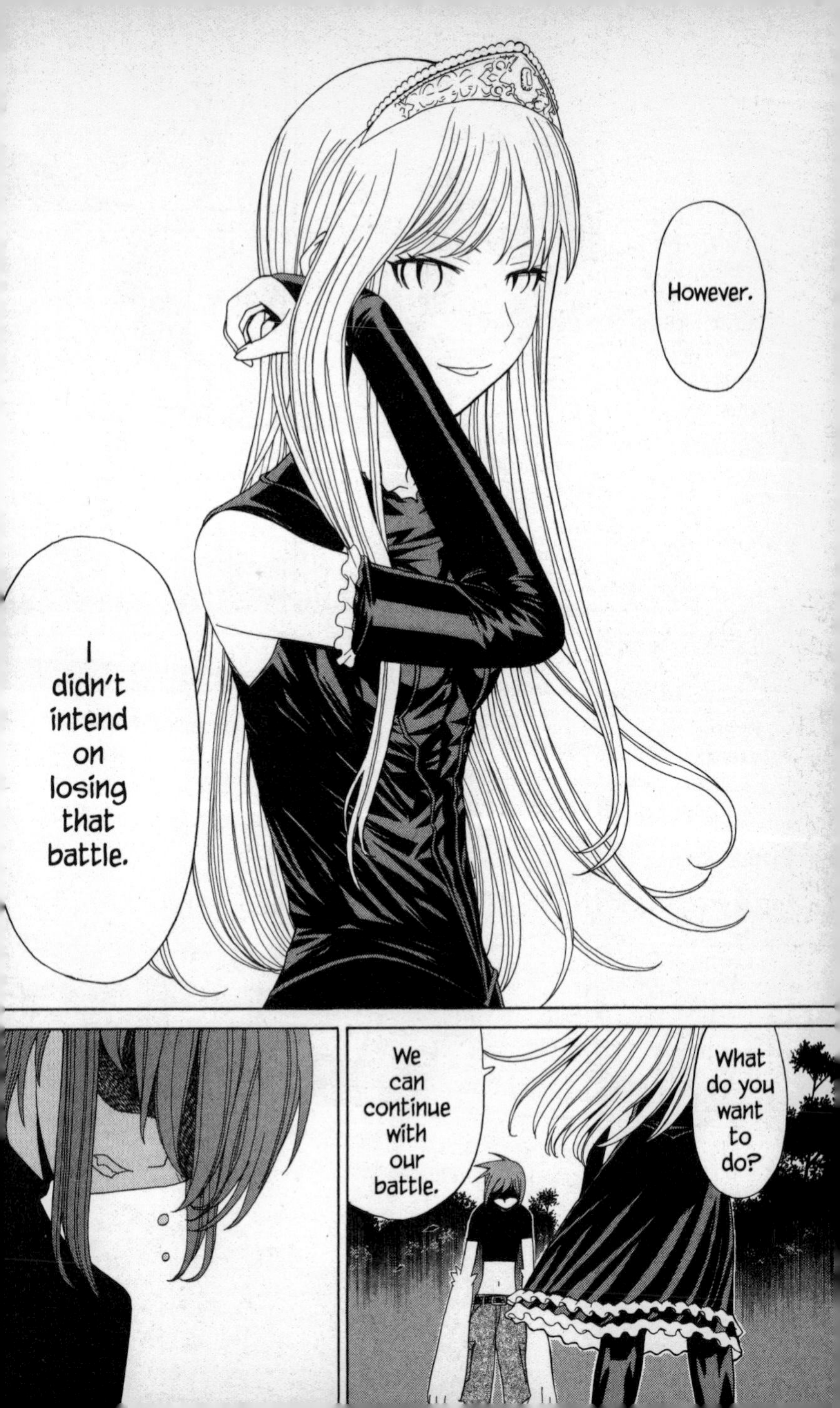
However.
I didn't intend on losing that battle.
What do you want to do?
We can continue with our battle.

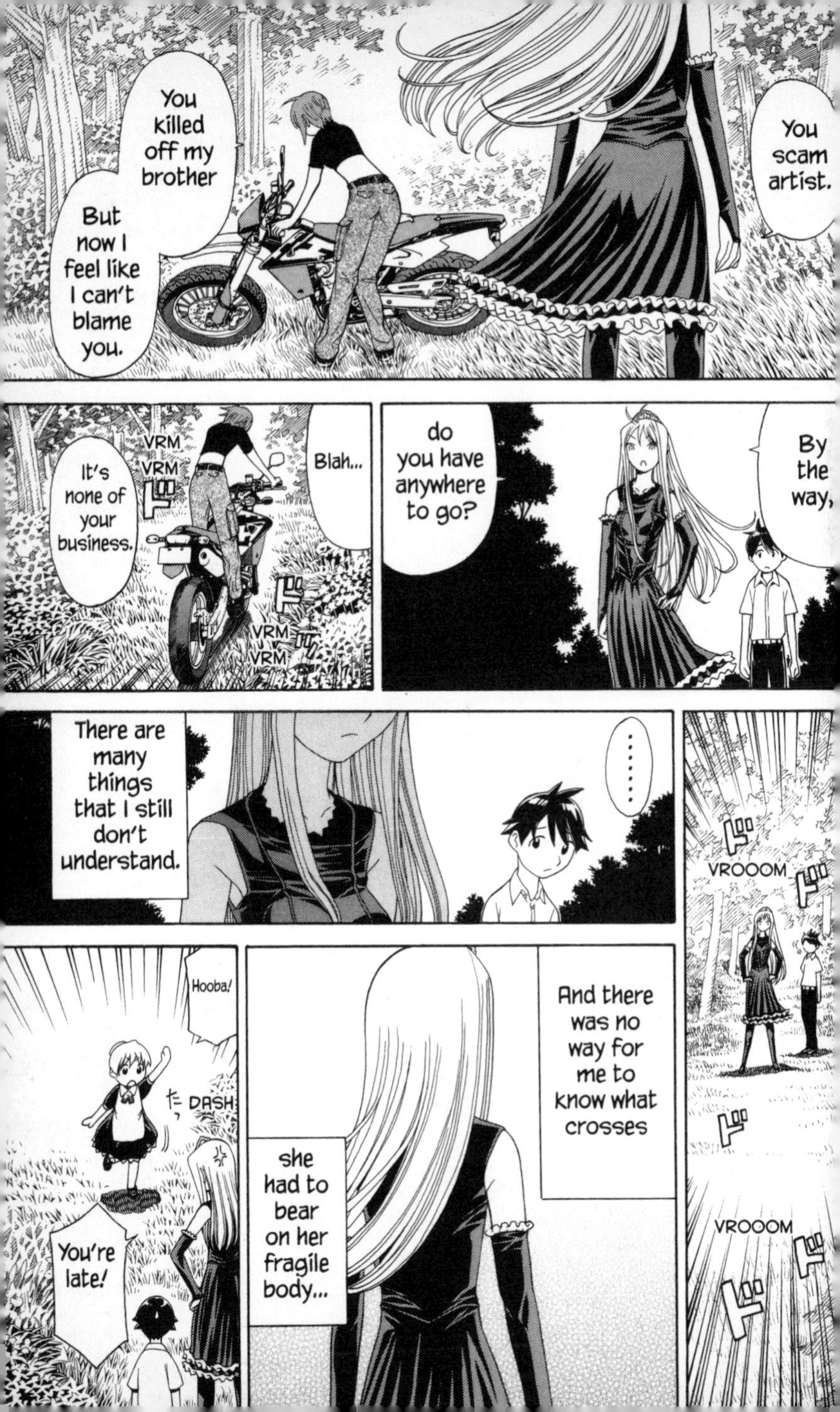
You scam artist.
You killed off my brother
But now I feel like I can't blame you.
By the way,
do you have anywhere to go?
Blah...
It's none of your business.
VRM VRM
VRM VRM
VROOOM
VROOOM
......
There are many things that I still don't understand.
And there was no way for me to know what crosses
she had to bear on her fragile body...
Hooba!
DASH
You're late!

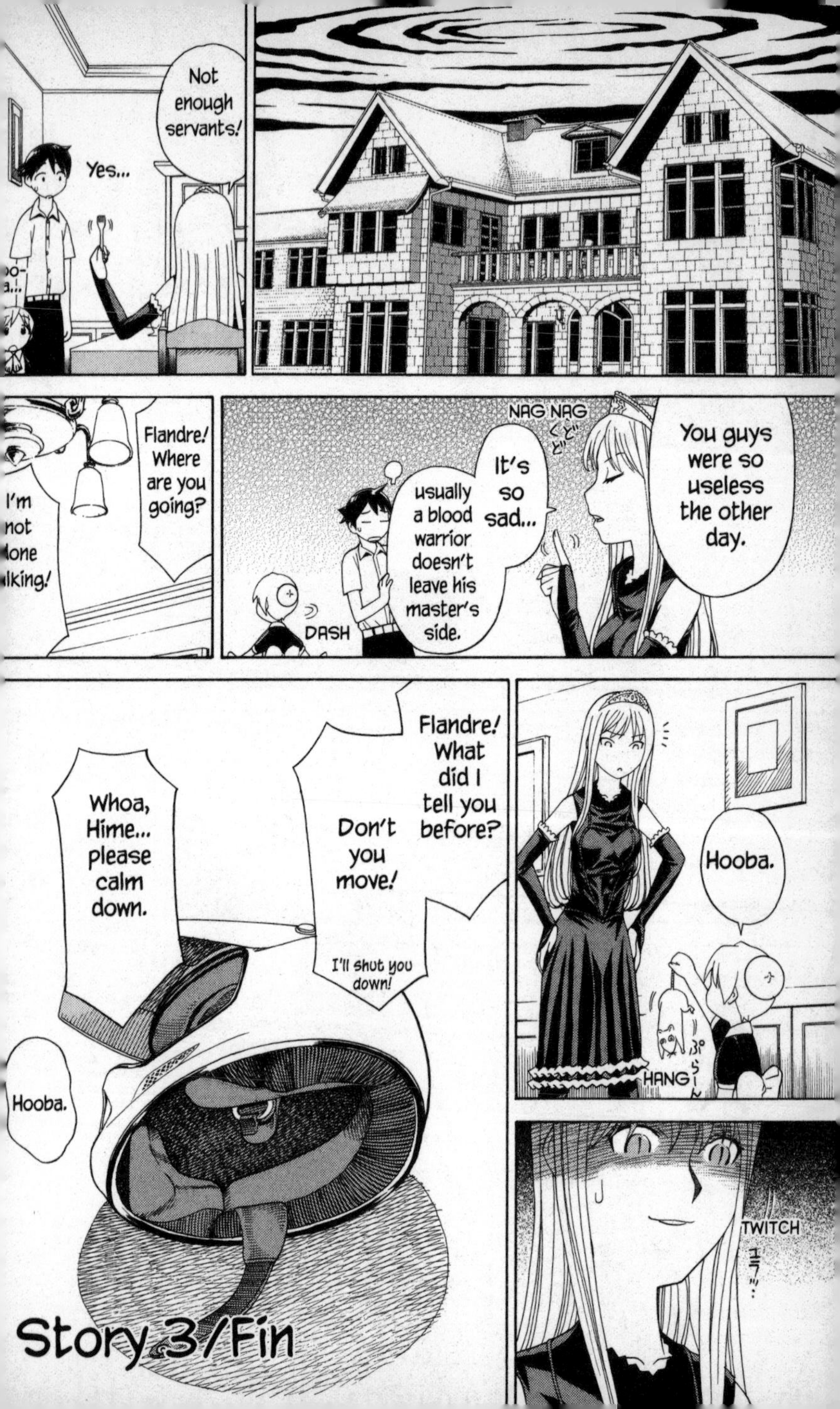
Not enough servants!
Yes...
You guys were so useless the other day.
NAG NAG
It's so sad...
usually a blood warrior doesn't leave his master's side.
DASH
Flandre! Where are you going?
Hooba.
HANG
TWITCH
Flandre! What did I tell you before?
Don't you move!
I'll shut you down!
Whoa, Hime... please calm down.
Hooba.
Story 3/Fin

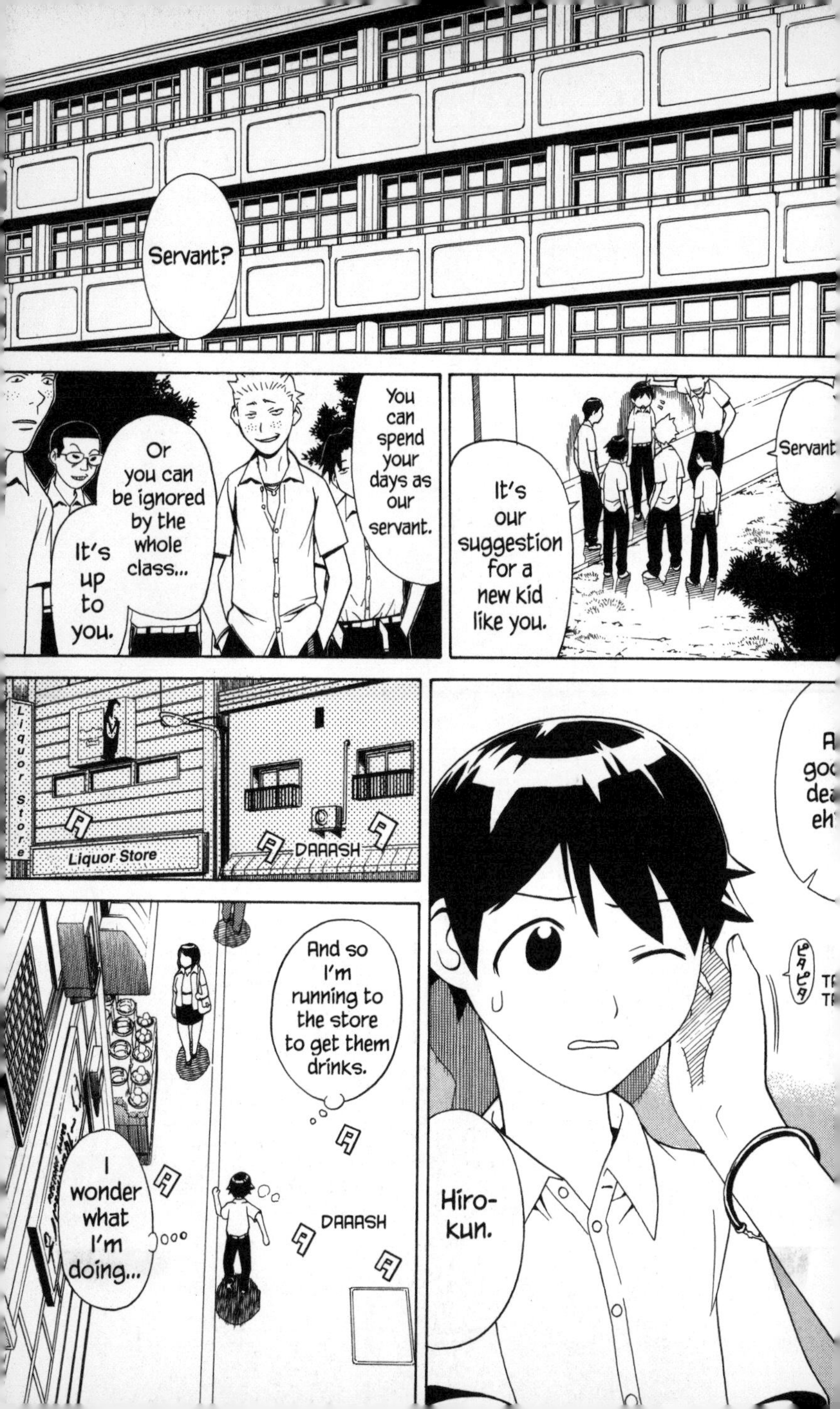
Servant?
Servant
It's our suggestion for a new kid like you.
You can spend your days as our servant.
Or you can be ignored by the whole class...
It's up to you.
Hiro-kun.
Liquor Store
Liquor Store
DAAASH
And so I'm running to the store to get them drinks.
DAAASH
I wonder what I'm doing...

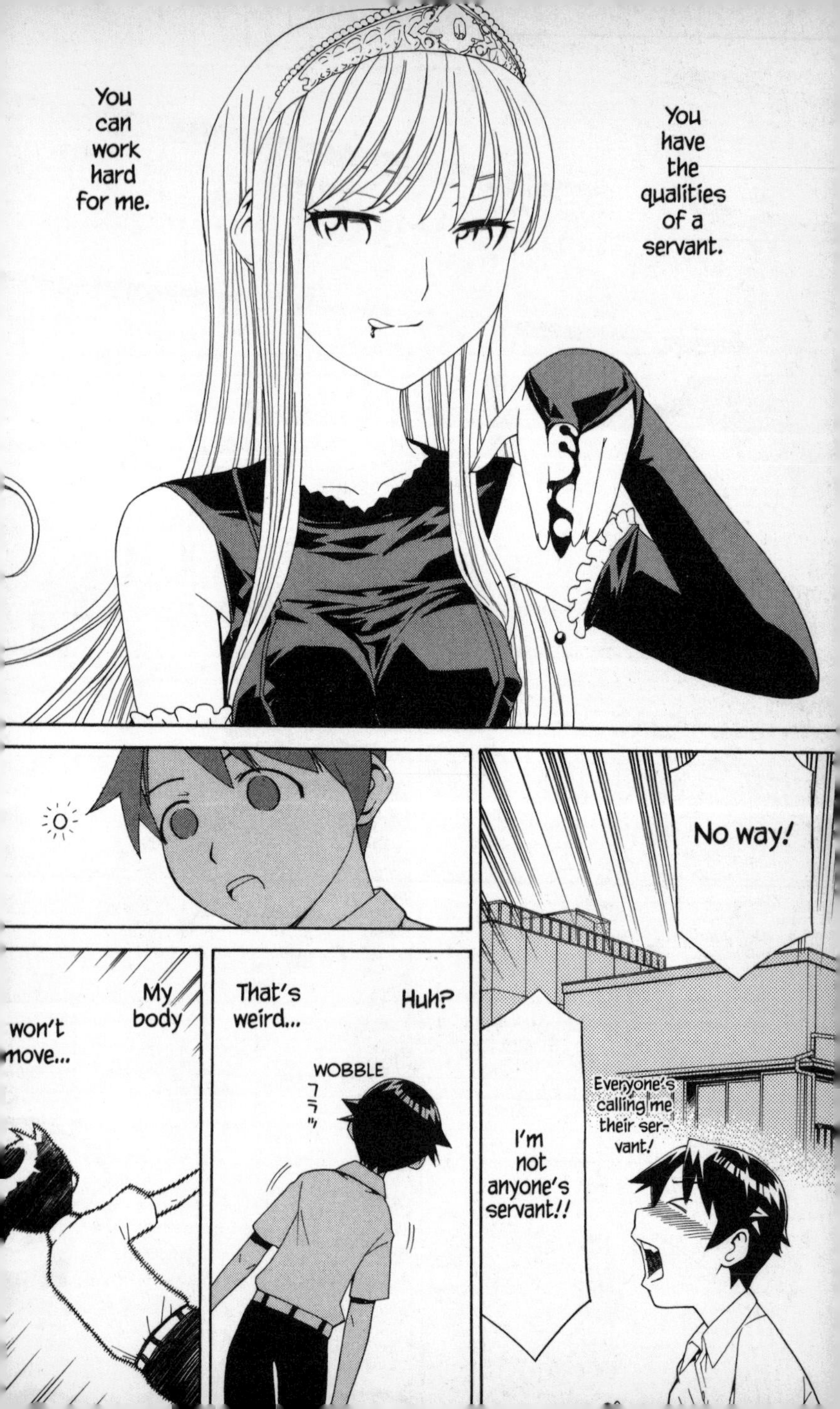

You have the qualities of a servant.
You can work hard for me.
No way!
Everyone's calling me their servant!
I'm not anyone's servant!!
Huh?
That's weird...
WOBBLE
フラッ
My body won't move...

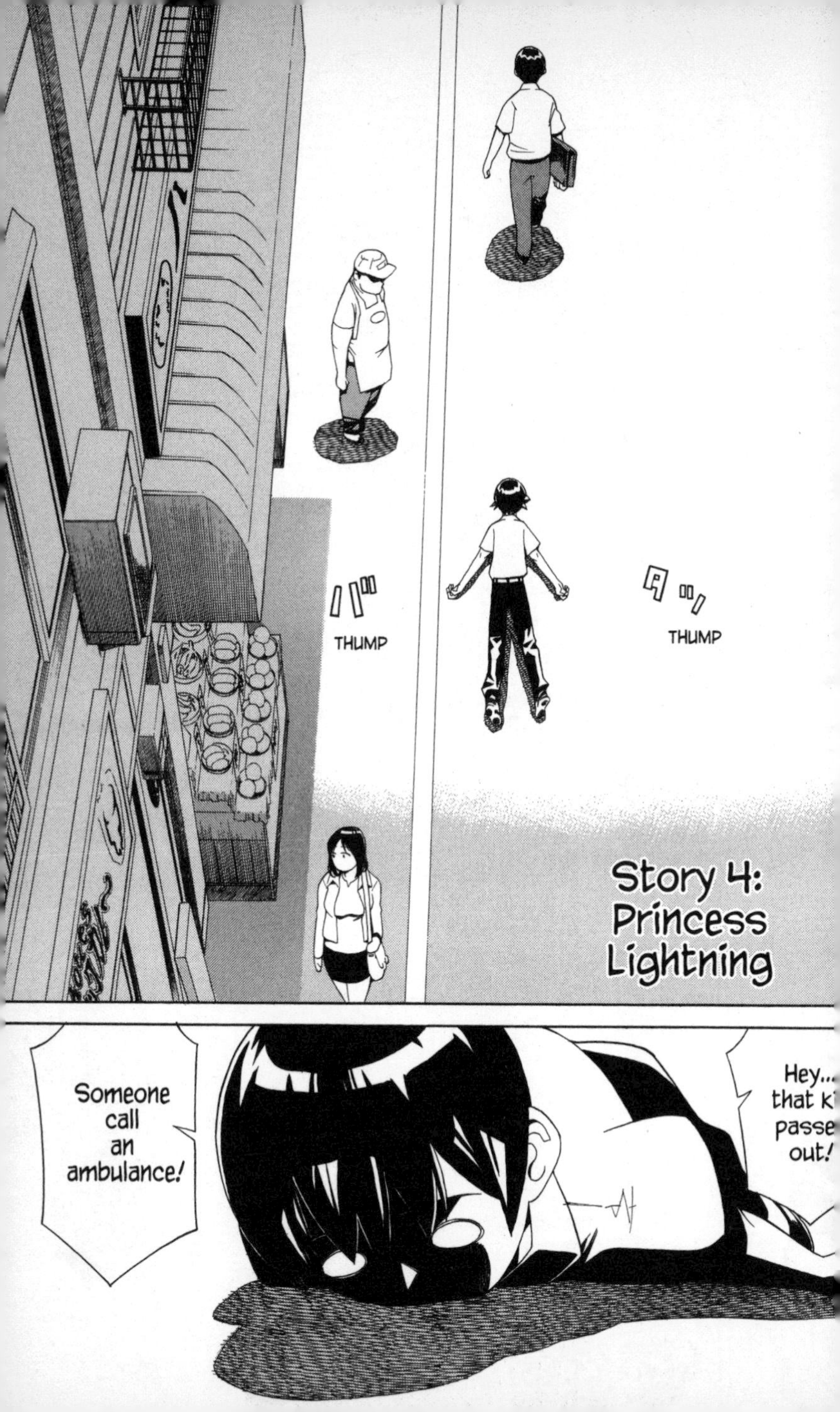
THUMP
Story 4: Princess Lightning
THUMP
Hey... that ki passe out!
Someone call an ambulance!

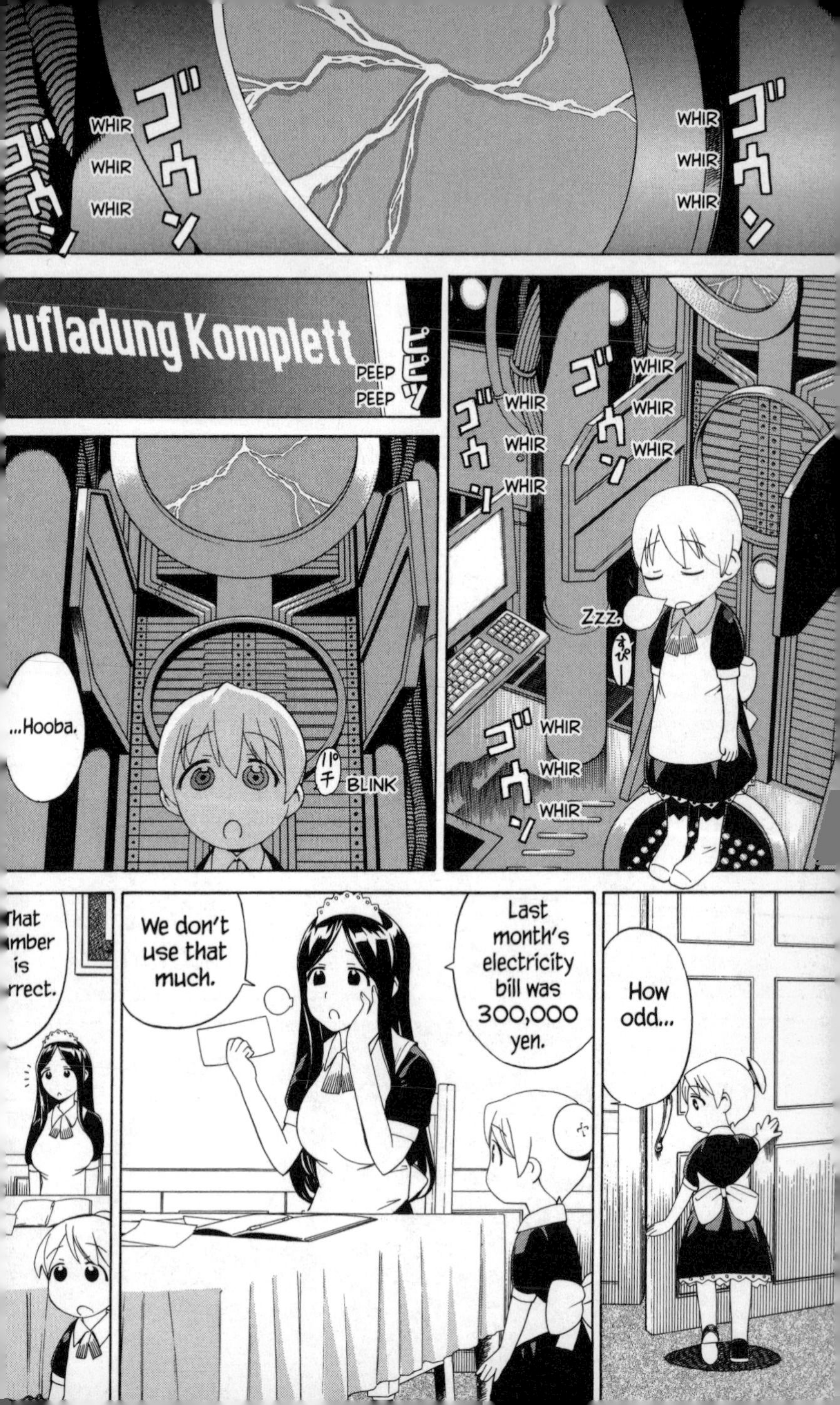
ゴウン
WHIR
WHIR
WHIR
ゴウン
WHIR
WHIR
WHIR
ゴウン
WHIR
WHIR
WHIR
ゴウン
WHIR
WHIR
WHIR
Zzz.
すぴー
ゴウン
WHIR
WHIR
WHIR
ufladung Komplett
ピピッ
PEEP
PEEP
...Hooba.
パチ
BLINK
How odd...
Last month's electricity bill was 300,000 yen.
We don't use that much.
That
mber
is
rrect.

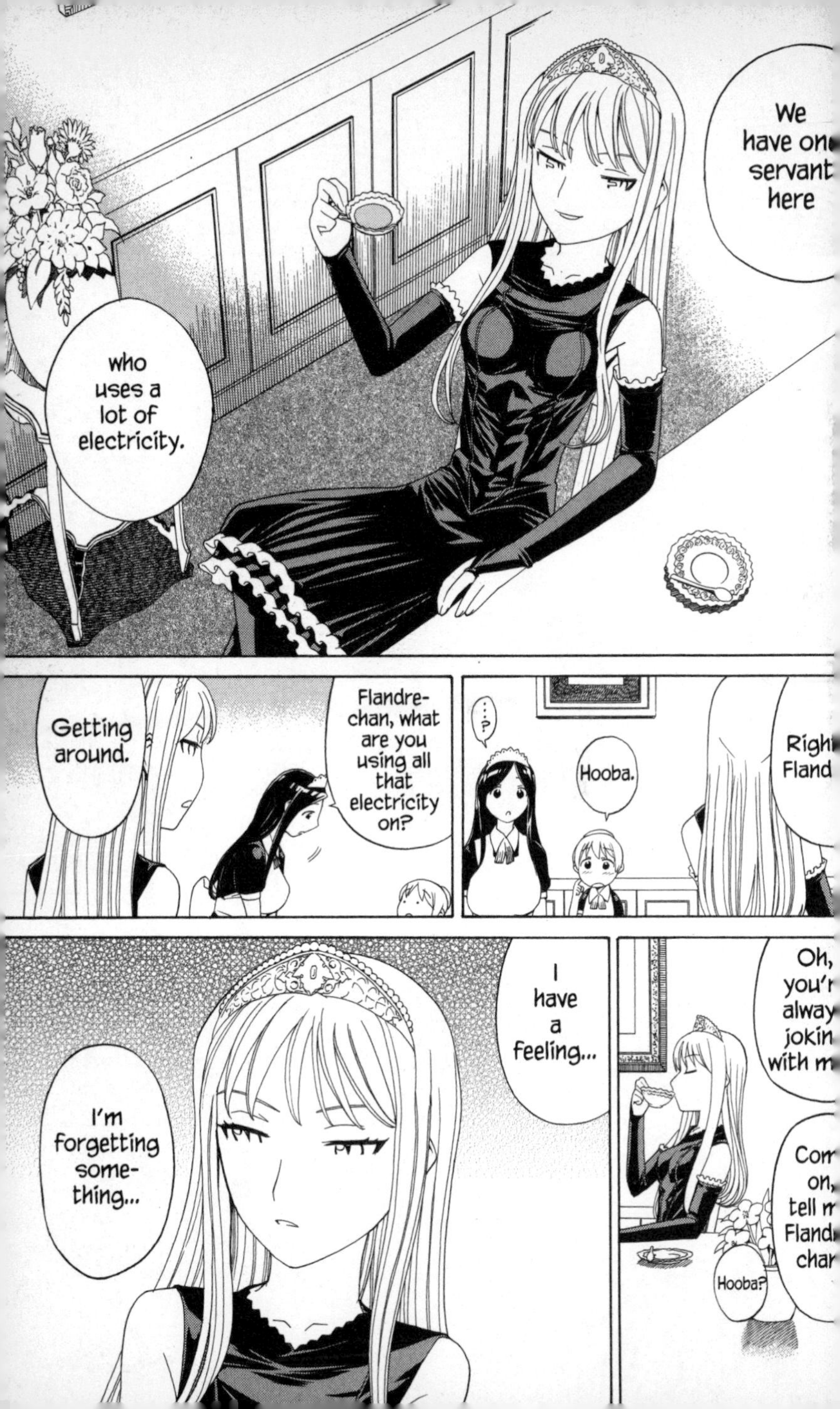

We have on servant here
who uses a lot of electricity.
Righ Fland
Hooba.
...?
Flandre-chan, what are you using all that electricity on?
Getting around.
Oh, you'r alway jokin with m
Com on, tell m Fland char
Hooba?
I have a feeling...
I'm forgetting some-thing...

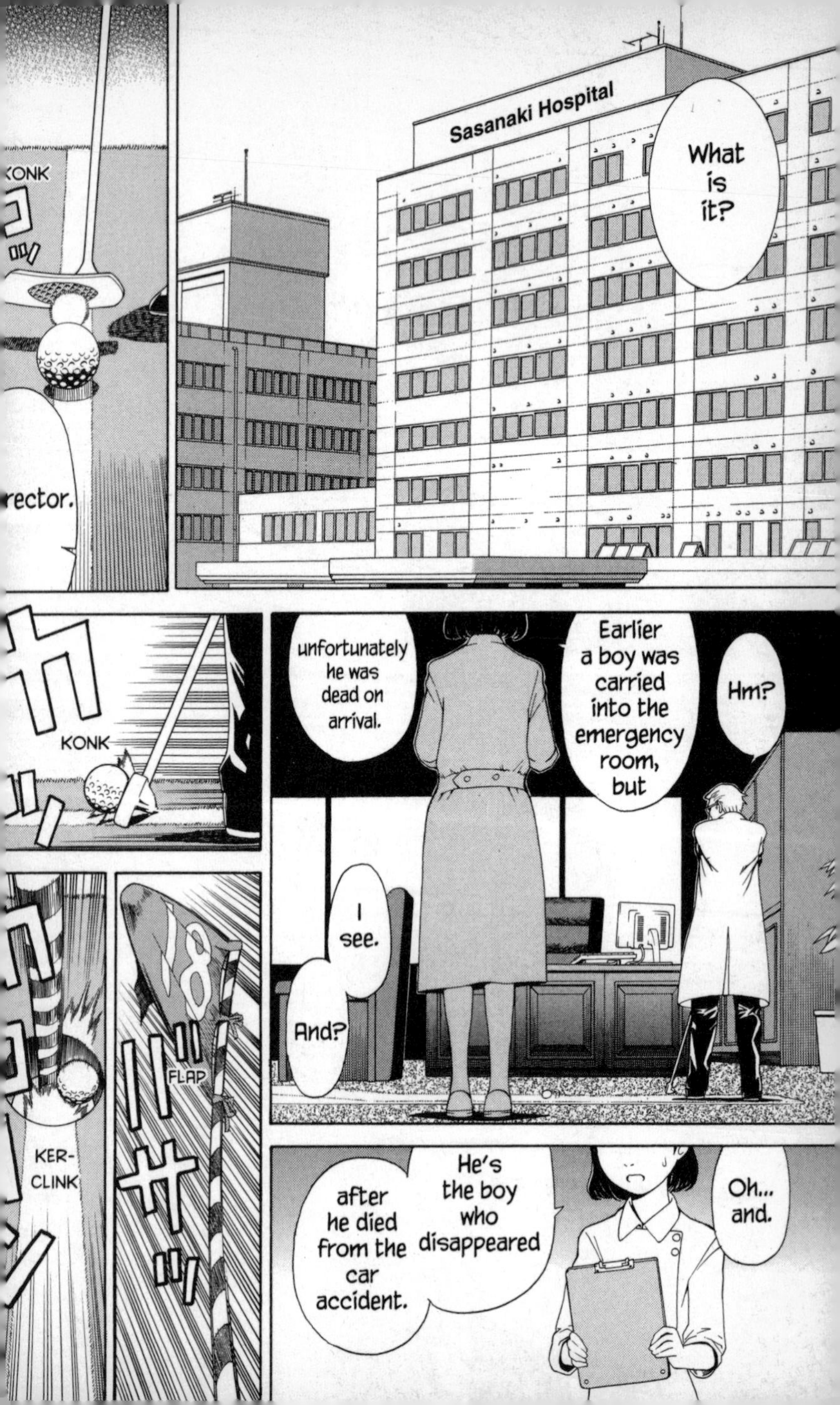
Sasanaki Hospital
What is it?
KONK
rector.
Hm?
Earlier a boy was carried into the emergency room, but
unfortunately he was dead on arrival.
I see.
And?
KONK
Oh... and.
He's the boy who disappeared
after he died from the car accident.
FLAP
KER-CLINK

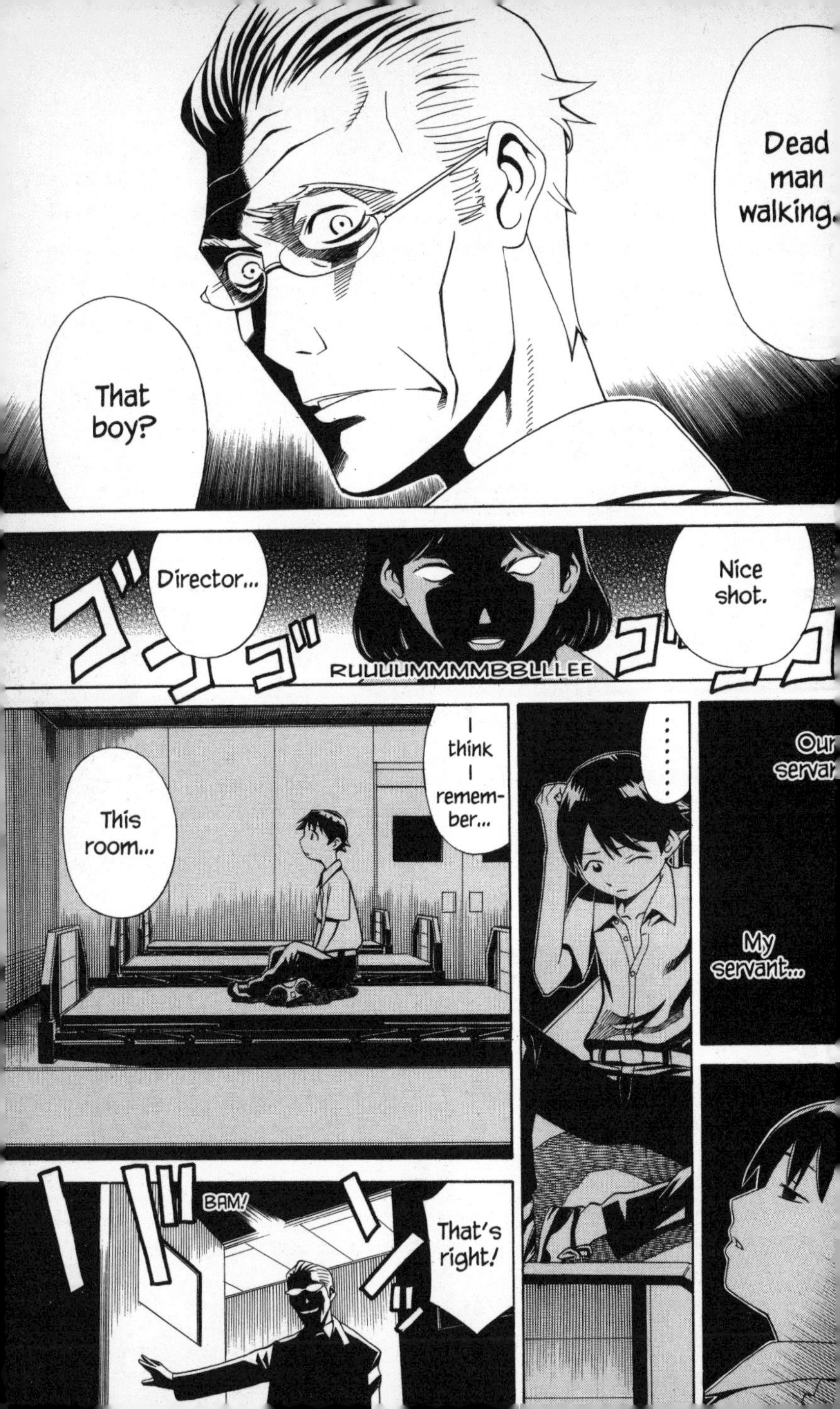

Dead man walking.
That boy?
Nice shot.
Director...
RUUUUMMMMBBLLLEE
Our servan
My servant...
......
I think I remember...
This room...
BAM!
That's right!

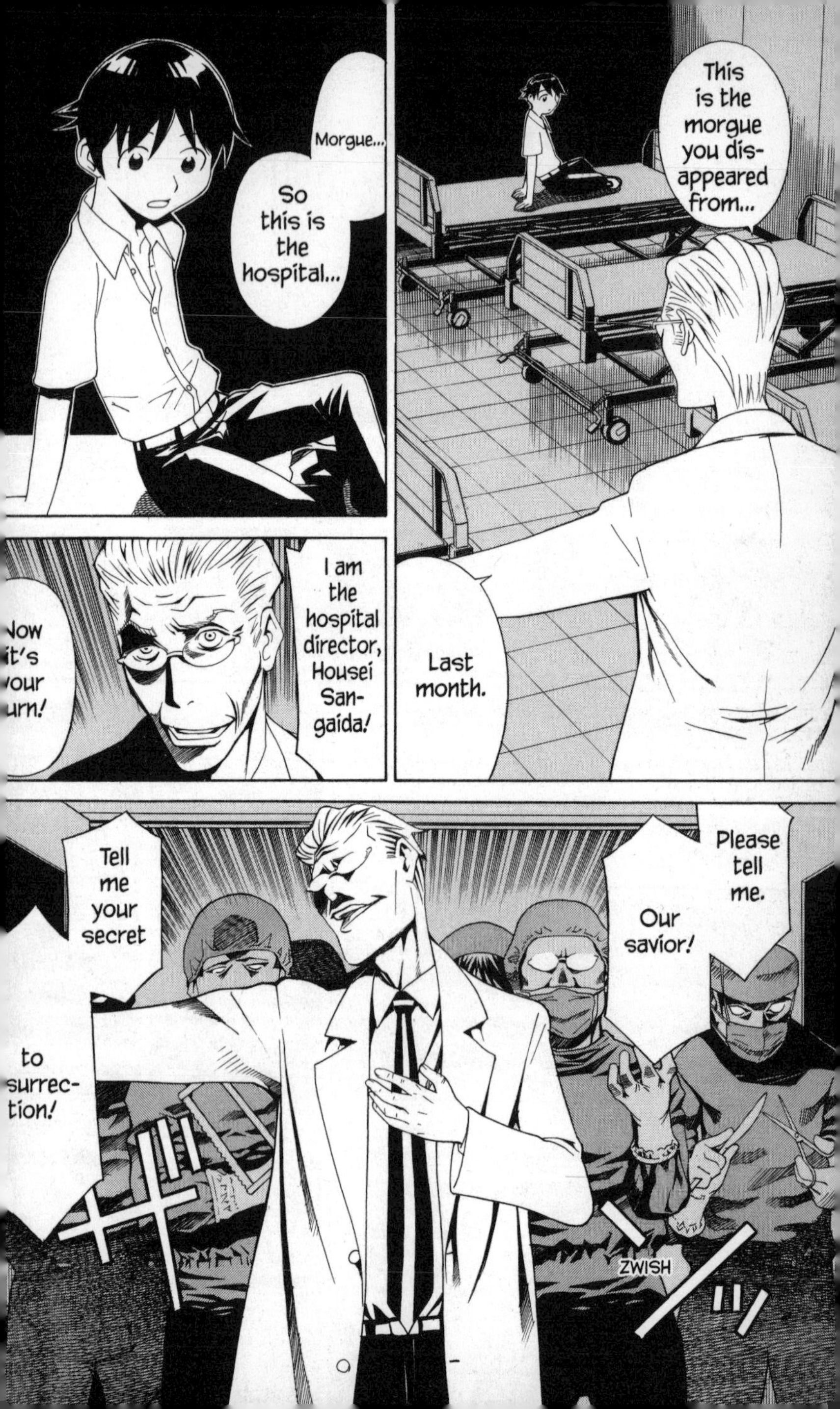
This is the morgue you disappeared from...
Morgue...
So this is the hospital...
Last month.
I am the hospital director, Housei Sangaida!
Now it's your turn!
Please tell me.
Our savior!
Tell me your secret
to resurrection!
ZWISH

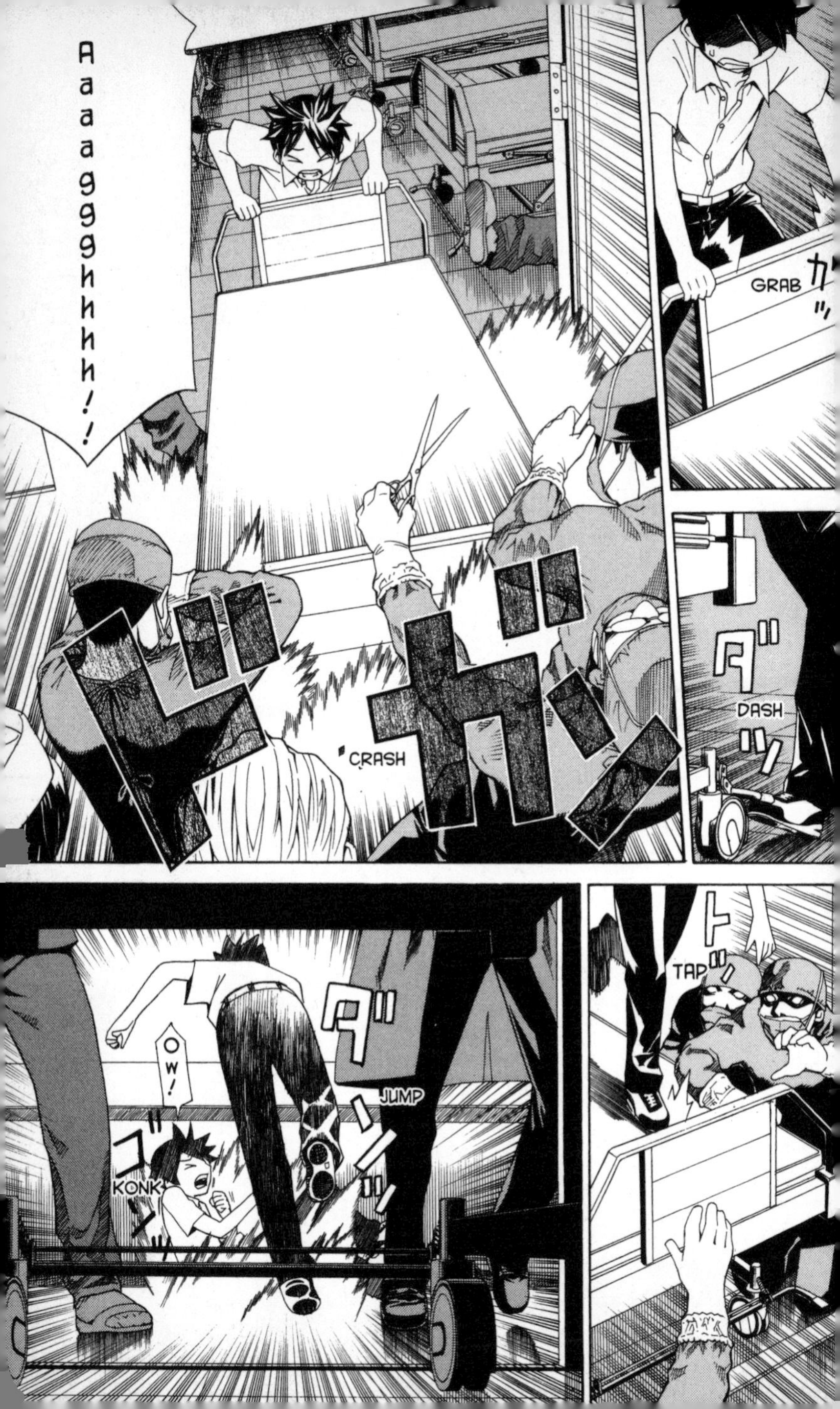
GRAB
カッ
DASH
ダッ
Aaaagghhhhh!!
CRASH
TAP
トッ
JUMP
ダッ
OW!
KONK
ゴッ

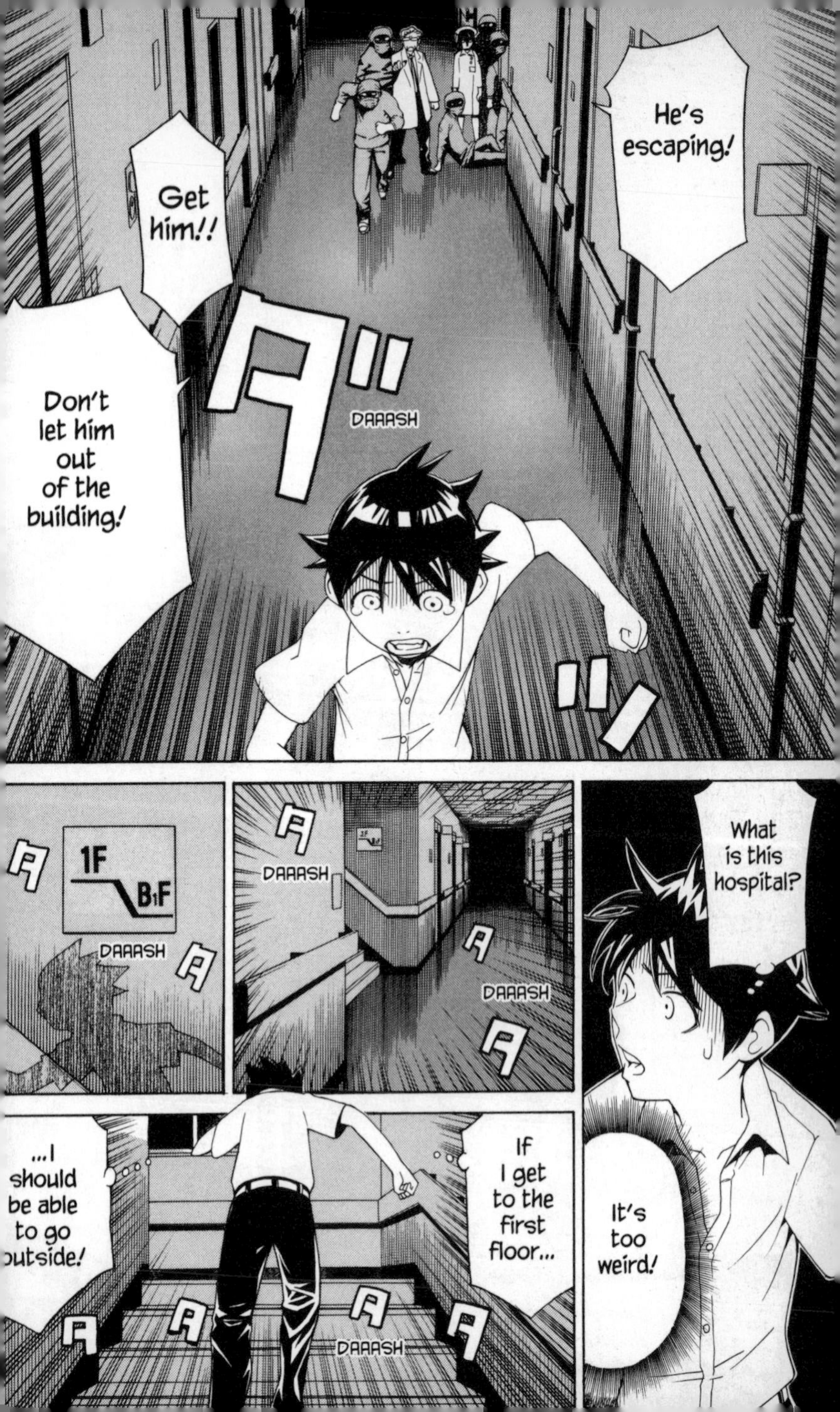
He's escaping!
Get him!!
Don't let him out of the building!
DAAASH
What is this hospital?
It's too weird!
DAAASH
DAAASH
1F
B1F
DAAASH
If I get to the first floor...
...I should be able to go outside!
DAAASH

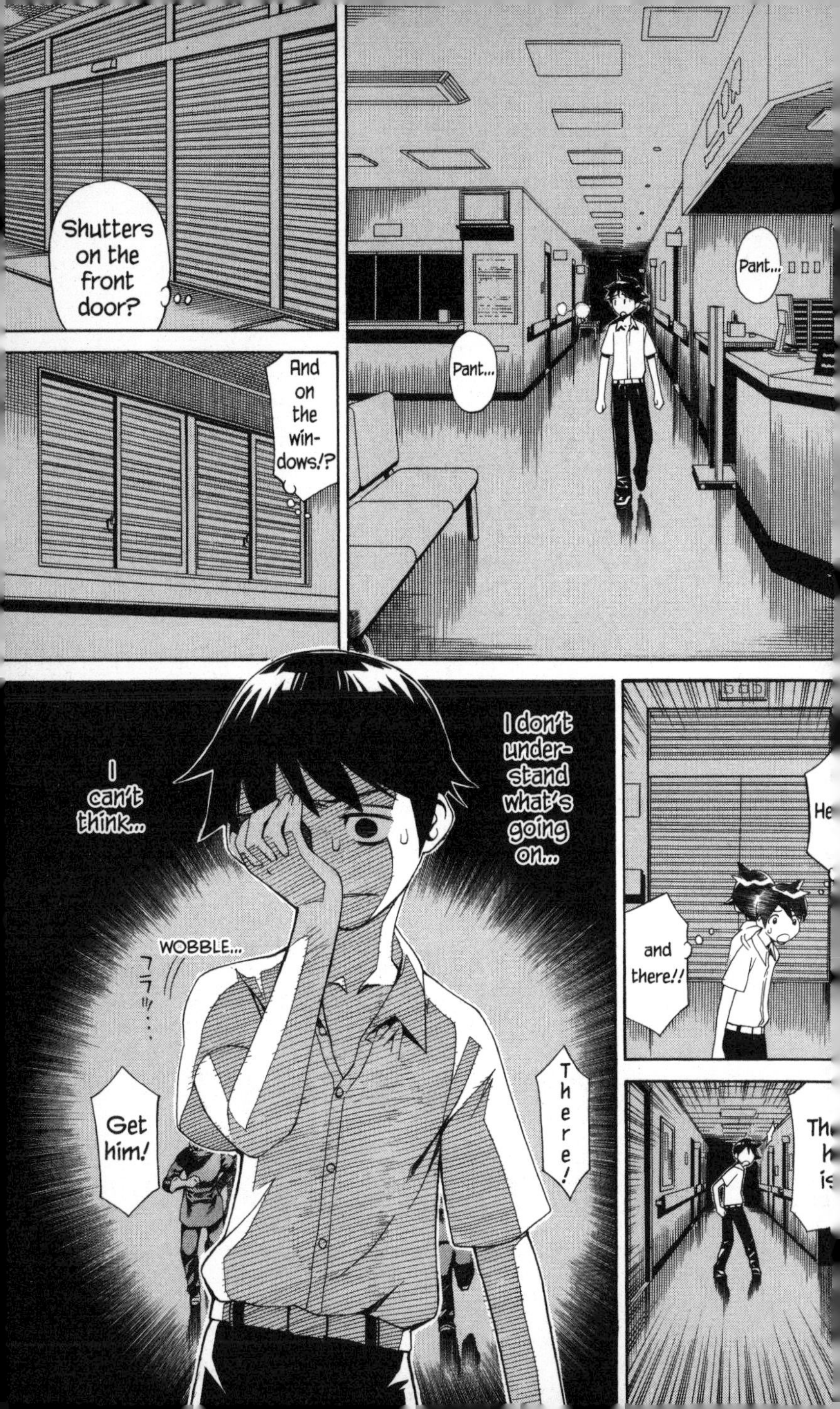
Pant...
Pant...
Shutters on the front door?
And on the win-dows!?
and there!!
I don't under-stand what's going on...
I can't think...
WOBBLE...
フラッ・・・
There!
Get him!

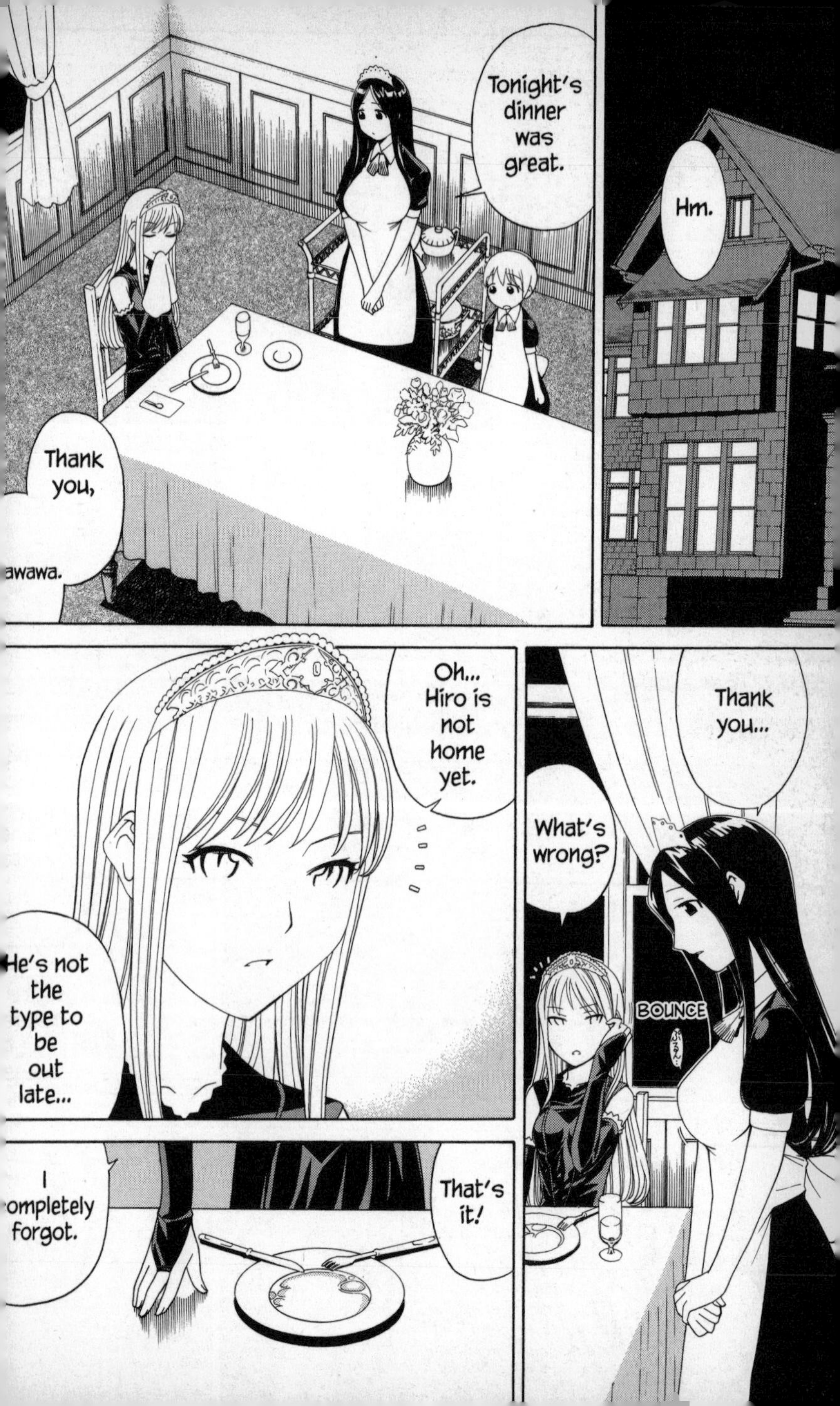
Hm.
Tonight's dinner was great.
Thank you, awawa.
Thank you...
What's wrong?
BOUNCE
ぷるん…
Oh... Hiro is not home yet.
He's not the type to be out late...
That's it!
I ompletely forgot.

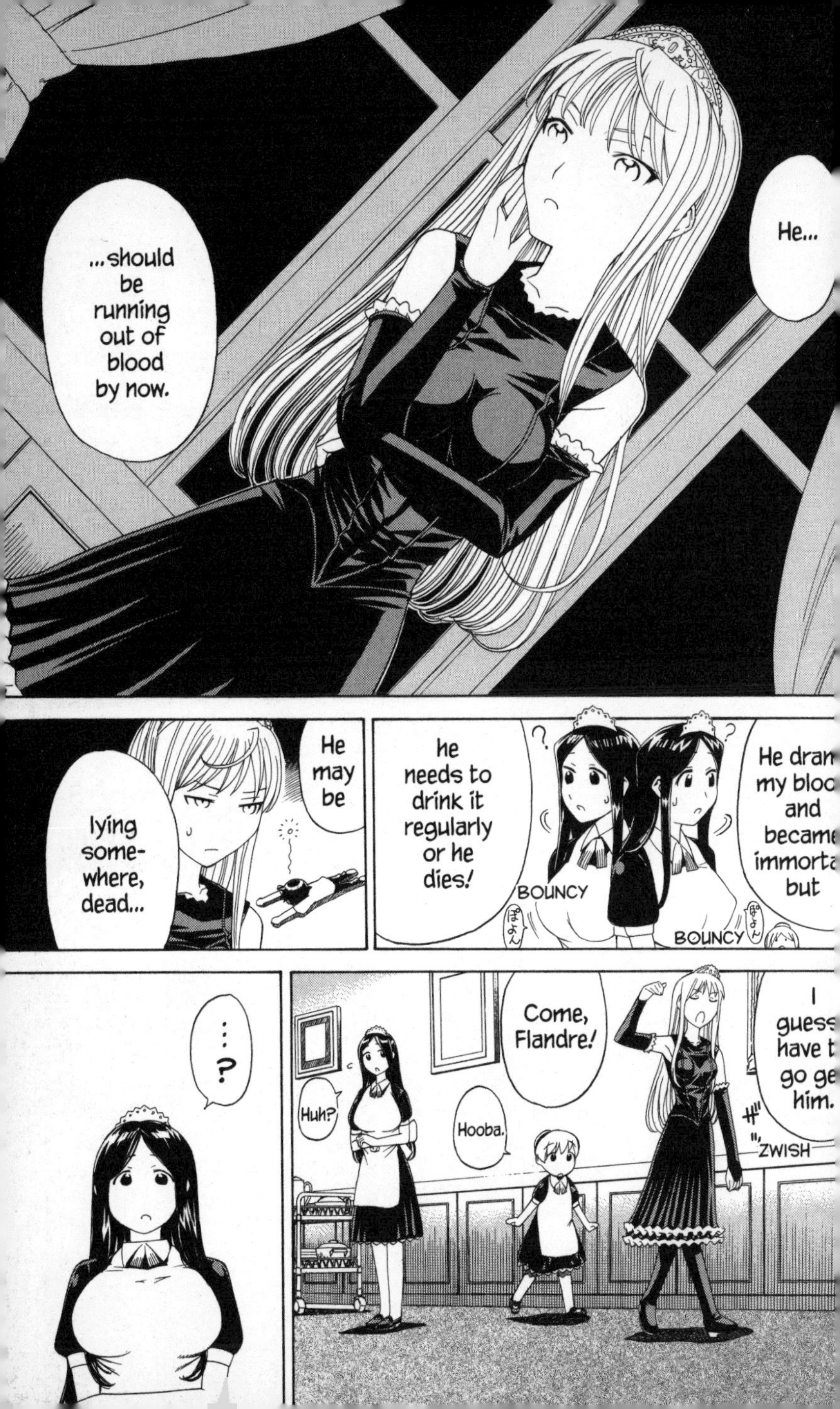

He...
...should be running out of blood by now.
He dran my bloo and became immorta but
he needs to drink it regularly or he dies!
BOUNCY
ぽよん
BOUNCY
ぽよん
He may be
lying some-where, dead...
I guess have t go ge him.
Come, Flandre!
ザ
ZWISH
Hooba.
Huh?
...?

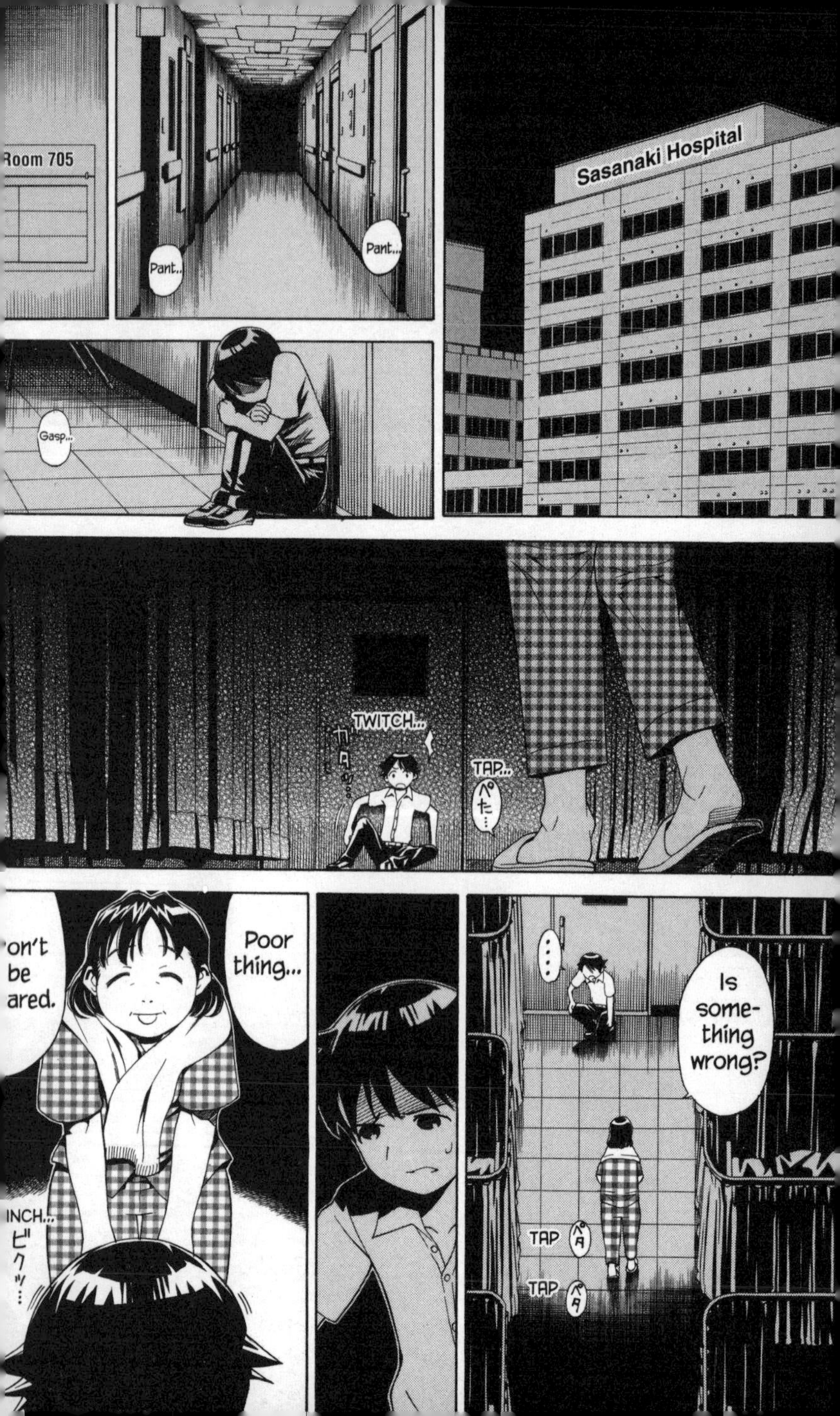
Sasanaki Hospital
Pant...
Pant..
Room 705
Gasp...
TAP...
ぺた...
TWITCH...
カタッ...
...
Is something wrong?
TAP
ペタ
TAP
ペタ
Poor thing...
'on't be
ared.
INCH...
ビクッ...

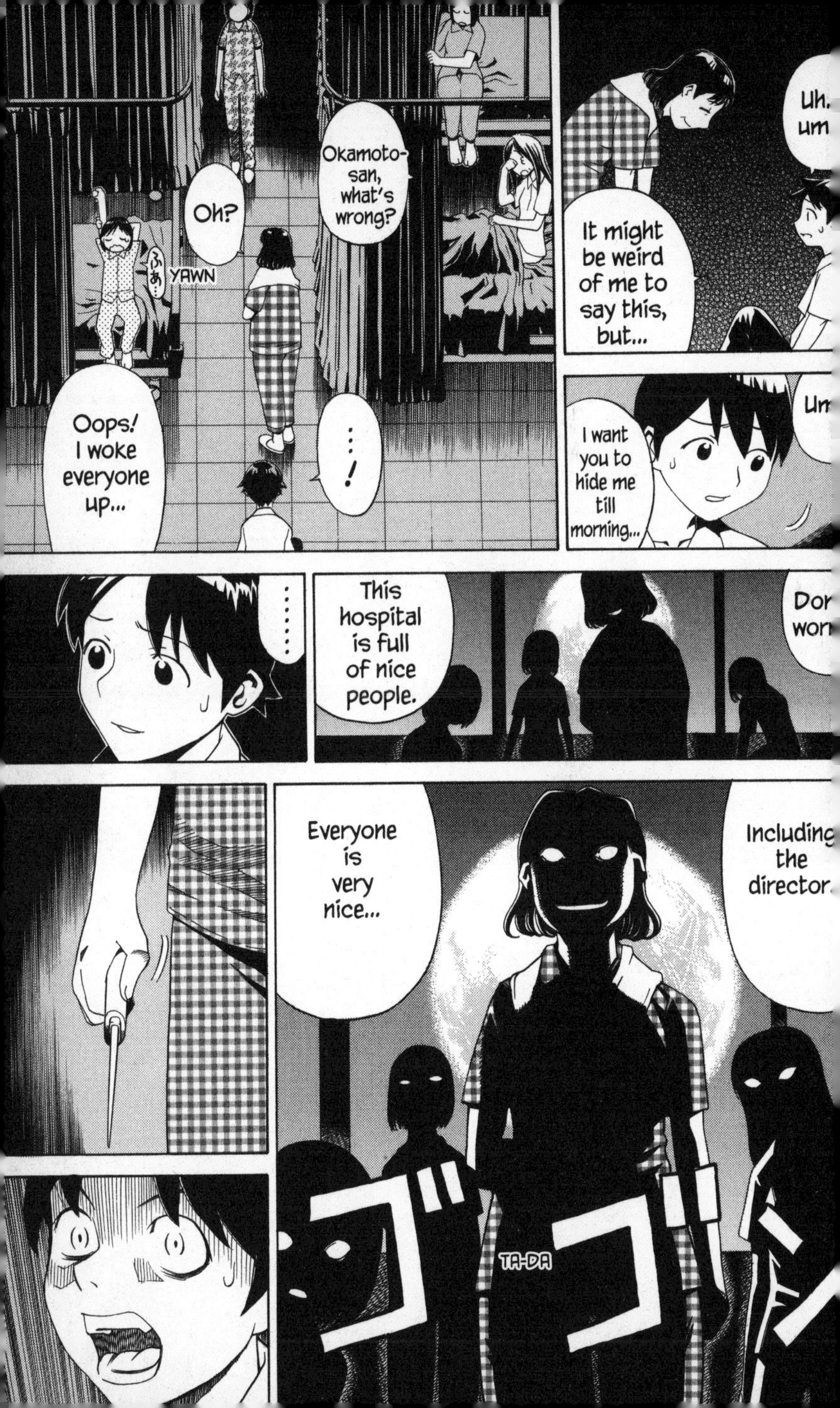

Uh. um
It might be weird of me to say this, but...
Um
I want you to hide me till morning...
Okamoto-san, what's wrong?
Oh?
ふぁ…
YAWN
...!
Oops! I woke everyone up...
Dor wor
This hospital is full of nice people.
......
Including the director.
Everyone is very nice...
TA-DA

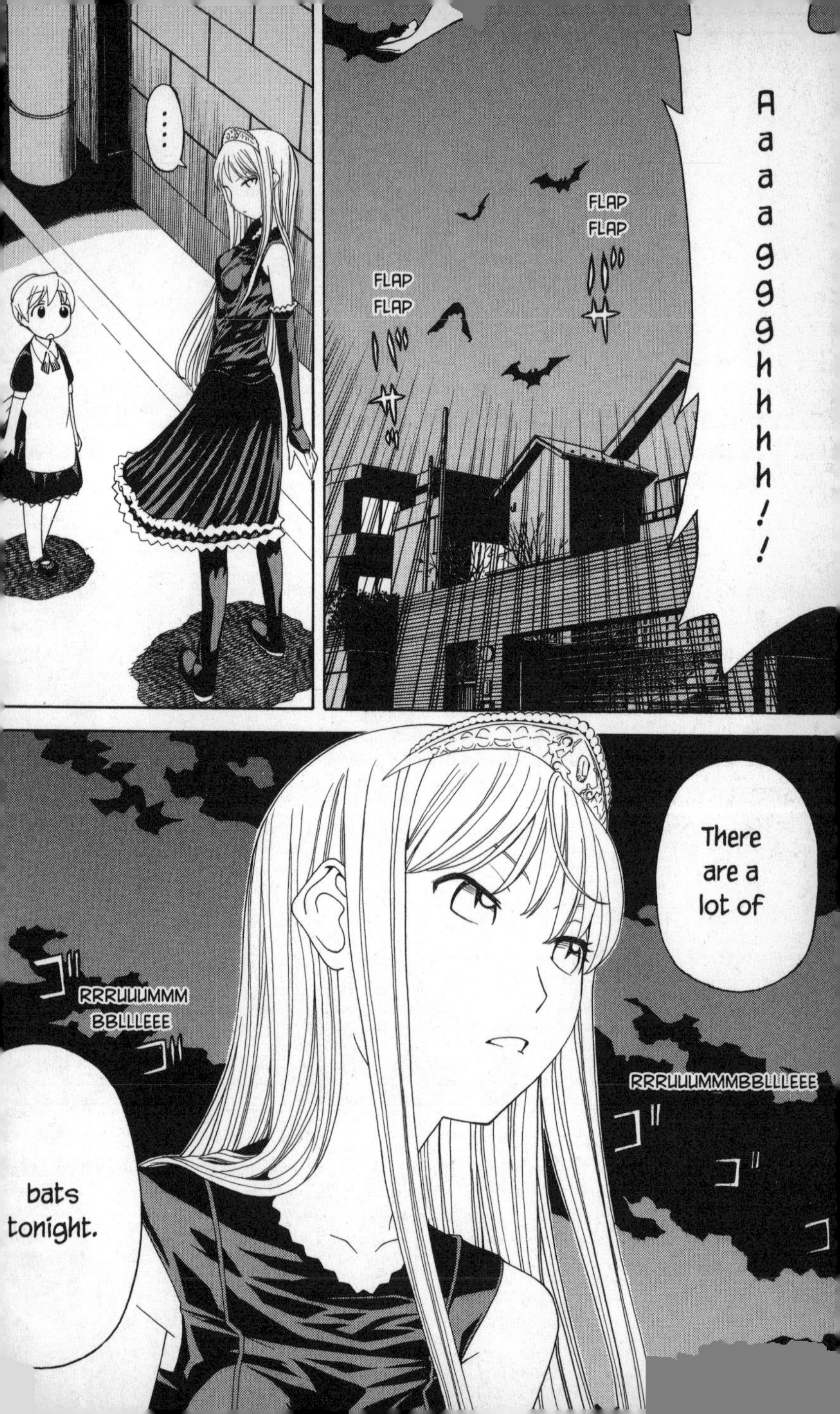
Aaaagghhhh!!
FLAP FLAP
FLAP FLAP
....
There are a lot of
RRRUUUMMMBBLLLEEE
RRRUUUMMM BBLLLEEE
bats tonight.

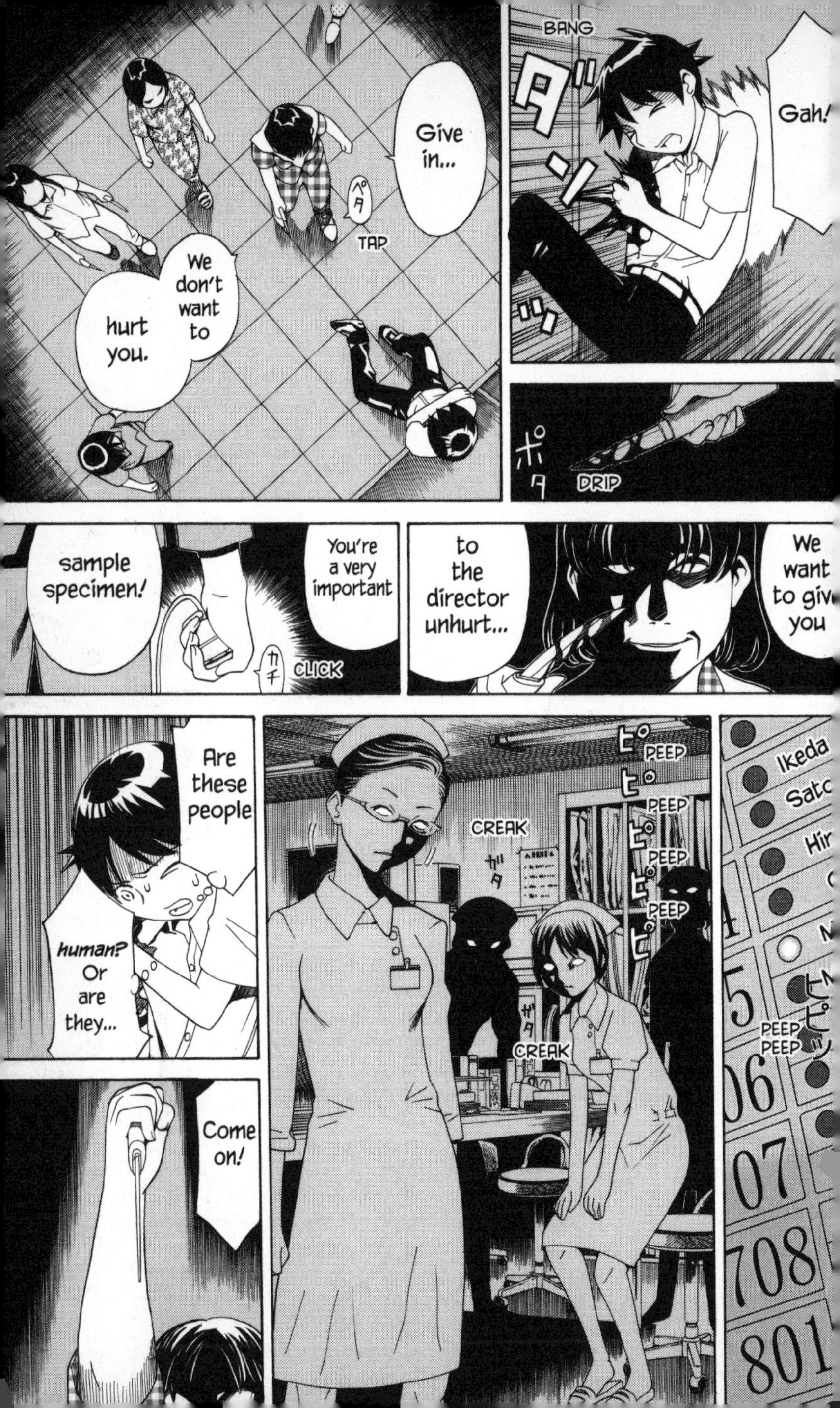
BANG
ダッ
Gah!
ポタ
DRIP
Give in...
ペタ
TAP
We don't want to hurt you.
We want to give you
to the director unhurt...
You're a very important
sample specimen!
カチ
CLICK
Ikeda
Sato
Hir
ピピッ
PEEP PEEP
5
06
07
708
801
ピ
PEEP
ピ
PEEP
ピ
PEEP
ピ
PEEP
ガタ
CREAK
ガタ
CREAK
Are these people *human?* Or are they...
Come on!

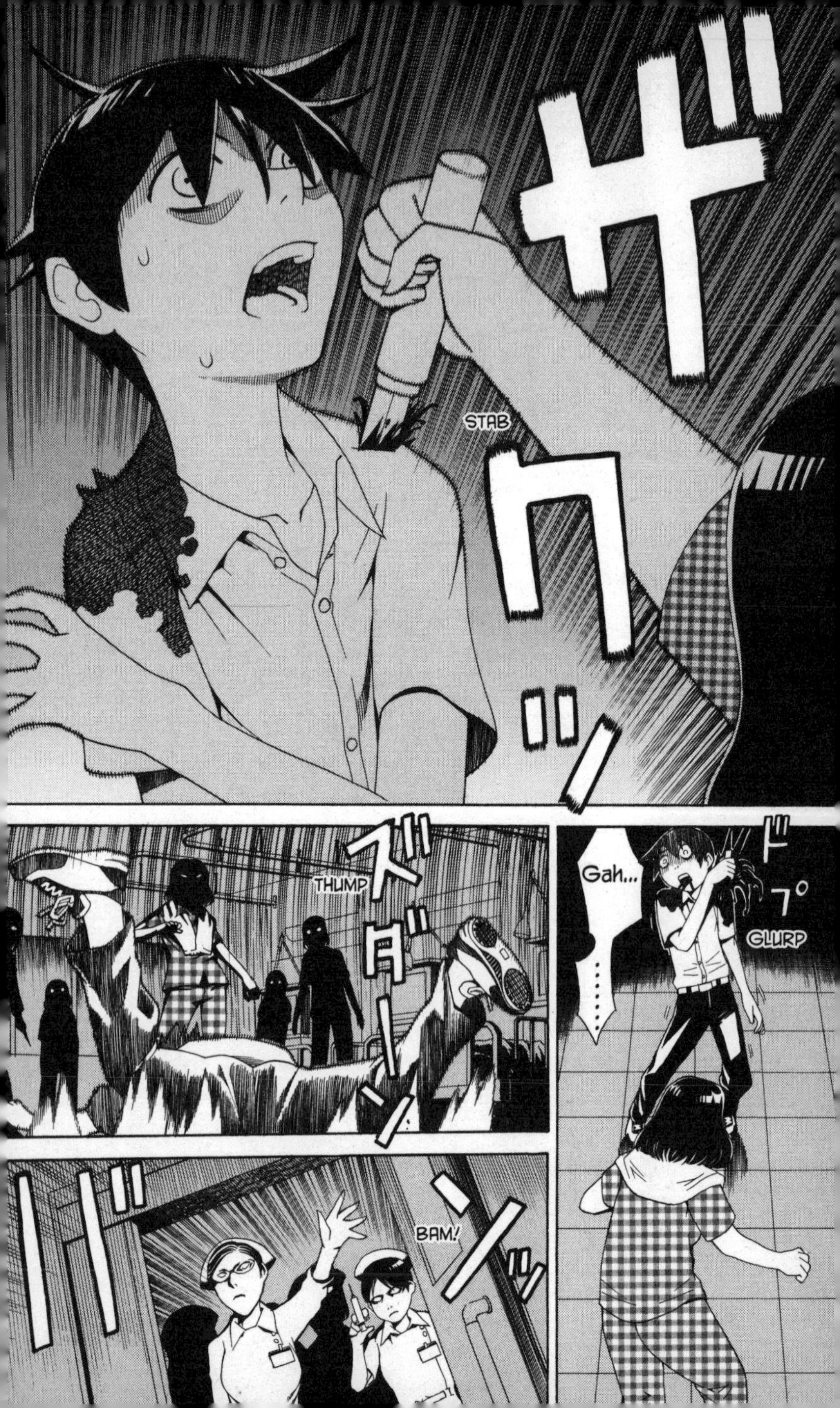
STAB
Gah...
......
GLURP
THUMP
BAM!

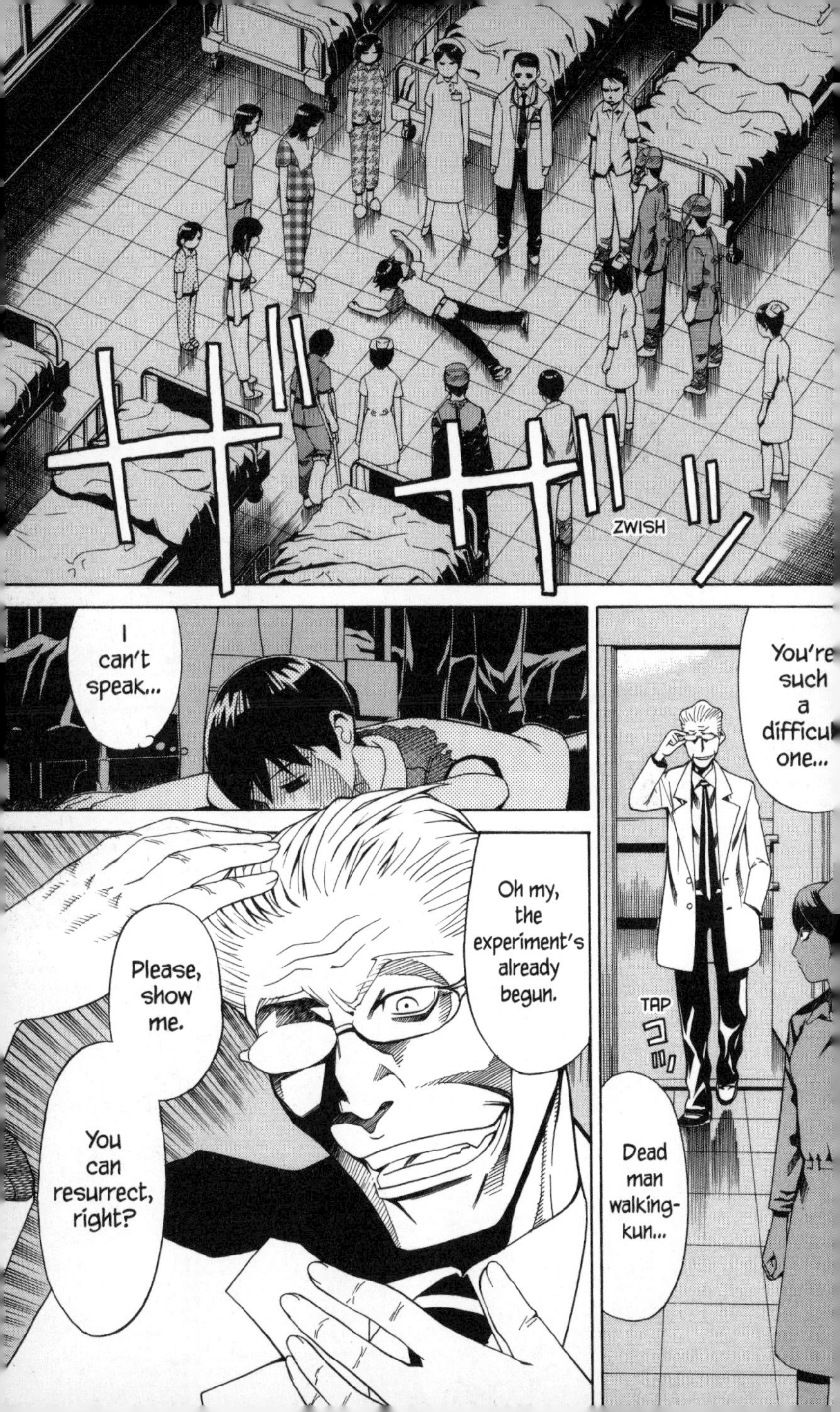
ZWISH
You're such a difficul one...
TAP
Dead man walking-kun...
I can't speak...
Oh my, the experiment's already begun.
Please, show me.
You can resurrect, right?

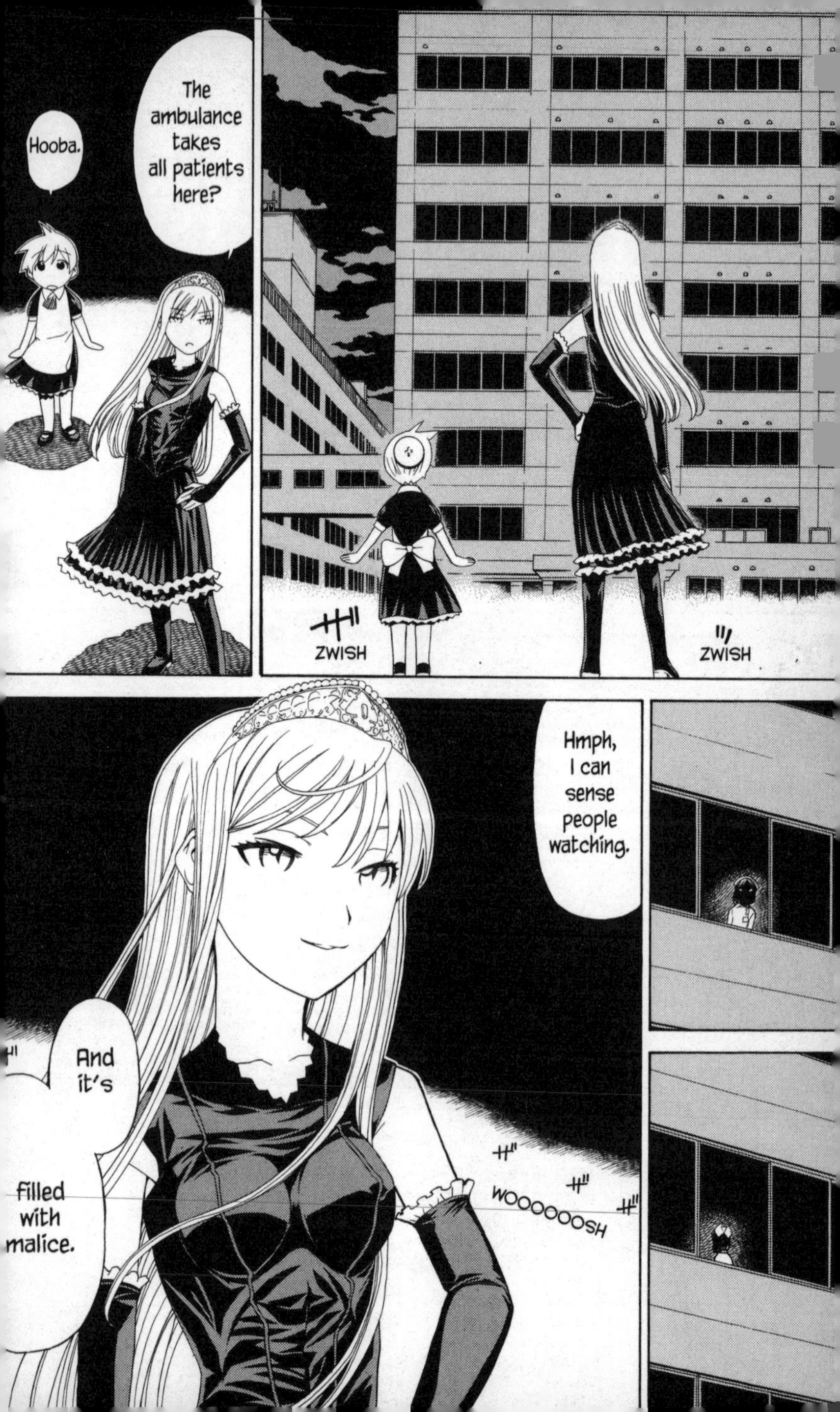
ZWISH
ZWISH
The ambulance takes all patients here?
Hooba.
Hmph, I can sense people watching.
WOOOOOOSH
And it's filled with malice.

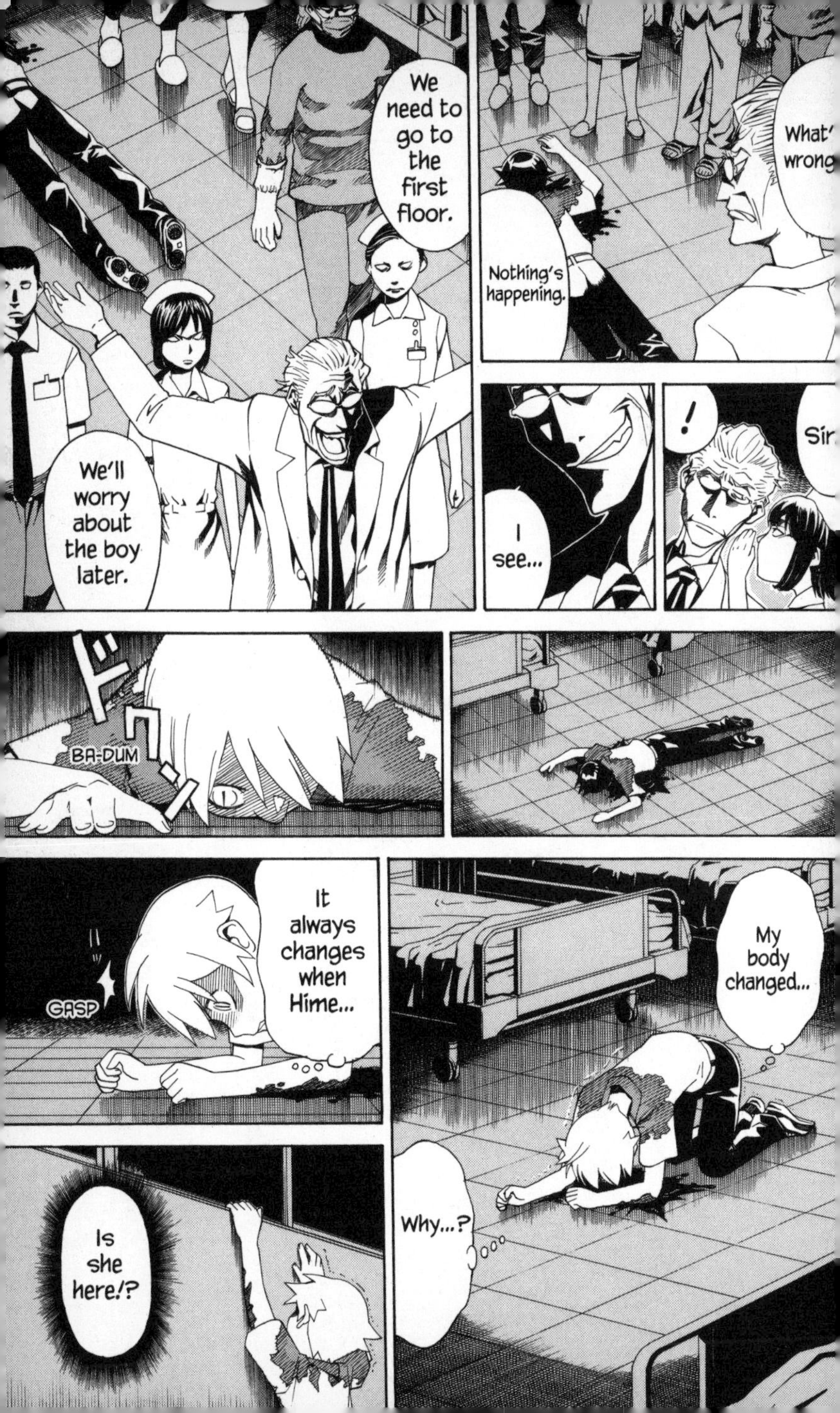
What'
wrong
Nothing's happening.
Sir
!
I see...
We need to go to the first floor.
We'll worry about the boy later.
BA-DUM
My body changed...
Why...?
It always changes when Hime...
GASP
Is she here!?

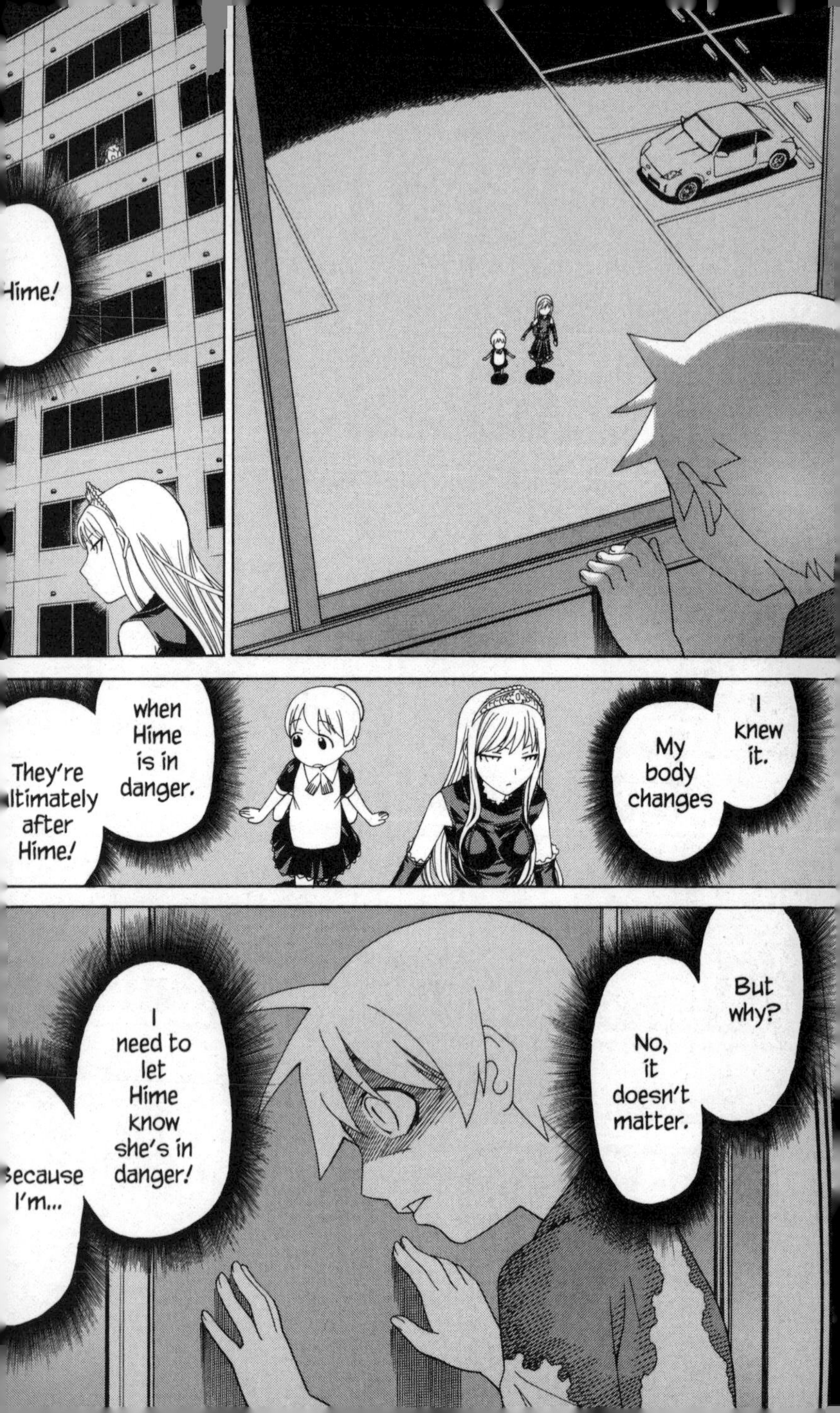
Hime!
I knew it. My body changes
when Hime is in danger.
They're ltimately after Hime!
But why?
No, it doesn't matter.
I need to let Hime know she's in danger!
ecause I'm...

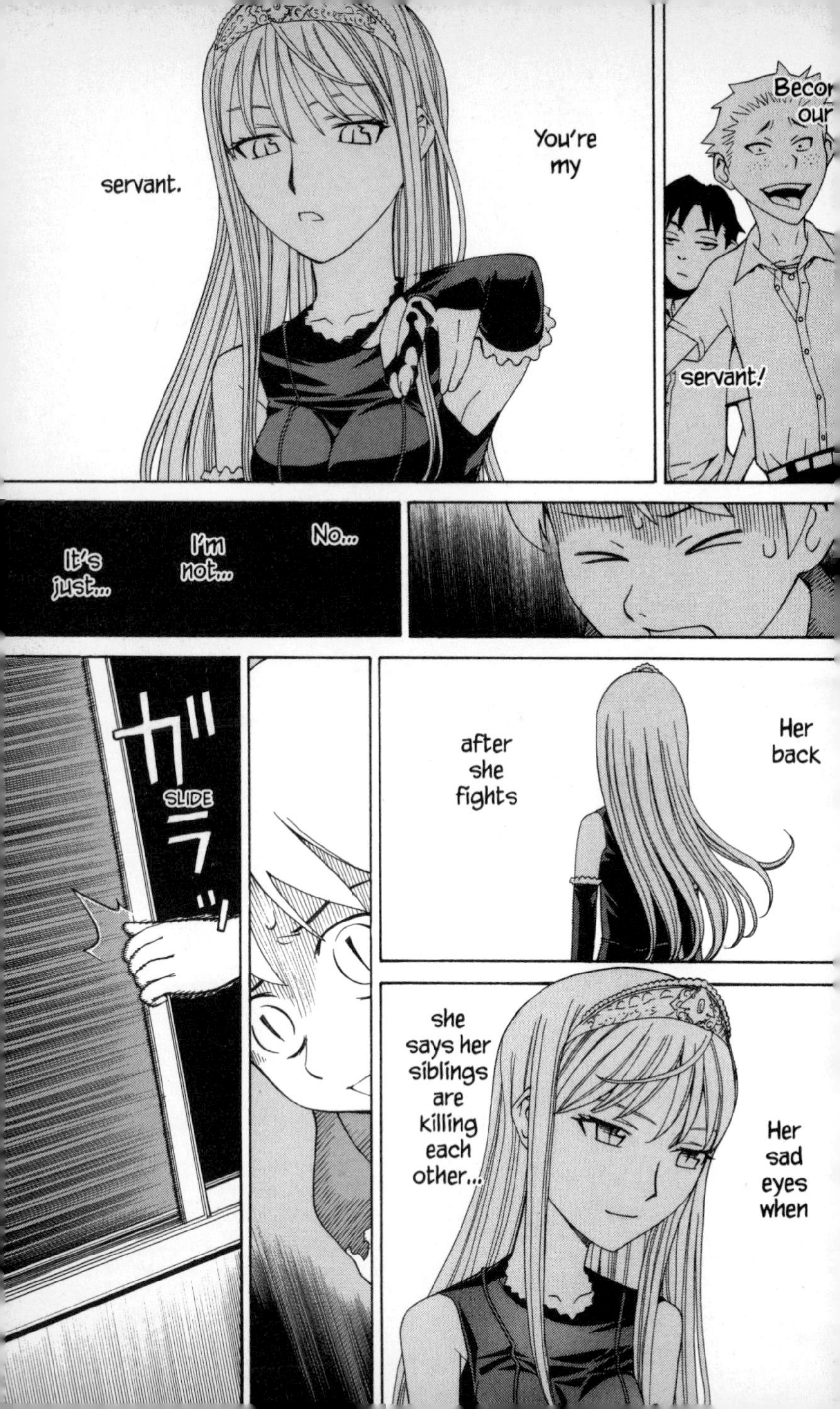

Becor our servant!
You're my servant.
No...
I'm not...
It's just...
Her back after she fights
Her sad eyes when she says her siblings are killing each other...
ガラッ
SLIDE

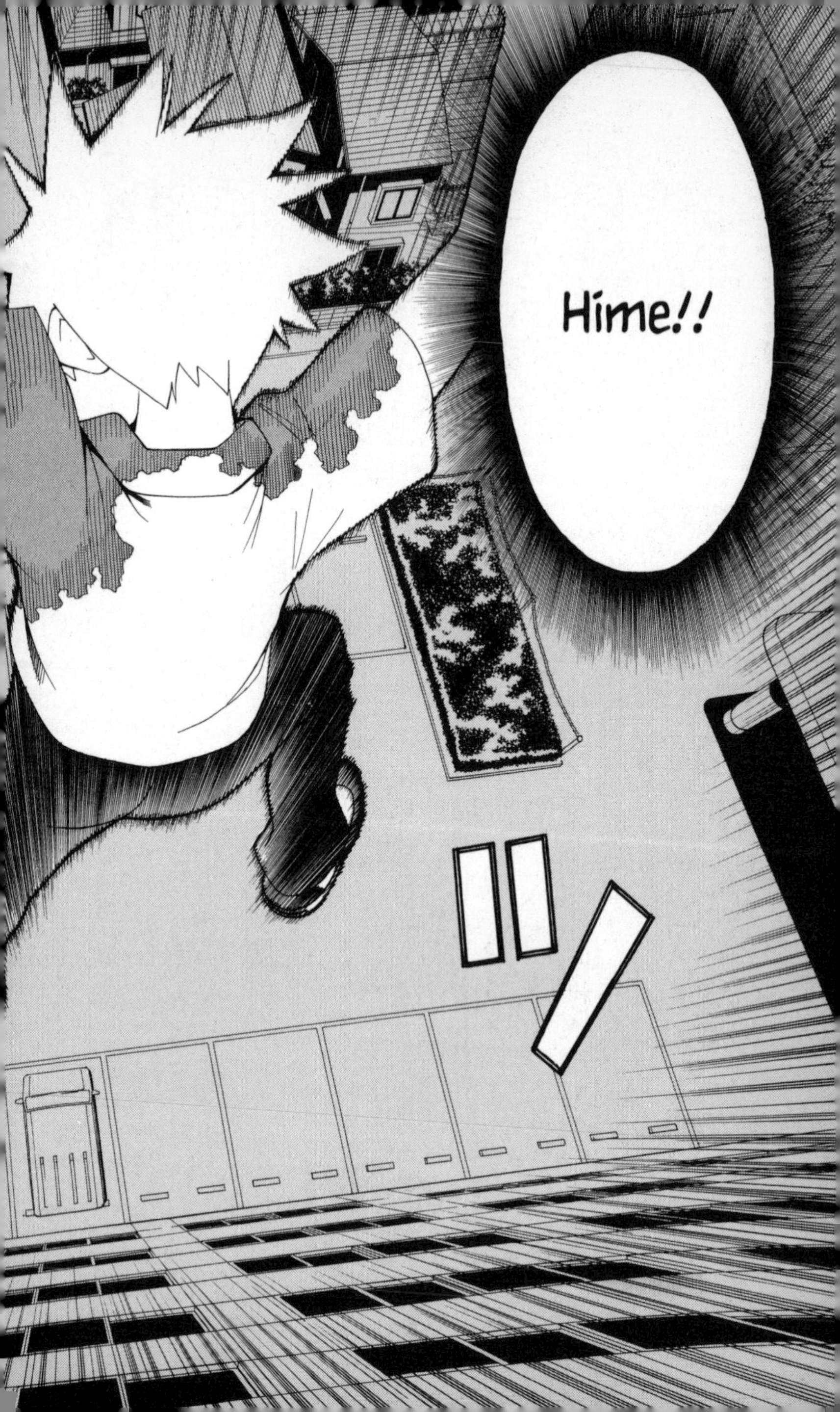
Hime!!

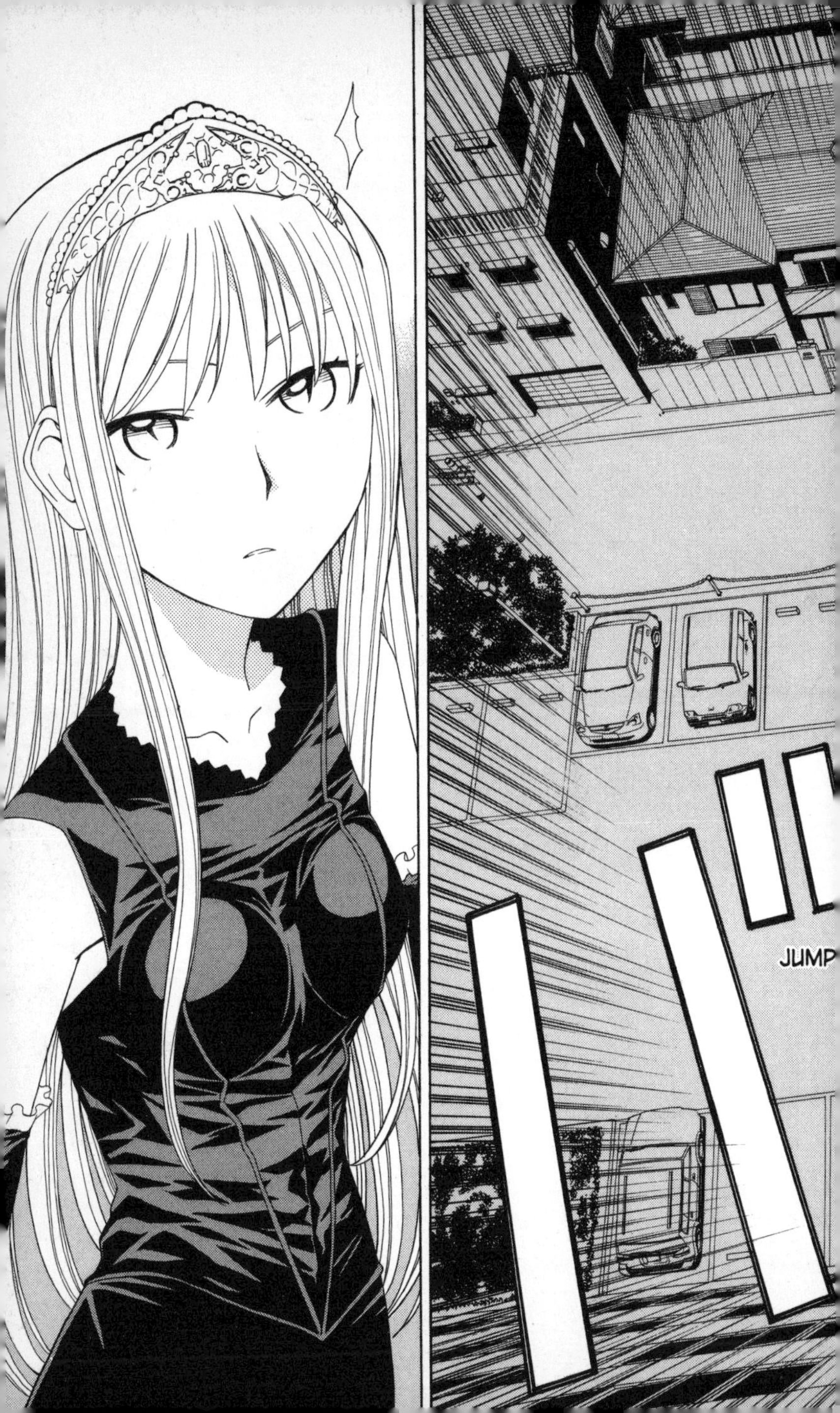
JUMP

Hiro?

I hear Hime's voice...

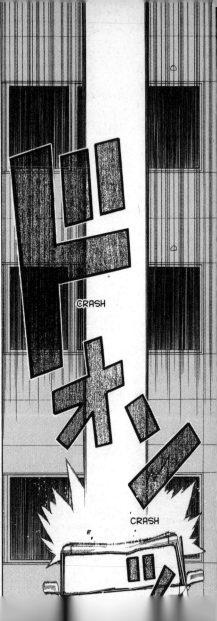

CRASH

CRASH

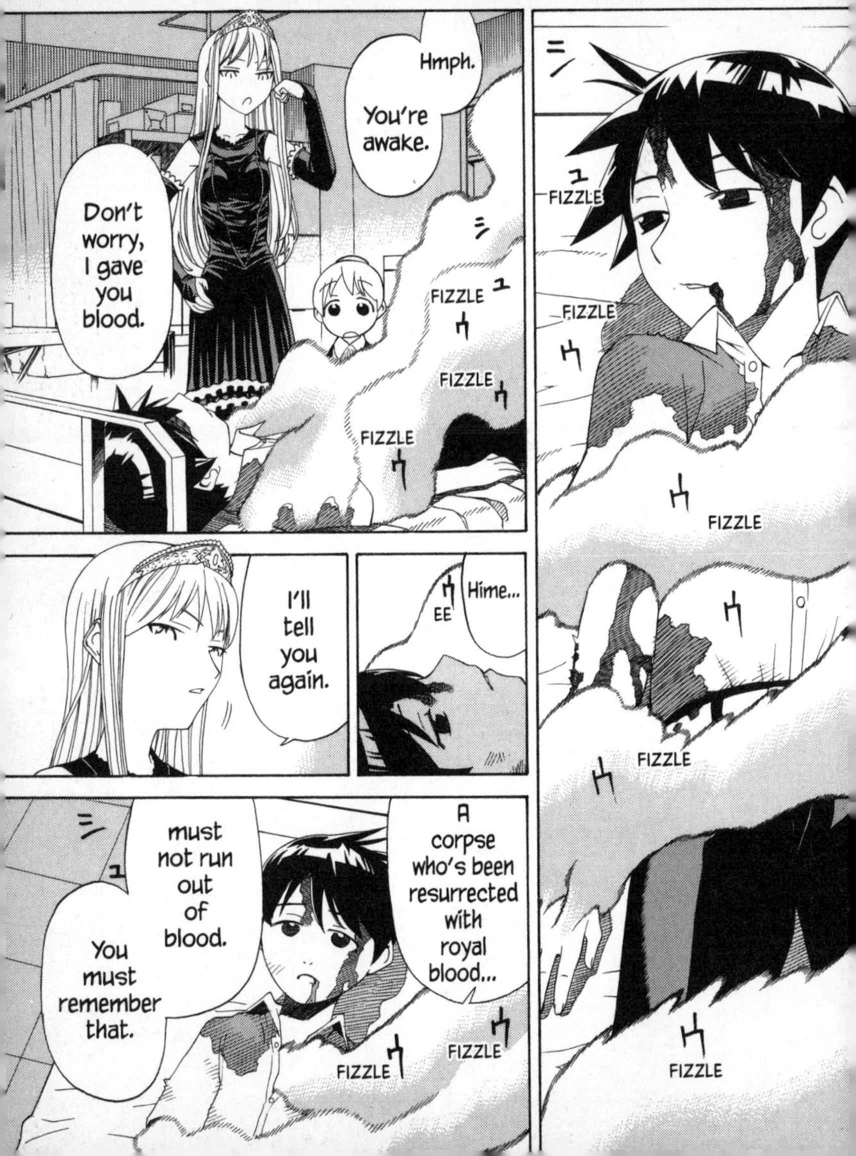
FIZZLE
FIZZLE
FIZZLE
Hmph.
You're awake.
Don't worry, I gave you blood.
FIZZLE
FIZZLE
FIZZLE
FIZZLE
FIZZLE
FIZZLE
Hime...
EE
I'll tell you again.
A corpse who's been resurrected with royal blood...
must not run out of blood.
You must remember that.
FIZZLE
FIZZLE

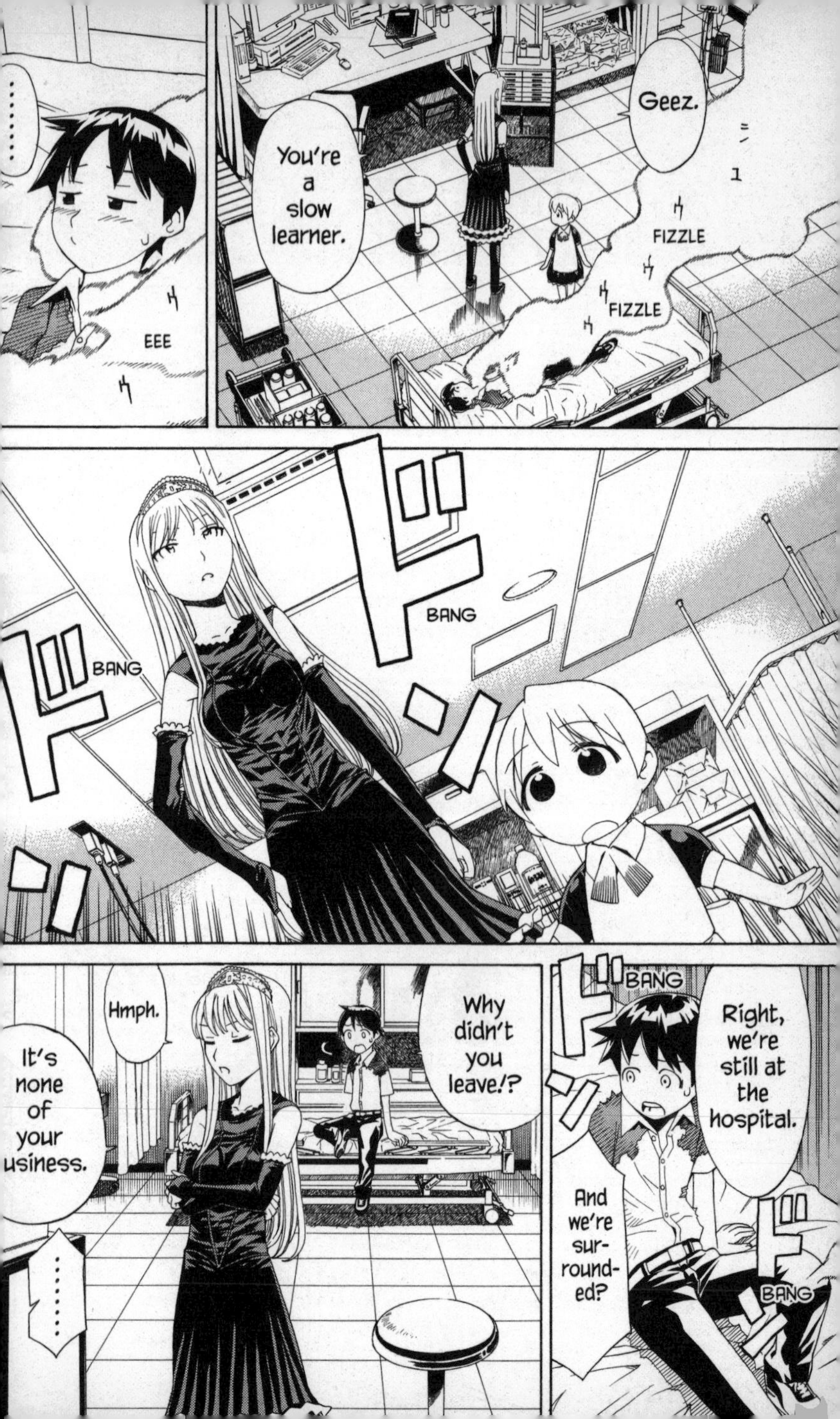
Geez.
You're a slow learner.
FIZZLE
FIZZLE
......
EEE
BANG
BANG
BANG
Right, we're still at the hospital.
And we're surrounded?
BANG
Why didn't you leave!?
Hmph.
It's none of your usiness.
......

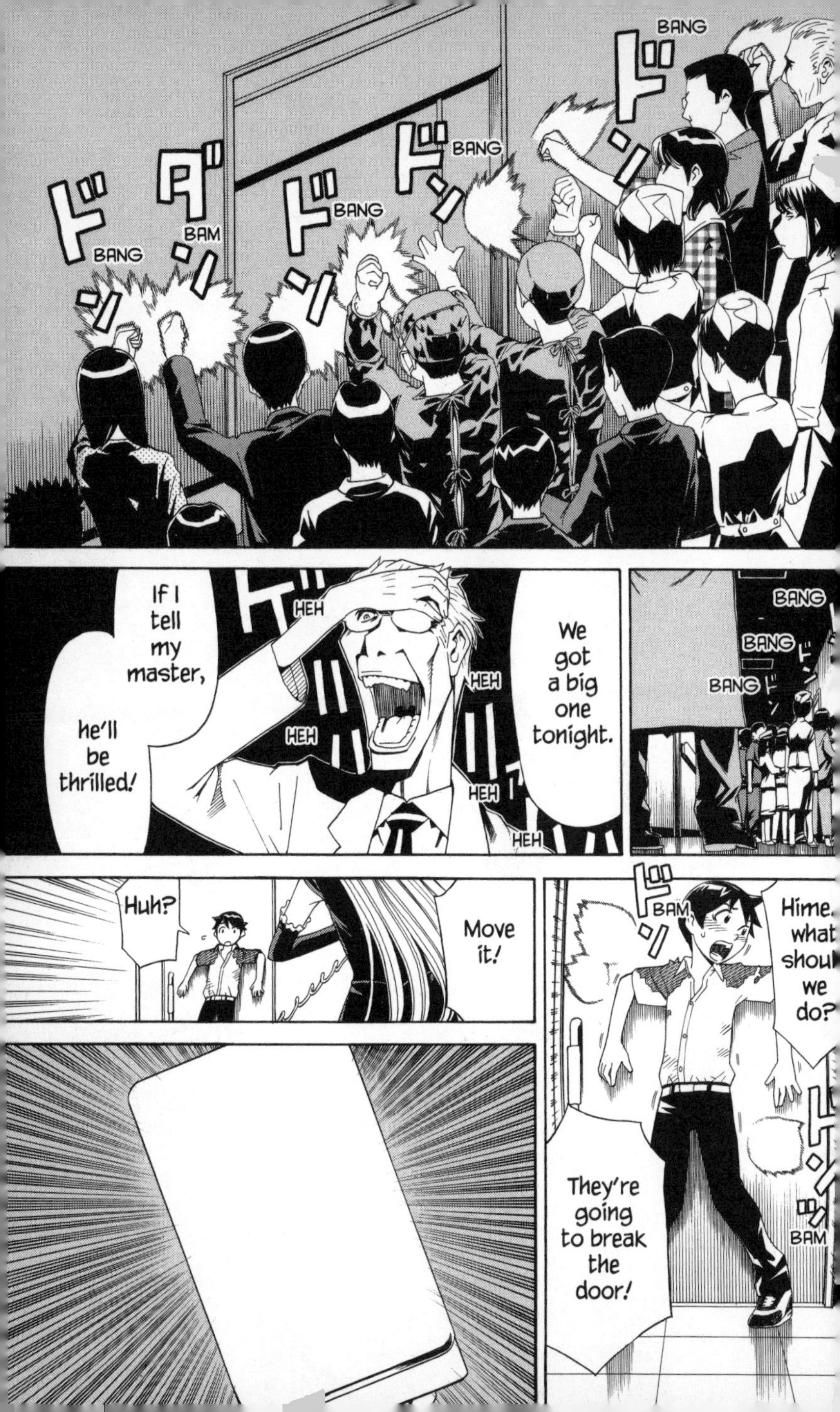

BANG
BANG
BANG
BAM
BANG
BANG
BANG
BANG
We got a big one tonight.
HEH
HEH
HEH
HEH
HEH
If I tell my master,
he'll be thrilled!
BAM
Hime, what shou we do?
They're going to break the door!
BAM
Move it!
Huh?

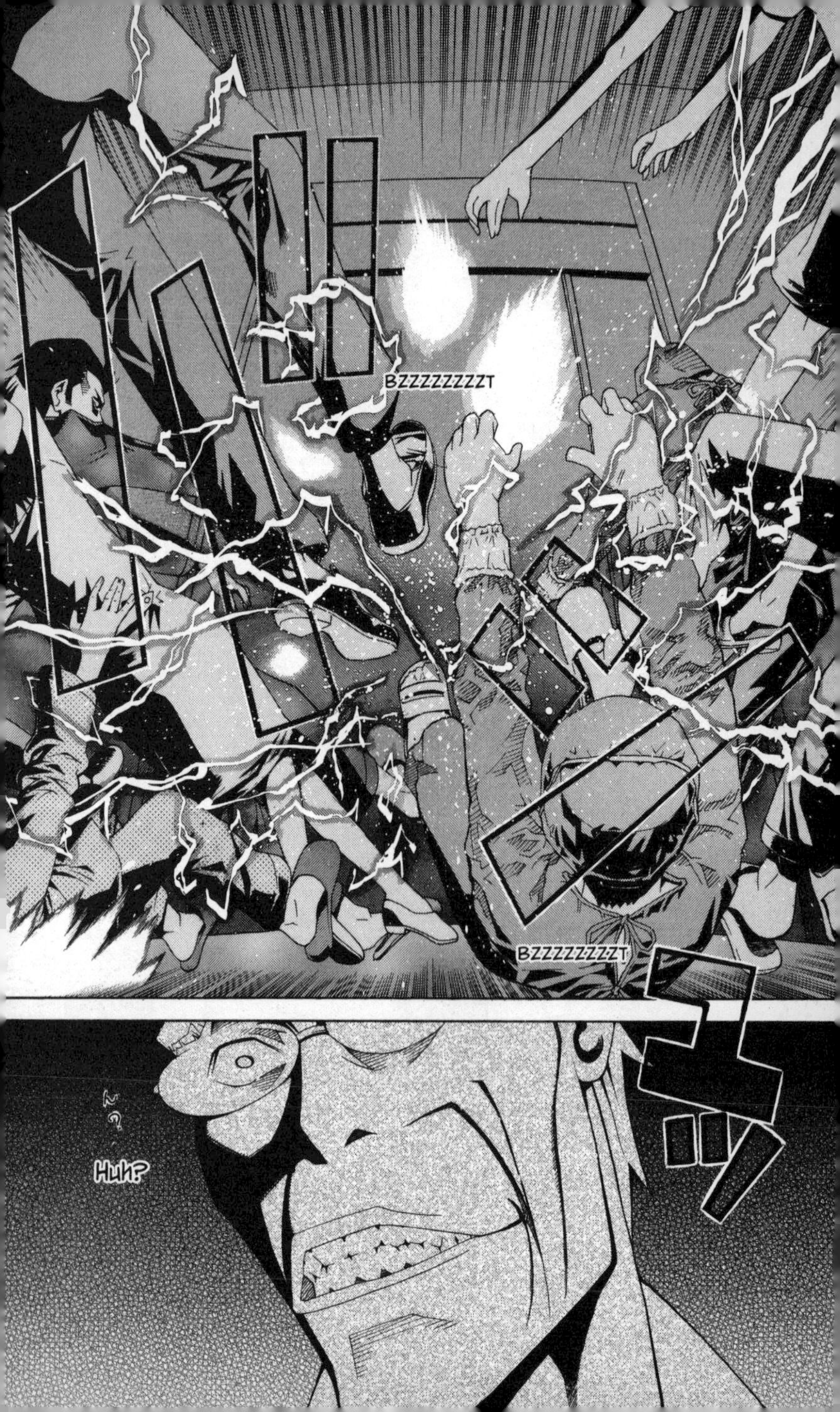
BZZZZZZZZZT
BZZZZZZZZZT
Huh?

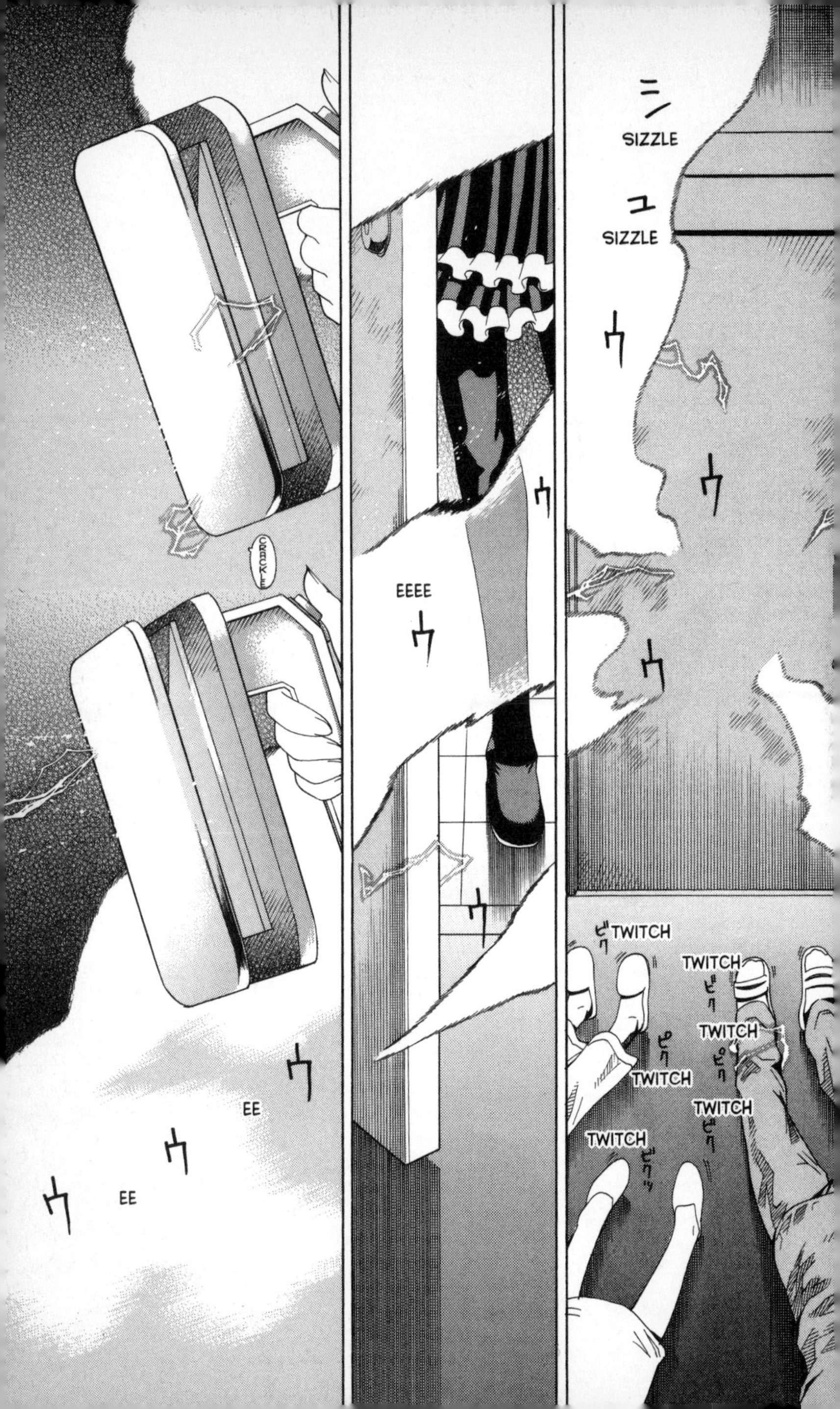
シ
SIZZLE
ュ
SIZZLE
ウ
ウ
ウ
TWITCH
ビク
TWITCH
ビク
TWITCH
ピク
TWITCH
ピク
TWITCH
ビク
TWITCH
ビクッ
ウ
EEEE
ウ
ウ
CRACKLE
ウ
EE
ウ
EE
ウ

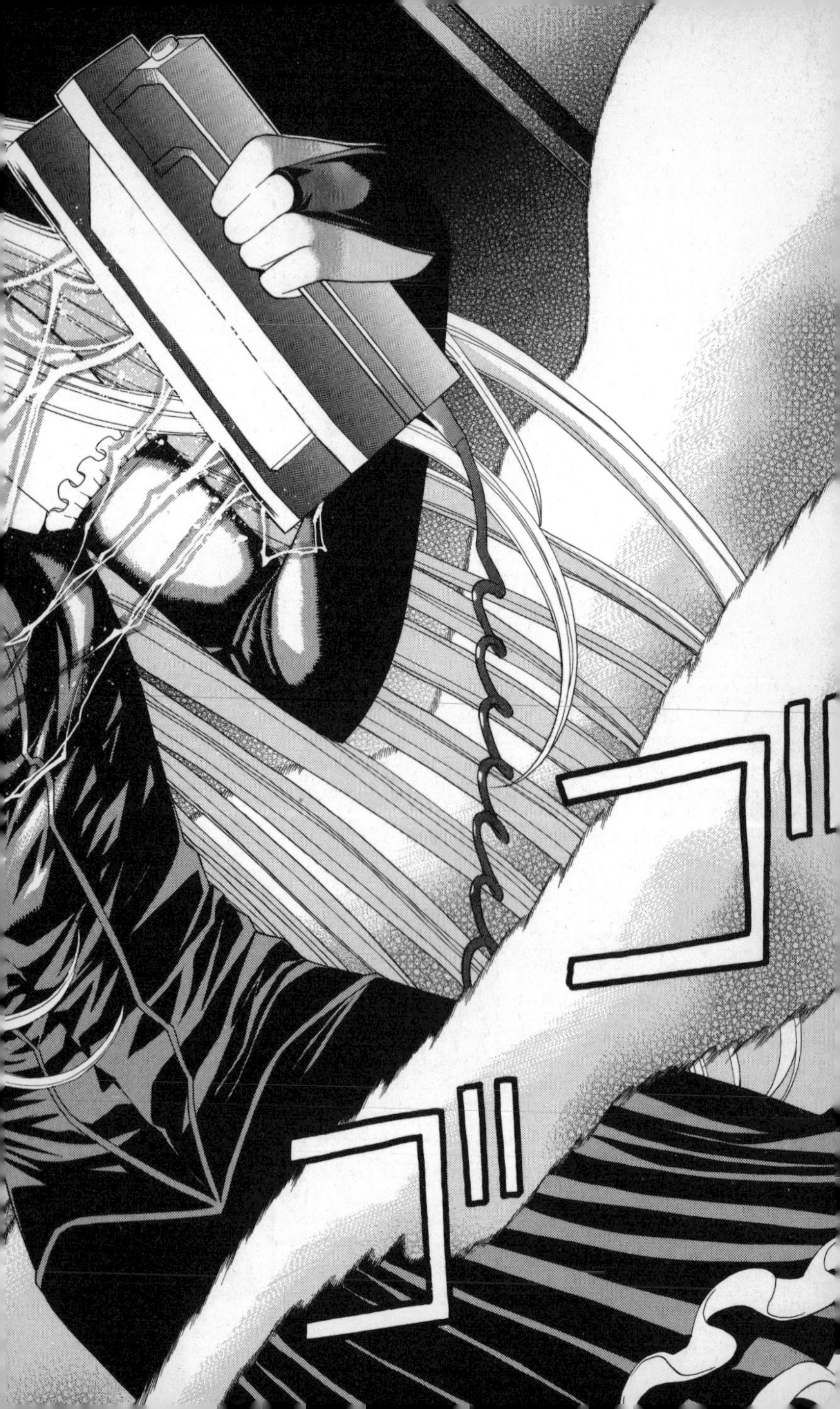
ゴ
ゴ

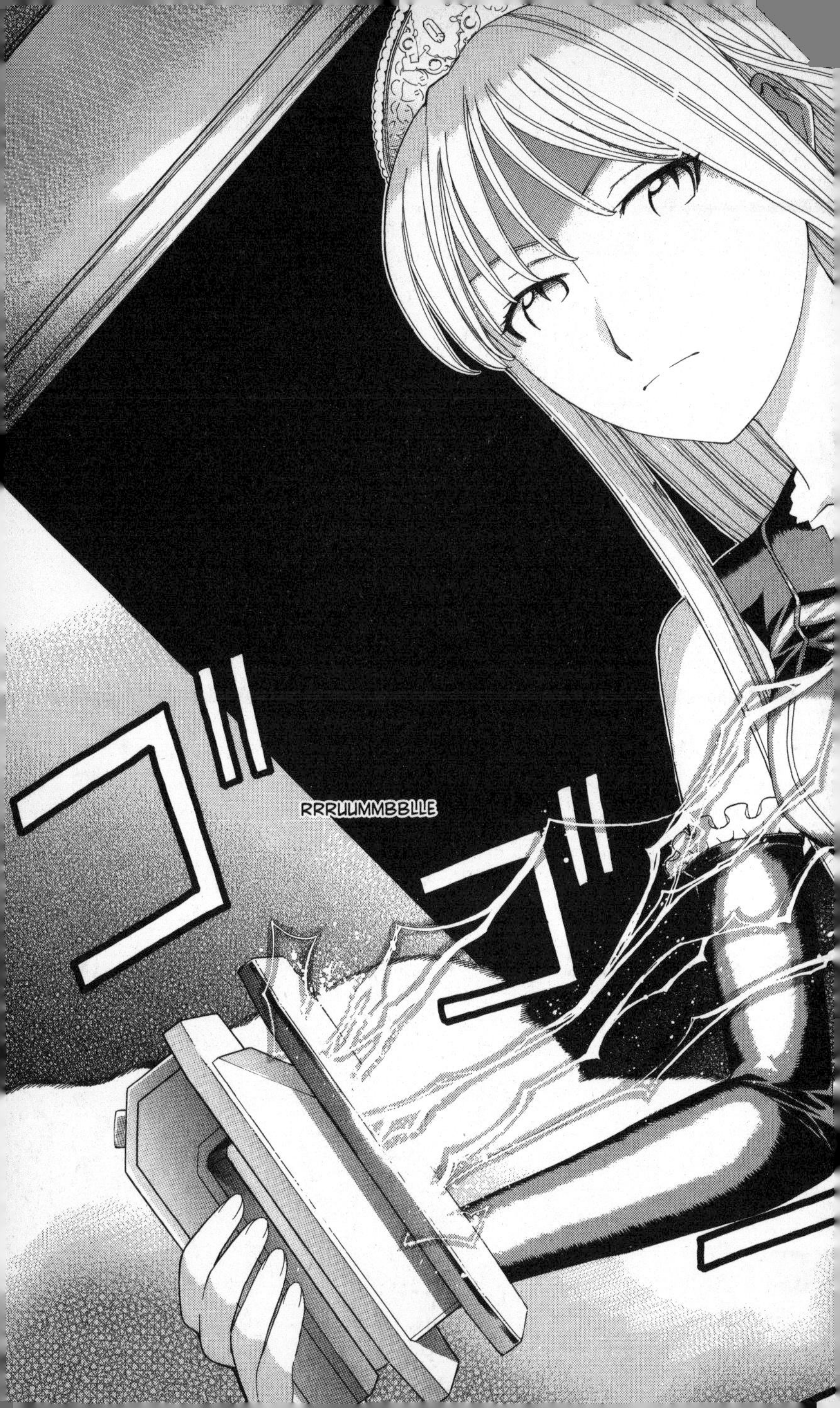

ゴゴゴ
RRRUUMMBBLLE

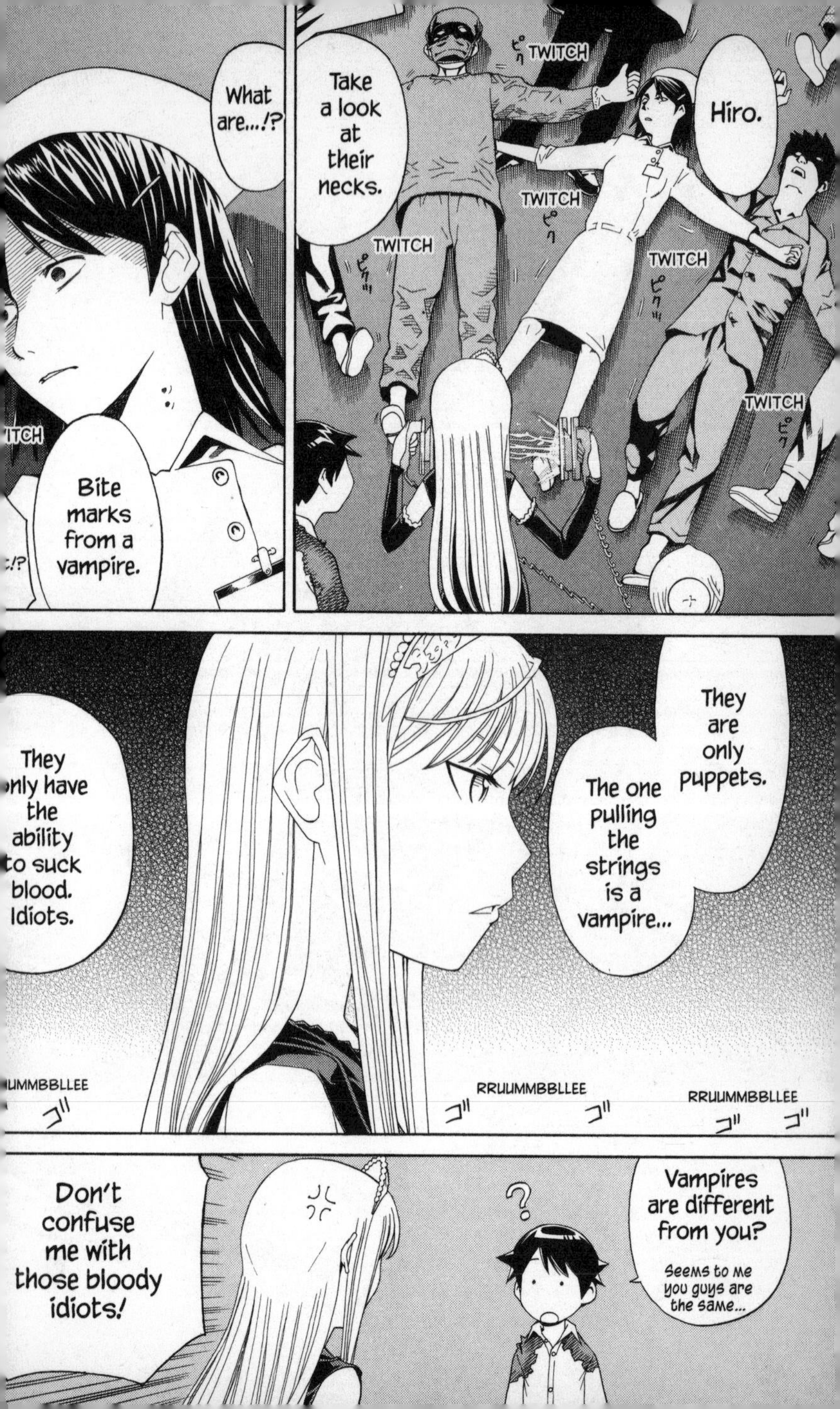
Hiro.
TWITCH
Take a look at their necks.
TWITCH
TWITCH
TWITCH
TWITCH
What are...!?
Bite marks from a vampire.
They are only puppets.
The one pulling the strings is a vampire...
They nly have the ability to suck blood. Idiots.
RRUUMMBBLLEE
RRUUMMBBLLEE
Vampires are different from you?
Seems to me you guys are the same...
Don't confuse me with those bloody idiots!

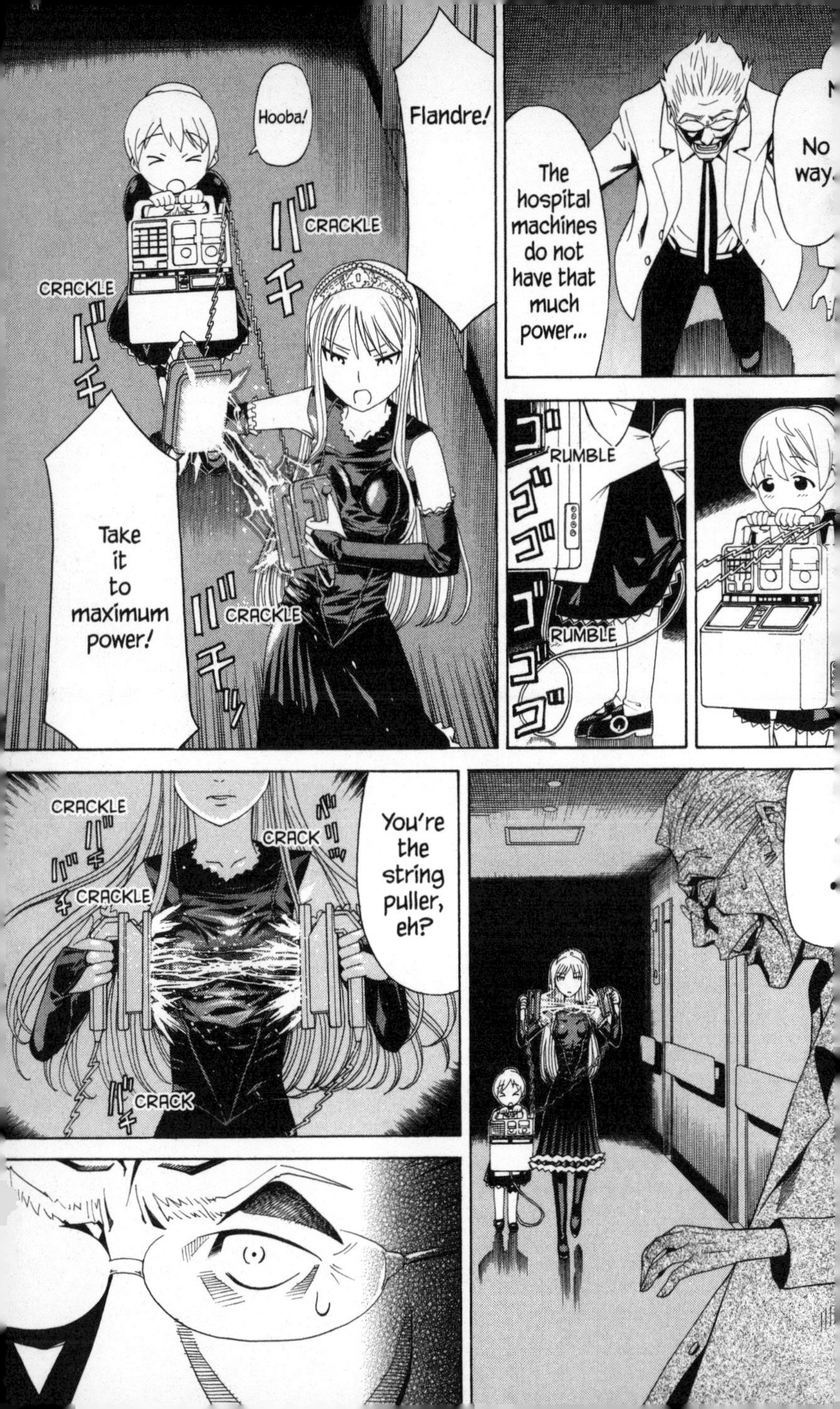
No way.
The hospital machines do not have that much power...
RUMBLE
RUMBLE
Flandre!
Hooba!
CRACKLE
CRACKLE
CRACKLE
Take it to maximum power!
CRACKLE
CRACK
You're the string puller, eh?
CRACKLE
CRACK

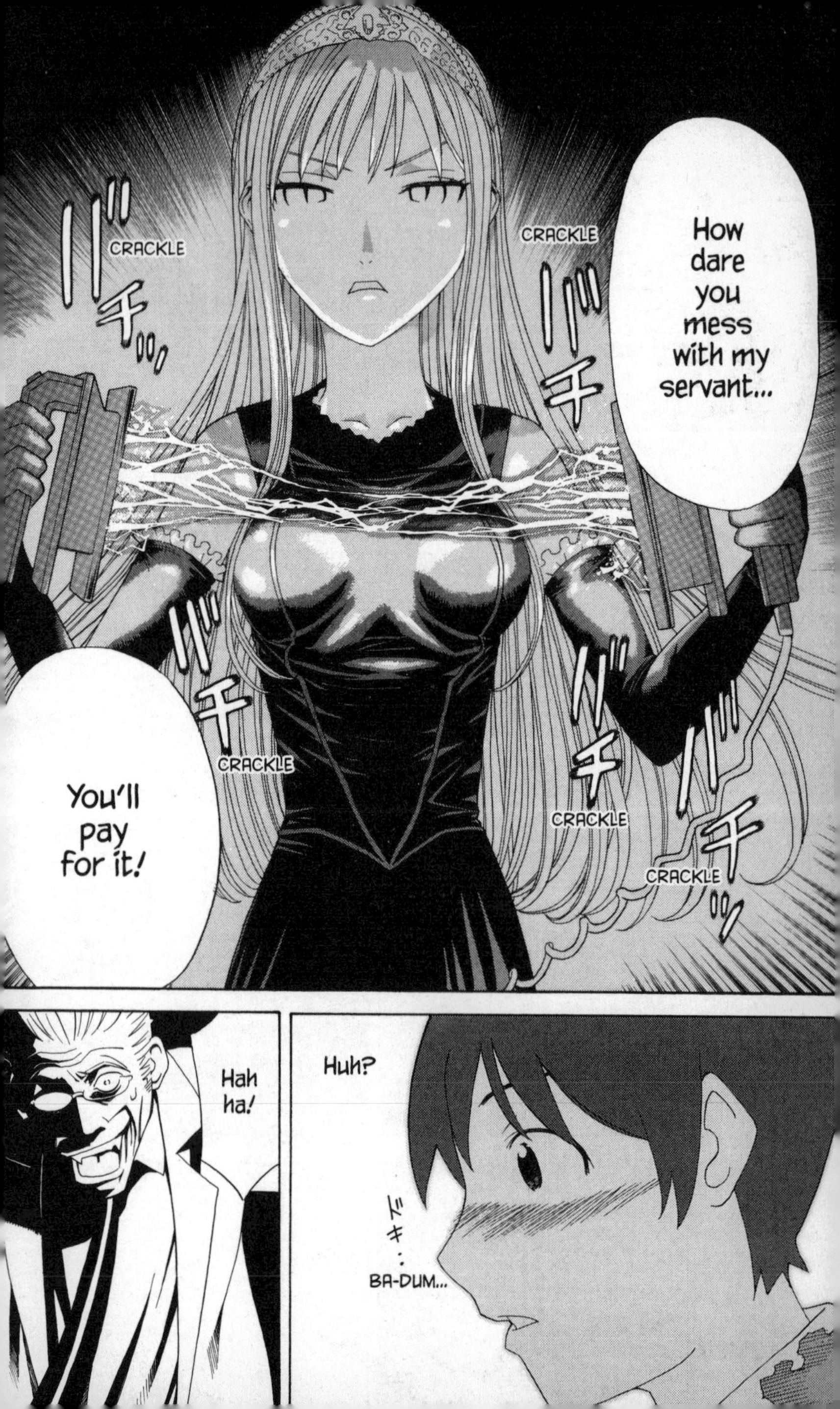
How dare you mess with my servant...
CRACKLE
CRACKLE
CRACKLE
CRACKLE
CRACKLE
You'll pay for it!
Huh?
BA-DUM...
Hah ha!

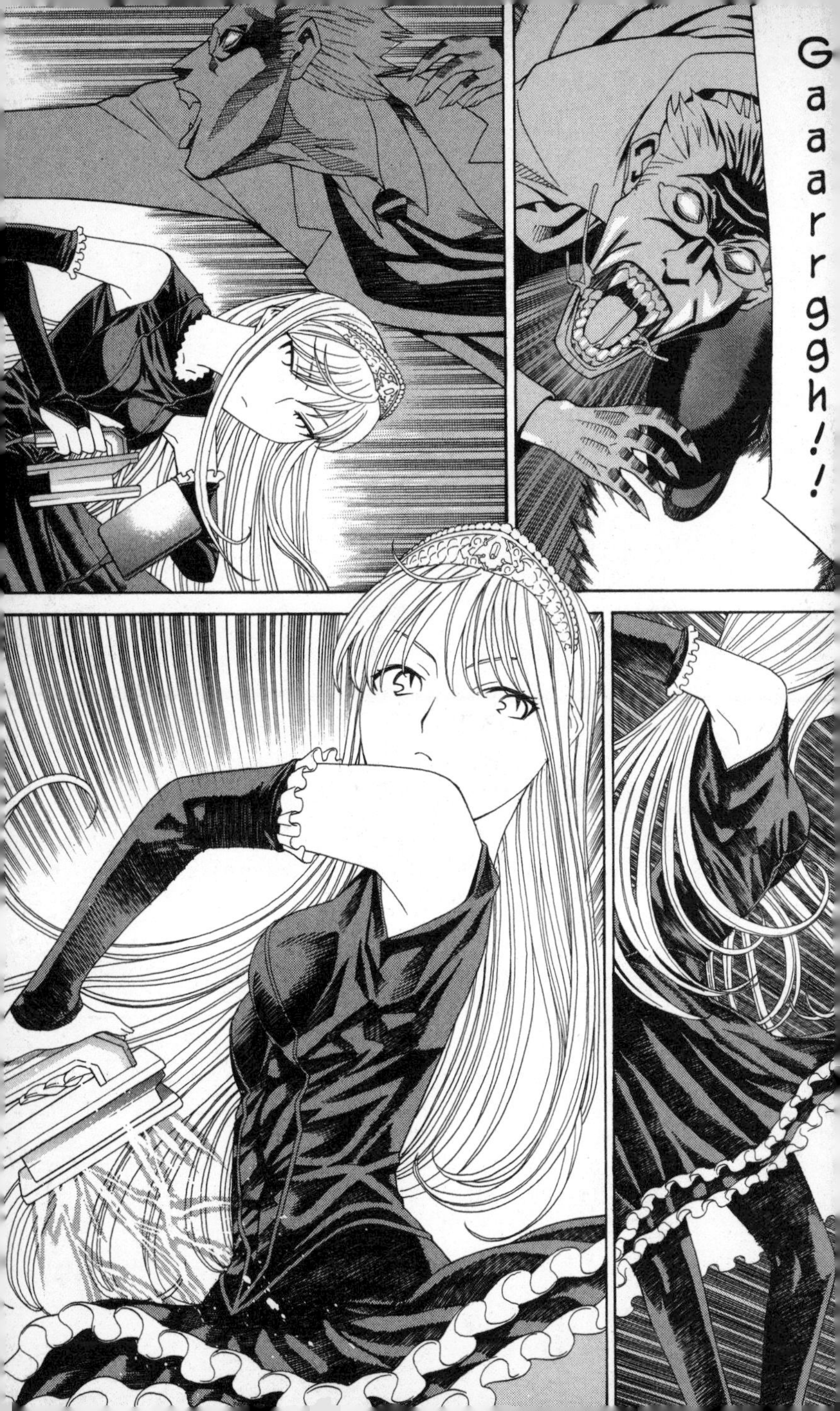
Gaaarrggh!!

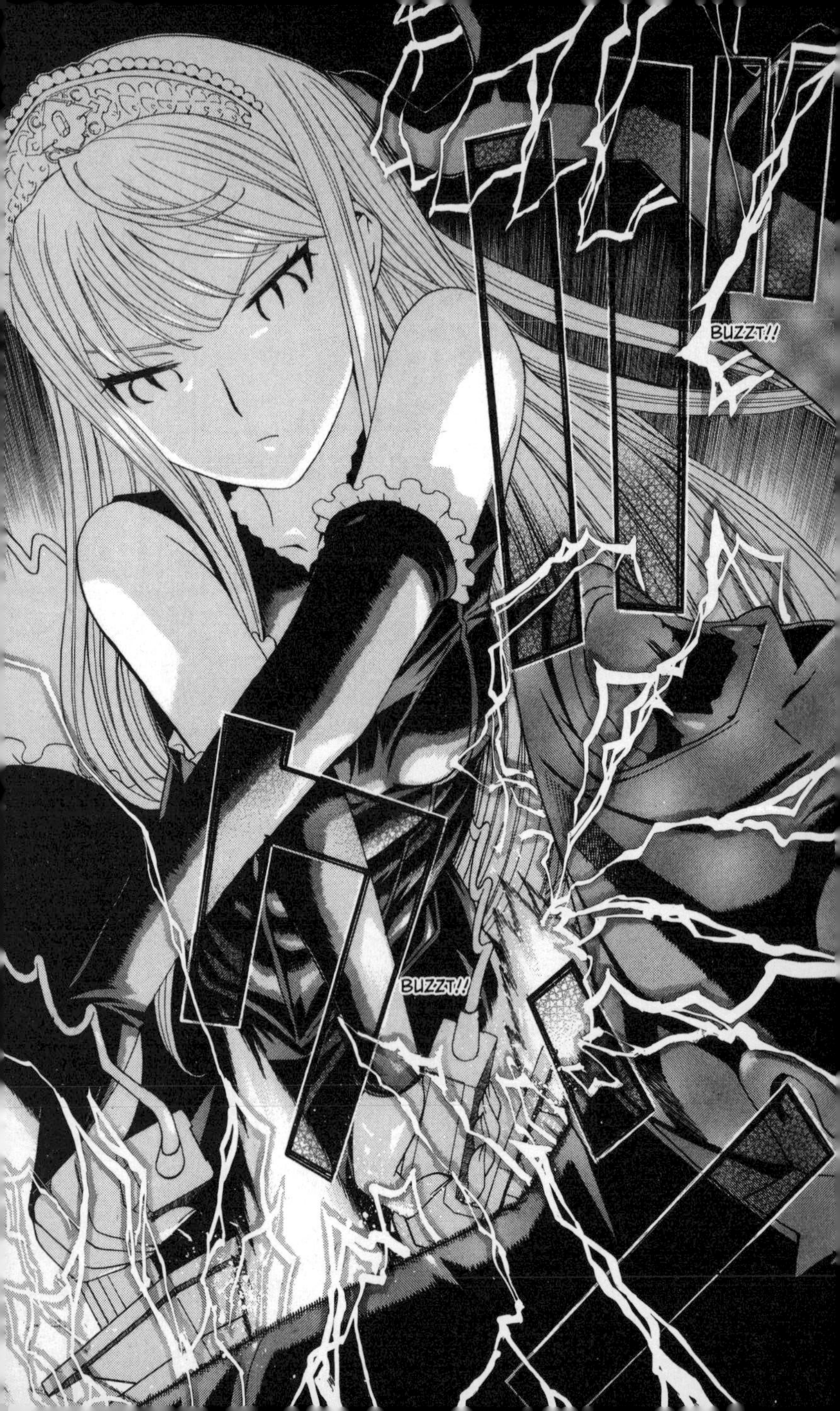
BUZZT!!
BUZZT!!

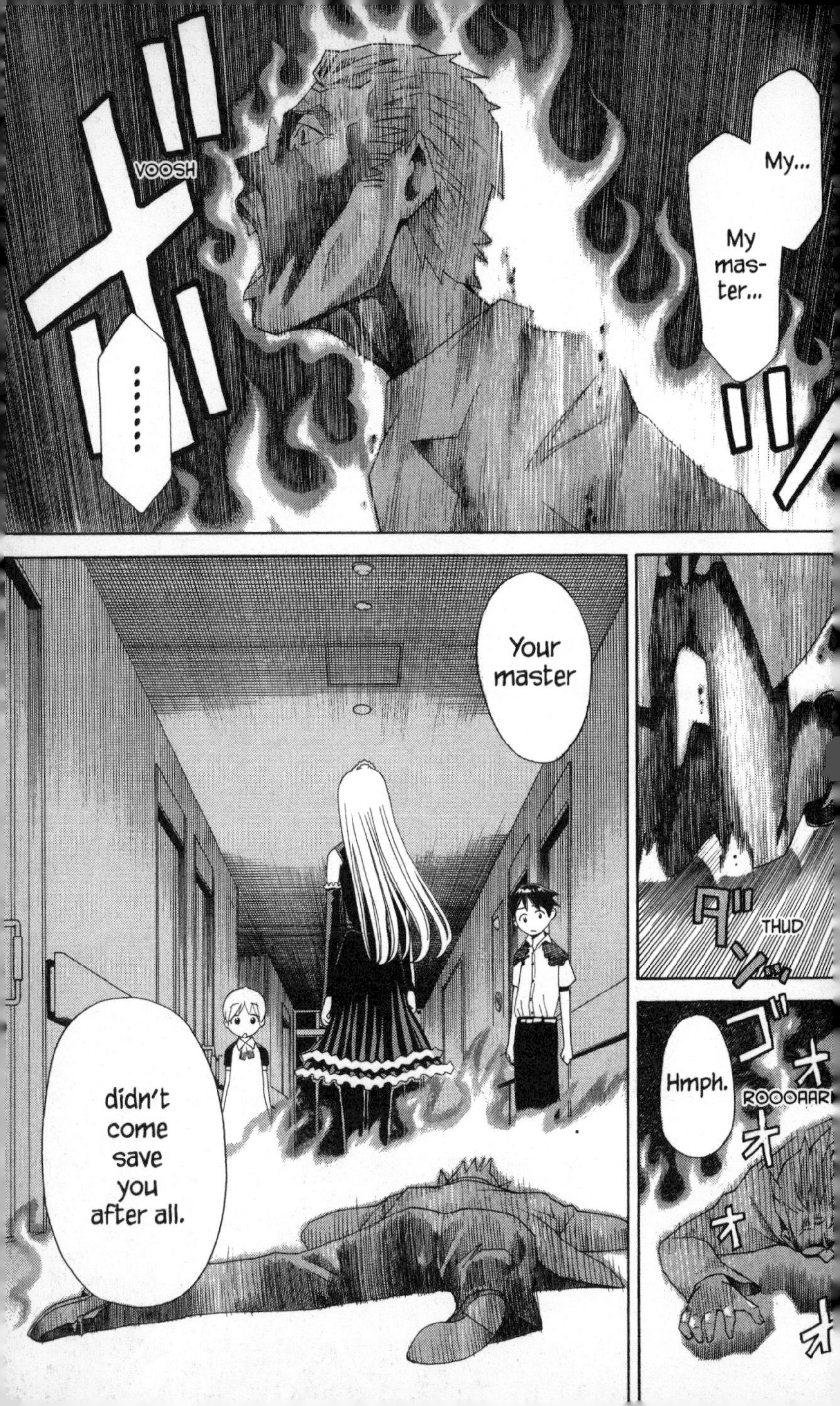
My...
My mas-ter...
VOOSH
......
THUD
Hmph.
ROOOAAR
Your master
didn't come save you after all.

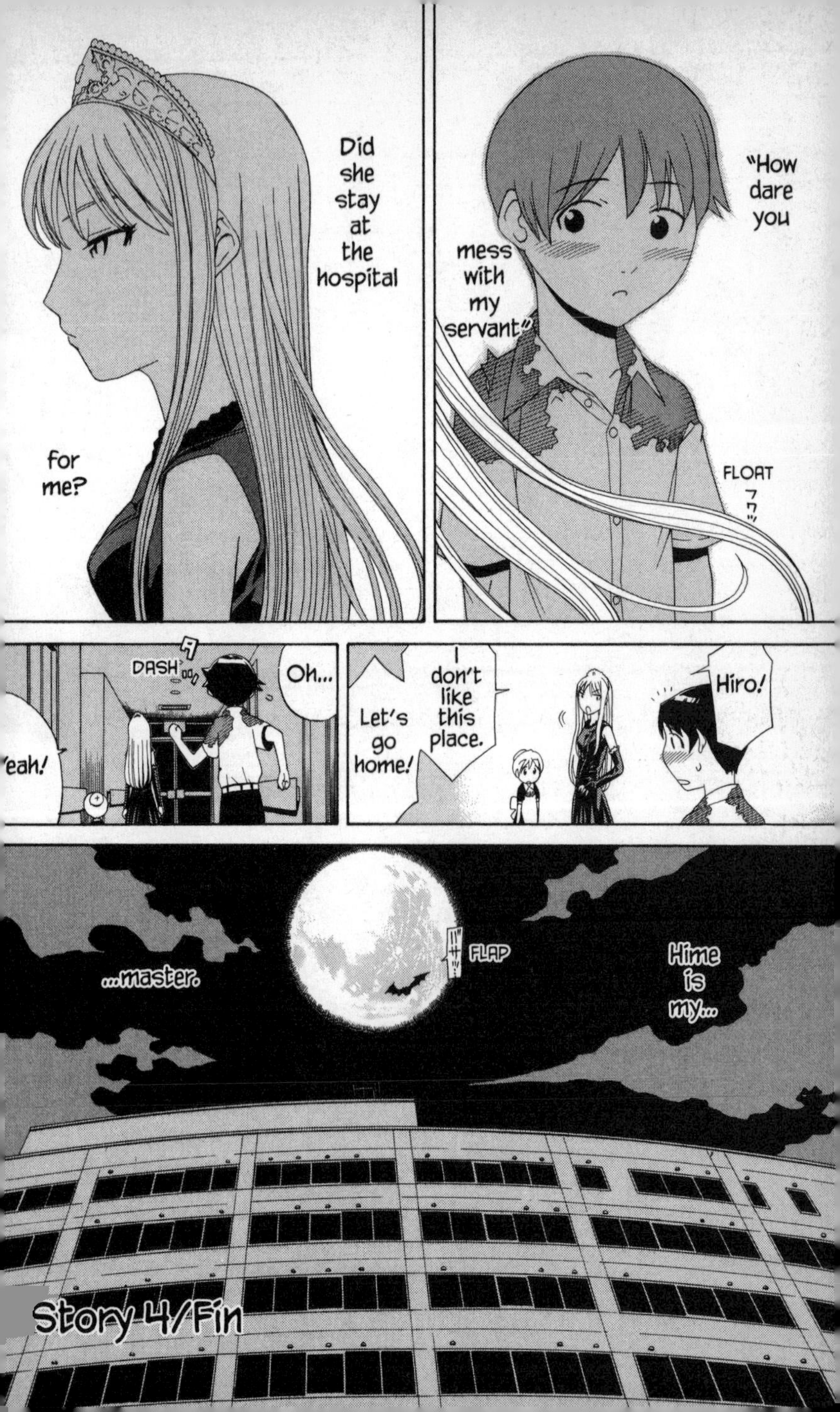
"How dare you
mess with my servant"
FLOAT
Did she stay at the hospital
for me?
Hiro!
I don't like this place.
Let's go home!
Oh...
DASH
eah!
Hime is my...
FLAP
...master.
Story 4/Fin

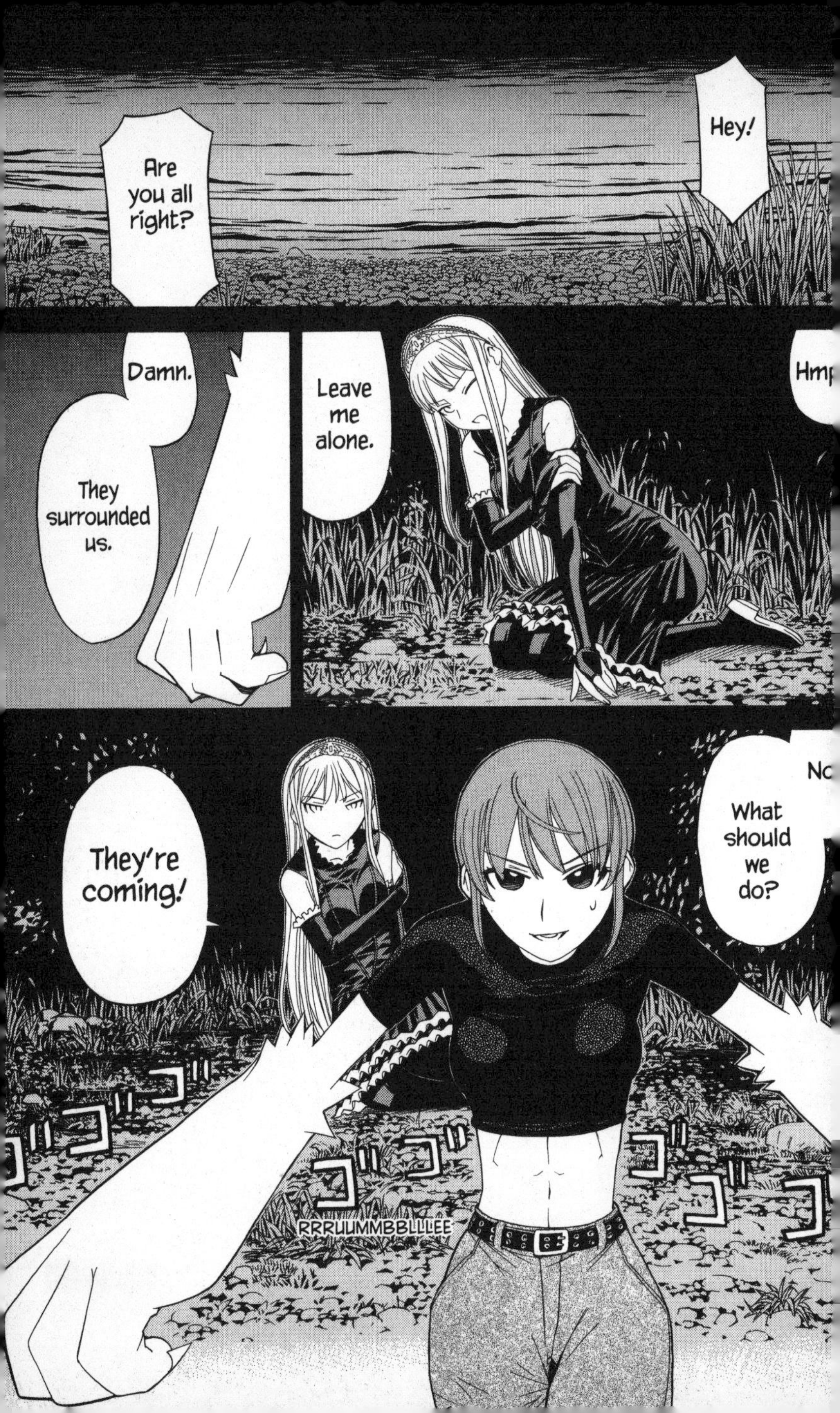
Hey!
Are you all right?
Hmp
Leave me alone.
Damn.
They surrounded us.
No
What should we do?
They're coming!
RRRUUMMBBLLLEE

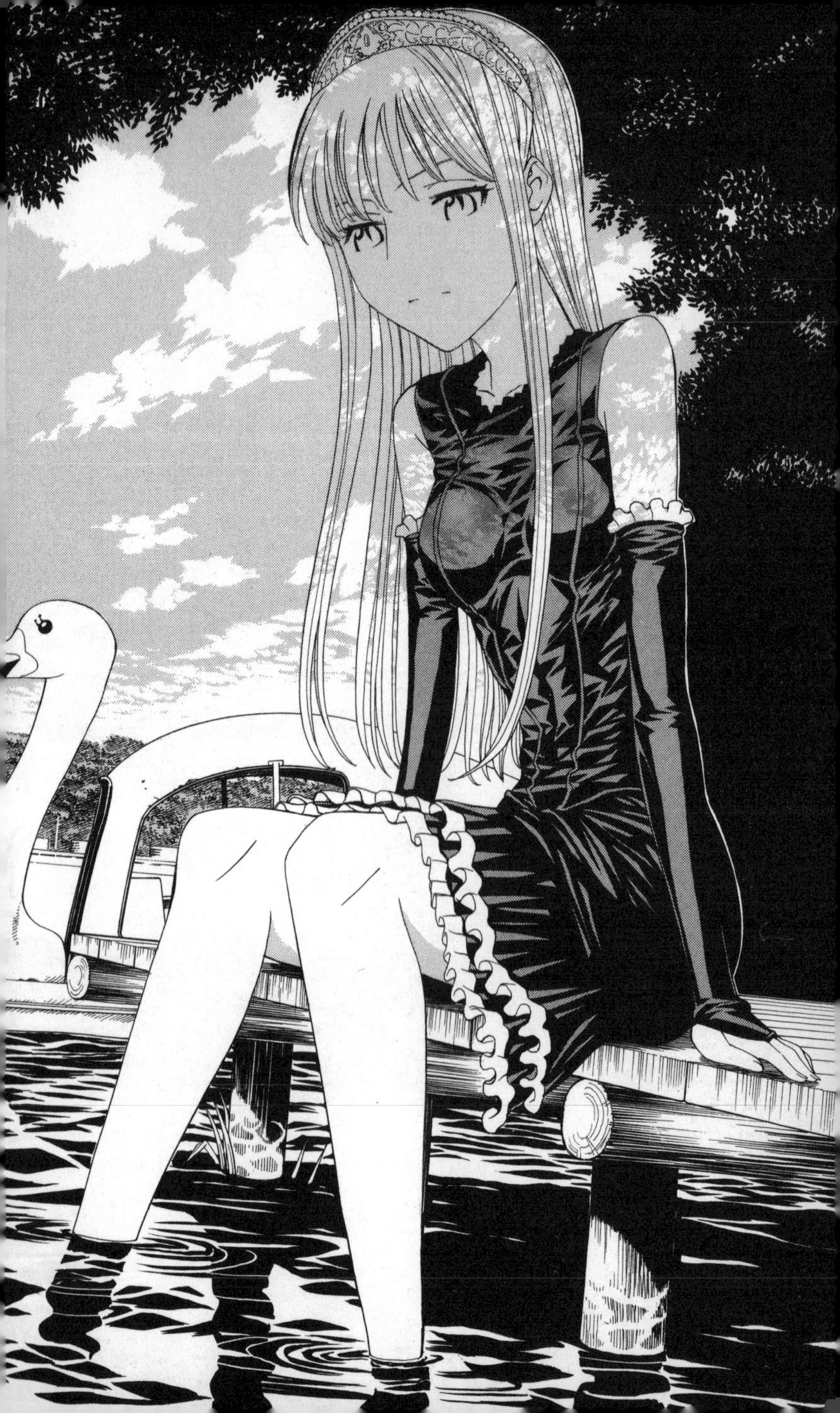

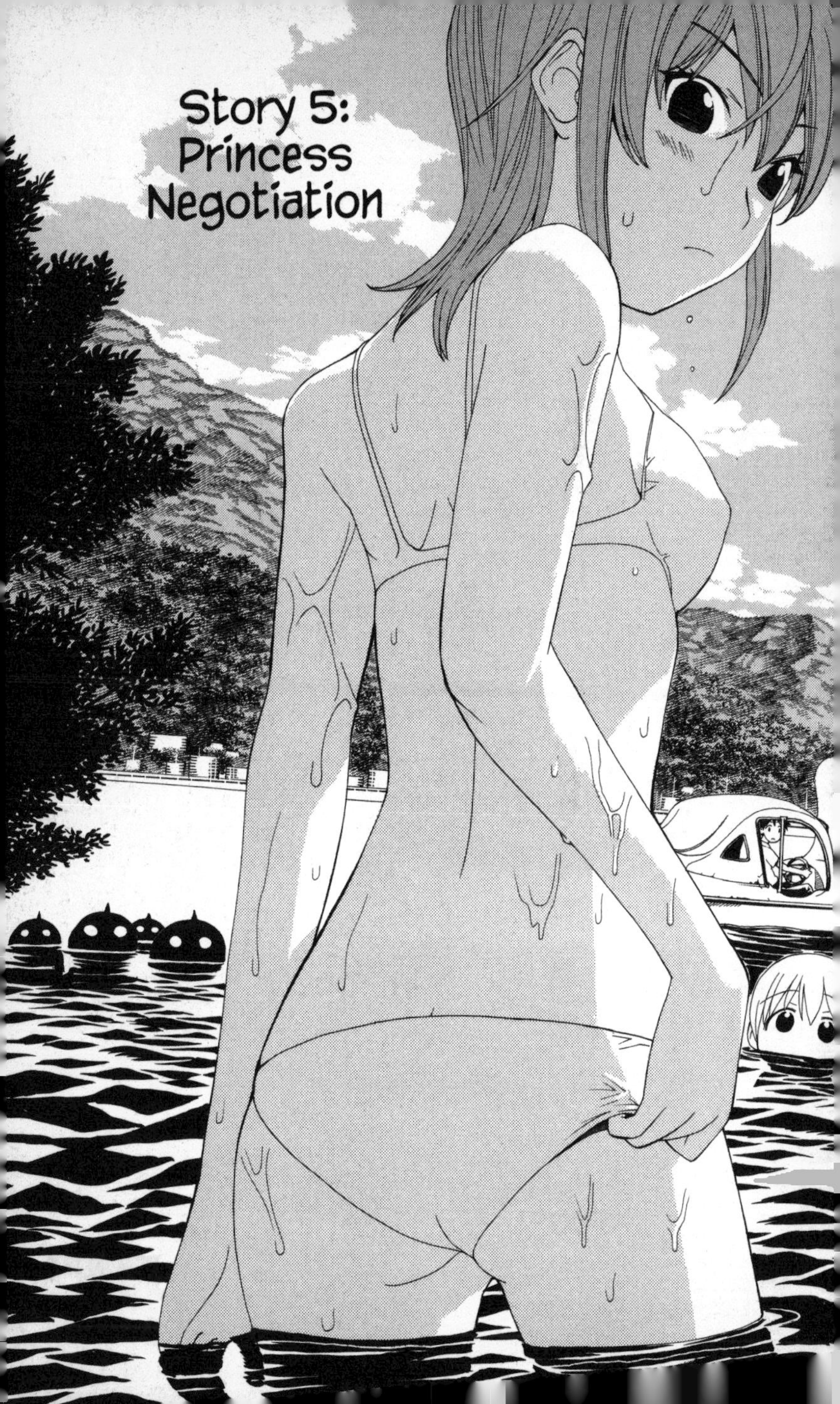
Story 5:
Princess
Negotiation

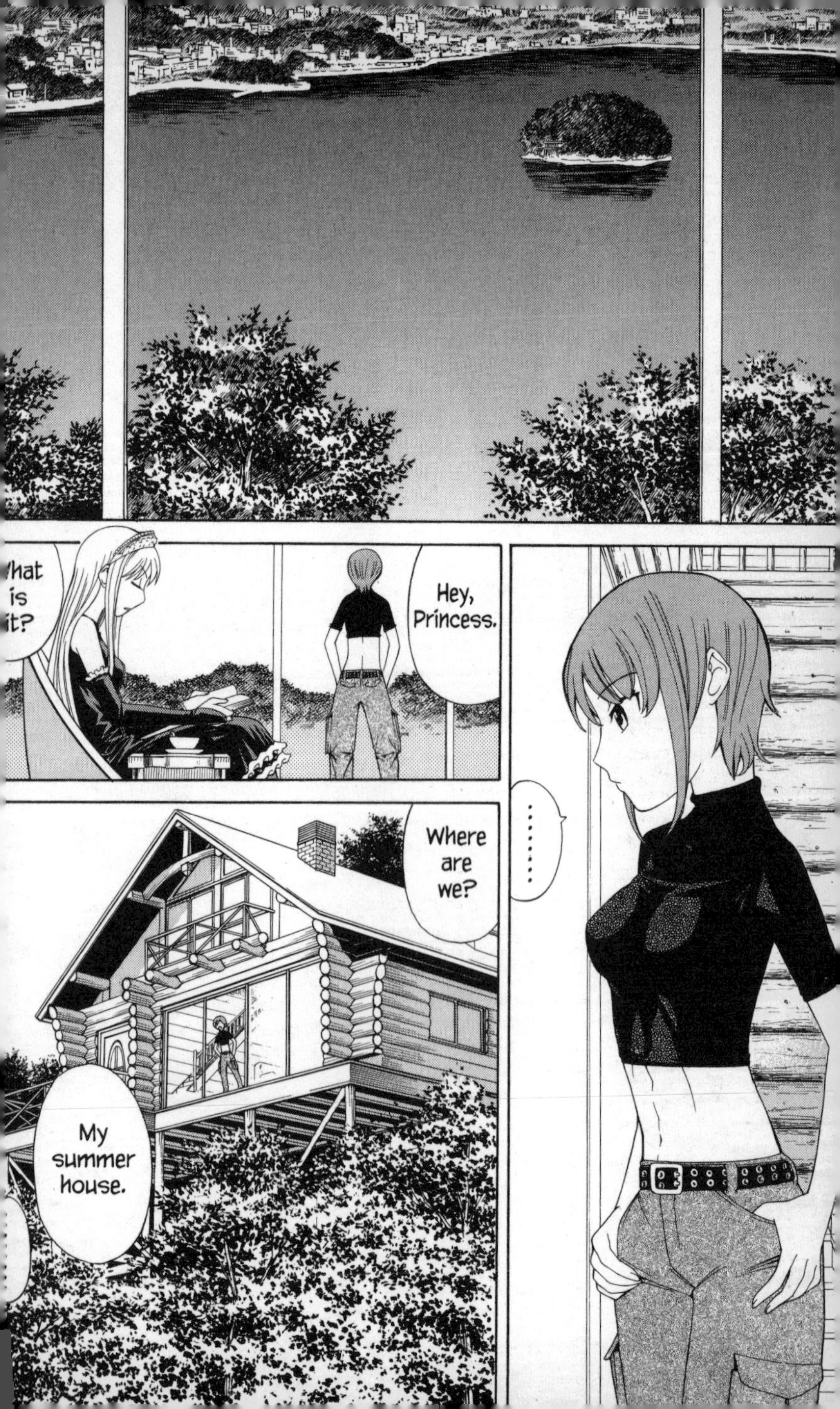
......
Hey, Princess.
What is it?
Where are we?
My summer house.

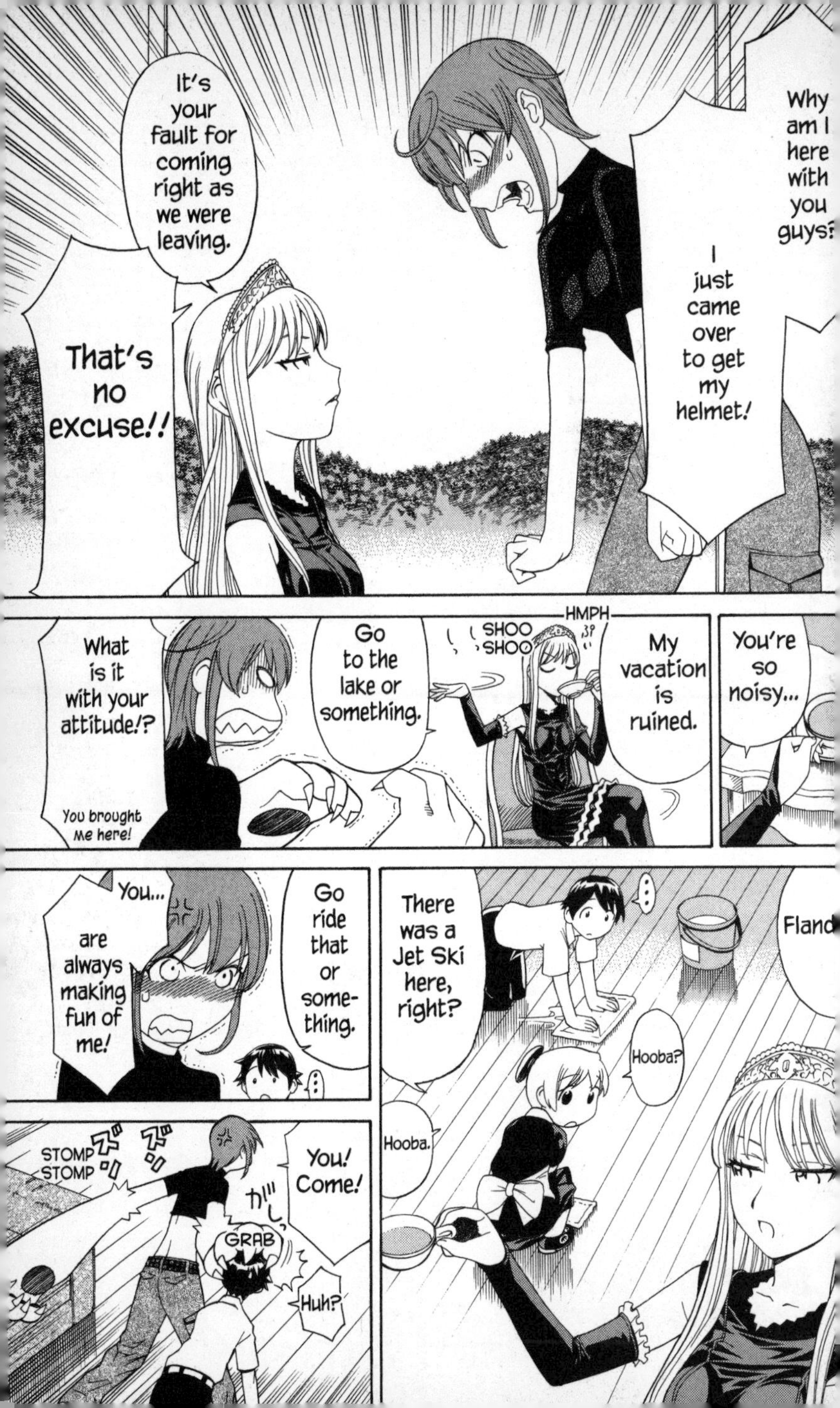

Why am I here with you guys?
I just came over to get my helmet!
It's your fault for coming right as we were leaving.
That's no excuse!!
You're so noisy...
My vacation is ruined.
HMPH
SHOO SHOO
Go to the lake or something.
What is it with your attitude!?
You brought me here!
Fland
There was a Jet Ski here, right?
...
Hooba?
Hooba.
Go ride that or something.
You...
are always making fun of me!
...
You! Come!
STOMP STOMP
GRAB
Huh?

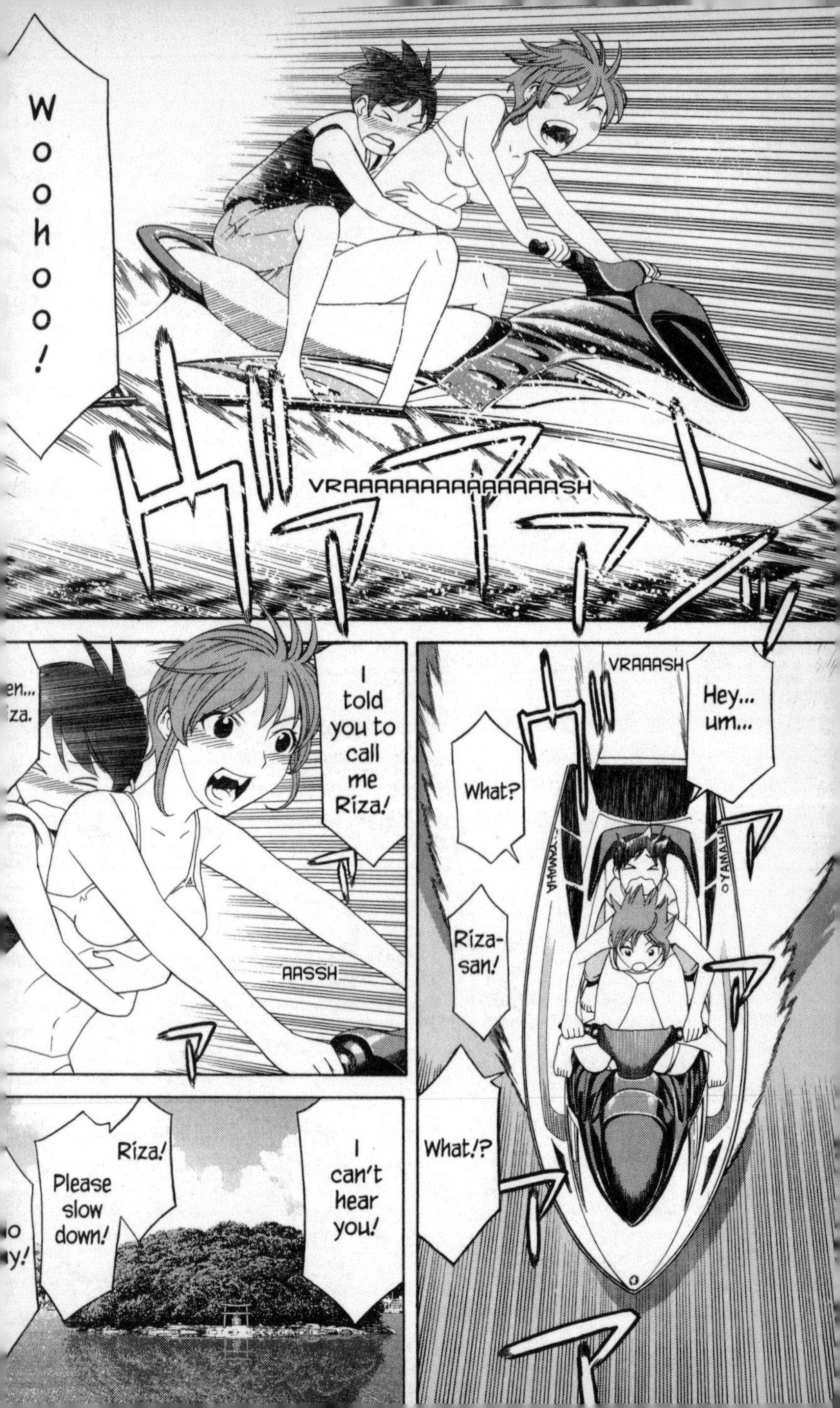
Woohoo!
VRAAAAAAAAAAAAAASH
VRAAASH
Hey... um...
What?
Riza-san!
What!?
I told you to call me Riza!
AASSH
I can't hear you!
Riza! Please slow down!

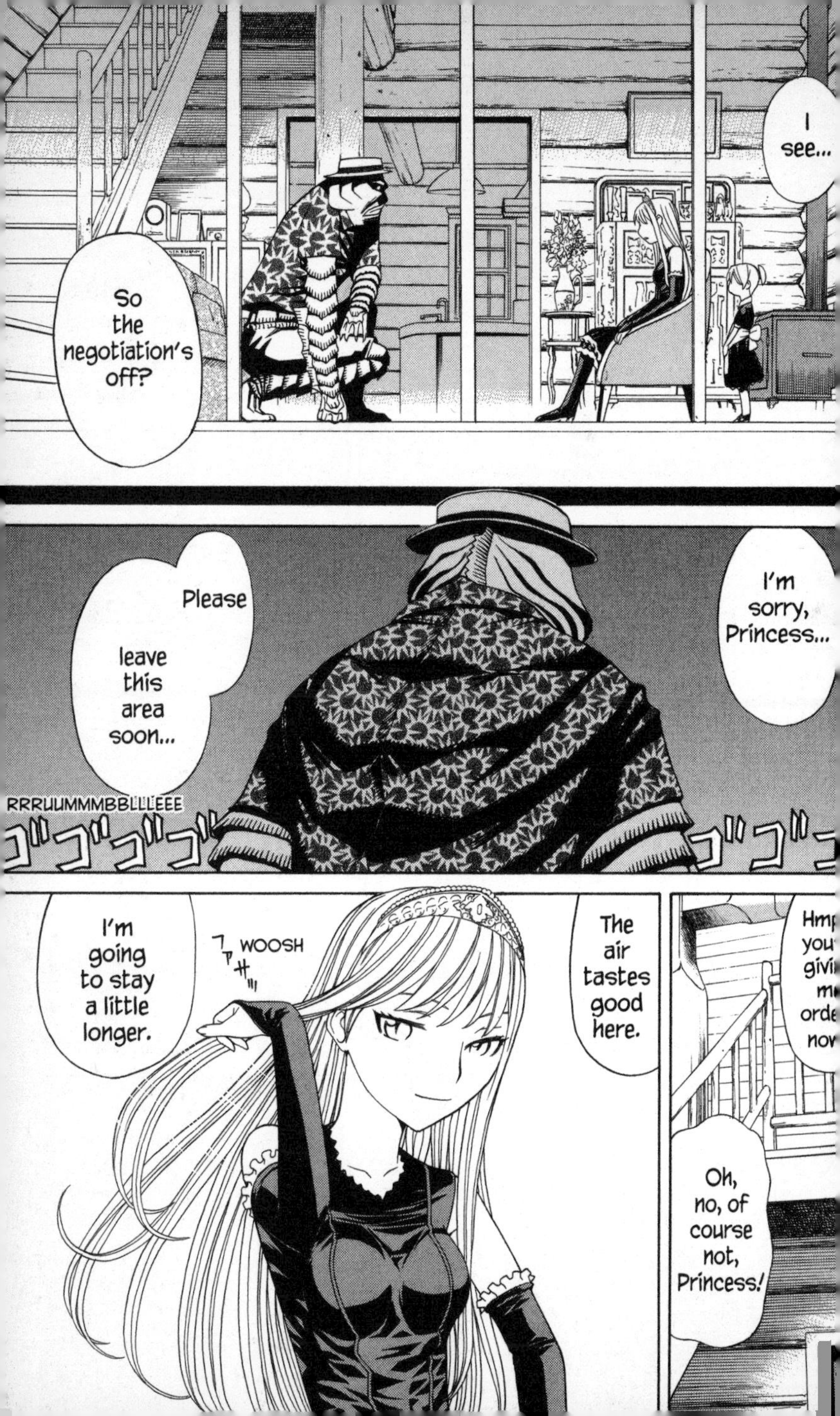
I see...
So the negotiation's off?
I'm sorry, Princess...
Please leave this area soon...
RRRUUMMMBBLLLEEE
ゴゴゴゴ
ゴゴゴ
Hmp you givi m orde now
Oh, no, of course not, Princess!
The air tastes good here.
WOOSH
I'm going to stay a little longer.

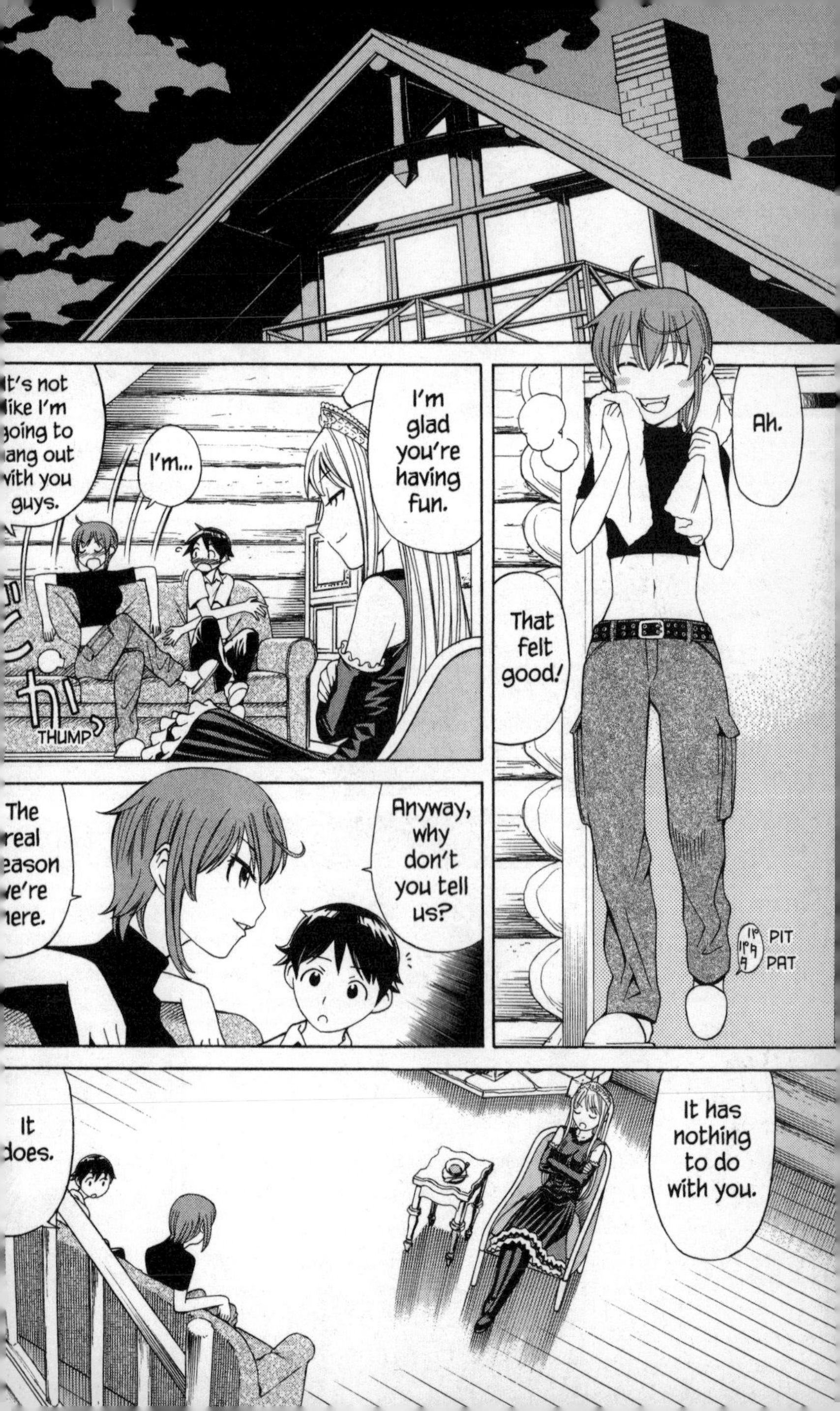

Ah.
That felt good!
PIT PAT
I'm glad you're having fun.
I'm...
t's not ike I'm going to ang out vith you guys.
THUMP
Anyway, why don't you tell us?
The real eason ve're iere.
It has nothing to do with you.
It does.

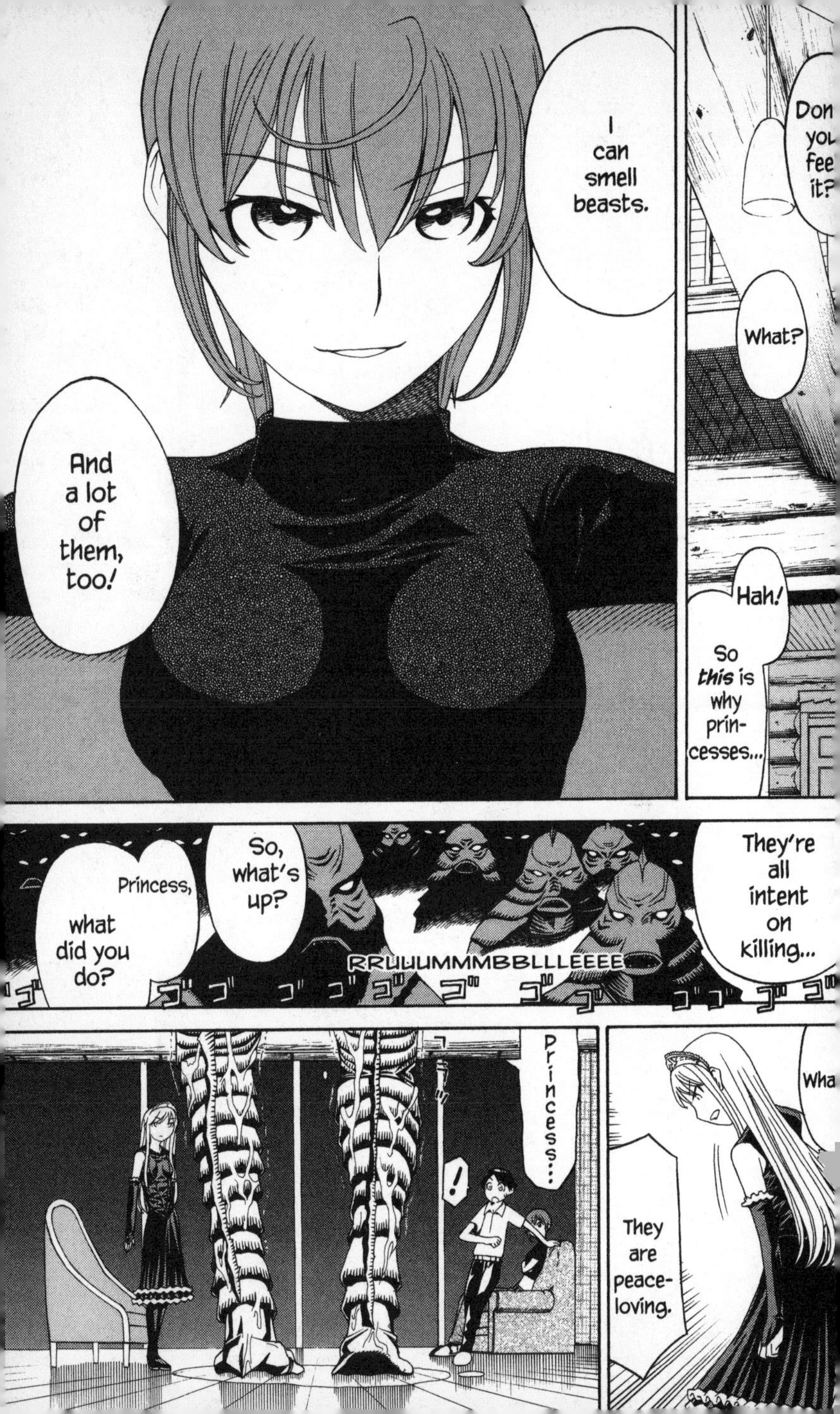

Don you fee it?
What?
Hah!
So this is why prin-cesses...
I can smell beasts.
And a lot of them, too!
They're all intent on killing...
RRUUUMMMBBLLLEEEE
So, what's up?
Princess, what did you do?
Wha
They are peace-loving.
Princess...
!

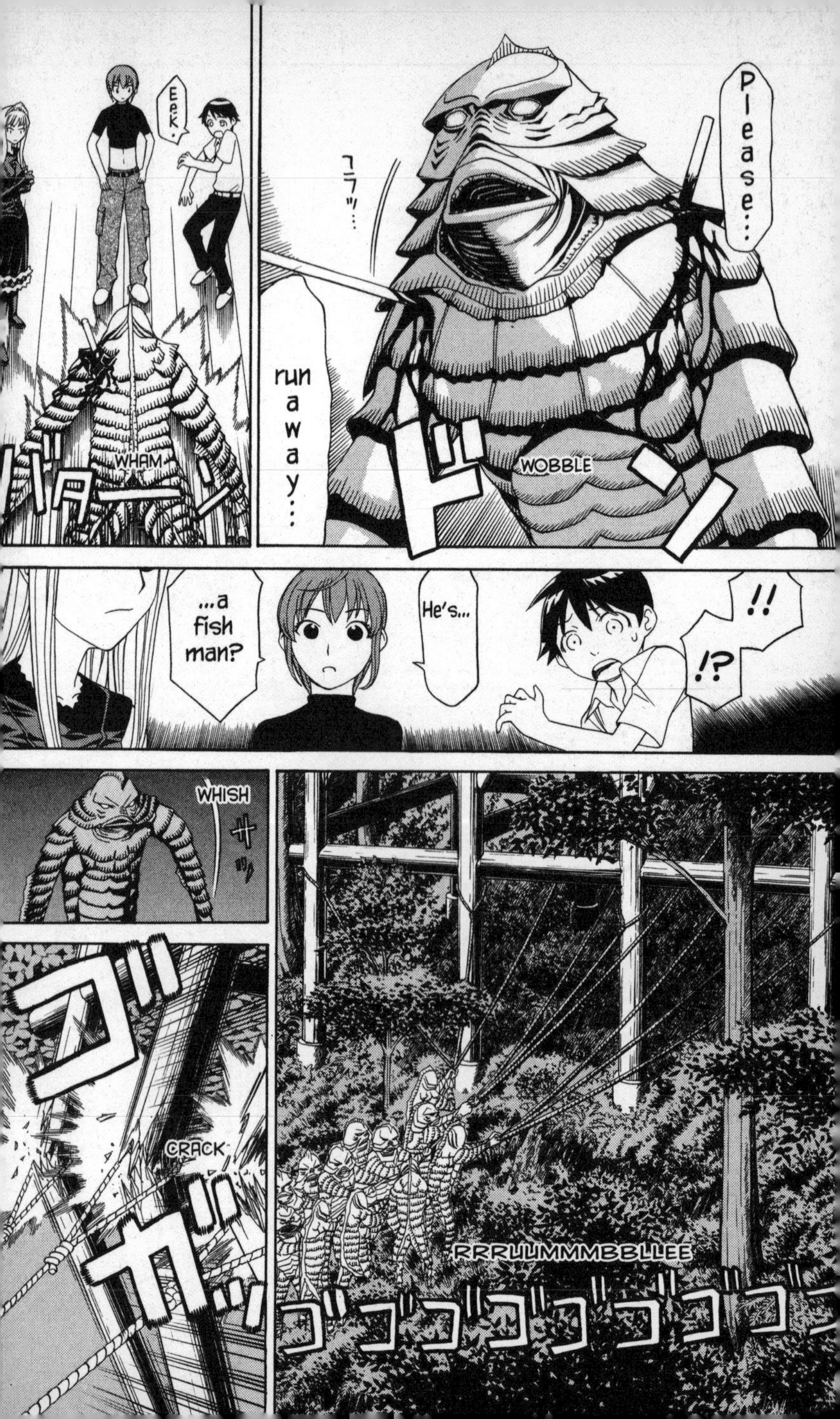
Please...
フラッ…
run away...
WOBBLE
Eek.
WHAM
!!
!?
He's...
...a fish man?
RRRUUMMMBBLLEE
WHISH
CRACK

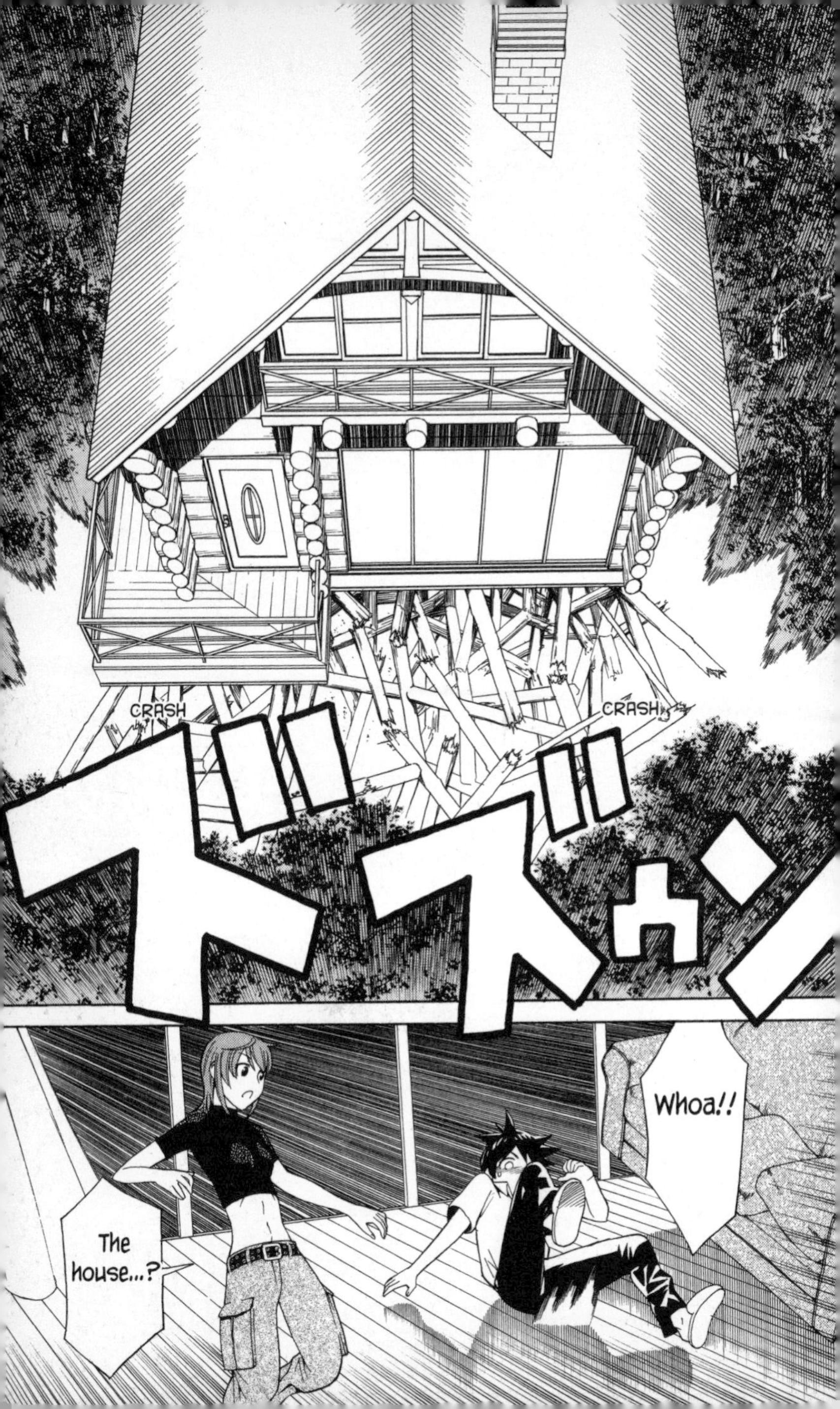
CRASH
CRASH
ズズゥン
Whoa!!
The house...?

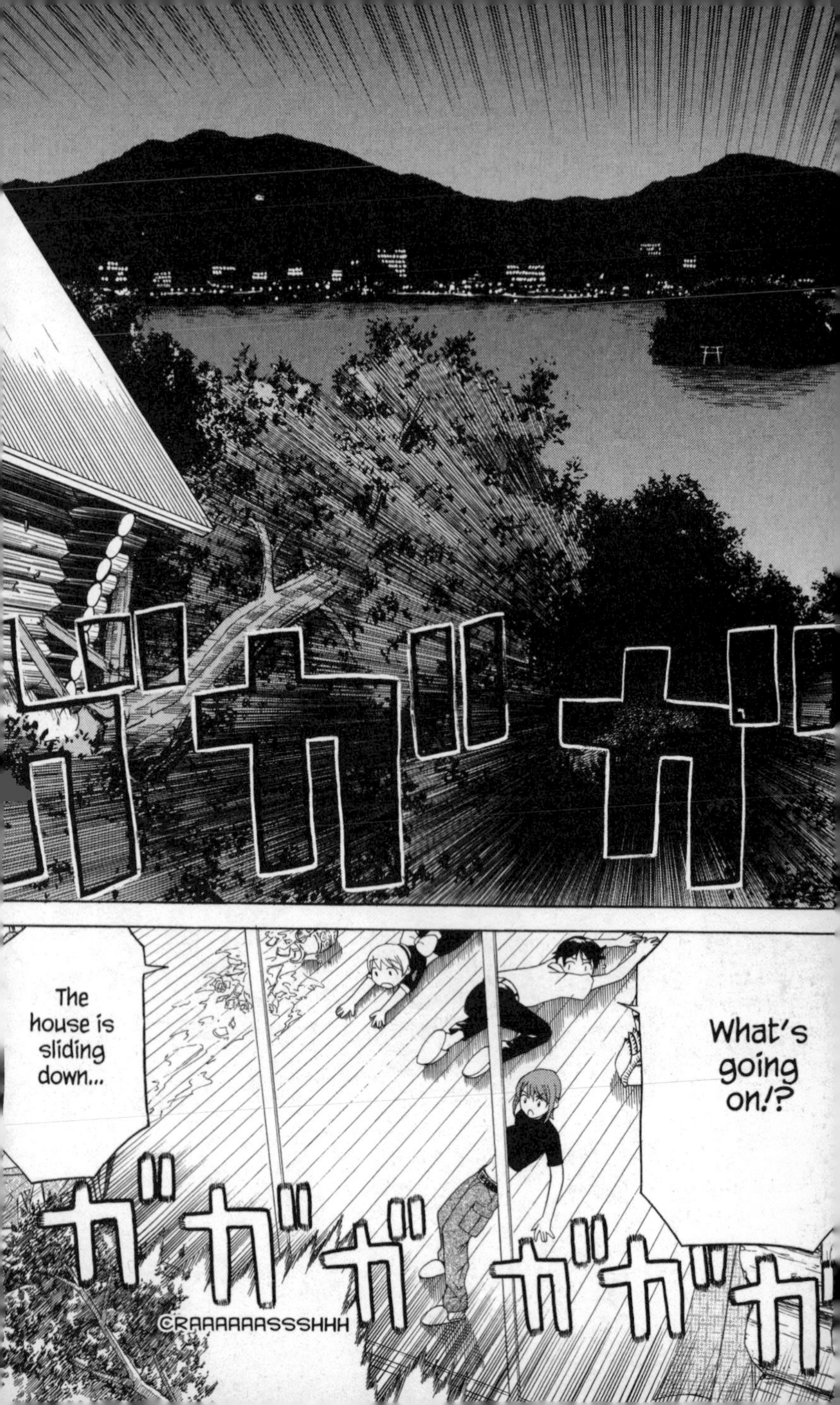
ガガガ
What's going on!?
The house is sliding down...
ガガガガガガ
CRAAAAAAASSSHHH

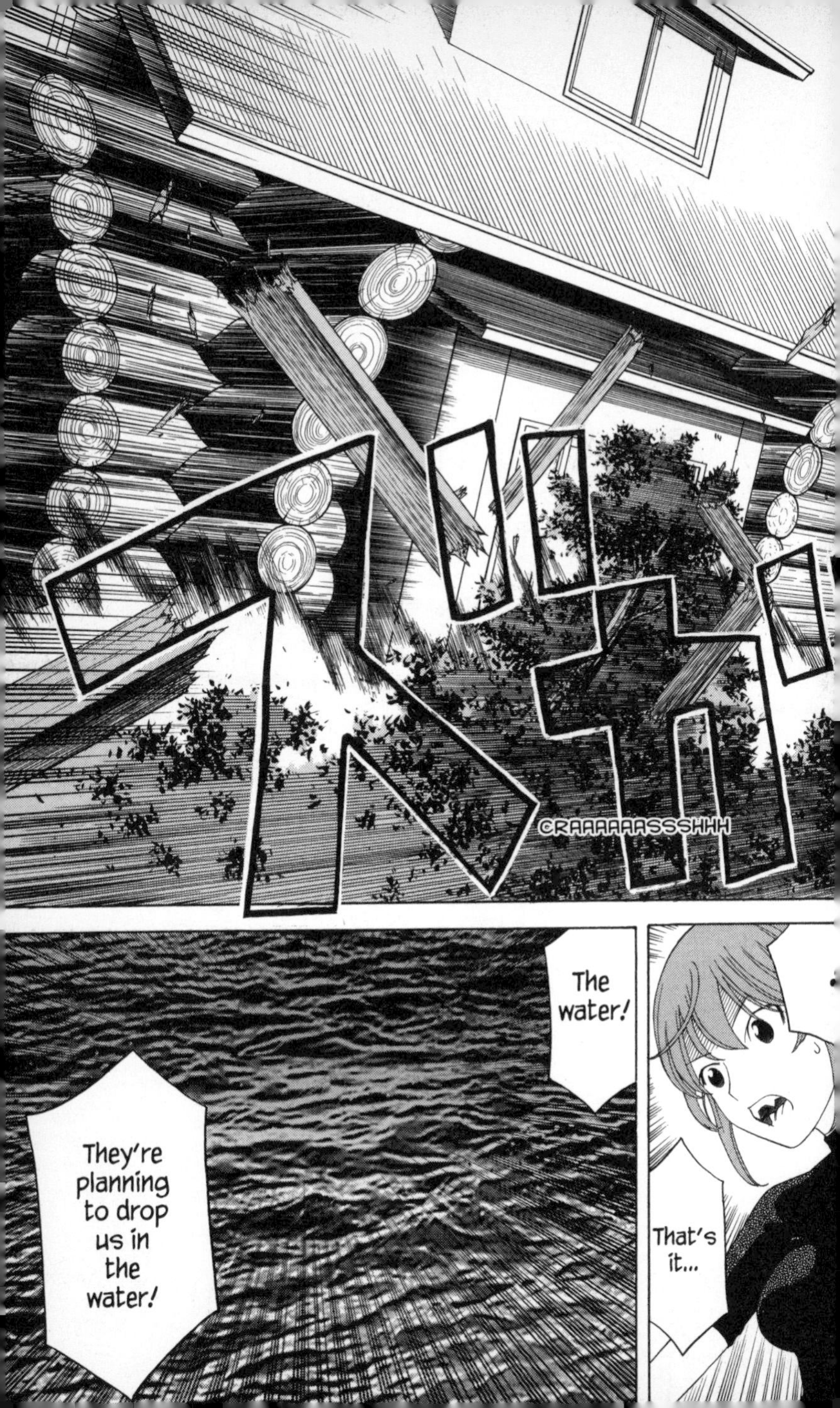
CRAAAAAASSSHHH
That's it...
The water!
They're planning to drop us in the water!

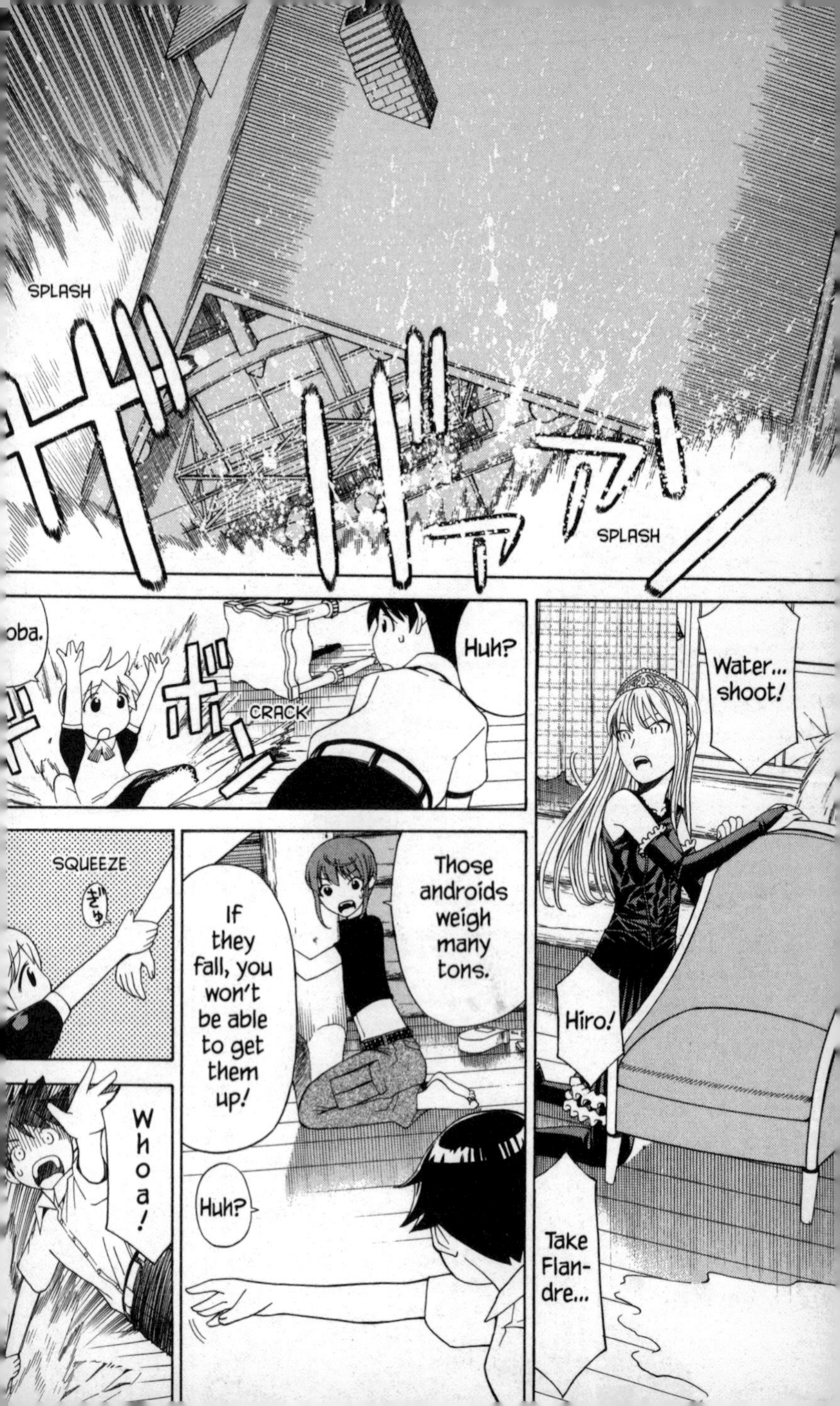
SPLASH
SPLASH
Water... shoot!
Hiro!
Take Flandre...
Huh?
CRACK
oba.
Those androids weigh many tons.
If they fall, you won't be able to get them up!
Huh?
SQUEEZE
ぎゅ
Whoa!

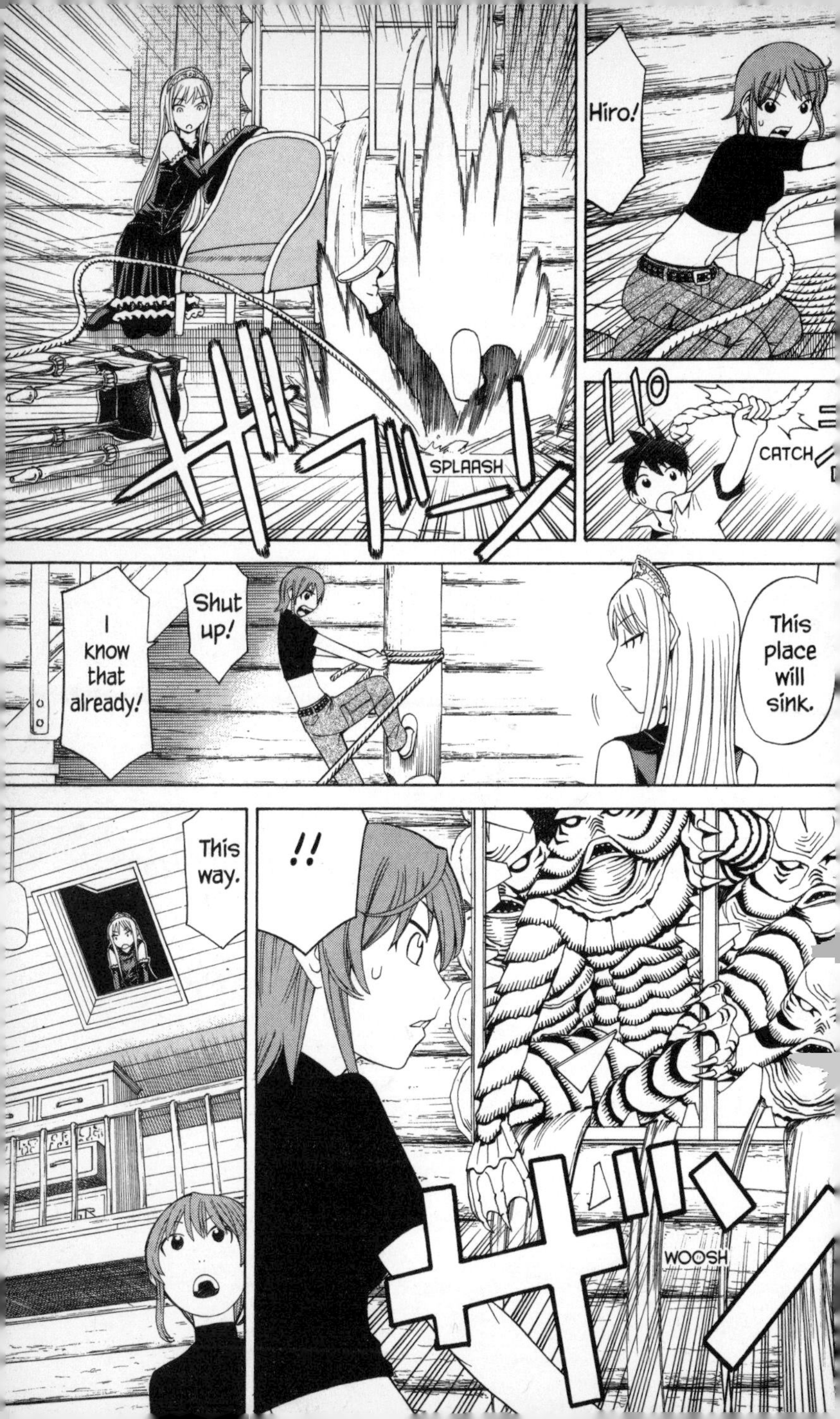
Hiro!
CATCH
SPLAASH
This place will sink.
Shut up!
I know that already!
WOOSH
!!
This way.

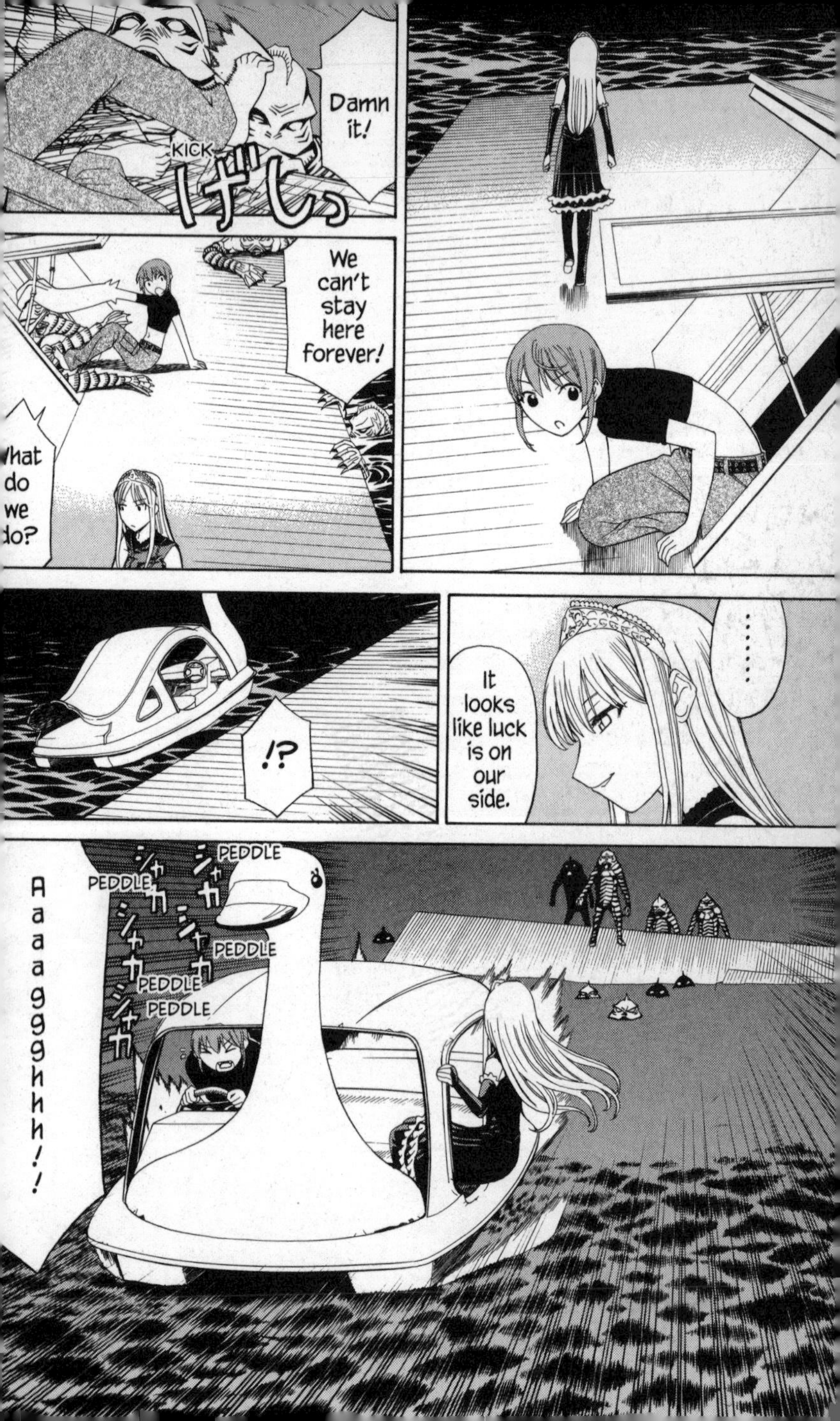
Damn it!
KICK
げしっ
We can't stay here forever!
What do we do?
......
It looks like luck is on our side.
!?
PEDDLE
シャカシャカ
PEDDLE
PEDDLE
シャカシャカシャカ
PEDDLE
PEDDLE
Aaaaggghhh!!

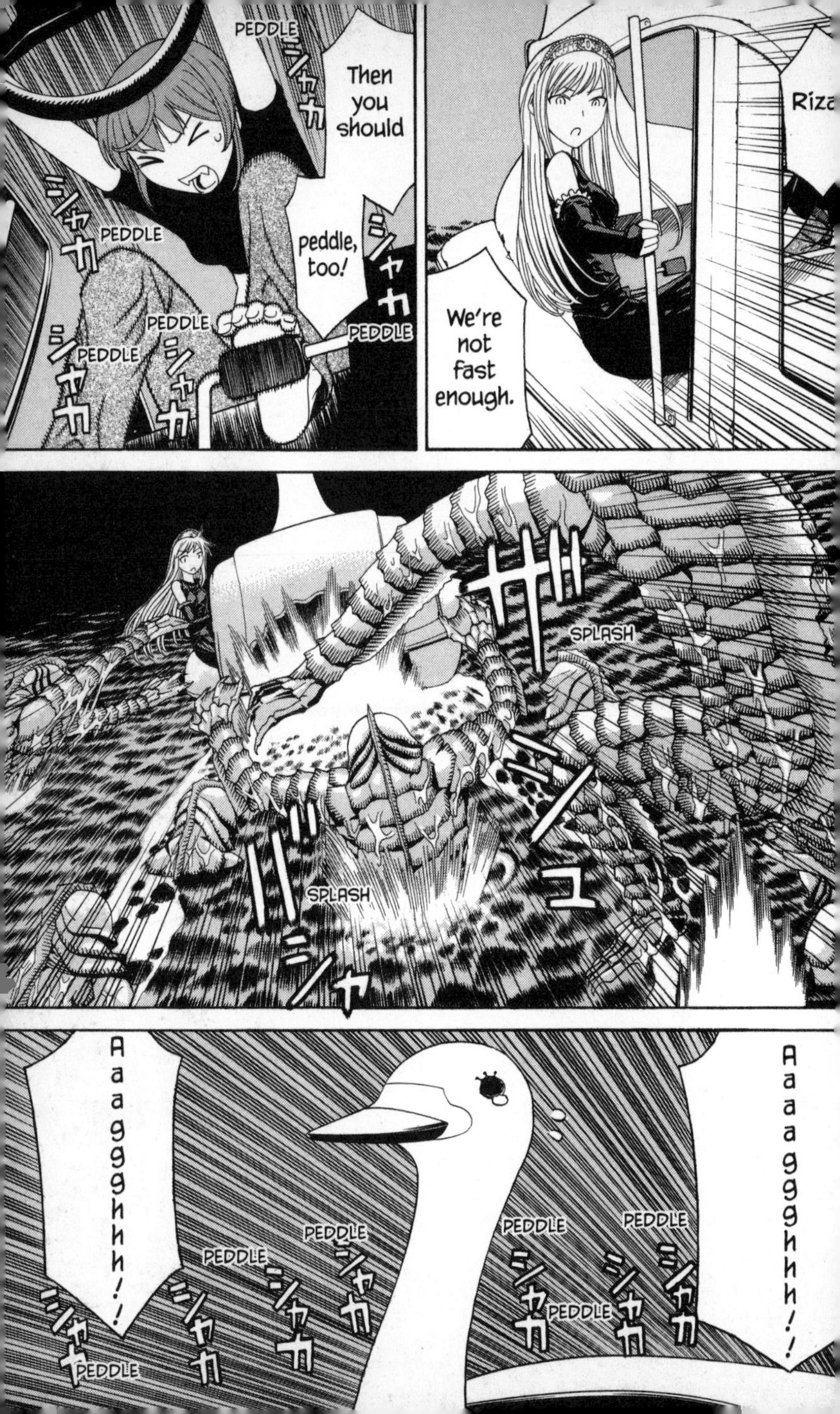
Riza
We're not fast enough.
PEDDLE
Then you should peddle, too!
PEDDLE
PEDDLE
PEDDLE
PEDDLE
SPLASH
SPLASH
Aaaaggghhh!!
PEDDLE
PEDDLE
PEDDLE
Aaaggghhh!!
PEDDLE
PEDDLE
PEDDLE

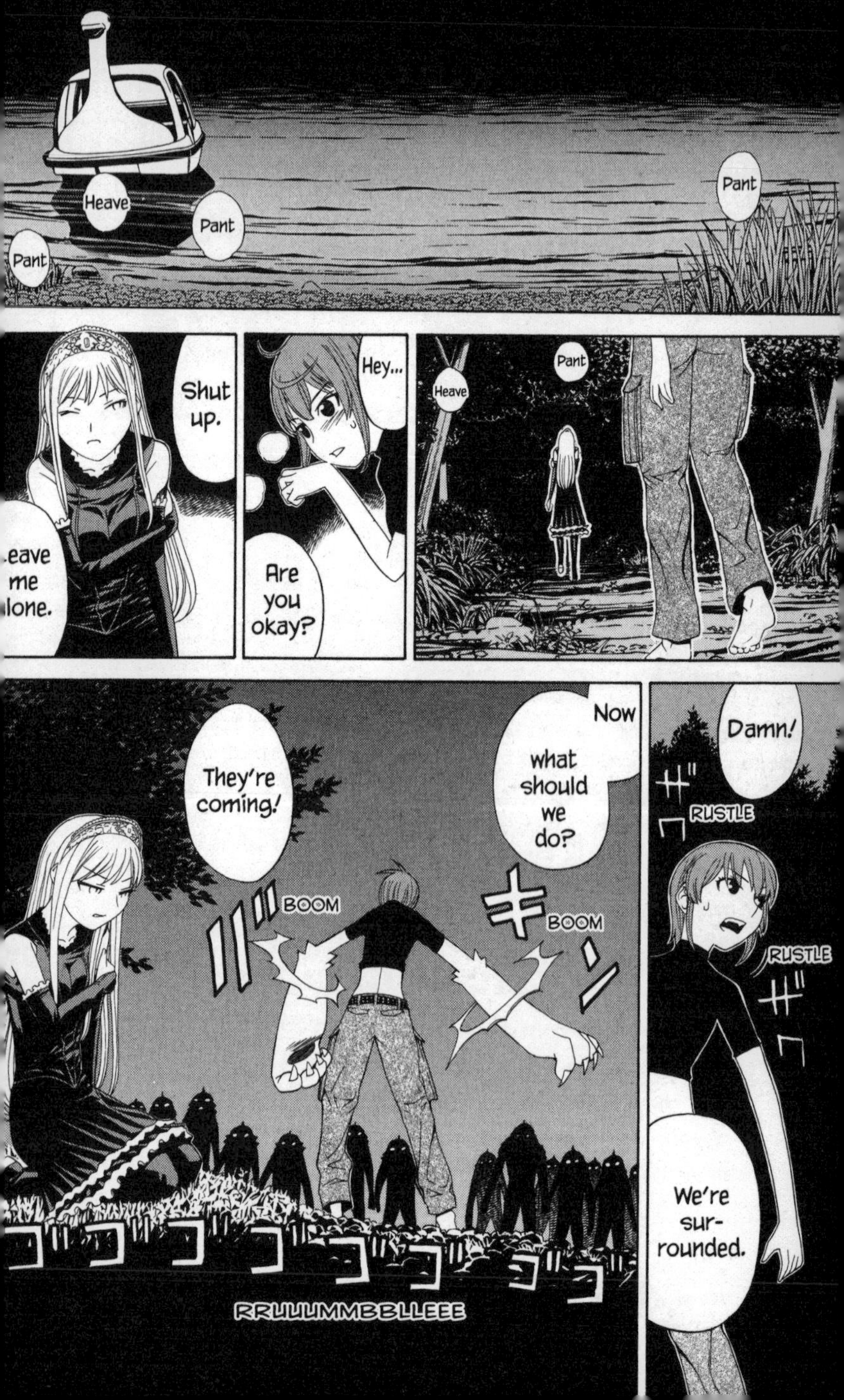
Pant
Pant
Heave
Pant
Pant
Heave
Hey...
Are you okay?
Shut up.
eave me lone.
Damn!
RUSTLE
RUSTLE
We're sur-rounded.
Now what should we do?
They're coming!
BOOM
BOOM
RRUUUMMBBLLEEE

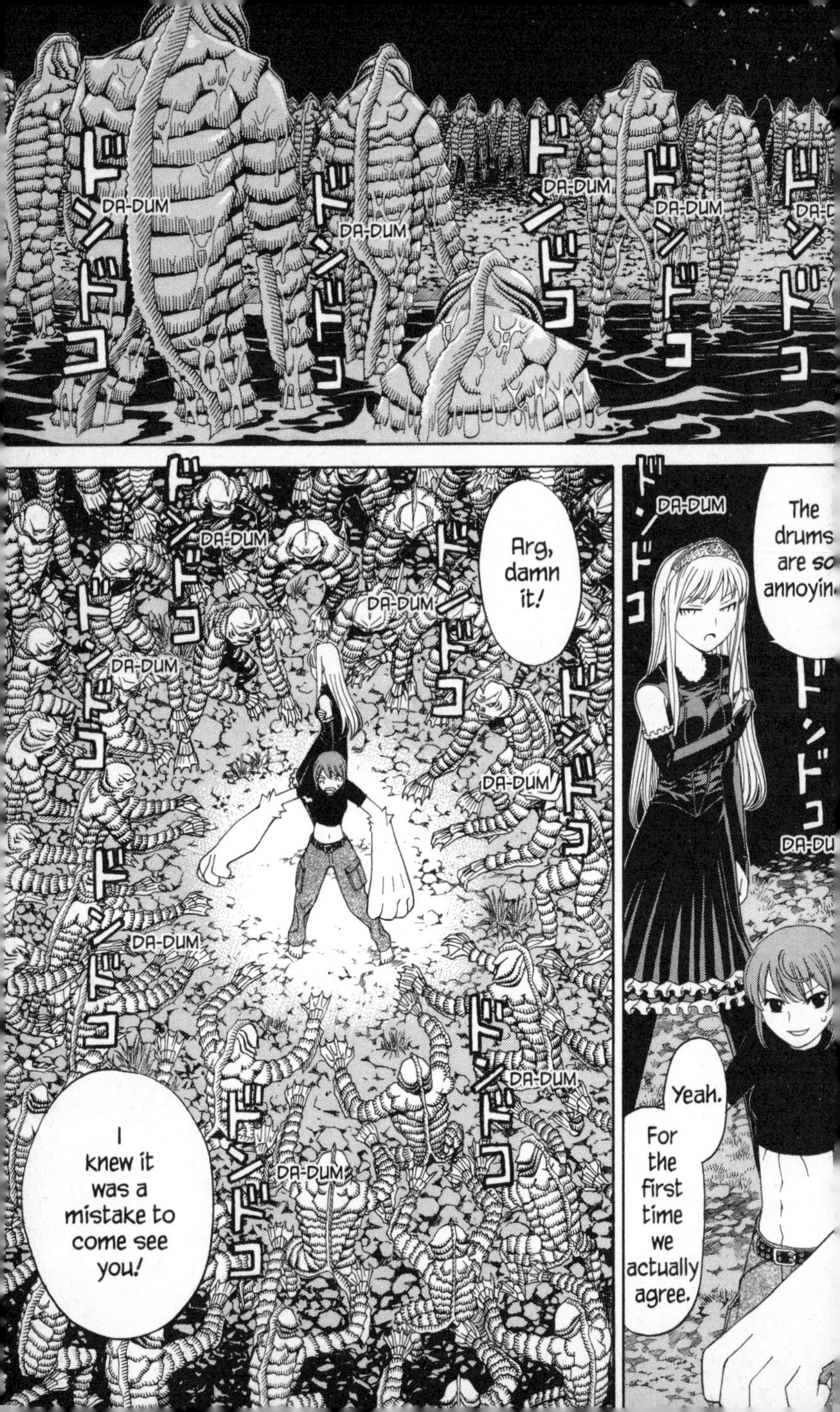
ドンドコ
DA-DUM
ドンドコ
DA-DUM
ドンドコ
DA-DUM
ドンドコ
DA-DUM
ドンドコ
DA-DUM
ドンドコ
DA-DUM
The drums are so annoyin
ドンドコ
DA-DU
Yeah.
For the first time we actually agree.
ドンドコ
DA-DUM
Arg, damn it!
ドンドコ
DA-DUM
ドンドコ
DA-DUM
ドンドコ
DA-DUM
ドンドコ
DA-DUM
ドンドコ
DA-DUM
ドンドコ
DA-DUM
ドンドコ
DA-DUM
ドンドコ
DA-DUM
I knew it was a mistake to come see you!

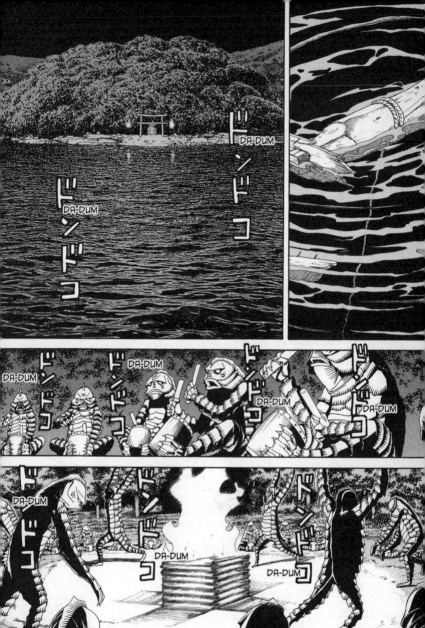

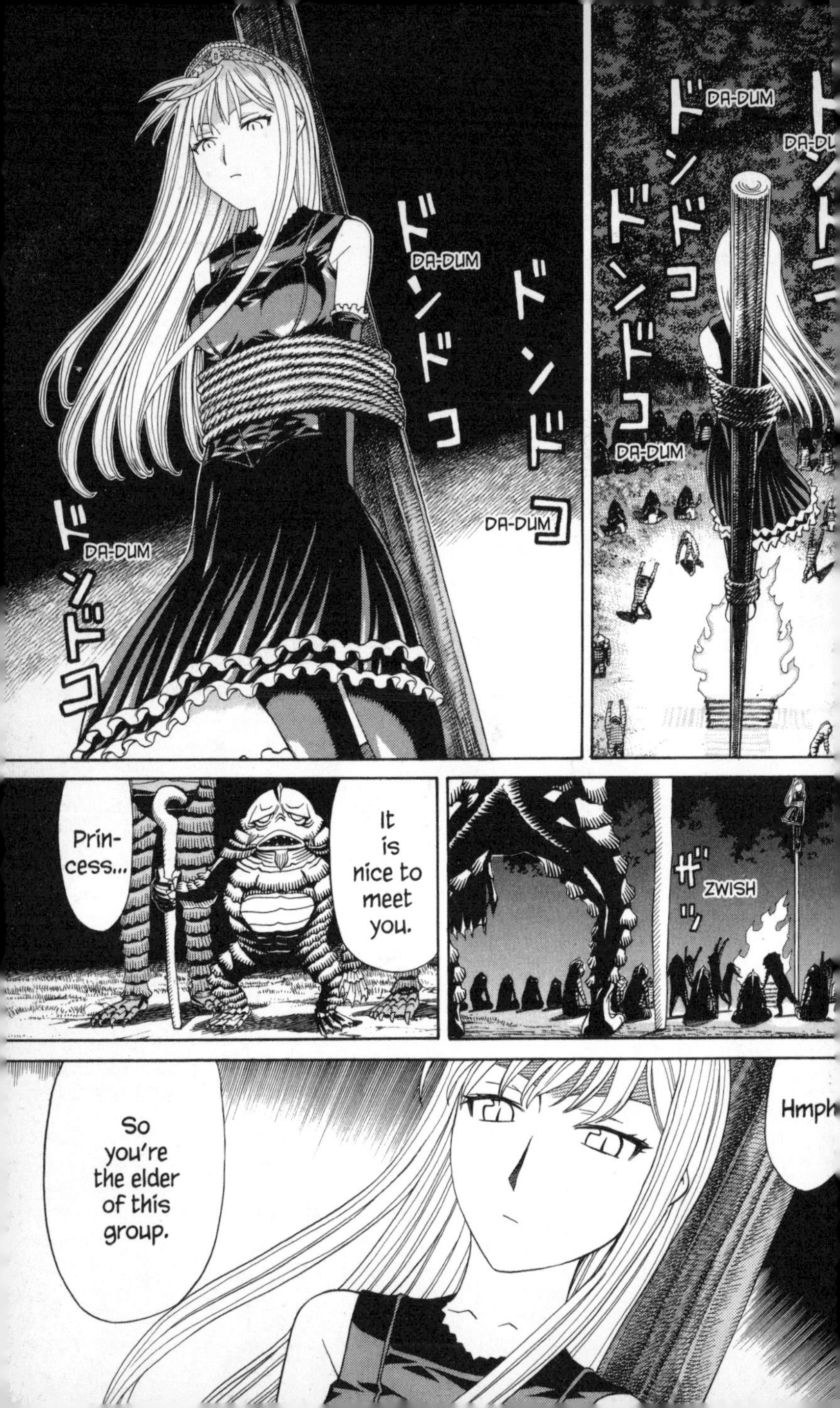
DA-DUM
DA-DUM
DA-DUM
DA-DUM
DA-DUM
DA-DUM
ZWISH
Prin-
cess...
It is nice to meet you.
Hmph
So you're the elder of this group.

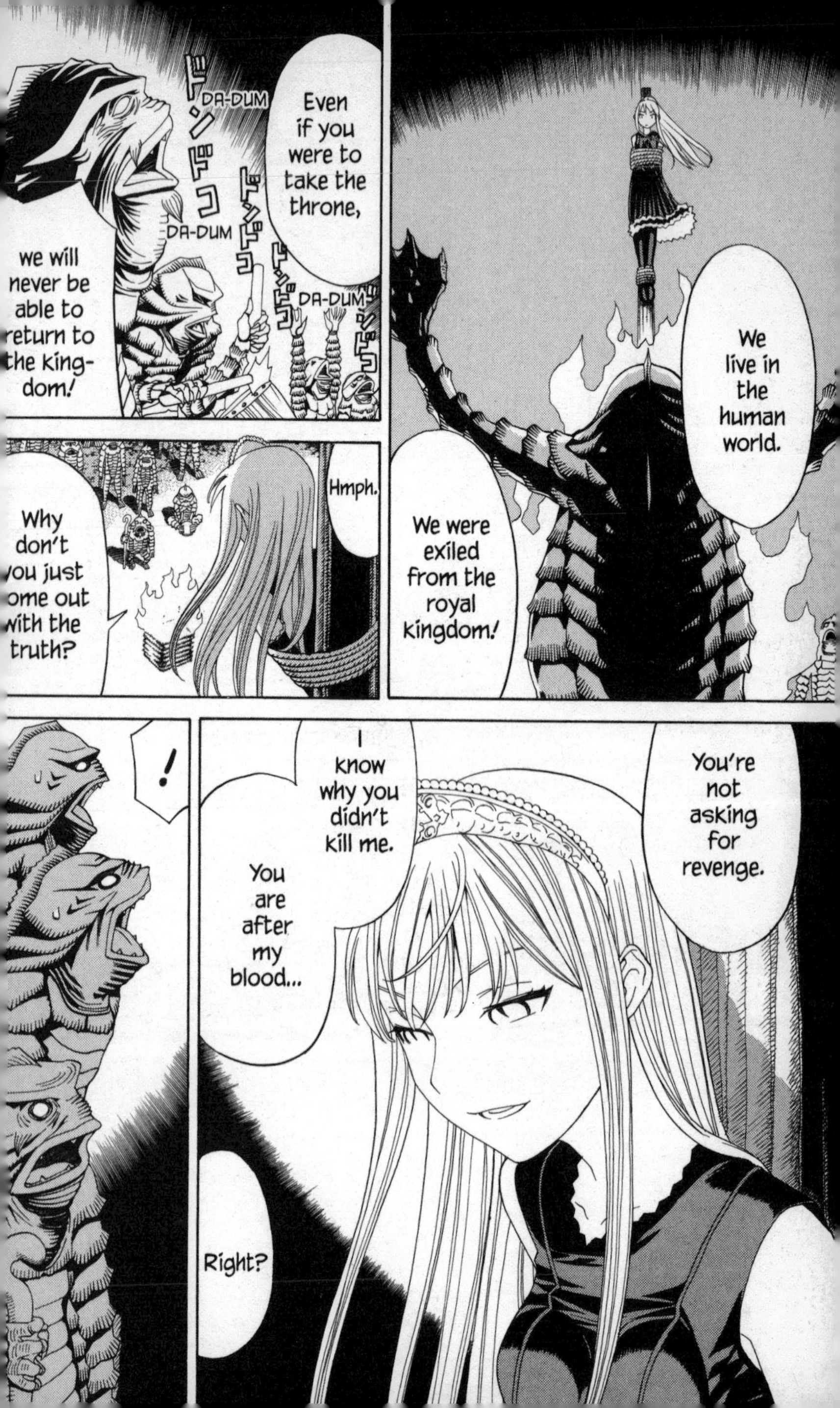
We live in the human world.
We were exiled from the royal kingdom!
Even if you were to take the throne,
DA-DUM
DA-DUM
DA-DUM
we will never be able to return to the king-dom!
Hmph.
Why don't you just come out with the truth?
You're not asking for revenge.
I know why you didn't kill me.
You are after my blood...
Right?
!

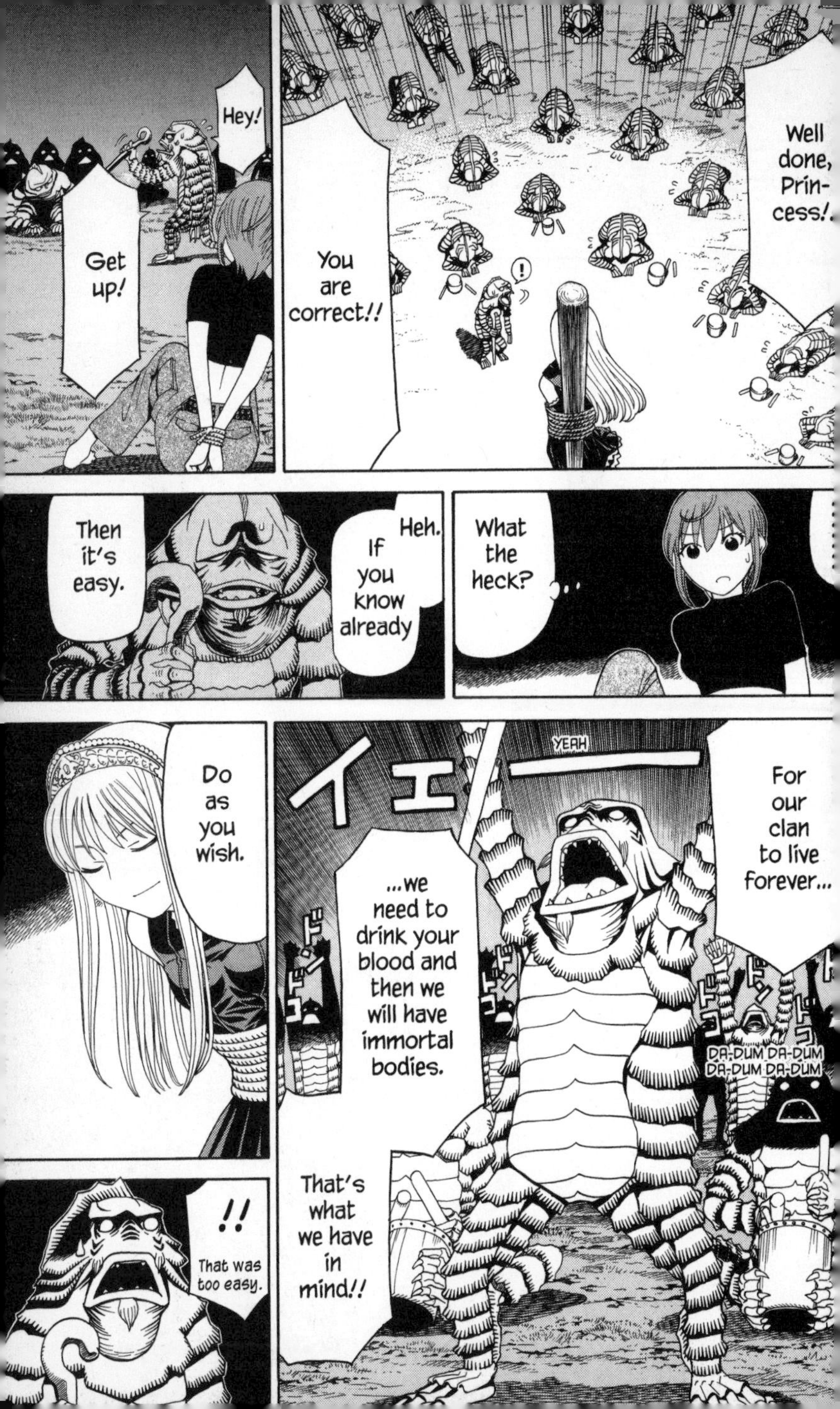

Well done, Prin-cess!.
You are correct!!
Hey!
Get up!
What the heck?
Heh.
If you know already
Then it's easy.
For our clan to live forever...
YEAH
...we need to drink your blood and then we will have immortal bodies.
DA-DUM DA-DUM DA-DUM DA-DUM
That's what we have in mind!!
Do as you wish.
!!
That was too easy.

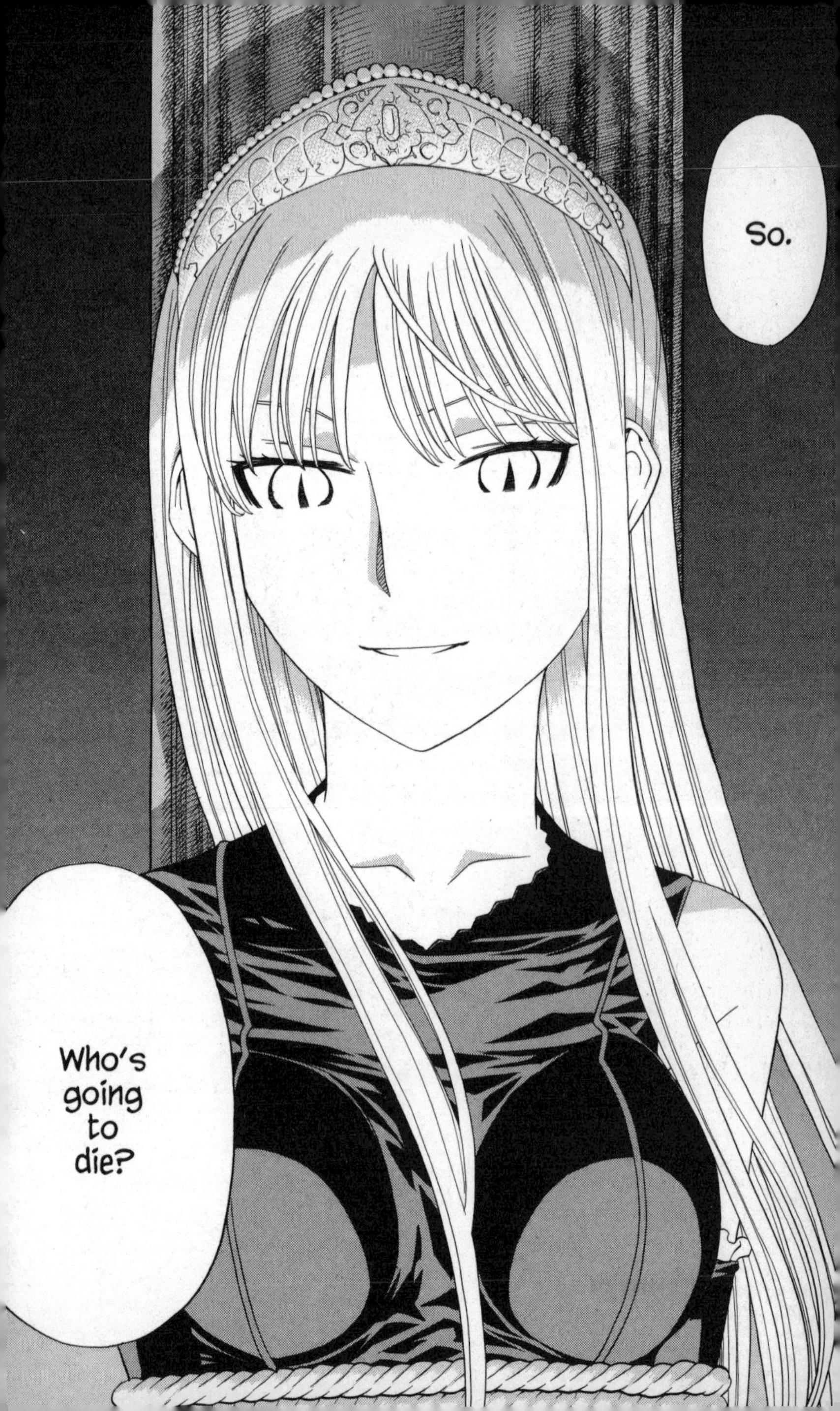
So.
Who's going to die?

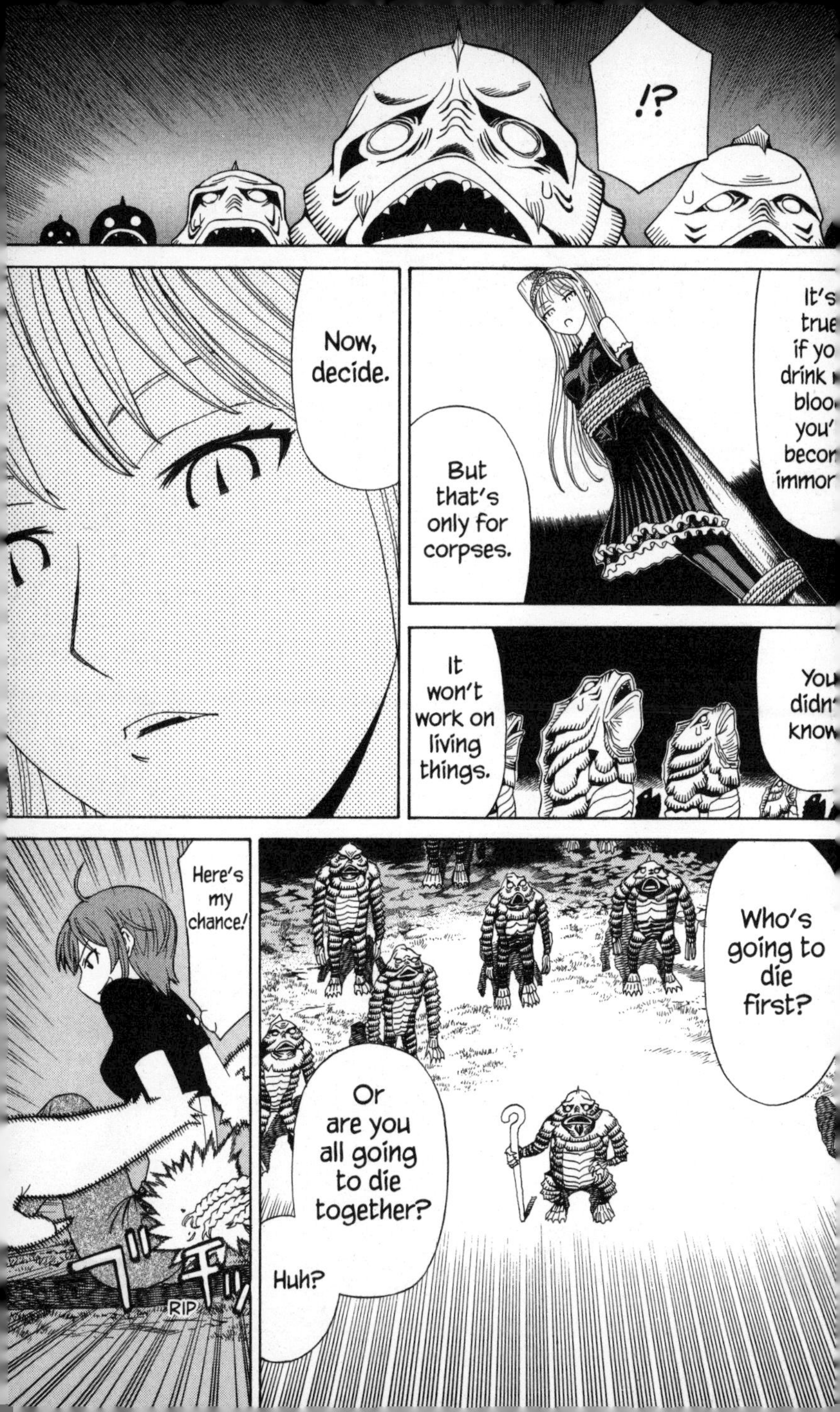
!?
It's true if yo drink bloo you' becon immor
But that's only for corpses.
You didn' know
It won't work on living things.
Now, decide.
Who's going to die first?
Or are you all going to die together?
Huh?
Here's my chance!
ブチッ
RIP

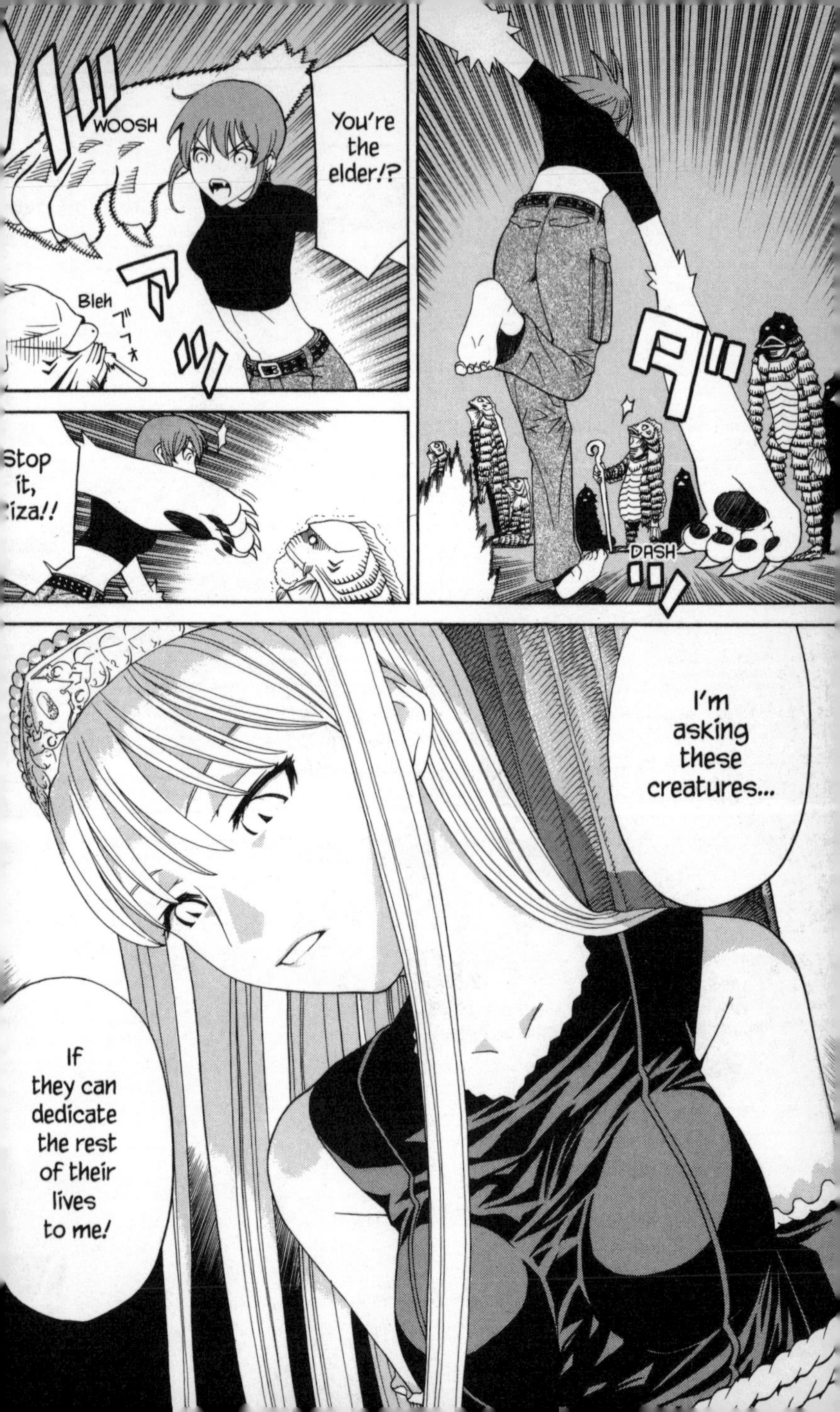
DASH
WOOSH
You're the elder!?
Bleh
Stop it, iza!!
I'm asking these creatures...
If they can dedicate the rest of their lives to me!

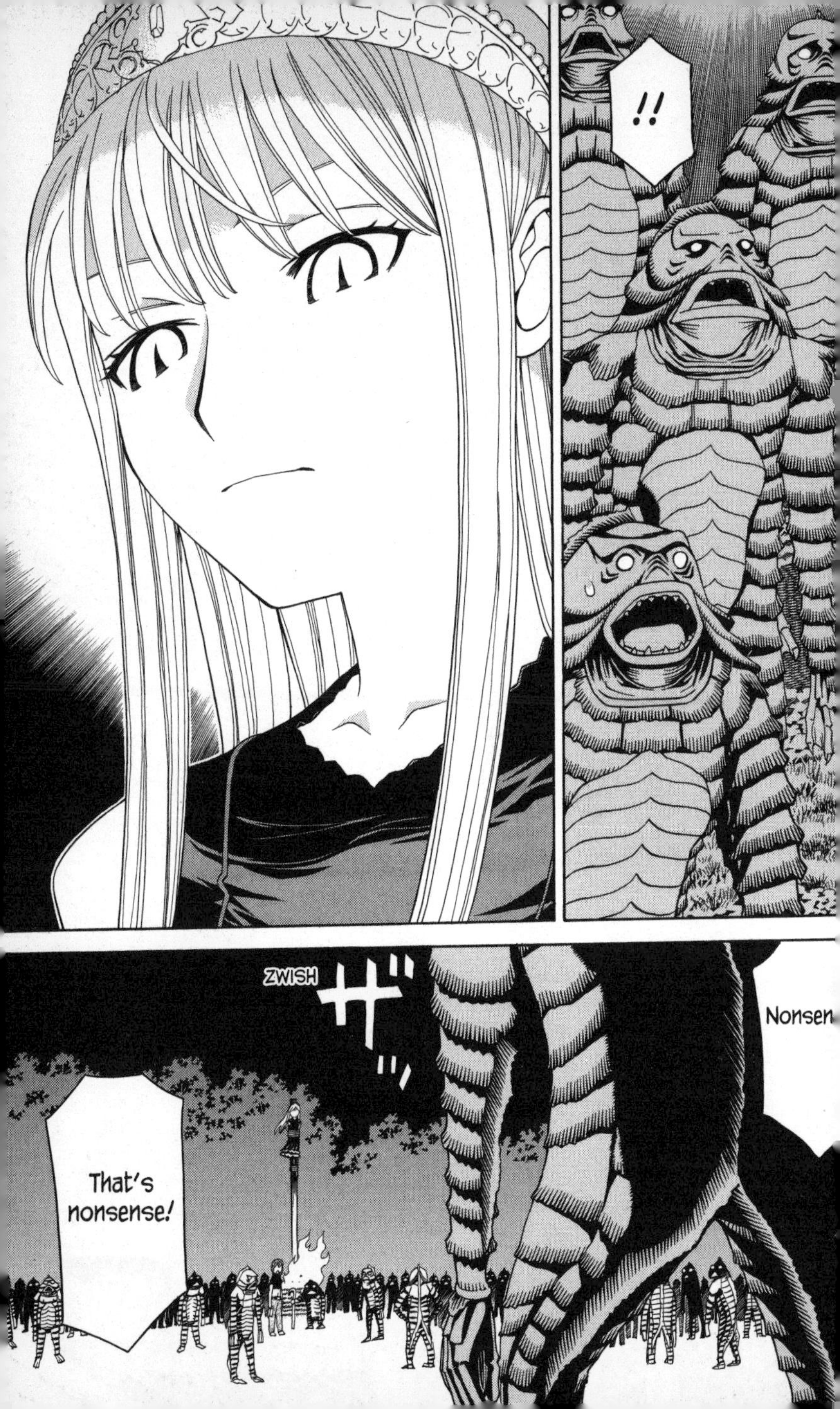
!!
Nonsen
ZWISH
That's nonsense!

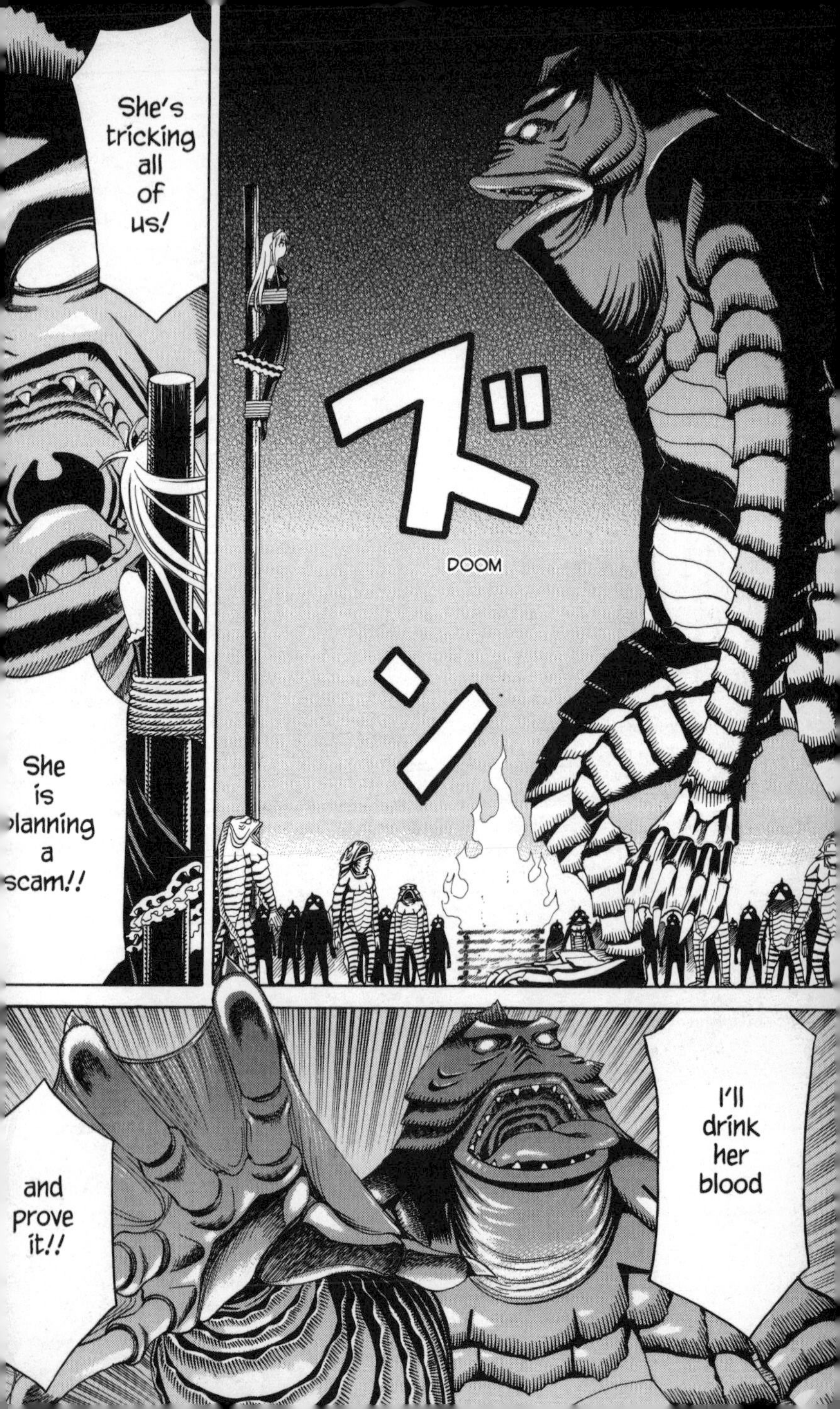
ズン
DOOM
She's tricking all of us!
She is planning a scam!!
I'll drink her blood
and prove it!!

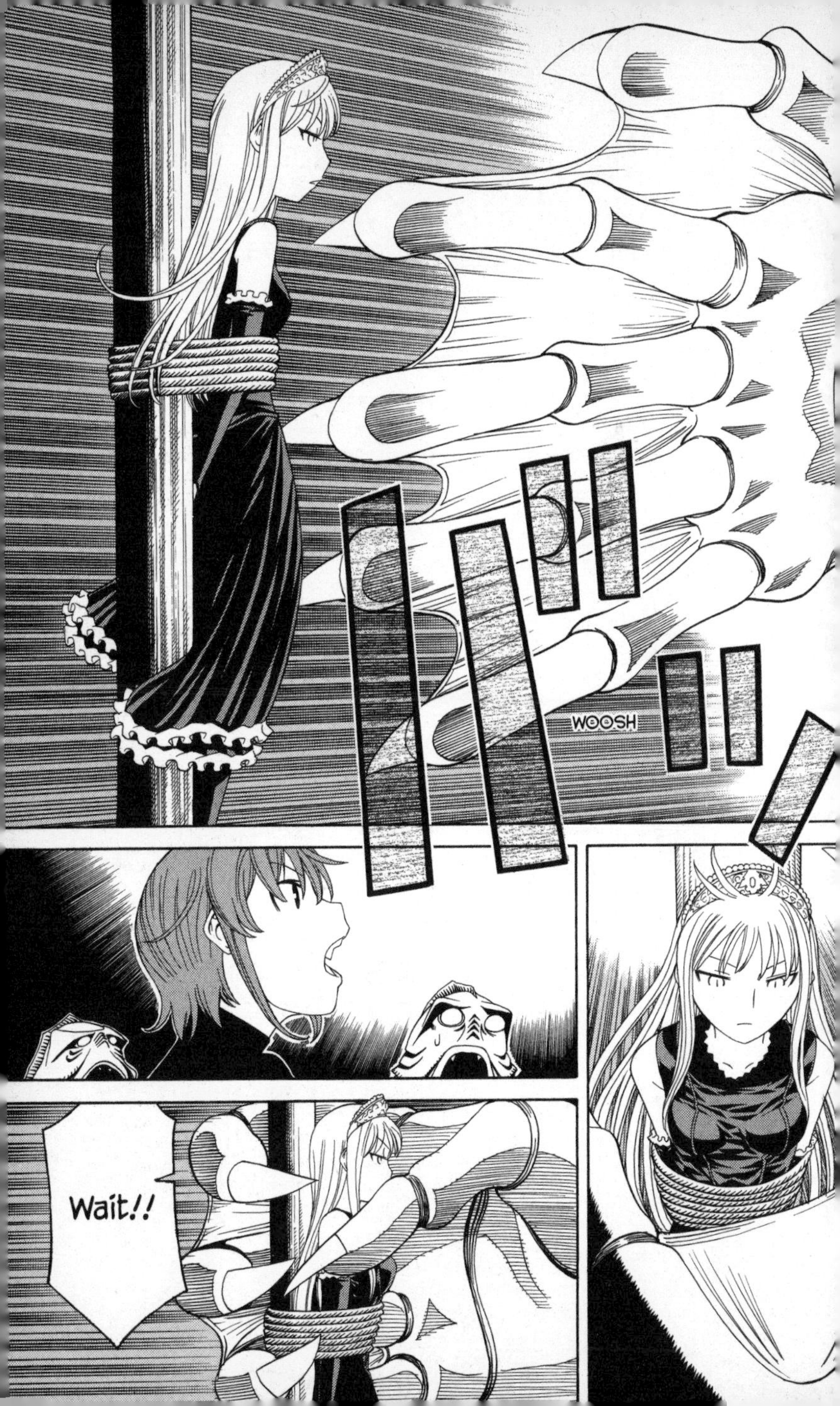
WOOSH
Wait!!

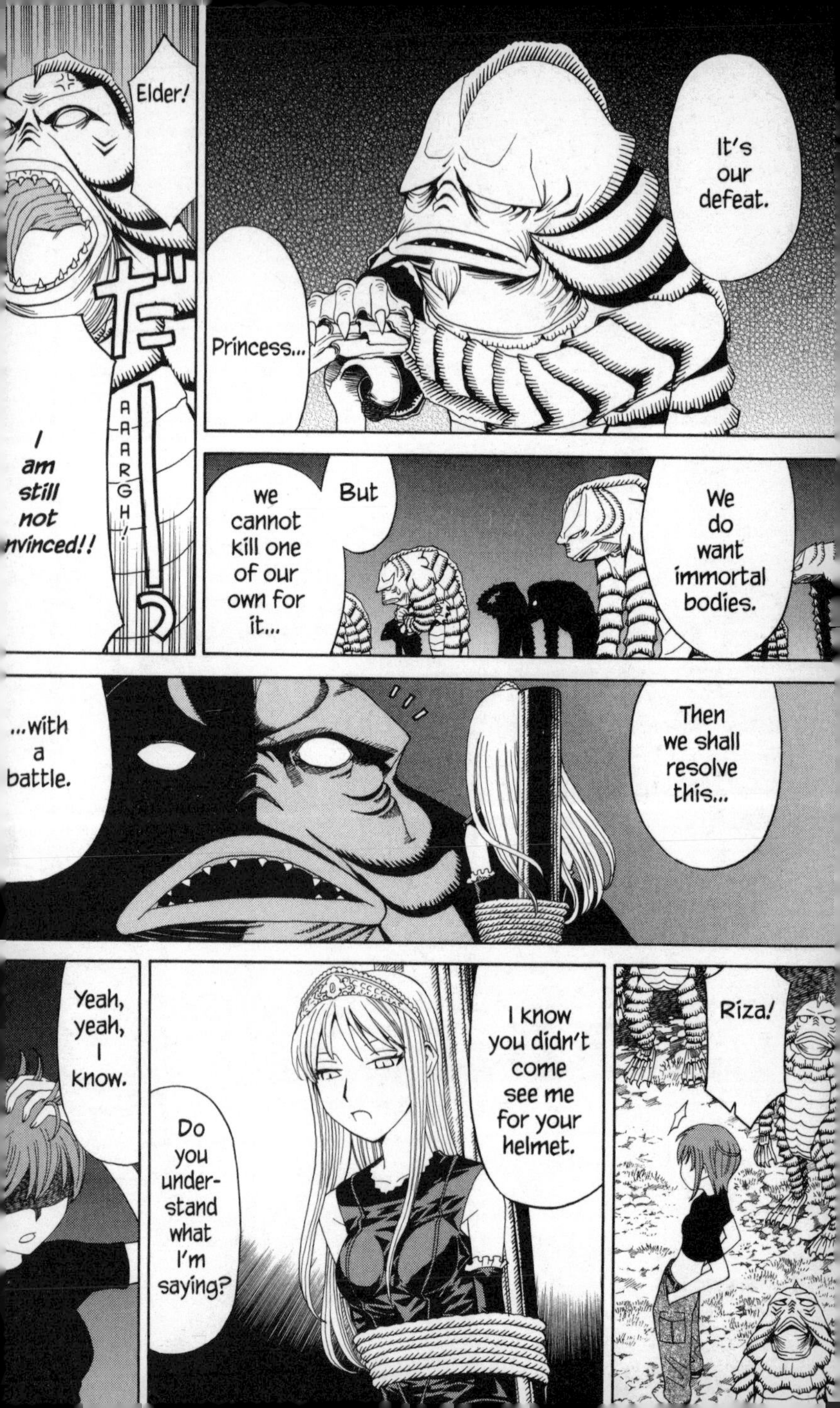
It's our defeat.
Princess...
We do want immortal bodies.
But
we cannot kill one of our own for it...
Elder!
AAARGH!
I am still not nvinced!!
Then we shall resolve this...
...with a battle.
Riza!
I know you didn't come see me for your helmet.
Do you understand what I'm saying?
Yeah, yeah, I know.

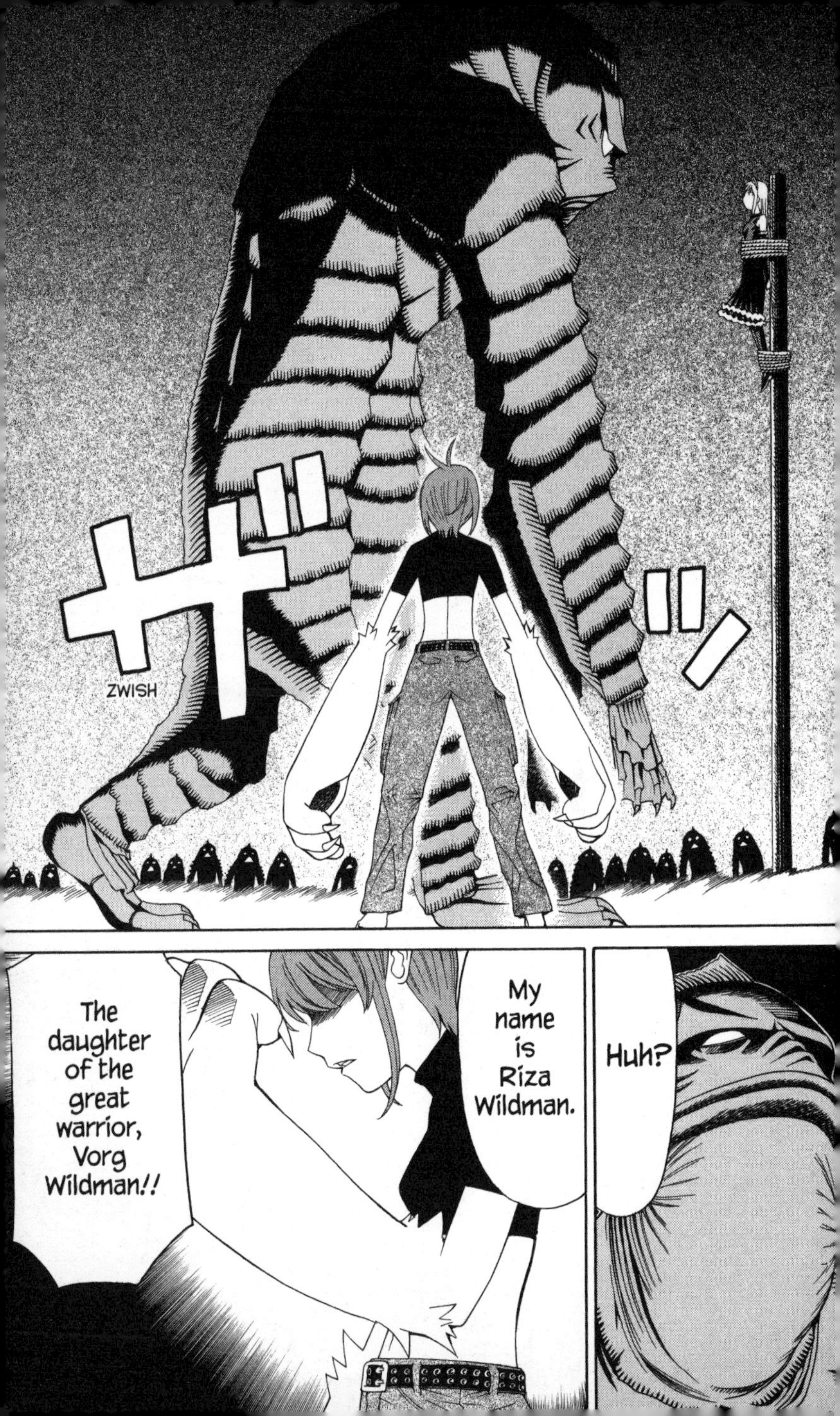
ZWISH
Huh?
My name is Riza Wildman.
The daughter of the great warrior, Vorg Wildman!!

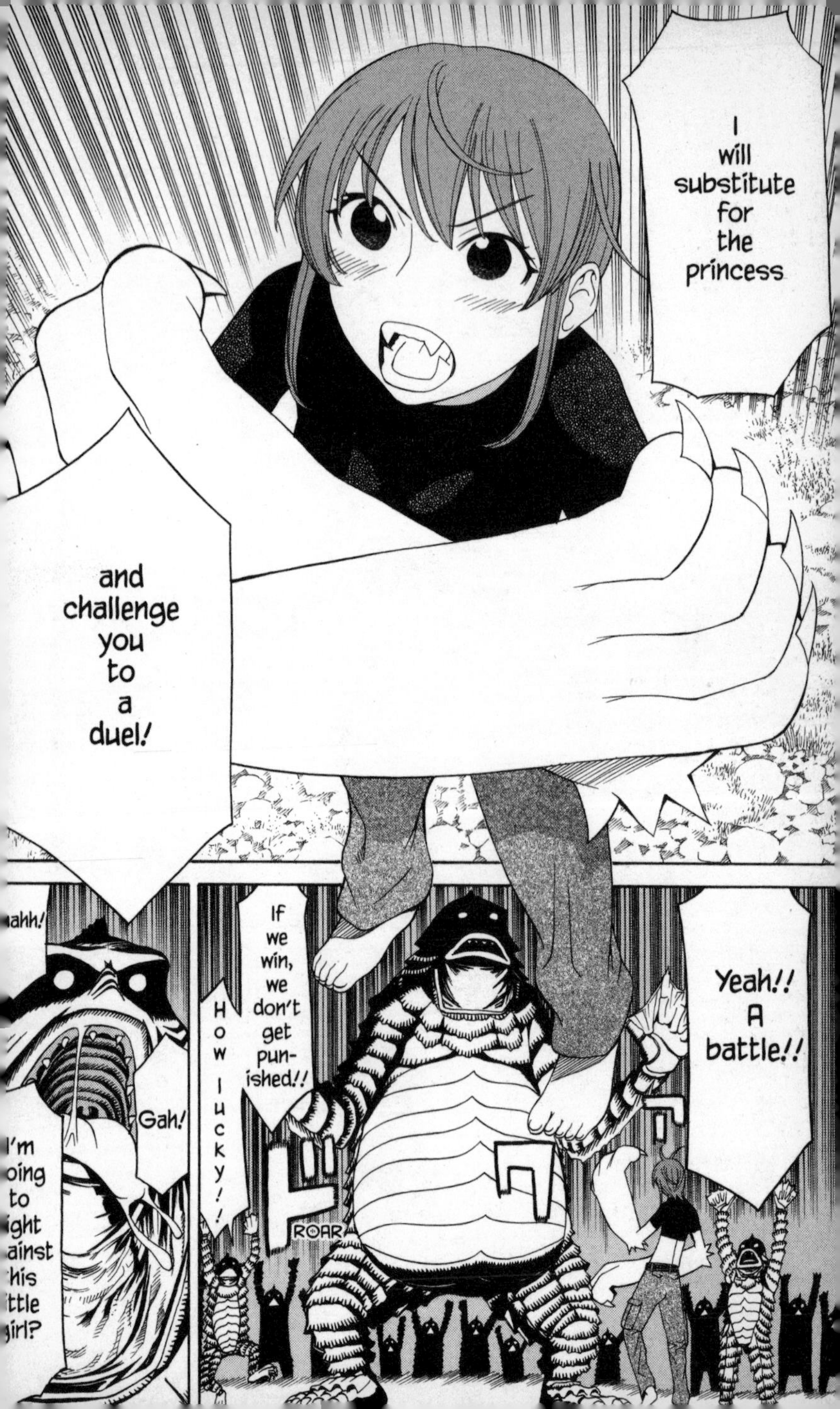

I will substitute for the princess
and challenge you to a duel!
Yeah!! A battle!!
If we win, we don't get pun-ished!!
How lucky!!
ROAR
ahh!
Gah!
I'm oing to ight ainst his ittle irl?

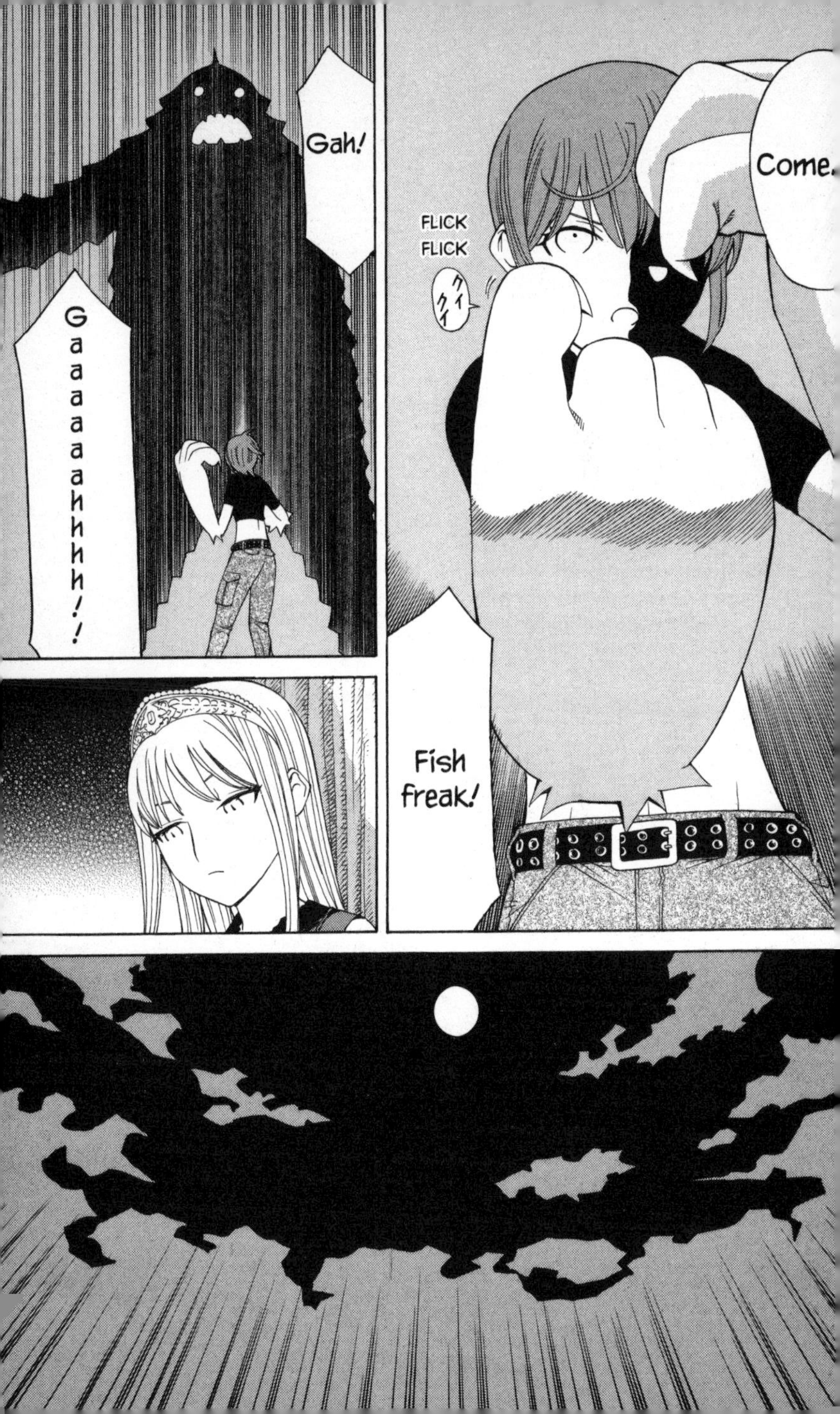
Come.
FLICK
FLICK
クイクイ
Fish freak!
Gah!
Gaaaaaahhhh!!

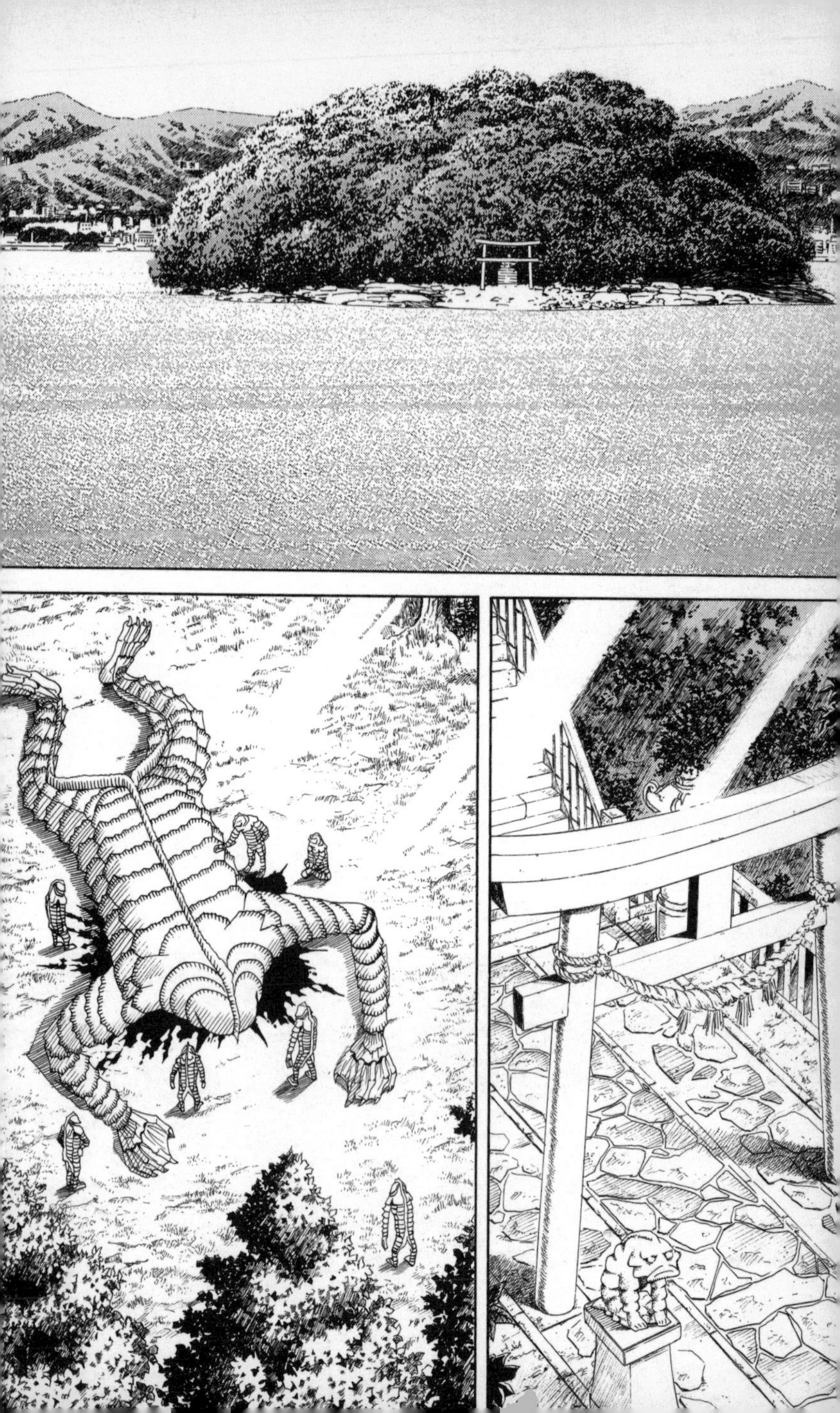

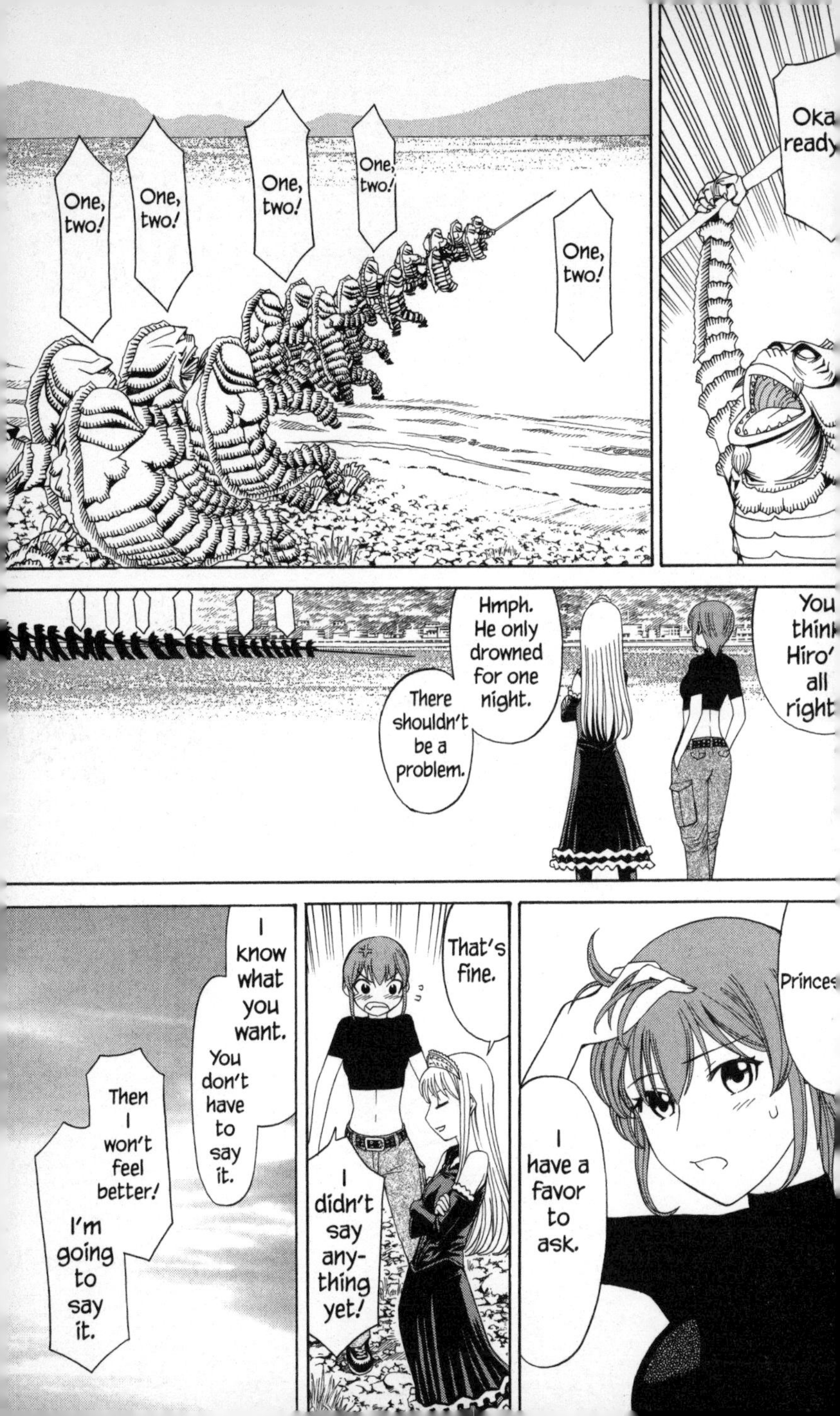
Oka ready
One, two!
One, two!
One, two!
One, two!
One, two!
You thin Hiro' all righ
Hmph. He only drowned for one night.
There shouldn't be a problem.
Princes
I have a favor to ask.
That's fine.
I didn't say any-thing yet!
I know what you want.
You don't have to say it.
Then I won't feel better!
I'm going to say it.

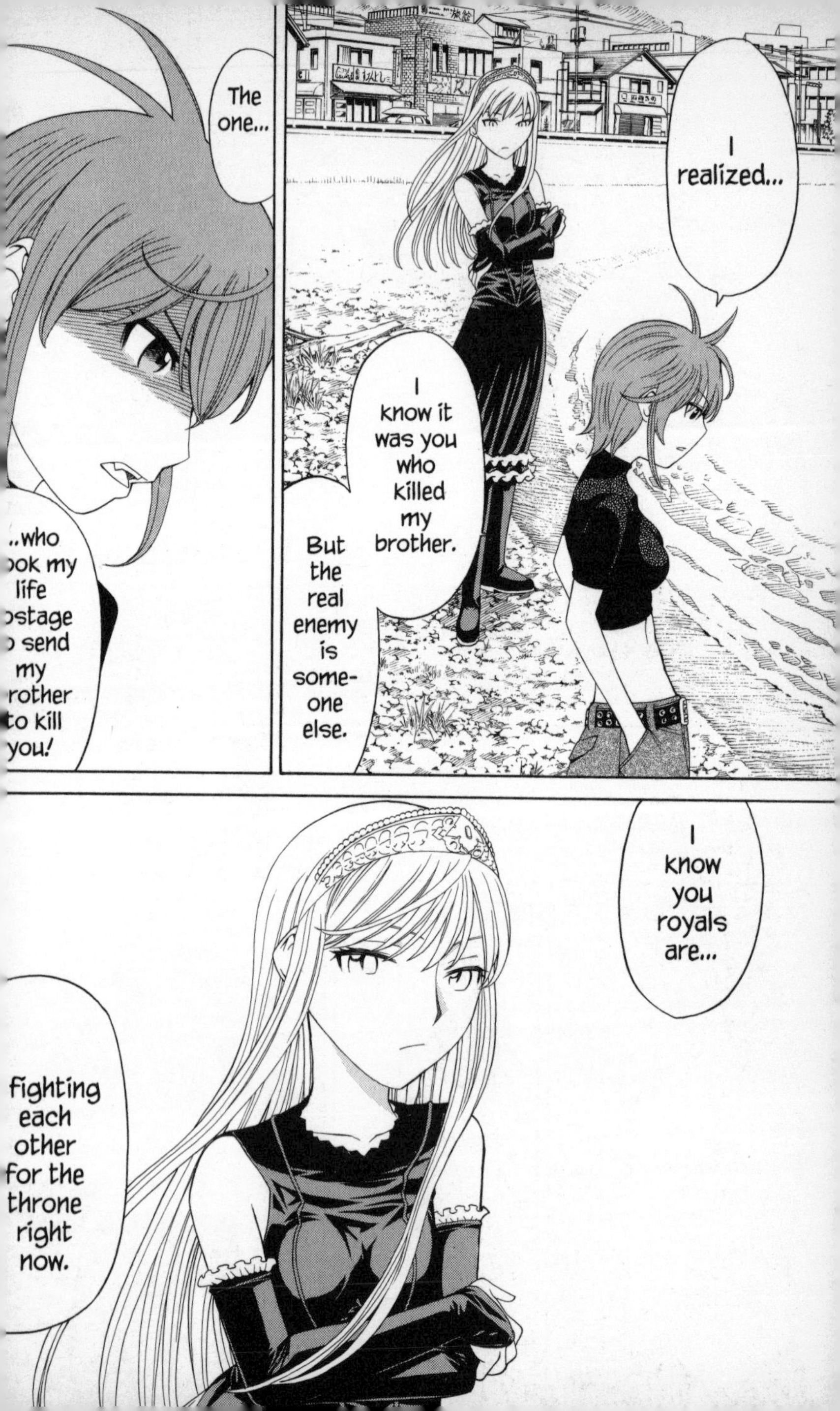
I realized...
I know it was you who killed my brother.
But the real enemy is someone-one else.
The one...
..who ook my life ostage o send my rother to kill you!
I know you royals are...
fighting each other for the throne right now.

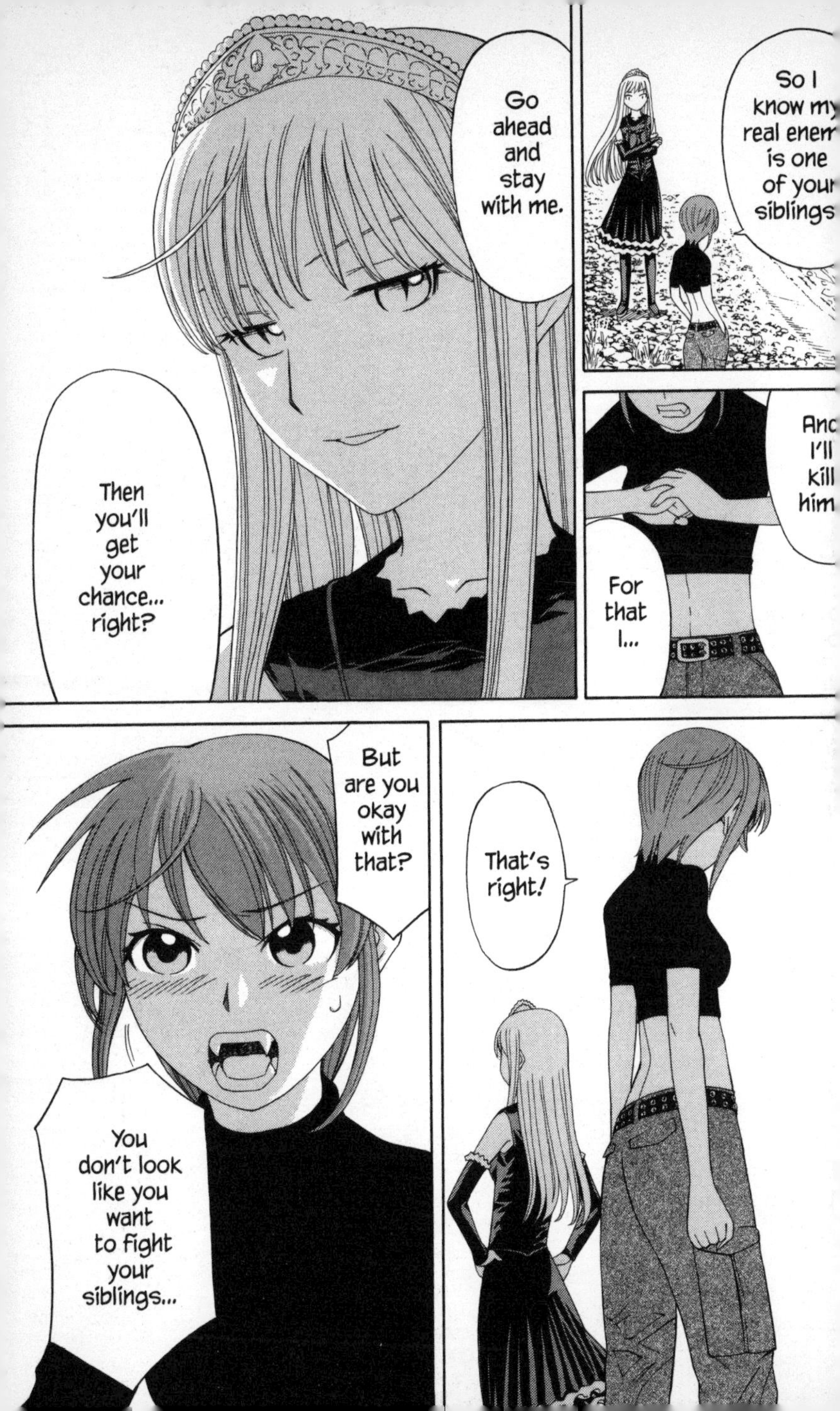
So I know my real enem is one of your siblings
And I'll kill him
For that I...
Go ahead and stay with me.
Then you'll get your chance... right?
That's right!
But are you okay with that?
You don't look like you want to fight your siblings...

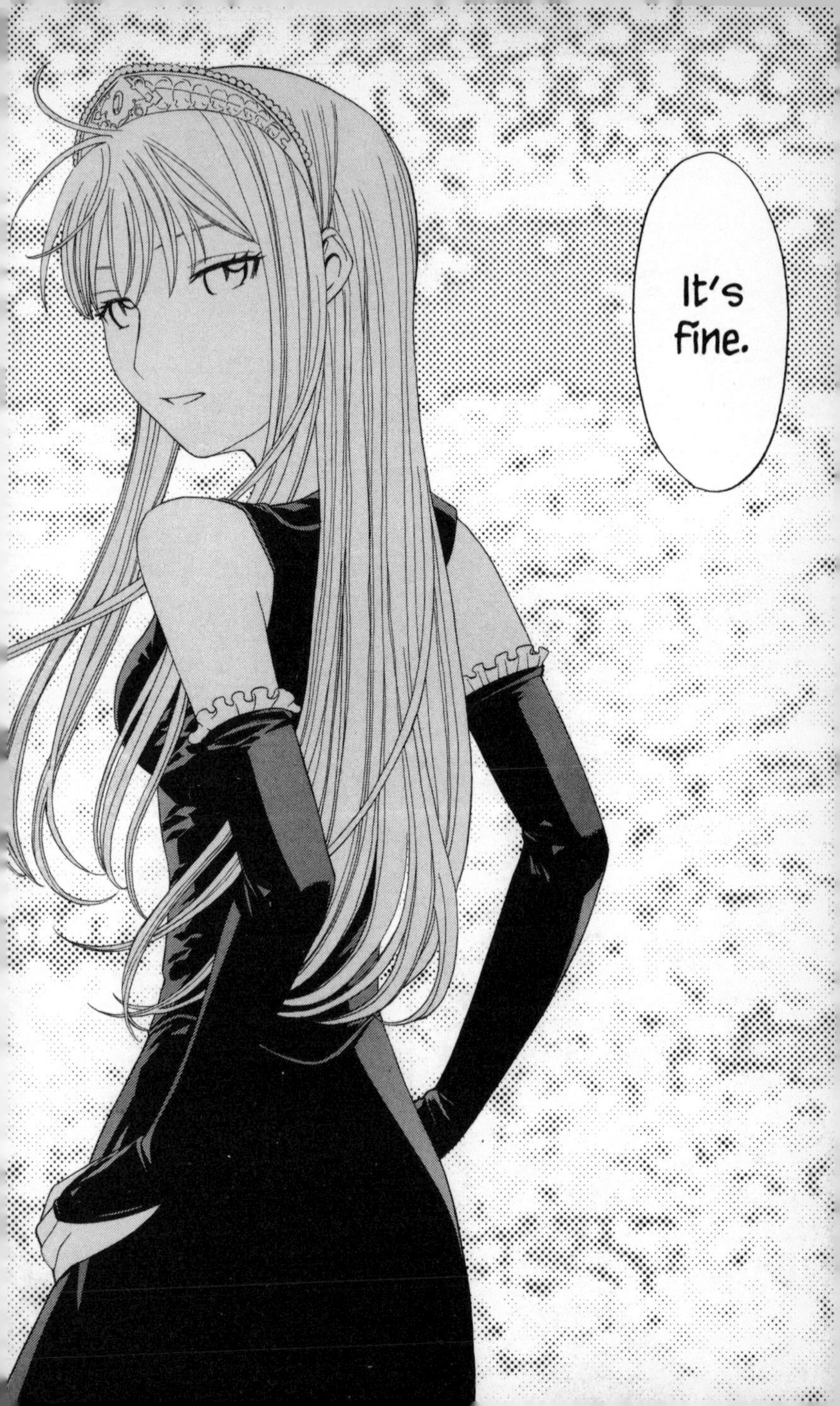
It's fine.

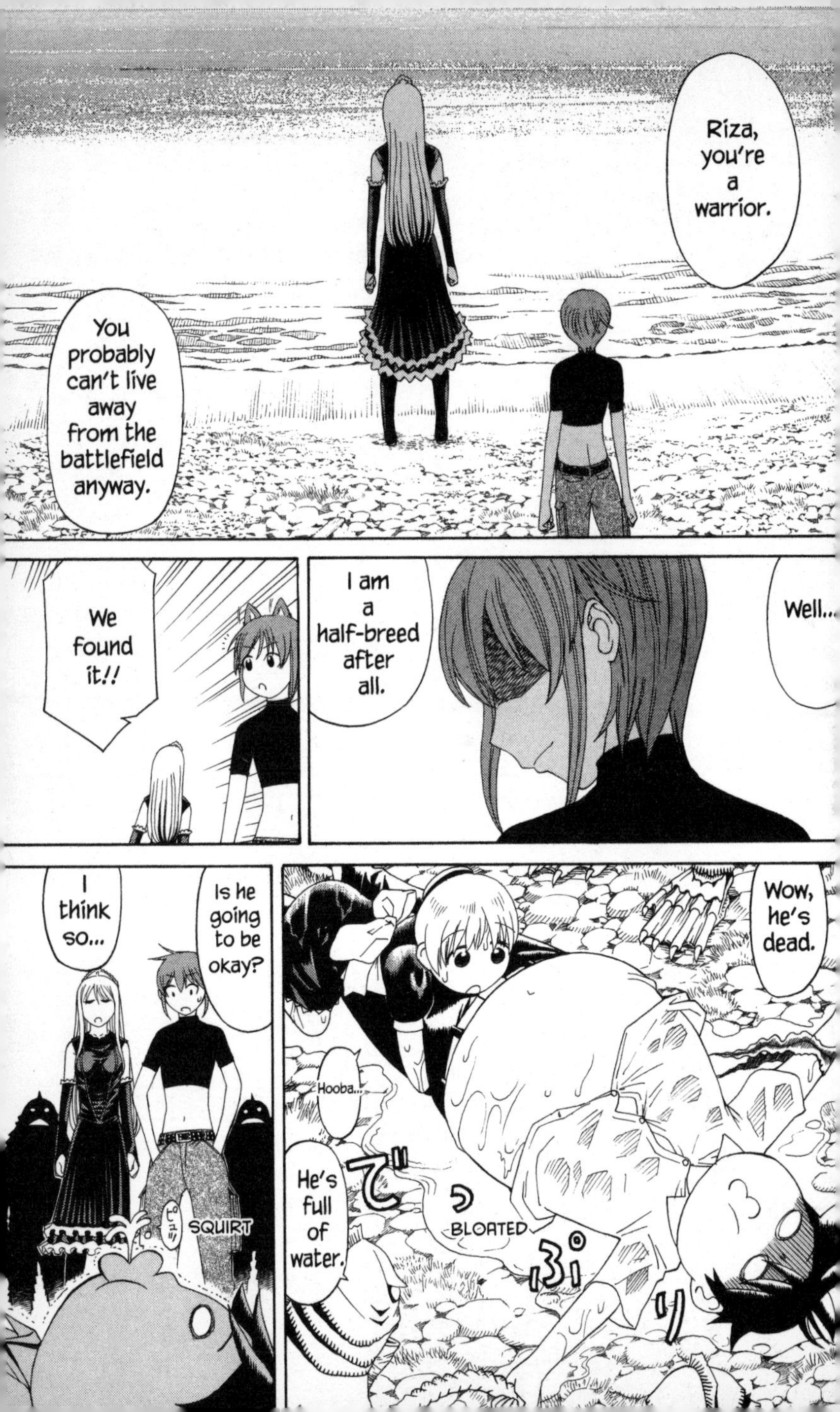
Riza, you're a warrior.
You probably can't live away from the battlefield anyway.
Well...
I am a half-breed after all.
We found it!!
Wow, he's dead.
Hooba...
He's full of water.
BLOATED
Is he going to be okay?
I think so...
SQUIRT

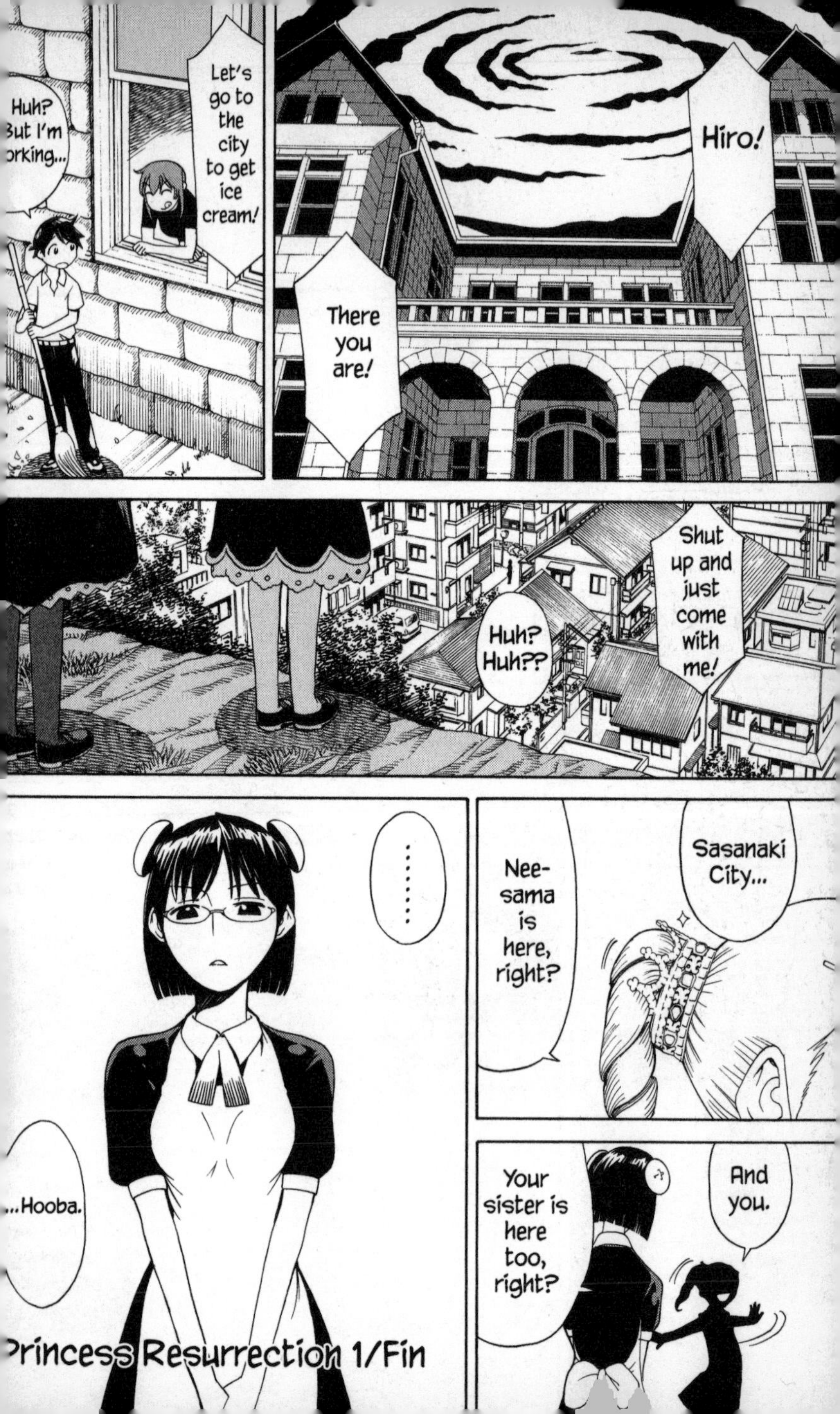
Hiro!
There you are!
Let's go to the city to get ice cream!
Huh? But I'm orking...
Shut up and just come with me!
Huh? Huh??
Sasanaki City...
Nee-sama is here, right?
And you.
Your sister is here too, right?
....
...Hooba.
Princess Resurrection 1/Fin

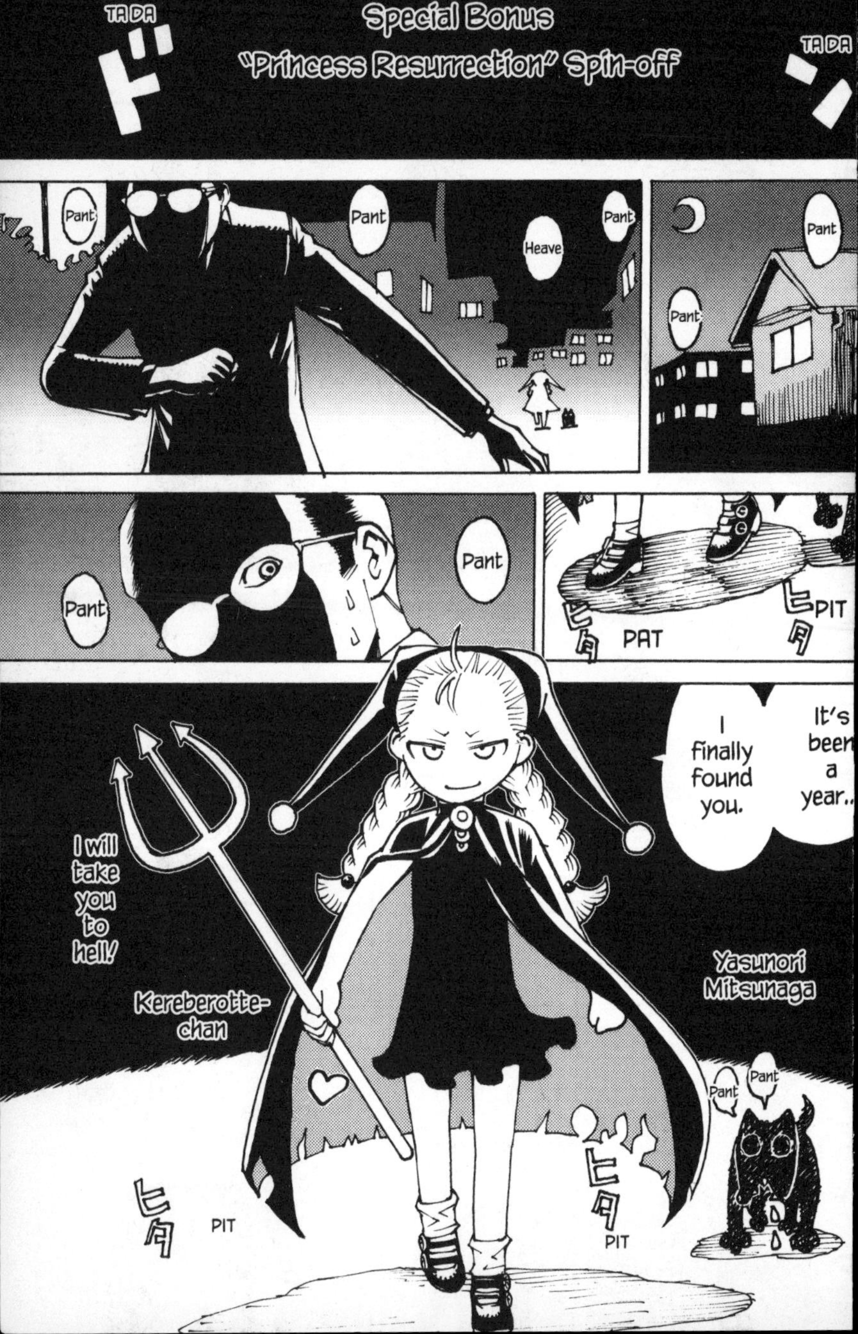
TA DA
TA DA
Special Bonus
"Princess Resurrection" Spin-off
Pant
Pant
Pant
Heave
Pant
Pant
PIT
PAT
Pant
Pant
It's been a year..
I finally found you.
I will take you to hell!
Yasunori Mitsunaga
Kereberotte-chan
Pant
Pant
PIT
PIT

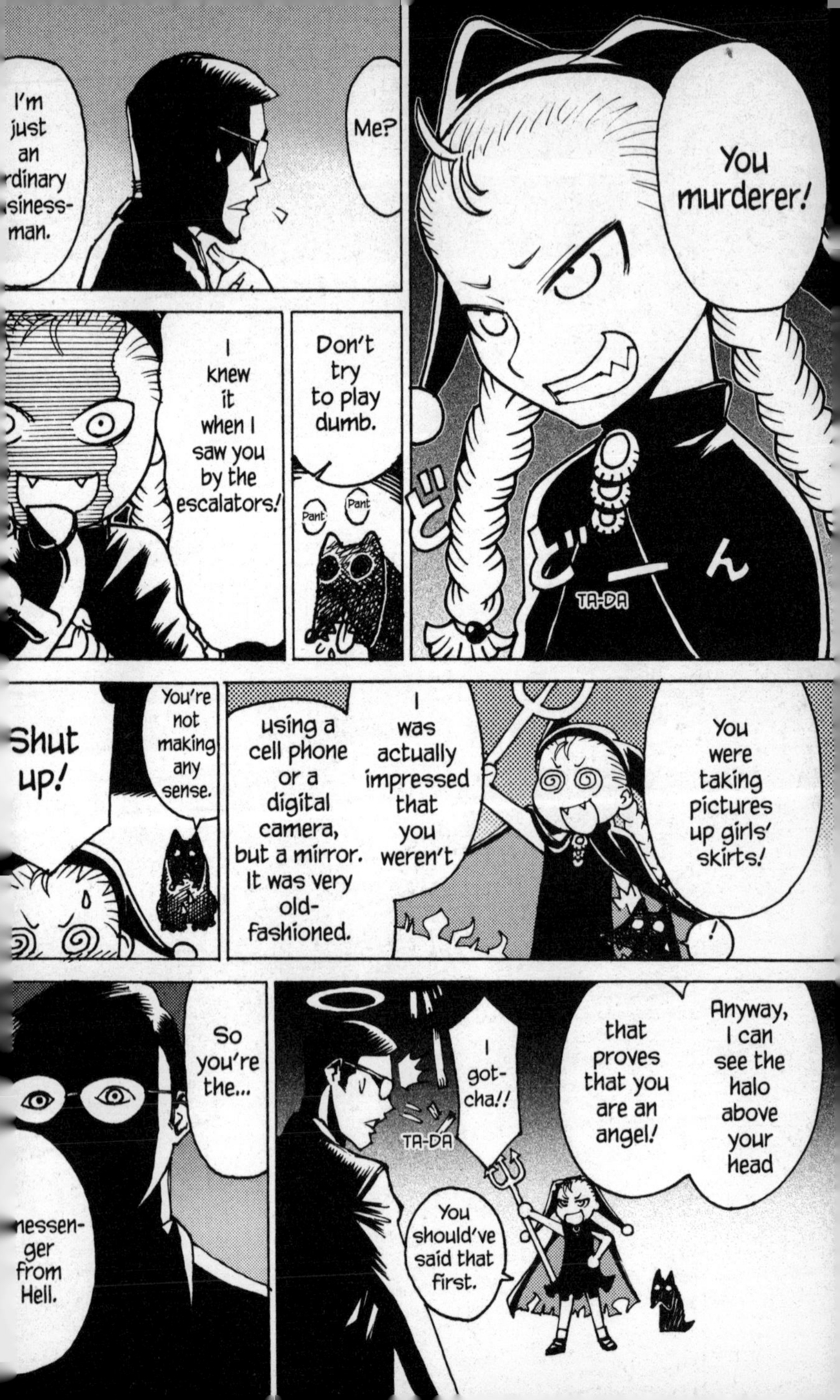

You murderer!
どーん
TA-DA
Me?
I'm just an rdinary siness- man.
Don't try to play dumb.
Pant
Pant
I knew it when I saw you by the escalators!
You were taking pictures up girls' skirts!
I was actually impressed that you weren't
using a cell phone or a digital camera, but a mirror. It was very old-fashioned.
!
You're not making any sense.
Shut up!
Anyway, I can see the halo above your head
that proves that you are an angel!
I got-cha!!
TA-DA
You should've said that first.
So you're the...
nessen-ger from Hell.

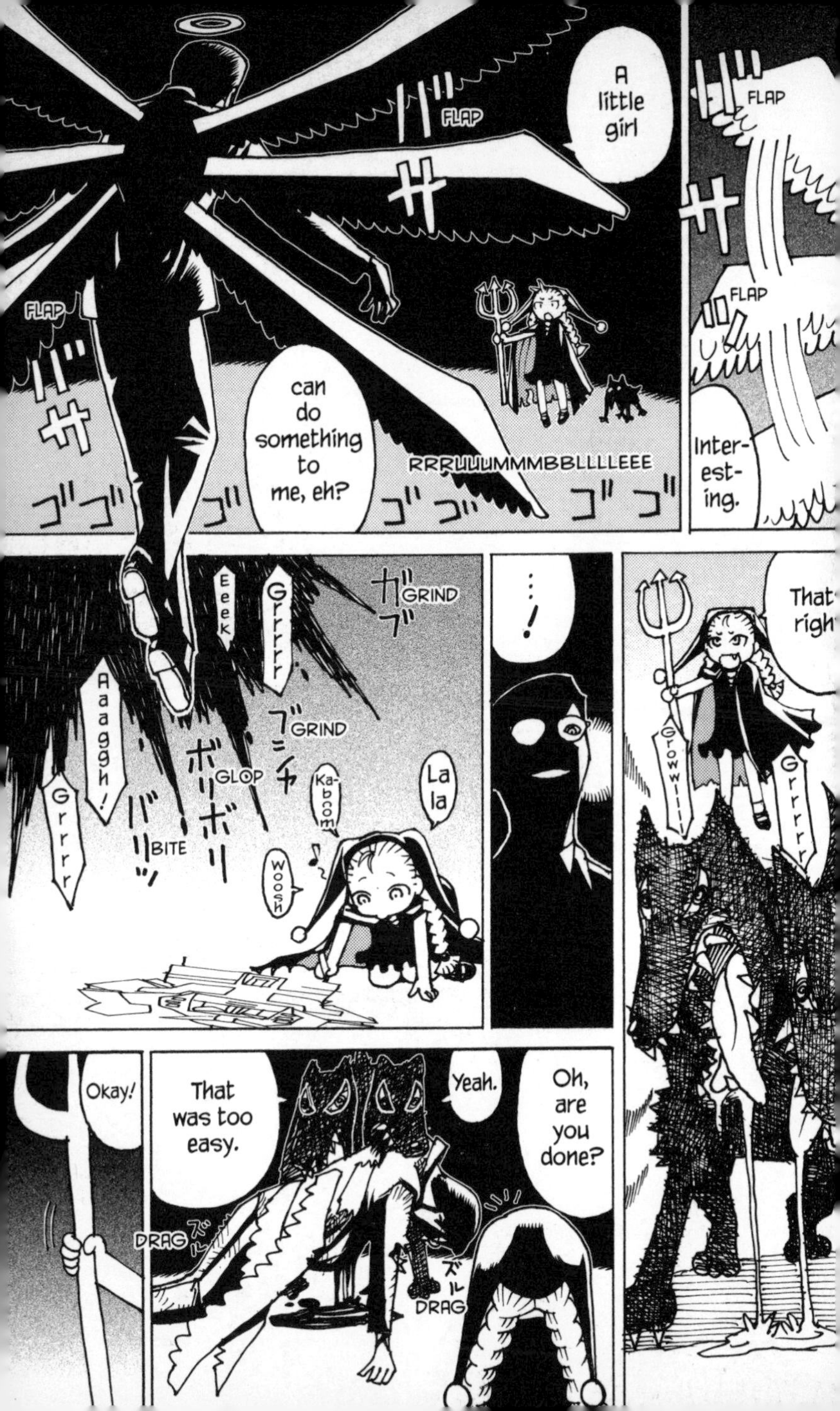

FLAP
FLAP
Inter-est-ing.
A little girl
FLAP
FLAP
can do something to me, eh?
RRRUUUMMMBBLLLLEEE
That righ
Growwl...
Grrrrr
...!
GRIND
Grrrrr
Eeek
Aaaagh!
GRIND
GLOP
La la
Ka-boom
Grrrr
BITE
Woosh
Oh, are you done?
Yeah.
DRAG
That was too easy.
DRAG
Okay!

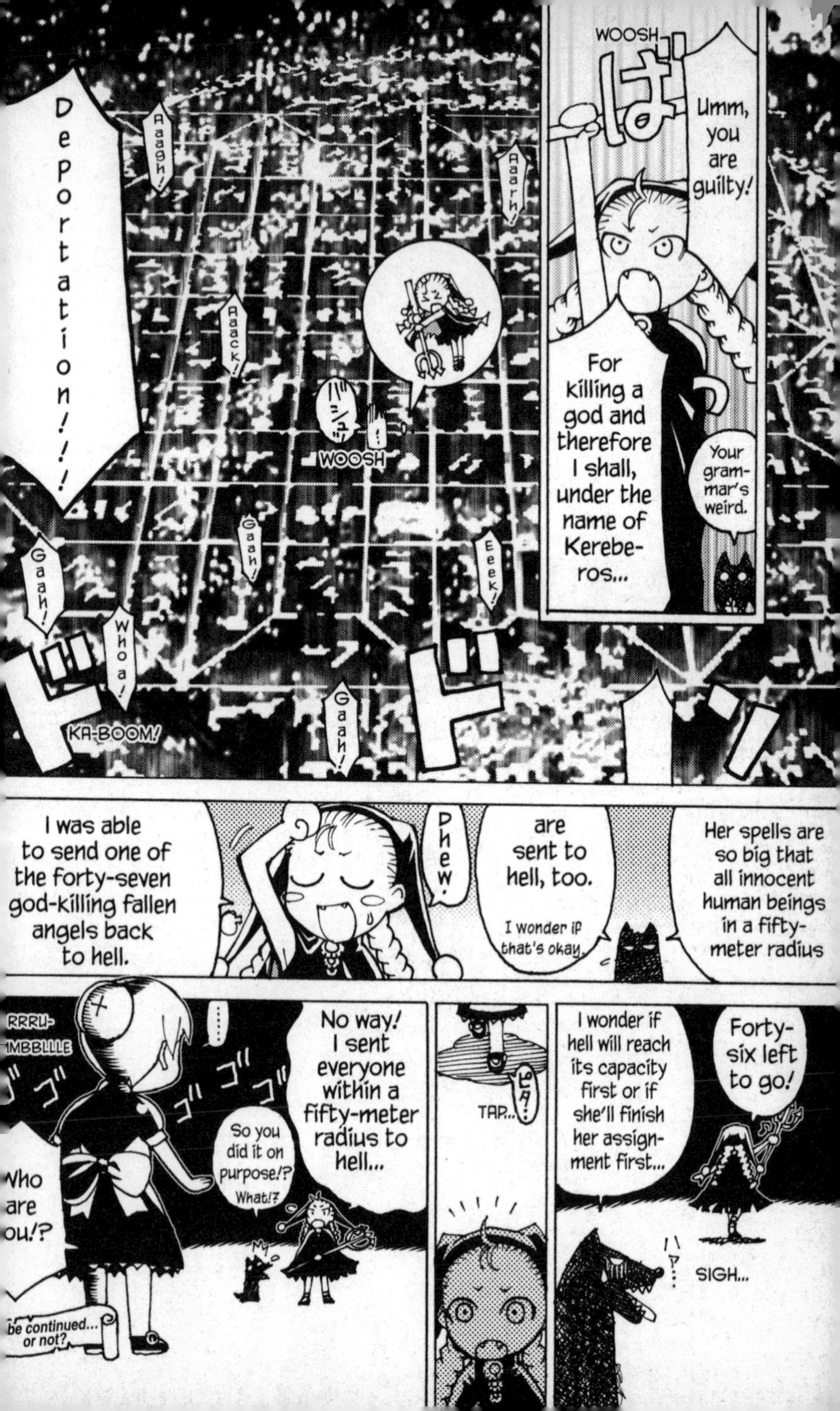

WOOSH
ば
Umm, you are guilty!
For killing a god and therefore I shall, under the name of Kerebe-ros...
Your gram-mar's weird.
Deportation!!!
Aagh!
Aaarh!
Aaack!
WOOSH
Gaah!
Eeek!
Gaah!
Whoa!
Gaah!
KA-BOOM!
Her spells are so big that all innocent human beings in a fifty-meter radius
are sent to hell, too.
I wonder if that's okay.
Phew!
I was able to send one of the forty-seven god-killing fallen angels back to hell.
Forty-six left to go!
SIGH...
I wonder if hell will reach its capacity first or if she'll finish her assign-ment first...
TAP...
No way! I sent everyone within a fifty-meter radius to hell...
So you did it on purpose!?
What!?
......
RRRU-MBBLLLE
Who are ou!?
be continued... or not?

Special thanks to
(in no particular order)
Rough and Road Motorcycles Co.
RABEE Co., Ltd
Fukuda Electronics Co., Ltd
CAGIVA Japan Co., Ltd
moto-Liaison

Princess
Resurrection

Translation Notes

Japanese is a tricky language for most Westerners, and translation is often more an art than a science. For your edification and reading pleasure, here are notes on some of the places where we could have gone in a different direction, or where a Japanese cultural reference is used.

Dear Hiro,
This is the mansion where you and your sister will be staying.
Here ♥
Farming Co-Op
Post Office
XX Bank
Book Store
North Exit
Sasanaki Station
TREMBLE
TREMBLE

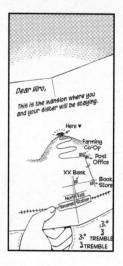

Sasanaki City, page 7

Hiro's looking at a map of Sasanaki City, which, much like the werewolves and invisible men you'll find in the pages of *Princess Resurrection*, is entirely fictional.

"H," page 44

In Japan, someone or something that's perverted is often said to be "H," which is pronounced *ecchi*. There are many theories about why this is so, but the most popular is that it is short for the word *hentai*, which means "perverted or having abnormal tendencies." *Hentai* is often used by English-speakers to describe pornographic material.

Today we have a new student.
Um, my name is Hiro Hiyorimi.
My initials are H.H., but I try not to be "H" as much.
SILENCE...
Your seat is over there.
Shoot, they didn't laugh.

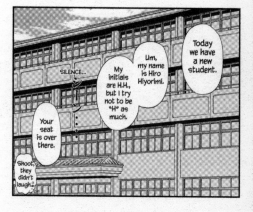

Maid outfit, page 61

Sawawa's wearing a maid's uniform because she really *is* a maid, but the girl in the café's surprise and delight at her outfit may have something to do with the "maid craze" that has swept Japan in recent years.

In Japan in 1993, the first video games featuring maids were released. This was probably the earliest depiction of maids in the anime/game culture, but it was not until 1997 when some popular *hentai* video games were released that the *otaku* really started to be interested in maids.

Afterward, anime/media companies started to have "maid cafés" during conventions, where girls dressed up as maids served drinks and light food. That later developed into "maid cafés" that are open year-round in major cities. Currently there are also "maid massages," where a girl dressed up in a maid costume gives you a massage.

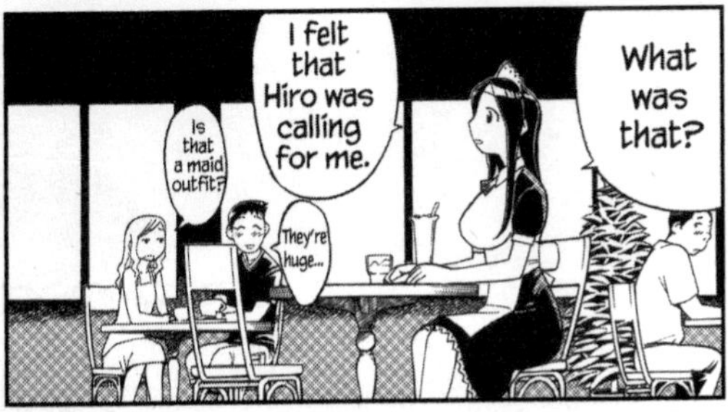
What was that?
I felt that Hiro was calling for me.
They're huge...
Is that a maid outfit?

Preview of Volume 2

We are pleased to present you with a preview of Volume 2 of *Princess Resurrection*. It will be available in English on August 28, 2007. For now you'll have to make do with the Japanese!

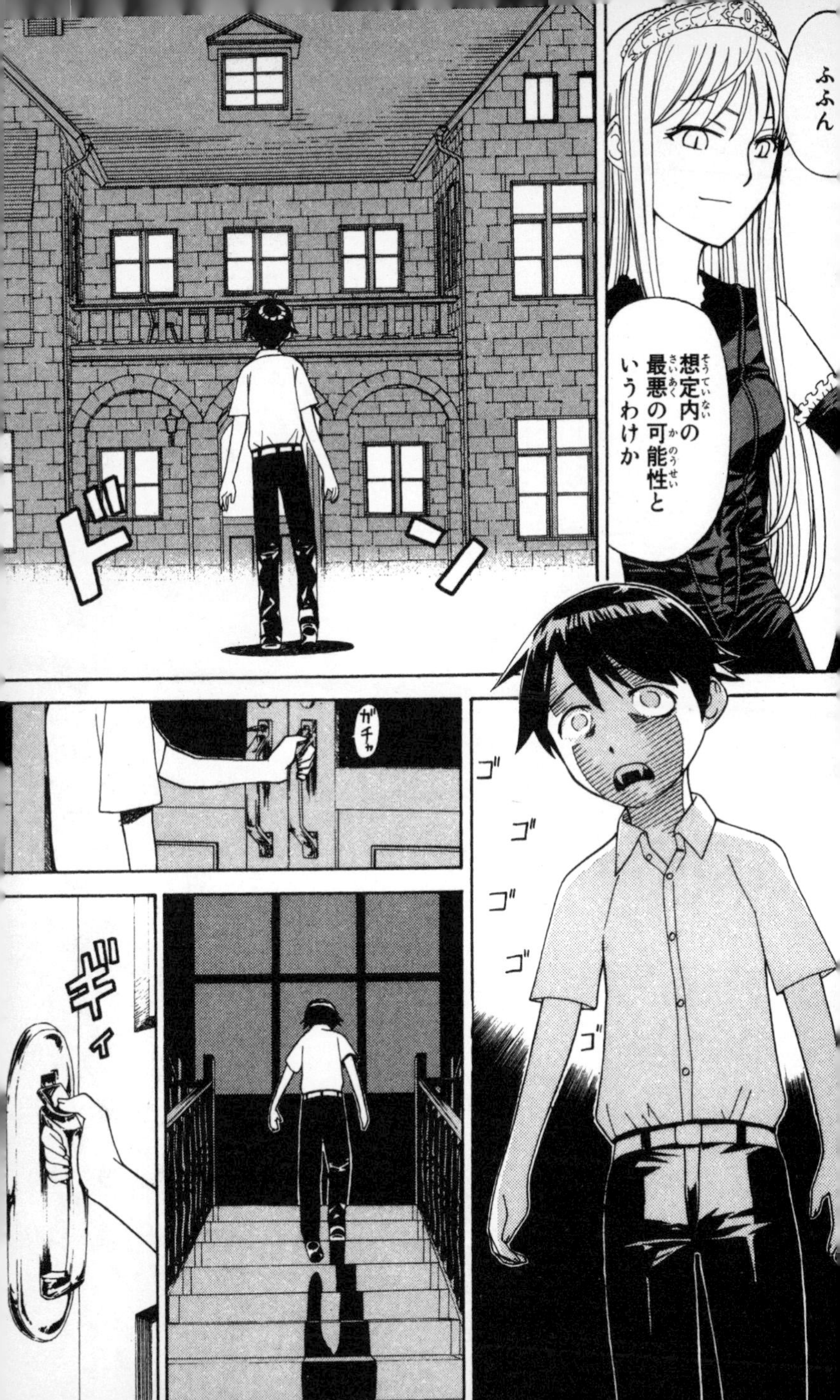

ふふん
想定内の最悪の可能性というわけか
ドー
ゴゴゴゴゴ
ガチャ
ギィ

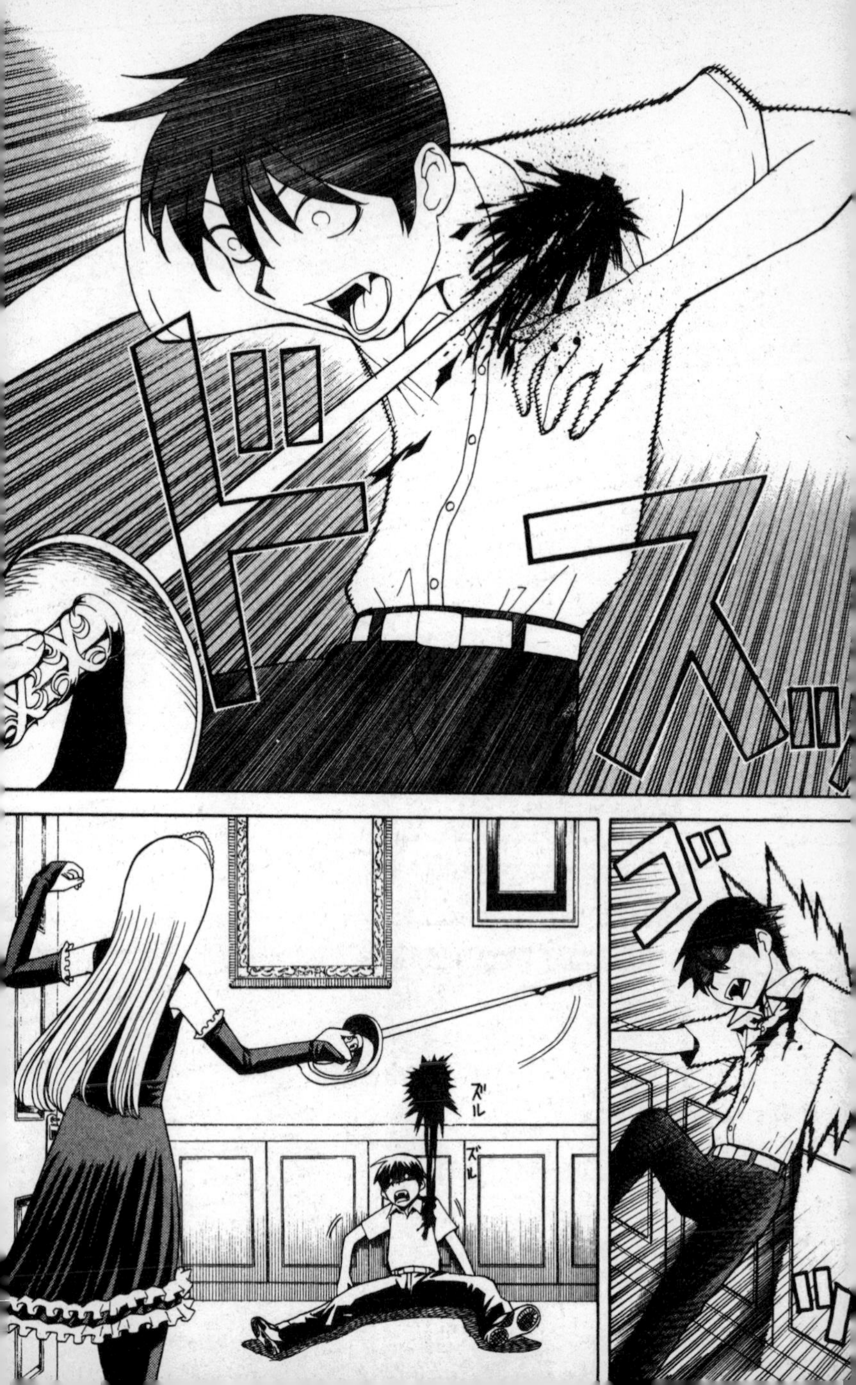
ドズ
ブ
ズル
ズル

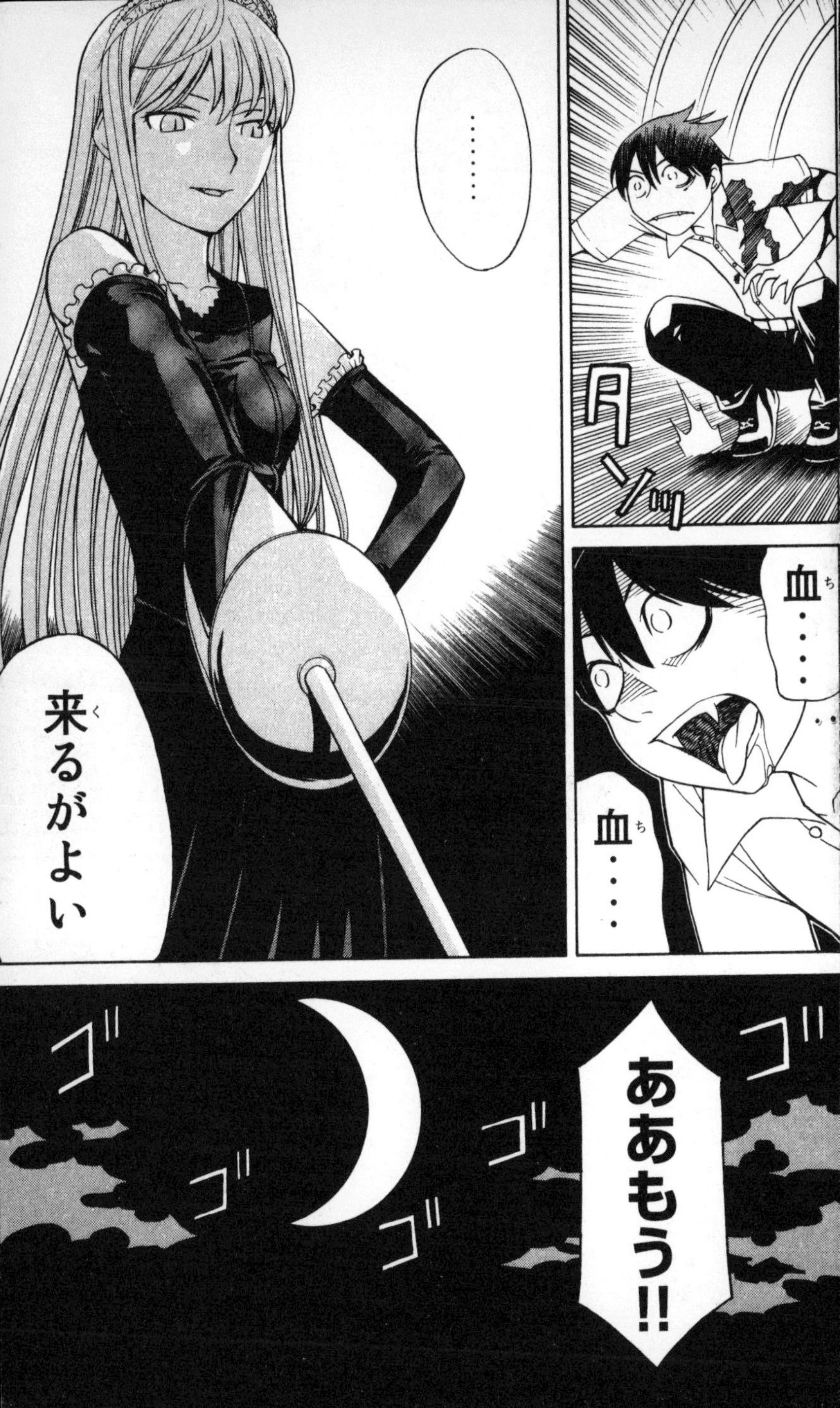
タンッ
血……
血……
……
来るがよい
ああもう!!
ゴゴゴゴゴ

DRAGON EYE

BY KAIRI FUJIYAMA

HUMANITY'S SECRET WEAPON

DRAGON EYE
1
KAIRI FUJIYAMA

Dracules—bloodthirsty, infectious monsters—have hunted human beings to the brink of extinction. Only the elite warriors of the VIUS Squad stand as humanity's last best hope.

Young Leila Mikami is one of the squad's most promising recruits, but she's not only training to battle the Dracules, she's determined to find the magical Dragon Eye, a weapon that will make her the most powerful warrior in the world.

Special extras in each volume! Read them all!

VISIT WWW.DELREYMANGA.COM TO:

- Read sample pages
- View release date calendars for upcoming volumes
- Sign up for Del Rey's free manga e-newsletter
- Find out the latest about new Del Rey Manga series

RATING T AGES 13+

DEL REY MANGA デルレイ

The Otaku's Choice™

Le Chevalier d'Eon

STORY BY TOU UBUKATA
MANGA BY KIRIKO YUMEJI

DARKNESS FALLS ON PARIS

A mysterious cult is sacrificing beautiful young women to a demonic force that threatens the entire country. Only one man can save Paris from chaos and terror, the king's top secret agent: The Chevalier d'Eon.

• Available on DVD from ADV Films.

Special extras in each volume! Read them all!

TOMARE!

止まれ

[STOP!]

You're going the wrong way!

Manga is a completely different type of reading experience.

To start at the *beginning,* go to the end!

That's right! Authentic manga is read the traditional Japanese way—from right to left, exactly the *opposite* of how American books are read. It's easy to follow: Just go to the other end of the book, and read each page—and each panel—from right side to left side, starting at the top right. Now you're experiencing manga as it was meant to be!